CARDINAL PELL, THE MEDIA PILE-ON & COLLECTIVE GUILT

Gerard Henderson

Connor Court Publishing

The Mass booklet containing the rite of service at Cardinal Pell's funeral and burial – St Mary's Cathedral, Sydney 2 February 2023.

The occasion was a packed-out affair with the Cathedral full and large crowds outside in the hot summer sun. It was televised by Sky News and live streamed. The principal celebrant was Archbishop Anthony Fisher OP, Archbishop of Sydney. (See chapter 12).

To my grandchildren

Published in 2021 by Connor Court Publishing Pty Ltd

Second Edition, 2022.

Third Edition, 2023.

Copyright © Gerard Henderson

All rights reserved. No part of this book may be reproduced or transmitted in any form or by any means, electronic or mechanical, including photo copying, recording or by any information storage and retrieval system, without prior permission in writing from the publisher.

Connor Court Publishing Pty Ltd
PO Box 7257
Redland Bay QLD 4165
sales@connorcourt.com
www.connorcourt.com

Printed in Australia

ISBN: 9781922449818

Front cover design: Paige Hally

CONTENTS

	FOREWORD	VII
1	GEORGE PELL v THE QUEEN: AN EPIC HIGH COURT CASE	1
2	MOB-RULE AND WITCH-HUNTS ON THE ROAD TO THE MAGISTRATES' COURT	39
3	THE TRIALS OF GEORGE PELL	63
4	THE APPEALS OF GEORGE PELL	93
5	FROM BALLARAT TO ROME AND OXFORD, BACK TO BALLARAT AND ON TO MELBOURNE	129
6	THE MEDIA PILE-ON COMMENCES	163
7	THE LEADERS OF THE PELL-ANTAGONISTS' BAND	195
8	STACKS ON THE PELL MILL – AND MORE ON STILL	247
9	ROYAL COMMISSION – OR ROMAN CATHOLIC COMMISSION?	297
10	VICTORIA POLICE'S OPERATION TETHERING – OR "GET PELL" – CAMPAIGN	361
11	THE FALLIBILITY OF MEMORY AND COLLECTIVE GUILT	395
12	A DEATH IN ROME - A BURIAL IN SYDNEY AS THE PILE-ON CONTINUES AND CARDINAL PELL'S FINAL REFLECTION	419
	APPENDIX 1: THE QUESTIONS ABOUT CARDINAL: THE RISE AND FALL OF GEORGE PELL WHICH LOUISE MILLIGAN DECLINED TO ANSWER	459
	APPENDIX 2: GAVIN SILBERT KC ON CARDINAL PELL AS "AN INNOCENT MAN"	464
	ENDNOTES	469
	ACKNOWLEDGEMENTS	476
	A NOTE ON THE THIRD EDITION	478
	INDEX	479

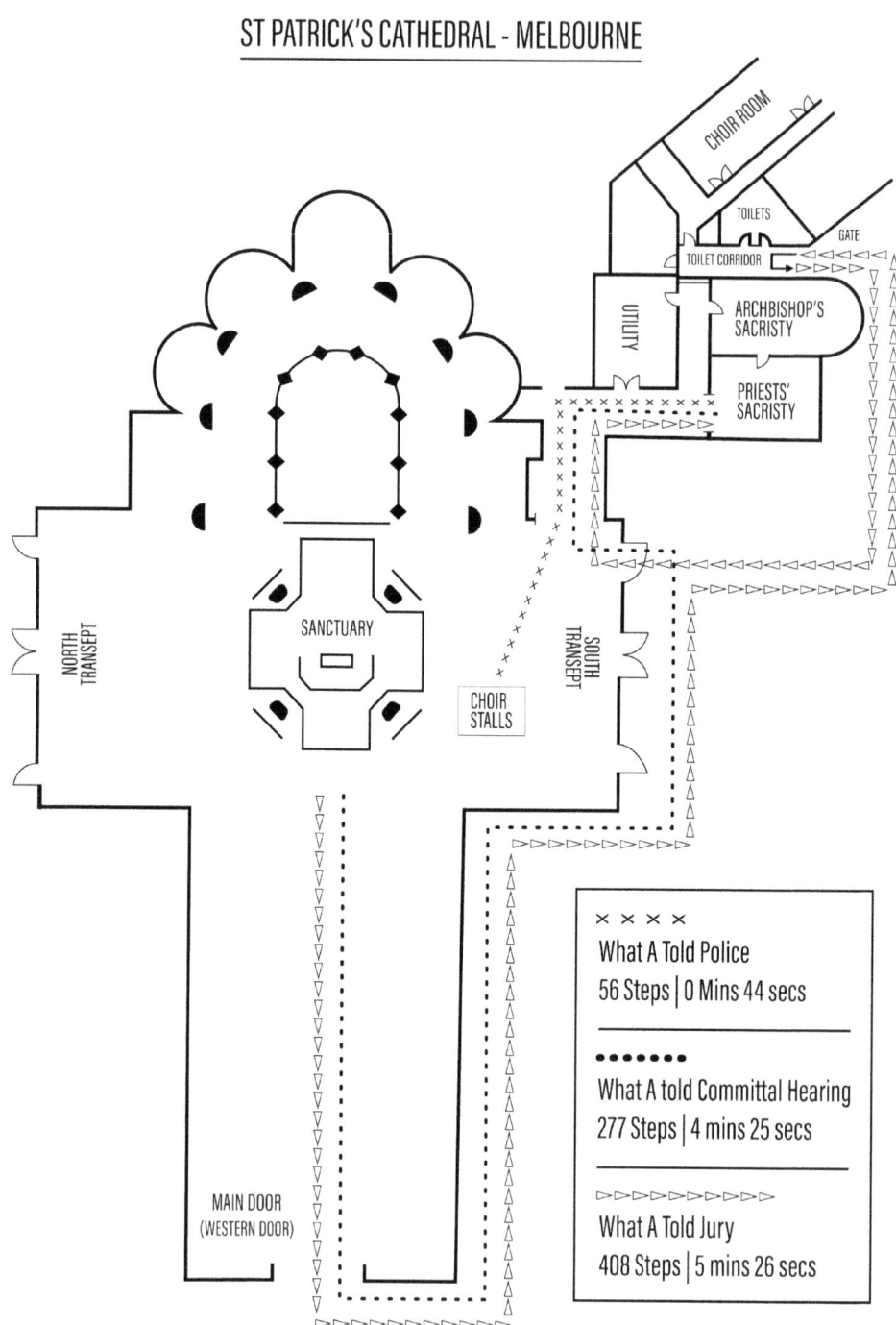

FOREWORD

The Hon John Howard OM AC

Gerard Henderson is a meticulous researcher, an engaging narrator, and an exemplar of the proverbial dog with a bone. Once he takes interest in something, he pursues it relentlessly.

He has applied these impressive skills to what he perceived to be the vilification of Cardinal George Pell by sections of the media and the wider community.

In his book *Cardinal Pell, The Media Pile-On & Collective Guilt* Henderson has painstakingly addressed not only the substance of the charges finally brought against the Cardinal, but other allegations which fell by the wayside. He has done so in a systematic, convincing fashion.

The sexual abuse of children, whether in a private home, a religious or other institution, sporting organisation, boarding school or indeed anywhere, is abhorrent. It is repulsive to our natural instincts of care and nurture for the young and vulnerable. Concern for the victims of abuse should always be uppermost.

Some institutions harboured and protected offenders. Given the large numbers within Catholic schools and institutions it was inevitable that there would be a heavy focus by official inquiries on those within the Church who had been involved in abuse. This has been painful for the Church and especially the great majority of priests and others who have served their faith in a blameless and dedicated fashion.

Cardinal George Pell is the most senior Catholic figure in Australia. He is a forthright and plain-speaking individual. He became a target for those who felt the Church had let them down and had been insensitive to the suffering of abused children. This occurred despite Pell's comprehensive initiative through the Melbourne Response which was designed to respond in a practical way to the abuse issue within the Archdiocese of Melbourne.

I never believed the charges ultimately brought against the Cardinal. That was based on my assessment of him as a man and the implausibility of the alleged offences having taken place within the circumstances which were alleged. I felt that justice had been served when the full bench of the High Court of Australia unanimously upheld his appeal and quashed the original convictions.

It is to his credit that Gerard Henderson has produced such a thorough, well argued book on an issue which gripped the attention of many Australians.

John Howard

5 November 2021

STATEMENT FROM CARDINAL GEORGE PELL
FOLLOWING THE HIGH COURT DECISION IN
PELL v THE QUEEN

I have consistently maintained my innocence while suffering from a serious injustice.

This has been remedied today with the High Court's unanimous decision.

I look forward to reading the judgment and reasons for the decision in detail.

I hold no ill will toward my accuser, I do not want my acquittal to add to the hurt and bitterness so many feel; there is certainly hurt and bitterness enough.

However my trial was not a referendum on the Catholic Church; nor a referendum on how Church authorities in Australia dealt with the crime of paedophilia in the Church.

The point was whether I had committed these awful crimes, and I did not.

The only basis for long term healing is truth and the only basis for justice is truth, because justice means truth for all…

Cardinal George Pell
7 April 2020

Cardinal Pell at Solemn Mass

At a Solemn Mass at St Patrick's Cathedral in Melbourne in December 1996, (then) Archbishop Pell would have been wearing the following clothes/garments: (i) underpants, (ii) singlet, (iii) trousers held up by braces and belt, (iv) shirt, (v) a long white seamless alb (robe) which is held in place by a cincture (a rope of cloth that is knotted) and reaches to the floor, (vi) a heavy chasuble (or cape) reaching well below the waist, (vii) a long stole which hangs from around the neck to below the waist and (viii) a purple zucchetto (small cap) worn on head under mitre. The only openings in an alb are small slits on the side to allow access to the pockets of trousers worn underneath. Some of the garments are heavy and difficult to put on and cardinals/archbishops/bishops have to be assisted by a monsignor or priest in robing. George Pell was fully robed when the alleged sexual abuses took place.

An alb cannot be parted – since it is seamless. Initially A said that Pell had parted his vestments – he later said that he had moved them to one side. Victoria Police did not inspect Pell's vestments worn in 1996, which are retained at St Patrick's Cathedral.

This photo depicts George Pell when Cardinal Archbishop of Sydney at a Solemn Mass in St Mary's Cathedral circa 2010. His vestments would be about the same as they were in Melbourne in the mid-1990s.

In procession at the beginning and end of Solemn Mass, he would have been wearing a mitre (a pointed hat) on his head and carrying a crozier which is a sacred (and costly) pastoral staff.

Credit: Image by Giovanni Portelli

1

GEORGE PELL v THE QUEEN: AN EPIC HIGH COURT CASE

"…It is evident that there is a significant possibility that an innocent person has been convicted because the evidence did not establish guilt to the requisite standard of proof."

- Chief Justice Susan Kiefel, High Court of Australia, 7 April 2020 – quoting from the judgment of all seven judges of the High Court – Chief Justice Susan Kiefel and Justices Virginia Bell, Stephen Gageler, Patrick Keane, Geoffrey Nettle, Michelle Gordon and James Edelman.

Judgment at a Time of Pandemic – the Chief Justice in Canberra, the Applicant in Prison

It was Tuesday 7 April 2020 at 10 am when the High Court of Australia delivered its order in the case of *George Pell* (the applicant) *v The Queen* (the respondent). Due to the partial lockdown in response to the COVID-19 pandemic, the Queensland-based Chief Justice Susan Kiefel sat alone in the court's Brisbane registry in the Harry Gibbs Building – rather than in Canberra where the court is based and most of its important decisions are delivered.

Cardinal George Pell sat alone in his cell in the maximum security Barwon Prison some 70 kilometres from Melbourne and close to the city of Geelong. He was in solitary confinement, for his own protection as a high profile convicted pedophile, and was spending some 23 hours a day in his cell.

For his first ten months of incarceration, the convicted man had resided in Cell 11 Unit 8 on the fifth floor of the Melbourne Assessment Prison (MAP) on the edge of the Melbourne CBD. His cell was around eight metres long and two metres wide and he was allowed outside for two 30 minute periods a day. He never saw or spoke to any of the other 11 prisoners in Unit 8. The concept of the MAP is that convicted prisoners spend up to three months there while the appropriate jail for them to serve their sentence is being assessed. The idea is that, where possible, no prisoner should be incarcerated in such harsh solitary confinement conditions for more than three months. Pell did ten months at the MAP.

On Friday 10 January 2020, the MAP's acting-governor visited Pell in his cell and advised that he would be transferred immediately to Barwon Prison. As is usual in such circumstances, no explanation was given. He was transported by prison van – handcuffed and with ankles shackled. The trip took just over an hour and Pell regarded the occasion as a psychological boon. As he put in his *Prison Journal* (Ignatius Press) the van "had three windows, nine inches by three inches, which...enabled me to watch a small slab of the outside world as we went West".

At Barwon Prison Pell was incarcerated in the Cell 17 Unit 3 at the Acadia High Security Unit. As he wrote at the time "prisoners wear a uniform of exactly cardinal red; I suppose this is progress from the darker green of MAP, the Muslim colour". Pell described his cell as about four times the size of that provided by the MAP with a yard attached where he could "stand in the sun and see the sky". He also had access to a common internal area – with a kitchen containing a refrigerator at one end and some gym equipment at the other.

At Barwon Prison, Pell was able to communicate with three other prisoners in his section through a glass aperture in the cell door if they happened to be in the common area outside his cell. Two of them were Muslim – Cardinal Pell came to regard his three fellow prisoners as friends. With respect to the two Muslim prisoners he has commented:

> We got on okay, no problem at all. They certainly regarded me as a fellow believer. And one of them said to me: "You know those guards – the ones that are nasty and unhappy". And I said "yeah". He said "They're the ones that don't believe in God".
>
> [Interview with the author, Saturday 25 July 2020.]

For the most part, however, Pell says that he was well treated by prison wardens while in both prisons. The prisoner was not offered – and never requested – alternative jail options when serving his time.

On the morning of Tuesday 7 April 2020, Cardinal Pell had served 405 days in prison – having been convicted on 11 December 2018 on five charges of historical child sexual abuse at St Patrick's Cathedral, Melbourne. His imprisonment commenced on 27 February 2019, following a period of bail for medical reasons.

There were around a dozen people in attendance when the Chief Justice delivered the High Court's order in a soft-spoken voice. First up, she advised that the applicant's special leave to appeal had been granted. There followed the announcement that the applicant's appeal, from the Supreme Court of Victoria's Court of Appeal, had been allowed. It all took less than a minute.

In a Sky News interview which aired a week after his release, Cardinal Pell told Andrew Bolt that, in the lead-up to the announcement he had tidied up his cell (hoping for some good news) and said his prayers. At about five minutes before the top of the hour he heard a fellow prisoner saying that Channel 7 News was reporting live on the event. So he switched on his television.

> *Cardinal Pell:* And so I took great pleasure in watching how disconcerted the reporter was when the word came through. The ap-

peal has been upheld. And the convictions are quashed. ... then a minute or so later, as it [the report] ended – seven nil, seven zero. So that was how I heard. And when it came through, one enormous cheer went up from outside. And then my two friends [who were in the common area] came knocking on the door, congratulating me.

Andrew Bolt: Two friends, one being a murderer.

George Pell: No, he's not. Well, I don't think he is. And one of the things I've become a bit interested in is people who were falsely condemned.

The reference is to Jason Roberts, who was serving a life sentence for murdering two police officers. He had won the right to appeal his sentence to the Victorian Court of Appeal and the decision was pending when Pell was released from Barwon Prison. In November 2020, the Victorian Court of Appeal (Justices T. Forrest, R. Osborn and A. Taylor) granted Roberts the right to a new trial due to the failure of Victoria Police to disclose evidence to the defendant during his first trial. However, Roberts was not granted bail and remained in jail pending the new trial.

The High Court's full judgment was immediately released – it was tweeted and published online. Due to the pandemic, international and interstate media were not able to attend the court – and the occasion was reported by just a few Brisbane journalists.

In his *Prison Journal* Pell recalled the moment after news of the High Court decision came through. Roberts and one of the Muslim prisoners came to his cell door and expressed their congratulations and best wishes. The other Muslim prisoner was in his cell but Pell farewelled him before he departed the Unit.

Pell recorded that he had no surge of elation but he punched the air a couple of times – and then prayed the *Te Deum*, the traditional prayer of thanks. He then said The Rosary in gratitude to God – since he did not want to be like the nine lepers. This was a reference to the New Testament parable of the ten lepers who were cured by Jesus Christ in a miracle – only one thanked Him.

The High Court's Full Bench

Pell v The Queen was an unusual unanimous decision written by the Chief Justice and her six colleagues. In order of seniority, they were Justices Virginia Bell (the court's most experienced criminal jurist), Stephen Gageler, Patrick Keane, Geoffrey Nettle, Michelle Gordon and James Edelman. The unanimity of the decision deauthorised any claim that the outcome in *Pell v The Queen* had anything to do with what some call the culture wars. Chief Justice Kiefel along with Justices Nettle, Gordon and Edelman were appointed by a conservative Liberal Party-Nationals Coalition government. Justices Bell, Gageler and Keane were appointed by a social democrat Labor government.

Those who watched the hearings in the High Court or read the transcript of proceedings would know how all judges were fully across the details of the case. Professor Jeremy Gans, one of Australia's most highly regarded criminal law legal academics, put out a *Twitter* thread shortly before Chief Justice Kiefel announced the High Court's decision. He commented that by the second day of the hearings every High Court judge had asked the Victorian Director of Public Prosecutions [Kerri Judd QC] "incredibly detailed questions about the evidence, especially the various 'alibi' and 'timing' witnesses". He added: "They were really on top of the factual details…way more than…Judd."

Remembering Other Wrongly Convicted Australians – Colin Campbell Ross and Lindy Chamberlain

Cardinal Pell's trial, conviction and ultimate acquittal is perhaps the most publicised criminal case in Australian legal history – even surpassing that of Lindy Chamberlain, Colin Campbell Ross and the Victorian bush-ranger, horse thief and murderer of three policemen Ned Kelly (1854-1880). Certainly the Pell Case was the one occasion where an Australian criminal process attracted so much international attention.

In October 1982, in the Northern Territory Supreme Court, a jury found Lindy Chamberlain (1948 -) guilty of murdering her nine-week old daughter, Azaria, around two years earlier at Uluru in central Australia. She claimed that a dingo had taken her baby. As *The Oxford Companion to the High Court of Australia* (OUP, 2001) states, few cases had generated as much public controversy. Like Pell, there was a media pile-on against Chamberlain which jurors must have noticed. Moreover, the accused was regarded by many as lacking empathy. And she was a believer who belonged to the unfashionable Seventh-day Adventist Church, a Protestant sect.

Ms Chamberlain's appeal against her conviction was dismissed by the High Court in February 1984. Five judges sat on the case and the decision went three to two. The dissenters were Justice Lionel Murphy and Justice William Deane. Lindy Chamberlain was released by the Northern Territory government in early 1986 after the discovery of new evidence. There followed a judicial inquiry which found that the jury verdict was unsafe.

Some words used by the High Court in *Pell v The Queen* – namely that it was evident that there is "a significant possibility that an innocent person has been convicted because the evidence did not establish guilt to the requisite standard of proof" – that is, beyond reasonable doubt – were taken (with acknowledgement) from Justice Deane's dissenting judgment in *Chamberlain v The Queen*. In doing so, the High Court sent a very direct message to the two most senior judges in Victoria whose decision it overturned – namely the Chief Justice of the Supreme Court of Victoria Anne Ferguson and the President of the Victorian Court of Appeal Chris Maxwell. It is noteworthy that Justice Mark Weinberg, who dissented when Pell appealed against his conviction in the Victorian Court of Appeal, also identified himself in his judgment with Justice Deane's dissent in *Chamberlain v The Queen*.

In December 1921, the 29-year old Colin Campbell Ross – who ran a somewhat seedy wine saloon in what today would be called the Melbourne Central Business District – was found guilty by a jury of raping and murdering a 12-year old girl, Alma Tirtschke. The Australian Wine Café, in the (then) Eastern Arcade, was a hang-out for criminals and prostitutes. Ross was a low-level criminal who did not exude empathy and was unlikely to impress a jury. As his entry in the *Australian Dictionary of Biography* attests, Ross' "courtroom behaviour, at first nonchalant, then truculent and finally angry, weakened the defence's case".

Ross had an alibi. But it could not withstand the testimony of several witnesses who benefited from rewards for providing evidence offered by the Victorian government (£1000) and *The Herald* (£250) – substantial amounts at the time equivalent to a total of around $100,000 in today's currency.

The convicted man appealed to the Full Court of the Supreme Court of Victoria which dismissed the application. Ross then appealed to the High Court of Australia. Four of the five judges rejected his application of special leave to appeal. The dissenting judge, Isaac Isaacs, granted leave to appeal and ordered a new trial – maintaining that the killing may not have been intentional and that it was open to the jury to enter a verdict of manslaughter. This was not a satisfactory dissent in view of the clear evidence that a murder (not a manslaughter) had occurred. The judges in the majority stressed the importance of jury verdicts to the legal system.

Ross was hanged at Melbourne Gaol on 22 April 1922, all the while protesting his innocence. In his book *Gun Alley: Murder, Lies and Failure of Justice* (Hardie Grant, 2012), Kevin Morgan expresses the view that Victoria Police fabricated the confession it maintained Ross had made. When it was proven decades later, following a DNA test, that the human hair produced by the prosecution to convict in the case did not belong to Ross, he was granted a posthumous pardon by the Victorian government in 2008. Some 86 years after his execution. This followed an inquiry by three Victorian Supreme Court judges.

The site of Ross' execution is now a museum called Old Melbourne Gaol, on the edge of Melbourne CBD. Visitors can see the condemned man's cell along with the trap-door through which he fell in what was a botched execution which led to the hanged man on the rope for between eight and twenty minutes before he died. It's the same site that saw the end of Ned Kelly who met his fate on 11 November 1880, two years before Ross was born.

The convictions by a jury of both Colin Campbell Ross and Lindy Chamberlain followed enormous adverse media publicity at the time – which made it inherently unlikely that either could receive a fair trial. Both decisions demonstrated that juries do not always get it right. In this case, there was a print media pile-on against Ross led by *The Herald*, the influential Melbourne evening newspaper, which even published the names and addresses of the jurors. After this, it became illegal to identify jury members. The Chamberlain case also received enormous publicity in all forms of media in those pre-internet days.

Victoria Police's "Get Pell" Campaign

In June 2015 the complainant – a man who was called "Witness J" at the Magistrates' Court and at the trial but referred to as "A" by the Victorian Court of Appeal and the High Court – made a complaint to Victoria Police alleging that Pell had committed sexual assaults on two occasions. He changed his version of events on a number of occasions – along with the dates of the alleged offences. In his *Prison Journal,* Pell wrote that his lawyers advised that A changed his story 24 times during the trial. In the end, Pell was charged with one set of offences in 1996 and a single offence in February 1997 in what became known as the Cathedral Trial.

1996 was the first year that A was at St Kevin's College in Melbourne – having won a scholarship there to perform in the choir, which also sang at St Patrick's Cathedral and elsewhere. The offences were alleged to have taken place at St Patrick's Cathedral where A was a choir boy. The Crown was never able to settle on a specific date when the crimes took place.

A's fellow chorister was "Witness R" – he was referred to by the Victorian Court of Appeal and the High Court as "B". B died of an accidental heroin overdose in 2014. There was common ground among the parties during Pell's trial in the County Court of Victoria that B's death was not related to the alleged offending by Pell. Moreover, evidence was submitted to – and accepted by – the County Court that B had told his mother that he had never been "interfered with or touched up" when a boy. B made a similar statement to his father, as revealed by Victoria Police. B's father advised Victoria Police that his son had told him that he had not been sexually abused.

On Christmas Eve 2015, the *Herald Sun*, Australia's top selling newspaper, ran a page one story that Victoria Police was interested in talking to any men who, when choristers at St Patrick's Cathedral between 1996 and 2001, had been sexually assaulted. This followed a media release by Victoria Police. *The Age* ran a similar report. The dates corresponded with Pell's period as Catholic Archbishop of Melbourne – i.e. between July 1996 and March 2001. No one came forward – leaving A as Pell's solitary accuser. It would seem that this was not what Victoria Police had anticipated.

Under cross examination at the committal proceedings in the Magistrates' Court, Detective Superintendent Paul Sheridan said that Victoria Police's SANO (Sexual Abuse Non-Government Organisations) Task Force had set up "Operation Tethering" in March 2013 to investigate whether any crimes committed by Pell had gone unreported. Victoria Police went looking for a crime before any crime had been complained of. A "Get Pell" campaign.

Sheridan also told the court it was over a year before a complaint was made to Victoria Police – it turned out to have been made by a man the day after he was discharged from a psychiatric hospital. Nothing came of this. The name of the operation speaks volumes. The common understanding of "tethering" relates to the activity by which an animal is fastened to a stake by a rope or chain in order to limit its range of movement. In March 2013, Pell was the Cardinal Archbishop of Sydney. According to Victoria Police, he should have been "tethered".

Clearly Victoria Police believed that Pell was an offender before any alleged offence had been identified.

The following exchange took place between Robert Richter QC and Detective Superintendent Paul Sheridan at the Magistrates' Court hearing on 28 March 2018:

> *Robert Richter:* Operation Tethering wasn't a "Get Pell" operation, was it?
>
> *Paul Sheridan:* Operation Tethering, as I understand it, commenced as an intel probe around what offences the cardinal may have committed....I guess you could term it the way you did but I wouldn't term it that way.

As Lucie Morris-Marr acknowledged in her book *Fallen: The inside story of the secret trial and conviction of Cardinal George Pell* (Allen & Unwin, 2019) – "the detective-superintendent did not deny the accusation" that this was a "Get Pell" operation. An important conclusion, since Morris-Marr is a Pell-antagonist.

A Roman Interview

In October 2016 three members of the Victoria Police flew business class to Rome to interview Pell – namely Deputy Commissioner (now Chief Commissioner) Shane Patton, Detective Superintendent Paul Sheridan and Detective Sergeant Christopher Reed. In February 2014, Pell had been appointed by Pope Francis to the newly created position of Prefect of the Secretariat for the Economy for the Holy See – a kind of treasurer or finance minister role in government. He lived in Piazza della Città (just outside Vatican City) . It was a comfortable apartment – but relatively modest by Rome standards. However, some of Pell's many journalist antagonists, most notably Peter FitzSimons of the *Sydney Morning Herald*, continually referred to the residence as a "$30 million mansion" – although they had not seen it. FitzSimons was part of the media pile-on against Pell.

The meeting was conducted at the Hilton Hotel, Fiumicino Airport, Rome on Wednesday 19 October 2016. Present in the room was Pell's legal adviser Michael do Rozario. Reed asked most of the questions with only occasional interventions by his superior Sheridan. Patton, the most senior member of the Victoria Police trio, did not attend the meeting – nor did Pell's barrister Robert Richter QC. Pell voluntarily agreed to make a statement and be interviewed – just as he had previously volunteered to give evidence at the Royal Commission into Institutional Responses to Child Sexual Abuse (see Chapter 9). Because he was resident in Rome, Pell was not compelled to appear before the Royal Commission. Also under Victorian law, no one is required to give an interview to Victoria Police. All Pell's statements were given willingly.

First up, Reed told Pell that he intended to interview him "in relation to the Victorian Australian offences of rape, buggery, indecent assault upon a male and an indecent act in the presence of a child under 16 years". Victoria Police spoke to Pell about his relations with nine boys (now men) when he was based in Ballarat and later Melbourne in Victoria. Most of the alleged offences which Victoria Police raised in Rome related to Ballarat and neighbouring areas.

Pell's initial statement and concluding remarks were emphatic as to his innocence – and his answers to a number of questions demonstrated the ignorance of Reed with respect to the propositions that were put. Early on Pell said that allegations had been made against him knowing that he was "the first person in the Western world to create a Church structure to recognise, compensate and help to heal the wounds inflicted by sexual abuse of children at the hands of some in the Catholic Church". The reference was to the Melbourne Response which Pell established in November 1996 within months of being appointed Archbishop of Melbourne. The Melbourne Response was established at the wishes of the Victorian government and in co-operation with Victoria Police – something which the police subsequently did not want to remember.

Towards the end of the interview, Reed asked Pell why his various accusers "may have made these allegations". Here's the reply:

> *Cardinal Pell:* It's something, obviously, to which I've really turned my mind... Now, unfortunately I think – well, I don't think, I've become a hate figure. I've become a symbol of the "Old Church", a scapegoat. I have been continually before the public. For some hours, I was at the Victorian Parliamentary Inquiry and then three times at the Royal Commission; the last time I was in the box for 19 hours.[1]
>
> *Christopher Reed:* Yes.
>
> *Cardinal Pell*: So, I am a bogeyman in the public imagination.
>
> *Christopher Reed:* Okay.
>
> *Cardinal Pell:* Now despite the fact, as I said, I was the first person to put together... any response around the world. So, for example, that's, we had our thing [the Melbourne Response] in place six years before the scandals that are detailed in the film *Spotlight* about Boston, which was in 2002.[2]
>
> *Christopher Reed:* So, do you think that that's the reason that –
>
> *Cardinal Pell:* [interrupting]: Well –
>
> *Christopher Reed:* [interrupting] – some of these could be – oh sorry, continue.
>
> *Cardinal Pell:* And the question about these [allegations] is to what extent they are simply diseased fantasy. I mean, we know that certainly that some of the people who made the accusation have been heavily into drugs and violence and that, you know, might or mightn't influence what they say. And then when you haven't got evidence, you've got to hypothesise. You know, to what extent have people been helped to put these things together in a certain way and there's a little bit of suggestion, won't go there, who knows? I mean, I wasn't going to bring this up but you've asked me, so I –
>
> *Christopher Reed:* No, that's, yeah fine. No, that's no problem.
>
> *Cardinal Pell:* So, I will go on. People were aware that in 2002 I

was accused of misbehaviour down at the Phillip Island.³ I mean a number of people would know that – and so mud can stick and they imagine that these other things. Although, the sort of details we've had here, there's nothing ambiguous about any of them. They're gross and explicit and mistaken. When you're hated so much, people can want to believe the worst of you. Now, I'm a well-known social conservative…

Victoria Police Charge Cardinal Pell

On 29 June 2017, the then Deputy Commissioner of Police Shane Patton gave a high profile media conference in which he announced that Cardinal Pell had been charged with an unspecified number of cases of historical child sexual abuse – some nine months after the Rome interview. No specific details were provided and no questions were taken. Initially the case was sent by Victoria Police to the Victorian Director of Public Prosecutions which sent the matter back to Victoria Police which sent the matter back to the DPP which sent the matter back to Victoria Police which sent the matter back to the DPP which sent the matter back to Victoria Police stating that it could lay charges against Pell if it wished. Which, eventually, it did.⁴

All up, the DPP sent the matter back to Victoria Police on three occasions before Victoria Police itself laid the charges. It was not a confident start to a prosecution. At any stage in the process the Director of Public Prosecutions could have advised Victoria Police to drop the case. It didn't happen. A counter-productive move – since the DPP was discredited by the time the case concluded.

In Rome, Victoria Police focused primarily on allegations concerning George Pell's time in Ballarat in the 1970s and early 1980s. The allegations concerning St Patrick's Cathedral were not the main focus. However, in time, the only charges that Pell faced involved his time in Melbourne.

In Rome, Victoria Police had only spent around 40 minutes talking to Pell about the St Patrick's Cathedral matter. It did not raise the alleged 1997 assault with him – only the alleged 1996 assaults. As Pell-antagonist Lucie Morris-Marr acknowledged in her book *Fallen*, "the police hadn't asked many questions nor had the questions been as detailed as expected". In fact, Victoria Police seemed unaware of the rituals and practices of the Catholic Church at solemn masses and the like. It seems that Victoria Police was intent on charging Pell irrespective of anything he might say in his defence.

Two Jury Trials – One Unanimous Verdict

The first Cathedral Trial commenced in the County Court of Victoria on 15 August 2018 and the jury was discharged on 20 September 2018 after failing to reach a verdict. The hearings took 17 days. The second Cathedral Trial commenced on 7 November 2018 and concluded on 11 December 2018 with a unanimous guilty verdict. The hearings in the re-trial took 22 days.

On 11 December 2018, the jury in the re-trial, after deliberating for almost four days, returned guilty verdicts on all of five charges. Four convictions related to the alleged offences committed at St Patrick's Cathedral in Melbourne on 15 December 1996 or 22 December 1996. Notably, it was the defence, not the prosecution, which identified the dates since, unbeknown to Victoria Police or the DPP initially, these were the only days when Pell participated in masses at the Cathedral in 1996 and early 1997.

The fifth conviction related to an alleged offence committed in the Cathedral on 23 February 1997 – again the date was suggested by the defence to Victoria Police and the DPP. The prosecution had not done research as to when Pell was involved in saying or attending Mass at St Patrick's Cathedral in late 1996 and early 1997. Pell was granted bail for medical reasons – he required bilateral knee surgery – and was not imprisoned until 27 February 2019. Pell's term of imprisonment commenced from that date – and concluded 405 days later.

When sentencing Pell some two months later in what is termed *DPP v Pell (Sentence)*, the trial judge stated:

> I must give full effect to the jury's verdict. It is not for me to second guess the verdict. What this means is that I am required to accept and act upon J's [i.e. A.'s] account. That is what the law requires me to do and that is what I will do.

Elsewhere in his sentencing remarks, the Chief Judge Peter Kidd made such comments as "by the jury's verdict, this offending occurred" and the "offending which the jury has found you have engaged in".

In an unusual move sometime after the trial, the Chief Judge sought, and obtained, an interview with co-presenter Waleed Aly on Network 10's *The Project*. Aly had been one of many journalists engaged in the media's Pell pile-on. It was an unusual intervention by a senior judge in a legal case which had not yet concluded. His Honour used the occasion to describe how the criminal law operated. He made it clear that he had no intention of discussing individual cases. However, this comment which aired on 15 October 2019, was revealing:

> *Waleed Aly:* I want to be clear, I'm not asking you about the Pell Case here. But there must have been times in your career where the jury has reached a decision that, if you were on the jury, you probably wouldn't have. And yet you've got to go out and sentence them. How do you do that?
>
> *Peter Kidd:* Well I'm not going to even engage in that question at all. Save to say this – that we as judges, we apply the law. And when a jury convicts somebody we're bound to sentence them. If trial judges were to more or less ignore verdicts of the jury then that would undermine the centrality of the role of the jury in our criminal justice system.
>
> *Waleed Aly:* I well understand you can't do that. [laughs] You're not in that position.
>
> *Peter Kidd:* If the accused wants to appeal, it's for the Court of Appeal to decide whether that verdict is unreasonable having regard to the evidence.

Chief Judge Kidd made it very clear that it was the role of trial judges to accept jury verdicts – and the role of appeal courts to decide if a verdict is unreasonable. The timing of Chief Judge Peter Kidd's decision to talk to *The Project* was interesting. It took place after the lodgement of Pell's Application for Special Leave to Appeal to the High Court on 17 September 2019. The submission, written by defence lawyers Bret Walker SC and Ruth Shann, was a meticulously argued document.

What Members of the Jury Decided

Unlike judges who sit at first instance or an appeal, juries are not required to give reasons for their decision. This is what the jury, in the re-trial of *DPP v Pell*, decided on 11 December 2018 that the defendant had done beyond reasonable doubt. And this is what the Victorian Court of Appeal, in a majority decision on 21 August 2019, held that it was reasonable for the jurors to have so done.

The first incident took place on 15 or 22 December 1996. Archbishop (as he then was) Pell conducted a Sunday Solemn Mass at St Patrick's Cathedral. At the end of the Mass there was a procession from the altar up the main aisle to the Main Door (also called the West Door). This continued outside the cathedral to the left and past the South Transept Door and headed towards the back of the cathedral where the archbishop, priests, altar servers and choristers were to disrobe. All turned left and entered the cathedral through the external metal door and the internal glass door down what is called the toilet corridor. All in the procession, except the choristers, turned left again past the archbishop's sacristy (which was not in use at the time) to the priests' sacristy and the workers' – or utility – room. The choristers, after passing through the glass door, turned right and moved to the Knox Centre nearby. The jury found that:

- Two of the boys, A and B, broke away from the procession near the metal door and, unnoticed by anyone, re-entered the Cathedral through the South Transept Door. Then, via an internal aisle, they headed to the priests' sacristy – which at this time was kept for the Archbishop's use due to the renovations at the Cathedral which had been underway for some years. There they found and drank some altar wine. It so happened that Pell entered the priests' sacristy in his full archbishop's gear, discovered the boys drinking wine, told them they were in trouble, extracted his penis from his heavy robes over his personal clothing and dragged B's face close to his genitals. This assault lasted a minute or two and took place while the door was open. This was the first charge.

- Soon after, while standing, Pell put his erect penis into A's mouth while A was crouching. This lasted about two minutes. This was the second charge.

- Then Pell told A to take off his pants and started to fondle his genitalia with his hands. This was the third charge.

- While the above was occurring, Pell touched his own genitalia with a hand and masturbated himself. This was the fourth charge. These latter two acts occurred over a minute or two.

Once Pell stopped the offending, A put his clothes back on, left the room with B and re-joined some of the choir who were in the Choir Room at the Knox Centre. It was not clear how they exited the Cathedral or how they re-entered the Knox Centre.

It was argued by the prosecution that the total time spent by Pell with the two choir boys in the priests' sacristy was between five and six minutes.

The second incident took place on Sunday 23 February 1997 – when there was an internal (not external) procession from the sanctuary at the foot of the altar to the priests' sacristy. The jury found that:

- On Sunday 23 February 1997, Pell presided over Sunday Solemn Mass at St Patrick's Cathedral – the mass was said by Fr Brendan Egan. The archbishop was in his official vestments. During an internal procession after Mass, of up to 50 choristers and altar servers, Pell moved from the back of the procession. He managed to identify A in the group near the priests' sacristy, pushed him up against a wall and squeezed his testicles for approximately two or three seconds. No one saw or reported this assault. This was the fifth charge. At the time all the choristers of about the same age dressed in identical burgundy soutanes buttoned to the feet with a white surplice on top – but Pell was able to identify A towards the front of the procession. George Pell is 192 centimetres tall – or 6 feet $3^{1/2}$ inches in the old imperial measurement.

In his dissenting judgment in the Victorian Court of Appeal, Justice Mark Weinberg – a former Commonwealth Director of Public Prosecutions and Australia's most experienced criminal jurist at the time – said that the evidence concerning the fifth charge was so weak that the matter should not have been prosecuted. His view was not taken up by Chief Justice Ferguson and President Maxwell. But all seven judges of the High Court reached a conclusion similar to that of Justice Weinberg.

There were many problems with the guilty verdict with respect to the first four charges. Evidence was given by Monsignor Charles Portelli (the master of ceremonies) and Mr Maxwell Potter (the sacristan) that Archbishop Pell had a habit of leaving the procession at the Main Door and speaking for ten or more minutes to parishioners.

The dates of 15 December and 22 December 1996 were the first occasions on which Pell had celebrated Sunday Solemn Mass in the Cathedral as the Archbishop of Melbourne – it had been undergoing renovations when he became archbishop in August of that year. The Crown's case was that, during his first or second Sunday Solemn Mass at the Cathedral, the fully robed Archbishop nicked off in the early stage of the procession without anyone noticing and without being interrupted by parishioners wishing to speak with him and headed to the priests' sacristy where – by chance – he found and assaulted two boys whom he did not know. A violent opportunistic attack on two unknown teenagers in a public place.

George Pell is an ambitious man. At age 55 he had become the Archbishop of Melbourne, culminating in a brilliant clerical career with further advancement likely. Also Pell, a theological conservative, is a stickler for ritual and ceremony. Sunday 15 December 1996 was the first occasion Pell had celebrated Sunday Solemn Mass in the Cathedral. There had been a very large crowd when he was consecrated Archbishop of Melbourne at the Exhibition Building the previous August. Many Catholics had attended the new archbishop's first and/or second (22 December 1996) Solemn Mass at St Patrick's Cathedral.

Yet the Crown's case was that, on one of these two dates, Archbishop Pell broke away from the procession and headed back to the priests' sacristy, for an unexplained reason, thus failing to meet with parishioners at the Main Door or even to remain with his Master of Ceremonies and others taking part in the procession. Yet no one noticed that the tall, high profile Archbishop of Melbourne, mitre on head and crozier in one hand, had gone missing-in-action. And no one explained why he left the procession. Since he had no reason to know that anyone would be in the priests' sacristy apart from, perhaps, the sacristan.

And then there was the matter of timing. Evidence given at the trial was that a period of around five to six minutes – described as private prayer time – was put aside after Mass finished and before the altar servers began removing sacred vessels from the altar and returning them to the priests' sacristy. This was to give those attending the Mass time to pray in silence before the cleaning-up commenced. The altar servers then went into action.

And here is the problem which Victoria Police, the DPP, Magistrate Belinda Wallington in the committal hearing and the majority of the Victorian Court of Appeal did not see. There was no time for the offending, outlined in the charges one to four, to have occurred. Victoria Police or the DPP or the Magistrate could have stopped the trial from proceeding – and Chief Justice Ferguson and President Maxwell could have quashed the jury's verdict. But no one did.

Under the existing law, it is all but impossible that a judge will "no case" a child sex abuse trial if the complainant has testified that a criminal sexual act occurred. Pell's lawyers did not put forward a "no case" submission at either of his trials.

In the procession after Solemn Mass, the altar servers (of which there were about six) were up the front followed by the choristers followed by the archbishop and his attendees at the rear. A and B were sopranos and, consequently, at the front of the choristers. The archbishop is almost last in the procession. Behind him are two altar servers responsible for the mitre and crozier respectively.

It's around 80 steps from the sanctuary at the base of the altar to the Main Door – a walk of about one minute and 20 seconds. Then, from the Main Door to the priests' sacristy, some 220 steps are required, taking just over three minutes. So those leading the procession would take around four and a half minutes to get to the priests' sacristy. But A said that he and B backtracked from inside the metal gate back through the South Transept Door and along an internal aisle to the priests' sacristy – another 120 steps taking around one minute and 15 seconds. Meaning that A and B would have taken around five and a half minutes to get from the sanctuary at the base of the altar to the priests' sacristy. (See the St Patrick's Cathedral map at the commencement of this chapter).

Max Potter, the cathedral sacristan, gave evidence that he would not open the sacristy until he was ready to start moving items from the altar – after the five to six minutes of prayer time. Two altar servers gave evidence that they would start removing items from the altar after returning to the priests' sacristy where they first bowed to the crucifix inside the sacristy before proceeding to clean up the altar after Mass.

If Pell had stopped at the Main Door and spoken to parishioners for even a couple of minutes, he could not have got to the priests' sacristy in time to assault A and B. Even if he had not stopped at the Main Door and proceeded direct to the priests' sacristy, there still would not have been time for the offending of around five to six minutes to have occurred. Since immediately after the five minutes or so that the procession would have taken, the altar servers, who were at the front of the procession, would have started clearing up after Mass – and the priests' sacristy would have been a very busy place indeed which provided no opportunity for sexual assault. Even if Pell had decided to take such an enormous risk on such an important and high-profile occasion.

As the High Court pointed out, the private prayer time (taking around five to six minutes) commenced at around the same time as the procession (also taking around five to six minutes). In short, there was no spare five or six minutes in which the offending could have taken place as described by A.

This was a most unusual case since, based on the five to six minutes in which the alleged crimes took place, the offender would not have had time to get to the scene of the crime where the alleged offences took place. Nor would the alleged victims – since both parties were in the same procession for some, most or all of the time.

Pell had told Victoria Police this in Rome in October 2016 – but it seems that Victoria Police had decided to charge Pell before arriving in Rome.

Cardinal Pell in 2016 & High Court in 2020 Compared

Right at the end of his Rome interview, Cardinal Pell had this to say – which was not challenged by the two members of the Victorian Police at the Hilton Hotel:

> *Paul Sheridan:* I don't have any other questions at all, thank you.
>
> *Christopher Reed:* I'll invite comment, Cardinal.
>
> *Cardinal Pell:* Good, I'd like just to say a word or two about the Sunday Mass at the Cathedral in Melbourne.
>
> *Christopher Reed:* Yes.
>
> *Cardinal Pell*: Now, for a start, there would be hundreds of people

present, even in the, there's a couple – two or three hundred, perhaps more, that's parishioners. Even when I started in '96, it built up as I went along. Now, we can get the count but I think there's 35, 40 people in the choir. There's 30 or 40 boys and I know, 10 or 15 adults.... On top of that, there would be half a dozen [altar] servers. In those early days I think they were adult servers. And I was always accompanied by a Master of Ceremonies. There would be incense, always incense, solemn music. So it was a big, a big operation.

And after the Mass...[we] would come out of the end of the procession ...we'd go out the Main [West] Door. As we said, I would stay there. They would go back, the servers would go into the sacristy and get rid of, divest themselves of the garments. And the choir boys would go into their robing room [in the Knox Centre] with their parents around and then they'd get off and go. And the choirmaster would make sure that the last one was gone. Now the sacristy after Mass is generally a hive of activity because you've – well you've the sacristan [Max Potter] there and often we had an assistant sacristan. If there were concelebrants [i.e. other priests], they would divest, the servers would get out of their vestments, the collectors would bring in the [money] collection, the sacristans and the assistants would be bringing the chalice and the vessels out from the altar.

Now, I was always accompanied by my Master of Ceremonies [Charles Portelli] after the Mass. So he would come around with me and help me unrobe – it was just the protocol. And then we would both go off together. The sacristan would always lock the wine away in the big safe, it was a very formidable safe – the rings and the pectoral crosses and that were kept there. The sacristan would stay around until he locked the sacristy....

You could scarcely imagine a place that was more unlikely to be committing pedophilia crimes than the sacristy of the Cathedral after Mass...

In its conclusion, the seven High Court judges delivered a finding which was consistent with the comments made by Cardinal Pell to Victoria Police in Rome three and half years earlier:

> It may be accepted that the Court of Appeal majority did not err in holding that A's evidence of the first incident did not contain discrepancies, or display inadequacies, of such a character as to require the jury to have entertained a doubt as to guilt. The likelihood of two choirboys in their gowns being able to slip away from the procession without detection; of finding altar wine in an unlocked cupboard; and of the applicant [Pell] being able to manoeuvre his vestments to expose his penis are considerations that may be put to one side. It remains that the evidence of witnesses, whose honesty was not in question, (i) placed the applicant on the steps of the Cathedral for at least ten minutes after Mass on 15 and 22 December 1996; (ii) placed him in the company of Portelli when he returned to the priests' sacristy to remove his vestments; and (iii) described continuous traffic into and out of the priests' sacristy for ten to 15 minutes after the altar servers completed their bows to the crucifix.
>
> Upon the assumption that the jury assessed A's evidence as thoroughly credible and reliable, the issue for the Court of Appeal was whether the compounding improbabilities caused by the unchallenged evidence summarised in (i), (ii) and (iii) above nonetheless required the jury, acting rationally, to have entertained a doubt as to the applicant's guilt. Plainly they did. Making full allowance for the advantages enjoyed by the jury, there is a significant possibility in relation to charges one to four that an innocent person has been convicted.

So the High Court found that "a jury acting rationally" would have "entertained a doubt as to the applicant's guilt" with respect to charges one to four. It made the same finding with respect to charge five – which involved the February 1997 procession with Pell at the rear. In coming to this conclusion, their Honours made the following comment:

> Weinberg JA [in his Court of Appeal dissent] considered that, had

the second incident occurred in the way A described it, it was highly unlikely that none of the many persons present would have seen what was happening or reported it in some way. His Honour concluded that it was not open to the jury to be satisfied beyond reasonable doubt of the applicant's guilt of the offence charged in the second incident.

The assumption that a group of choristers, including adults, might have been so preoccupied with making their way to the robing room as to fail to notice the extraordinary sight of the Archbishop of Melbourne dressed "in his full regalia" advancing through the procession and pinning a 13 year old boy to the wall, is a large one....

It is unnecessary to decide whether A's description of the second incident so strains credulity as to necessitate that the jury, who saw and heard him give the evidence, ought to have entertained a reasonable doubt as to its occurrence. The capacity of the evidence to support the verdict on this charge suffers from the same deficiency as the evidence of the assaults involved in the first incident.....

The unchallenged evidence of the applicant's invariable practice of greeting congregants after Sunday solemn Mass, and the unchallenged evidence of the requirement under Catholic church practice that the applicant always be accompanied when in the Cathedral, were inconsistent with acceptance of A's evidence of the second incident. It was evidence which ought to have caused the jury, acting rationally, to entertain a doubt as to the applicant's guilt of the offence charged in the second incident. In relation to charge five, again making full allowance for the jury's advantage, there is a significant possibility that an innocent person has been convicted.

It is noteworthy that the High Court dismissed the February 1997 charge in a mere nine brief paragraphs. It was not the Victorian Court of Appeal's finest hour – the same can be said of Victoria Police and the Victorian Director of Public Prosecutions.

The High Court of Australia

The Full Court of the High Court of Australia which sat on Pell v The Queen – Justices Michelle Gordon, Patrick Keane, Virginia Bell, Chief Justice Susan Kiefel and Justices Stephen Gageler, Geoffrey Nettle and James Edelman.

Karina Carvalho and Greg Craven

On 7 April 2020, ABC TV's Karina Carvalho interviewed Greg Craven (who, due to the pandemic, was not in a studio). Professor Craven said that, in reporting the Pell Case, the ABC "got it hopelessly wrong". Ms Carvalho replied: "I'd say ABC management would vigorously reject those accusations." Quelle Surprise!

Free at Last – But Not From Enemies

Soon after Chief Justice Susan Kiefel handed down the High Court's unanimous judgment in *Pell v The Queen*, Cardinal Pell was picked up by Kartya Gracer, one of his solicitors and, sitting in the back seat, driven from Barwon Prison to Melbourne. His principal solicitor, Paul Galbally proceeded to Melbourne in his own car. On leaving Barwon Prison, Pell noticed some 20 cameras on the far side of the road – the required distance due to COVID-19 social distancing rules. Victoria Police cars accompanied the Pell party at a distance and there were two media helicopters overhead.

It was three days before Good Friday (marking the death of Jesus Christ on the cross) and five days before Easter Sunday (marking Christ's resurrection from the dead). That Christ was dead and had risen is a central tenet of the teachings of the Catholic Church. As St Paul's epistle to the Corinthians puts it: "And if Christ be not risen again, then is our preaching vain; and your faith is also vain" – Corinthians 15.14 (The *Holy Bible*, Douay Version, 1956).

The freed man headed to the Carmelite Monastery in Stevenson Street, Kew – a suburb in eastern Melbourne – and close to *Raheen* where Daniel Mannix had resided as Archbishop of Melbourne. The Carmelites, an enclosed order of nuns who devote themselves to a life of prayer, were invited to set up a convent in Melbourne in the early 1920s by the Irish-born Dr Mannix. The first Carmelite monastery was founded in Sydney from France. Initially the Carmelites set up in Mason Street, Hawthorn and moved to Kew when the new monastery was completed in 1929.

Dr Mannix arrived in Australia in 1913 as Coadjutor Archbishop of Melbourne with a right to succeed Archbishop Thomas Carr. He became archbishop in May 1917 and died in office on 6 November 1963, at 99 years of age. George Pell is a successor to and an admirer of Daniel Mannix – Australia's most controversial religious leader of his time. He had a strong influence on Pell.

Plans had been made to get Pell's party inside via the monastery's back entrance on a side street – rather than through the main entrance on Stevenson Street so as to avoid the media pack. Cardinal Pell was greeted by the Mother Prioress at the back door leading into the Sisters' quarters – he was filmed by a hovering helicopter. As Sister Mary of Christ described the occasion in an email to the author dated 17 January 2021:

> His Eminence was very quiet and a bit dazed in a way as he walked through our cloister to his destination. He had been there before, of course.

Pell had lunch in the visitors' cottage and said his first Mass in over 400 days later that afternoon in the public Chapel. Two nuns from the monastery choir attended. It so happened that the relics of St Therese of Lisieux and her parents – Saints Zelie and Louis Martin – were on display in the Chapel, having been stranded there due to the pandemic. Chris Meney, Pell's friend and second cousin (who had driven down from Sydney), served Mass.

Meney had arrived in the convent with a bottle of Wolf Blass red wine which was shared at dinner over a meal of steak and three vegetables. In his *Prison Journal* Pell wrote it was a good wine, but he didn't enjoy it much. And so ended what Pell called his first day of liberation.

Pell said Mass again the next morning, had breakfast and, with Meney driving, departed the convent shortly before 10 am. He had intended to stay in Victoria longer to catch up with relatives and friends but, due to the demonstration outside the monastery, Pell decided to leave the convent.

With Meney driving, Pell headed to the Good Shepherd Seminary in Homebush, Sydney. This had been his Sydney residence after returning from Rome. He was followed all the way by media crews. First stop was at Glenrowen in Northern Victoria, Ned Kelly's home town. Pell spoke to the journalists – excusing his informal dress and, in an ironic way, reminding them of the social distancing requirements. Next stop Goulburn in southern New South Wales. Pell and Meney noticed that NSW Police were more helpful than Victoria Police in ensuring that the media pack kept a safe distance from their car.

There was another interaction with the media at the Good Shepherd Seminary, where Pell was greeted by the rector Fr Danny Meagher. There were some demonstrators. In his *Prison Journal* Pell reflected that he had adapted well to solitary confinement and now had to find a new equilibrium in a locked down society. He added that in some ways his 405 days in prison was a good preparation for the degree of isolation required by health authorities during a pandemic.

On the night of 7 April, St Patrick's Cathedral, Melbourne had been vandalised with graffiti spray-painted on its doors. The messages included "No Justice Pedophile Rapist" and "No Justice 4 Victim". Protest ribbons were also placed on the fence. On the same night ribbons and a child's toy were placed on the entrance gate of the Carmelite Monastery. In time, the fence outside the Good Shepherd Seminary was also decked with protest ribbons. The continuing protests indicated that many of Pell's opponents had not accepted the High Court's decision.

Pell's Media Antagonists Deny the Presumption of Innocence

Immediately after Chief Justice Kiefel's statement in Brisbane, ABC presenter Barrie Cassidy tweeted about Pell that "the High Court has found there was not enough evidence to convict; it did not find him innocent". He added: "You are then entitled to maintain your view and you are under no obligation to apologise for holding those views." Melbourne Radio 3AW presenter Justin Smith, another Pell-antagonist, tweeted "Not guilty; but far from innocent." It is not clear whether either Cassidy or Smith had read the High Court's judgment when they put out their tweets. In any event, both demonstrated profound ignorance about the presumption of innocence that prevails under common law.

The following morning on ABC Radio National *Breakfast*, presenter Fran Kelly expressed surprise that the High Court had overturned a jury verdict and a court of appeal decision. She had to be told by her guests that it is "not unheard of" for the High Court to overthrow a jury verdict (Victorian barrister Matt Collins QC) and that it is "not unusual" for the High Court to uphold an appeal against an appeal court (Professor Rick Sarre, University of South Australia). Fran Kelly seemed surprised – yet the High Court had overturned a jury verdict and an appeal in the court decision in *Fennell v The Queen* in an unanimous five to zero decision the previous September. Kelly seems to have been unaware of this.

On Wednesday 8 April 2020, Nine Newspapers (*Sydney Morning Herald, The Age*) ran a number of articles on *Pell v The Queen*. Nine columnist and former long-term ABC presenter Jon Faine wrote a piece which commenced as follows:

> The High Court decision to allow the appeal of Cardinal George Pell will send shivers through the entire Australian criminal justice system. Their Honours have given hope to anyone who has been convicted by a jury. They have effectively said that doubt can be entertained even when the principal witness in court is unshaken in their testimony.
>
> The scales of justice are being re-calibrated. The balance has shifted. Trials will be different and appeals as well. It has never before been the role of an Appeal Court to substitute their view for the jurors. Now it is. No one in Australia has ever spent so much money trying to undo the sworn evidence of a single witness. Millions of dollars were invested – no stone left unturned.

This was an extraordinarily ignorant comment – especially for someone with a law degree who, albeit briefly, practised law. In *Tyrrell v The Queen* on 15 March 2019, the Victorian Court of Appeal overturned a jury verdict on a historical child sexual assault matter. And in *Fennell v The Queen* on 11 September 2019 the High Court overturned both a jury verdict and a Queensland Court of Appeal decision. Neither Tyrrell nor Fennell had access to considerable amounts of money to defend themselves.

Moreover, as Justice Weinberg pointed out in his dissenting judgment in the Victorian Court of Appeal, not everyone regarded A as unshaken in his testimony. At least two and probably more jurors in the first trial did not regard A as a compelling witness. Nor did Justice Weinberg who, like all the jurors, viewed A's testimony on a video.

On the same day journalist and author Malcolm Knox wrote an article in Nine Newspapers which was headed: "Consider 12 victims of the Pell verdict" which concluded as follows:

> Much focus, since Pell has been freed, has fallen on the victims of abuse in the Catholic Church committed by those other than Pell. There is another group of mistreated people here: the 12 who actually heard the evidence. Juries have no lobby group, no institutional backing, no voice.
>
> Amid other indignities the legal system visits on jurors, it compels them to suffer this insult in silence. But they are us. We citizens are potential jurors, and our response to future requests for our time might be: If you won't trust us, why should we trust you?

Another extraordinarily ignorant comment. Not only is Malcolm Knox suggesting that every jury verdict should be upheld. He is also saying that the plight of a dozen anonymous jurors who have their decisions overturned can be compared with that of a wrongly convicted person who spent over a year in solitary confinement.

On 11 April 2020, the editorial of the leftist *The Saturday Paper*, editor-in-chief Erik Jensen, consisted of a mere 25 words under the heading "A Note On George Pell" – it occupied the whole editorial space:

> George Pell has not been found innocent. It is wrong to say so. The High Court accepted his appeal on the basis of reasonable doubt.

Erik Jensen's editorial was misleading. It is part of the Australian legal system that a person is presumed innocent unless found to be guilty. It is the common law's presumption of innocence. Anyone who is not convicted of a crime is innocent of that crime. The concept is defined in the *Lexis Nexis Butterworths Concise Australian Legal Dictionary*:

> Presumption of innocence. A rule of the criminal law that every person is presumed innocent of a criminal charge until proven guilty. The presumption can only be rebutted if the prosecution discharges the general burden of proving guilt beyond reasonable doubt.

But many Pell-antagonists – like Cassidy, Smith and Jensen – refused to accept the High Court's decision in this instance. While others, like Faine and Knox, refused to accept that juries can make mistakes.

Pell's critics, who were disappointed with the High Court's decision, looked forward to the publication of the non-redacted version of the report of the Royal Commission into Institutional Responses to Child Sexual Abuse concerning the diocese of Ballarat and the archdiocese of Melbourne. The Royal Commission's findings with respect to Pell had been withheld pending the outcome of the criminal proceedings against him. They were released on Thursday 7 May 2020 and are discussed in Chapter 9.

Cardinal Pell's Supporters Speak Out

As examined in Chapters 6, 7 and 8, the overwhelming media comment on Cardinal Pell was either hostile or avowedly critical. However, as Pell acknowledged in his statement after his conviction was quashed by the High Court, there was a small number of commentators who spoke up for him. The list includes, in alphabetical order, Janet Albrechtsen, Peter Baldwin, Andrew Bolt, Frank Brennan, Greg Craven, Peter Craven, Peta Credlin, Rowan Dean, Miranda Devine, Monica Doumit, James Franklin, John Finnis QC, David Flint, the British academic Chris S Friel, Shelley Gare, Kathryn Greiner, Anne Henderson, Gerard Henderson, Peter Hoysted, Jeff Kennett, Paul Kelly, Peter Kurti, Tess Livingstone, Malcolm McCusker QC, Warren Mundine, Tom Percy QC, John Roskam, Angela Shanahan, Lyle Shelton, the late Fr Paul Stenhouse, Ramesh Thakur, Amanda Vanstone, the American commentator George Weigel, Peter Westmore and Keith Windschuttle – many of whom were not baptised Catholics, including agnostics and atheists and many of whom who did not agree with Pell. Most of this group received little media coverage for their views – some were effectively "cancelled" by the ABC.

Interviewed by Sky News' Kieran Gilbert on Wednesday 8 April 2020, Frank Brennan (the son of one-time Chief Justice of the High Court Sir Gerard Brennan) launched a withering critique of the contemporary legal system in Victoria:

> *Frank Brennan:* …I think in Australian society, there are basically three groups of people when it comes to Cardinal Pell. There are those who revile him. And it wouldn't matter what any court said, it wouldn't change their opinion. There are those who think he's absolutely wonderful and idolise or canonise him. And it wouldn't matter what any court said that wouldn't change their view. But then I think there's the vast majority of Australians who say: "Well, we want the processes of the law to work themselves through if there is an allegation which is made against someone of his standing." And I think that's precisely what the High Court has done.
>
> The tragedy in this case is that the policing that was done by the Victoria Police in this particular case was very shoddy. The supervision of the brief by the Director of Public Prosecutions of Victoria was shoddy. The way the Director of Public Prosecutions [Kerri Judd QC] conducted herself, particularly in the High Court, was appalling. And so what we've had is a situation where it's been very difficult for people to get a ready resolution of matters.

Fr Brennan concluded his 15 minute interview by stating that, in this case, the rule of law had not been extended without fear or favour:

> …Sure, I've had all sorts of fights with Cardinal Pell in the past and I'll probably have some more in the future. They'll be about esoteric theological points in the Catholic Church which won't need to worry your viewers. But I couldn't care whether I like him or dislike him – whether his theology is the same as mine or not. If a

prominent citizen like that is going to be targeted by the police, by the DPP, and then given second rate treatment by an appeal court, I say I've got a job to do to be out there and say the rule of law should apply to everyone. Including one George Pell, even though he's a cardinal of the Catholic Church.[5]

Not long after the High Court decision was handed down, Professor Greg Craven appeared on the ABC TV News channel. Interviewed by Karina Carvalho, Craven criticised the Victorian legal system which had made Pell's charging, and subsequent conviction, possible:

> *Karina Carvalho:* Thank you so much for your time today. You've been a staunch supporter of Cardinal George Pell. Does this decision made you feel vindicated in your ongoing support?
>
> *Greg Craven:* I don't think it's a question of vindicated one way or the other. It's not a surprising decision. This was a case that always had a "reasonable doubt" a mile-wide. It shouldn't have been prosecuted. It should not have resulted in a guilty verdict and I think most lawyers thought that, sooner or later, once it got to the High Court this was the default setting. I think the question is why such a case was prosecuted and what damage it did.

After criticising the media's coverage of the case, and particularly that of the ABC and Nine, Craven continued:

> *Greg Craven:* ... What has happened today is the High Court unanimously, seven-nil, said the Victorian justice system got it hopelessly wrong. And restored a person who has been consistently referred to by a variety of media, including leading members of the ABC, as a convicted pedophile. Which he is now not, nor can it be said. That's the news of the day. It is astonishing that there is an organisation like the ABC which places so much emphasis on its trust is rapidly now trying to divert attention from the fundamental fact that you've got it hopelessly wrong –
>
> *Karina Carvalho:* [interjecting] I'd say management would vigorously reject those accusations...

The ABC would, wouldn't it? – to paraphrase Mandy Rice-Davies' comment during the Profumo Affair of 1963. Greg Craven's point, made to a hostile interviewer, was that the ABC had been a player in the Pell Case – and that ABC management would not address this.

Then, writing in the *Sydney Morning Herald* on Saturday 11 April 2020, barrister Greg Barns SC rejected the Malcolm Knox argument that the High Court had made the jury's job redundant. He maintained that all the High Court did in *Pell v The Queen* was to restate the law:

> The jury system is regarded as a bedrock institution in the Australian legal system, as it is in others that have adopted the English common law framework. And the right to be judged by your peers is something which the legal system and legislatures have been very reluctant to interfere with because of this central importance. But we live in the age of Twitter and Facebook. Long gone is the reticence that the community, including the media, once had in discussing individuals facing criminal proceedings. The potential for jurors to have knowledge about a case they are selected to decide upon is self-evident.
>
> It raises an important question. Should Pell, given the hostility of the media, have had the option a trial by judge alone? This was not available to him in Victoria but would have been in NSW, South Australia, the ACT, Queensland and Western Australia. Not because of Pell's position but because such a right should be available to every person in Australia, irrespective of where they happened to be charged....
>
> One will never know whether the jurors in the Pell Case were influenced by the negative media. This does not mean they did not undertake their task to the best of their ability and with good conscience. But is it good enough to work on the hunch that a person's liberty and reputation should be in the hands of 12 individuals about whom nothing is known, and in circumstances where no reasons have to be provided as to why they find a person guilty or not guilty? This is a point made often by Malcolm McCusker QC, a leading West Australian barrister and Kim Beazley's predecessor as governor of that state.

After the Verdict – Responses from Cardinal Pell, A, Pope Francis and Victorian Labor Premier Daniel Andrews

Despite the humiliation of being convicted for pedophilia and having to sign the sex offenders' register before going to prison – and despite his long incarceration for a crime he did not commit – Cardinal Pell was gracious in victory. His Eminence issued a statement, shortly after his release, saying that he was relieved by the decision but bore no ill-will towards his accuser A. Here it is in full:

> I have consistently maintained my innocence while suffering from a serious injustice. This has been remedied today with the High Court's unanimous decision. I look forward to reading the judgment and reasons for the decision in detail. I hold no ill will toward my accuser, I do not want my acquittal to add to the hurt and bitterness so many feel; there is certainly hurt and bitterness enough. However my trial was not a referendum on the Catholic Church; nor a referendum on how Church authorities in Australia dealt with the crime of paedophilia in the Church. The point was whether I had committed these awful crimes, and I did not. The only basis for long term healing is truth and the only basis for justice is truth, because justice means truth for all.
>
> A special thanks for all the prayers and thousands of letters of support. I want to thank in particular my family for their love and support and what they had to go through; my small team of advisors; those who spoke up for me and suffered as a result; and all my friends and supporters here and overseas. Also my deepest thanks and gratitude to my entire legal team for their unwavering resolve to see justice prevail, to throw light on manufactured obscurity and to reveal the truth. Finally, I am aware of the current health crisis [COVID-19]. I am praying for all those affected and our medical frontline personnel.
>
> Cardinal George Pell

For his part, A issued a statement on the website of his lawyer Vivian Waller of Waller Legal.[6] It commenced:

> I respect the decision of the High Court. I accept the outcome. I understand their view that there was not enough evidence to satisfy the court beyond all reasonable doubt that the offending occurred. I understand that the High Court is saying that the prosecution did not make out the case to the required standards of proof. There are a lot of checks and balances in the criminal justice system and the appeal process is one of them. I respect that. It is difficult in child sexual abuse matters to satisfy a criminal court that the offending has occurred beyond the shadow of a doubt.

In fact, in Victoria and elsewhere there are numerous former Catholic priests and brothers who are serving long sentences in prison having been found guilty by a jury, beyond reasonable doubt, of child sexual assault. Moreover, most appeals in child sexual abuse cases are not successful.

In Vatican City, Pope Francis put out this tweet – sympathising with the fate of those who are falsely accused:

> *Pope Francis:* In these days of #Lent, we've been witnessing the persecution that Jesus underwent and how He was judged ferociously, even though He was innocent. Let us #PrayTogether today for all those persons who suffer due to an unjust sentence because of someone had it in for them.

And then there was the statement of Victorian Labor Party premier Daniel Andrews who effectively challenged the unanimous decision of the High Court in *Pell v The Queen*. This is what Mr Andrews had to say – in full:

> I make no comment about today's High Court decision. But I have a message for every single victim and survivor of child sex abuse: I see you. I hear you. I believe you.

Soon after, Melbourne University's Professor Jeremy Gans put out the following tweet:

> *Jeremy Gans:* This is a quite odd official statement apparently in response to a High Court ruling in a Victorian criminal case, espe-

cially one that has always been the subject of significant community debate, as well as division within (and now between) the courts.

Premier Andrews' statement was certainly odd. As Professor Gans pointed out at the time, the Pell Case had always been the subject of significant debate, including within the Victorian Court of Appeal. It demonstrated the animosity held by the head of government in Victoria – who leads the Victorian Labor Party's socialist left faction – towards Cardinal Pell.

This was evident even before the High Court decision. On 3 December 2019, when the Pell Case was before the High Court, former prime minister Tony Abbott visited the cardinal in the Melbourne Assessment Prison. Abbott was door-stopped by Channel 7 News reporter Brendan Donohoe (who later worked for Daniel Andrews) as he left the prison and declined to answer questions – except to say that he had been visiting a friend. The following day – speaking as the premier of Victoria – Daniel Andrews described the visit as "shameful, absolutely shameful" and added:

> If you want to go visiting child sex offenders, then surely you'd think for a moment [that] this is something bigger than you and him and your friendship. Lives have been destroyed. It's appalling. I wouldn't have done it.

This was an improper intervention by a State premier – especially since the legal matters against Cardinal Pell had yet to be finalised and were before the High Court. Also, it is part of the corrections system in Australia that prisoners have a right to receive visitors in accordance with prevailing requirements.

In Premier Andrews' view, a complainant is always a "victim" who must be believed. In which case, the State of Victoria might as well abolish trials – along with appeals – in current and historical child sexual abuse cases. Most complaints of child sexual assault are true. However, some are not – of which the Pell Case is a recent example.

Some complainants, for whatever reason, have clear "recollections" of events that never happened. A recent example of which is the John Francis Tyrrell Case in Victoria (see Chapter 4). Some others do not tell the truth – as in the "Nick" case in Britain which saw Carl Beech sentenced to a lengthy jail term in 2019 for making false allegations of child sexual abuse against high profile figures in British society, living and dead – including Lord Bramall and the late Ted Heath. Initially the Metropolitan Police believed Beech's claims – describing them as "credible and true" and declared he was a victim – which did huge reputational damage to Beech's alleged abusers, both living and dead.

According to Daniel Andrews, Tyrrell and Pell should be rotting in prison – while the lying Carl Beech should be living free in comfort, having received financial compensation from the British taxpayer for his concocted suffering.

What Premier Andrews and other Pell-antagonists failed to recognise was that the pre-trial hysteria critical of Pell, going back over a decade, was likely to influence a jury. Clearly the introduction of trial by judge alone acknowledges that juries can get it wrong. Something that Premier Andrews refused to concede in child sexual abuse cases since he maintains that a complainant is always a victim. It speaks volumes for the state of justice in contemporary Victoria that its premier would effectively deny the common law presumption of innocence to one of the best known Victoria-born Australians.

Magistrates and judges can make mistakes. However, unlike juries, they have to give reasons for their decisions. This makes it possible for an accused to at least understand on what grounds he/she has been convicted "beyond reasonable doubt" and, where appropriate, lodge an appeal which takes issue with the reasons for the decision.

It is noteworthy that Cardinal Pell became a free man after his case was removed from the jurisdiction of the State of Victoria and its police, prosecution and judicial systems – to the High Court of Australia.

2

MOB-RULE AND WITCH-HUNTS ON THE ROAD TO THE MAGISTRATES' COURT

"…over the last period we have witnessed, outside of this court and within our community, examples of a "witch-hunt" or "lynch mob" mentality in relation to Cardinal Pell. I utterly condemn such behaviour. That has nothing to with justice or a civilised society…"

- Chief Judge Peter Kidd, County Court of Victoria, 13 March 2019

The Warnings of Chief Judge Kidd and Judge Ellis

Cardinal George Pell was the defendant or appellant in seven cases/applications in the Australian legal system. First there was *The Police v George Pell* in the Magistrates' Court of Victoria. Followed by the trial and then re-trial of *Director of Public Prosecutions v George Pell* in the County Court of Victoria. Followed by *DPP v Pell (Evidential Ruling No. 1)* in the County Court. Followed by *George Pell v The Queen* in the Supreme Court of Victoria's Court of Appeal. Followed by an application for special leave to appeal to the High Court of Australia. Followed by *Pell v The Queen* in the High Court.

Anti-Pell protest outside the County Court of Victoria

In sentencing Cardinal Pell on 13 March 2019, Chief Judge Peter Kidd condemned the "witch hunt" and "mob rule" mentality which had prevailed outside the Victorian Magistrates' Court (during Pell's committal hearings) and the Victorian County Court (during Pell's trial and re-trial). But no Victorian authority attempted to disperse "the mob" when the legal proceedings were underway. *(Photo by Michael Dodge via Getty Images)*

Belinda Wallington, Louise Milligan, Lyn Allison and Magistrate Pauline Spencer outside the ABC studio

On Monday 14 May 2017, the topic for The Conversation Hour on ABC Radio Melbourne 774 was "George Pell allegations and Law Week". The program presenter was Jon Faine – with former Democrats Senate leader Lyn Allison as his co-host. The Cardinal author Louise Milligan was interviewed first. After that a discussion took place between Magistrate Belinda Wallington, Magistrate Spencer, Jon Faine and Lyn Allison. Cardinal was formally launched on 17 May 2017. The Police v Pell hearings commenced in the Magistrates' Court on 6 March 2018 with Magistrate Wallington presiding.

Pell's hearing before the High Court in Canberra on 11-12 March 2020 was a relatively quiet affair. A few opponents and supporters (primarily Vietnamese Australians) held placards outside the court but that was all. There were no major protests by Cardinal Pell's opponents – partly because the hearing was in Canberra and the applicant was not in court but in prison. When the High Court's judgment was handed down a month later it was a very quiet affair due to the pandemic and all that. But it is unlikely that High Court hearings in Canberra or Brisbane, absent a pandemic, would have led to scenes like those Pell experienced outside the Magistrates' Court and the County Court of Victoria. The atmosphere in Melbourne was different.

The committal hearing before the Magistrates' Court and the County Court trials were often wild affairs as the accused, his several advisers and legal team were frequently abused and jostled before and after sittings of the courts, despite police protection.

For example, Lucie Morris-Marr reported that early in the committal proceedings "a female protestor screamed at the Cardinal: 'Go to hell, George Pell' as he was swallowed up by an international scrum and large police presence on his arrival at the court". Writing in *The New Daily* on 26 February 2019, after the suppression order concerning Pell's conviction at the Cathedral Trial was released, Morris-Marr reported:

> Cardinal George Pell was verbally attacked on Tuesday [26 February 2019] amid angry and violent scenes in Melbourne after it was revealed he had been found guilty of sexually abusing two choirboys. Outside the County Court of Victoria members of the public shouted "you're a monster" and "scum" as the 77-year-old was led to a waiting car amid a huge media scrum. Multiple officers from Victoria Police had to hold back the furious onlookers who pushed towards the cardinal after a media blackout on the high-profile case was lifted on Tuesday morning…Katrina Lee, the executive advisor for the Archdiocese of Sydney, was seen physically pushing away one man as she protected the cardinal.

Neither Magistrate Belinda Wallington, nor the Victorian DPP (initially John Champion SC and from March 2018 Kerri Judd QC), nor the Victorian Attorney-General Jill Hennessy, nor Victorian Premier Daniel Andrews criticised such violations of the rights of a defendant to a fair and orderly hearing and trial. Nor did Chief Judge Peter Kidd before Pell was convicted and sentenced.

However, in *DPP v Pell (Sentence)* on 13 March 2019 when Pell was sentenced, Chief Judge Peter Kidd spoke out for the first time against the mob mentality that had accompanied the defendant's trial. It was a powerful rebuke to Pell's opponents who had demonstrated and verbally abused him outside the court and within the community – which was televised live:

> As I directed the jury who convicted you in this trial, you are not to be made a scapegoat for any failings or perceived failings of the Catholic Church. Nor are you being sentenced for any failure to prevent or report child sexual abuse by other clergy within the Catholic Church. You have not been charged with or convicted of any such conduct or failings.
>
> This leads me to say something to other victims of clerical or institutional sexual abuse who may be present in court today or watching or listening elsewhere. This sentence is not and cannot be a vindication of your trauma. Cardinal Pell has not been convicted of any wrongs committed against you. Cardinal Pell does not fall to be punished for any such wrongs. I recognise that you seek justice, but it can only be justice if it is done in accordance with the rule of law. For me to punish Cardinal Pell for the wrongs committed against you would be contrary to the rule of law and it would not be justice at all....
>
> Finally, with respect to these preliminary observations, over the last period we have witnessed, outside of this court and within our community, examples of a "witch-hunt" or "lynch mob" mentality in relation to Cardinal Pell. I utterly condemn such behaviour. That has nothing to do with justice or a civilised society. The Courts stand as a bulwark against such irresponsible behaviour.

The Chief Judge's condemnation of the witch-hunt or lynch mob mentality, both outside Pell's trials and within the Australian community, was a voice in the wilderness. His comments were not highlighted in the media and they did not prevent a recurrence of such behaviour immediately after the sentencing judgment or when Pell's appeal was heard by the Victorian Court of Appeal. During Pell's committal hearings and trials, Victoria's police, legal and governmental institutions did not stand as a bulwark against irresponsible behaviour.

Also unheeded was His Honour's other warning – namely that Cardinal Pell was not responsible for all victims of clerical sexual abuse. The Chief Judge recognised that victims of child sexual assault seek justice – but warned that it would not be justice if Pell were punished for the crimes of others. The message was that one of the most senior figures in the Catholic Church in Australia should not bear a collective guilt for the crimes of others.

Archbishop Philip Wilson's Trial

It is a sad fact that two of the leaders of the Catholic Church in Australia who, in the 1990s and 2000s, did much to tackle the crime of clerical child sexual abuse – Cardinal George Pell (born 1941) and Archbishop Philip Wilson (born 1950) – were both convicted of offences regarding children. Both had their convictions overturned on appeal. As previously mentioned, Pell set up the Melbourne Response in 1996. For his part, Wilson took a leading role in facing up to child sexual abuse when he was Archbishop of Wollongong in 1996-2001 and, subsequently, as Archbishop of Adelaide from 2001 to 2018. Wilson also played an important role in improving the Catholic Church's response at a national level to clerical child sexual abuse. The other high-ranking Catholic Church official who played a significant role at the time was Bishop Geoffrey Robinson (1937-2020) in Sydney.

In July 2018, Archbishop Wilson was found guilty in the Newcastle Local Court by Magistrate Robert Stone of covering up child sexual abuse in the Maitland-Newcastle diocese when he was a junior priest aged about 25. Due to the vagaries of Section 316 in the *NSW Crimes Act*, Wilson's conviction turned on his failure to have a reasonable excuse for not reporting the matter to NSW Police during the period April 2004 to January 2006. Wilson was sentenced to 12 months to be served in home detention. The offence occurred in 1971 and Wilson was alleged to have been told about it by the victim in 1976.

During the *NSW Director of Public Prosecutions v Wilson* trial and on the day of Wilson's conviction, there was a large media contingent along with anti-Wilson protestors outside the court. It was a smaller version of the mobs which Pell faced at the Melbourne Magistrates' Court and the County Court of Victoria.

In spite of the national and international media coverage, the NSW Department of Justice refused to release even a redacted version of Magistrate Stone's judgment. As the lawyer and Jesuit priest Fr. Frank Brennan found out, the magistrate's decision could only be accessed by travelling to Newcastle (120 kilometres north of Sydney) and taking notes of a 59 page judgment while sitting in the waiting area of the court registry.

On 3 July 2018, the night of Wilson's conviction, the case was discussed on the influential ABC TV program *The Drum*. Julia Baird was in the presenter's chair as, variously, *The Saturday Paper's* Karen Middleton along with commentators Dee Madigan, Megan Motto and Stephen O'Doherty paid out on Archbishop Wilson without mentioning that he had a right of appeal. At one stage Dr Baird commented that "there seems to be a consensus on the panel here". There sure was – since, earlier in the discussion, the presenter herself had criticised the Catholic Church's "obstructive clericalism". No one on the panel was in court when Magistrate Stone's judgment was handed down and no one had read his decision.

On 6 December 2018, Judge Roy Ellis in the NSW District Court in Newcastle upheld Wilson's appeal and quashed his conviction. His Honour is very experienced in hearing matters relating to the sexual abuse of children as a result of his time as a crown prosecutor and, later, a judicial officer. Judge Ellis found that the prosecution had not proved its case beyond reasonable doubt.

Judge Ellis held that Wilson was an honest witness – as was the complainant.

However, he found that the complainant had given evidence that was, at times, inconsistent and unreliable. His Honour also noted that the Crown relied solely on the evidence of the complainant who claimed to have spoken to Wilson in 1976 and that there was "no other independent evidence to support his allegations". In this sense the case turned on memory. Psychologist Professor Richard Kemp was called as an expert witness. His evidence was unchallenged by the prosecution and accepted by the court.

Professor Kemp made the following points, among others. Namely, (i) delay will reduce the chances of accurate recall, (ii) a person typically forgets details of a conversation rather than that it took place, (iii) there is a tendency to have a memory of what was intended to be said but not actually said and (iv) that it is not possible to reliably distinguish between accurate, false or distorted memories in the absence of evidence.

In his judgment on 6 December 2018, Judge Ellis also warned about making assumptions. It was the prosecution's case that the defendant "must have" remembered, between 2004 and 2006, speaking with the complainant some four decades earlier. His Honour said: "A statement or conclusion to the effect that 'He must have!' does not and can never equate to proof beyond reasonable doubt".

This was a severe criticism of a Crown prosecution in this case and of the magistrate's decision by an experienced judge. But His Honour's decision was generally overlooked by the media – and not mentioned at all on *The Drum*, despite the fact that Fr Brennan appeared on the program soon after Wilson's acquittal and had read the decision of both the magistrate and the judge. Brennan was not invited to discuss the Wilson acquittal.

It was reported that some present in the court in Newcastle when the judgment was handed down yelled in disgust at Judge Ellis' decision. According to *The Guardian*, as His Honour left the bench, an onlooker called out: "Bullshit – that's a disgrace." There was a small demonstration outside the court during which the complainant severely criticised the judgment.

Within hours of the decision and, presumably before he had read and considered the 42 page judgment, NSW Coalition attorney-general Mark Speakman asked the NSW DPP to consider an appeal. After consideration, the DPP declined to appeal – which was not surprising in view of the strength of Judge Ellis' judicial logic in this instance along with the lack of evidence. Subsequently, Mr Speakman sought independent legal advice about the possibility of an appeal. Not surprisingly, this also came to naught – but that such a move was envisaged demonstrated the pressure on politicians to act in accordance with the demands of complainants and their supporters in historical child sexual abuse cases. At the time of his conviction, Archbishop Wilson was the highest ranking member of the Catholic Church world-wide to have been found guilty of offences with respect to historical child sexual assault.

Judge Ellis' decision in the Wilson Case was delivered just five days before the jury reached its decision in the re-trial of *DPP v Pell*. Judge Ellis said what few judicial officers have been prepared to say, in Australia or elsewhere, concerning the media's influence on judicial independence, particularly in child abuse cases:

> ...Following the Royal Commission into Institutional Responses to Child Sexual Abuse, our community is far more informed in terms of the morally deficient practices previously adopted by some religious institutions on some occasions to deal with sexual abuse allegations. There is no doubt that sexual abuse of children by members of the clergy and attempts to prevent publication of such abuse either on an individual or institutional basis is not only morally reprehensible but it is also contrary to the basic principles of Christianity. Clearly the public is now far better informed on

these issues because of the publicity the media has given, and rightly given, to these issues.

However, it is important to appreciate that the media's interest in the prosecution of institutional sexual abuse or its cover up should not be permitted to undermine judicial independence and the rule of law. The potential for media pressure to impact judicial independence may be subtle or indeed subversive in the sense that it is the elephant in the room that no one sees or acknowledges or wants to see or acknowledge. This is not a criticism of the media but rather a recognition that intended or not, the mere presence of large numbers of members of the media from all around Australia and indeed potentially the western world carries with it an undoubted pressure on the Court.

This may amount to perceived pressure for a Court to reach a conclusion which seems to be consistent with the direction of public opinion, rather than being consistent with the rule of law that requires a court to hand down individual justice in its decision making process. In practice complying with legal principles may well result in a verdict that is perhaps inconsistent with media or community expectations given more recent trends in public and media opinions. But if the verdict is a true representation of justice in the individual case then it is community or media expectations that must be dashed not the hopes of an individual that he or she will receive a fair trial and that the verdict will provide justice in their case in accordance with legal principles that operate in Australia.

His Honour also drew an emphatic division between the defendant and the institution for which he worked. He said: "It is fair to say that the Catholic Church as an institution has had a lot to answer for in terms of its historical self-protective approach to children complaining of sexual abuse at the hands of some of its priests." But Judge Ellis made the point that, when a defendant appears before a court, they are "an individual who has the same legal rights as every other person in the community". His Honour went on to say that it was not for him "to punish the Catholic Church for its institutional moral deficits or to punish Philip Wilson for the sins of the now deceased [offender]

James Fletcher by finding Philip Wilson guilty simply on the basis that he is a Catholic priest".

Like Chief Judge Kidd, Judge Ellis expressed concern about the presence of the notion of collective guilt in such high profile cases. Namely, the irrational view that the likes of Pell and Wilson should be held guilty for the crimes of others. This, along with the witch-hunt and lynch mob mentality, was capable of impacting judicial independence. To paraphrase Oscar Wilde, this is the (legal) truth that dare not speak its name. It was present in the case of Cardinal George Pell.

Magistrates' Court of Victoria: The Police v George Pell – 26 charges

The Victorian Director of Public Prosecutions decided not to prosecute George Pell on historical child sexual assault charges but advised Victoria Police that it could do so if it wished. When Victoria Police announced its decision to prosecute Pell in July 2017, the Victorian DPP John Champion SC said that his office would conduct the legal proceedings, commencing in the Magistrates' Court. John Champion was appointed to the Victorian Supreme Court by the Andrews government in December 2017 – and replaced by Kerri Judd QC. As Frank Brennan wrote in *The Weekend Australian* on 11-12 April 2020, from the time Champion made the decision "the office of the DPP went to extraordinary lengths trying to cobble together a case".

Victoria Police's prosecution of George Pell commenced in the Melbourne Magistrates' Court on 6 March 2018 and concluded on 17 April 2018. Magistrate Belinda Wallington handed down her findings on 1 May 2018. Mark Gibson SC, the Senior Crown Prosecutor, led the case for the prosecution assisted by Angela Ellis. Robert Richter QC appeared for the defence assisted by Ruth Shann.

On the final day of the hearings, Her Honour responded to a defence submission to throw out all the charges. Robert Richter said the most serious complaints "ought to be regarded as impossible and the lesser charges should be dismissed because of problems with the complainants' credibility". Ms Wallington responded that questions of credibility and reliability were for a jury to decide "except when you get to the point where credibility is effectively eliminated". It was a low bar indeed – and demonstrated the power of Victoria Police to lay charges and get them into court despite having a very weak case. This meant, in this instance, that Victoria Police could inflict massive reputational damage on someone like George Pell on the basis of scant evidence – provided its case had even a shred of credibility.

At the commencement of her findings on 1 May 2018, Magistrate Wallington had this to say:

> The test for committal in Victoria is set out in s.4(4) of the *Criminal Procedure Act*. If the evidence is not of sufficient weight to support a conviction, the court must discharge. If in the opinion of the court the evidence is of sufficient weight, it must commit the accused for trial. A court tasked with determining a committal, needs to bear in mind that it is fundamental to our system of criminal justice in relation to allegations of serious crimes tried by jury, that the jury is the constitutional tribunal for deciding issues of fact.
>
> Where there are competing inferences of guilt and innocence, the courts should not discharge merely because there is a reasonable hypothesis consistent with innocence. Although the committal court is empowered to assess the credibility and reliability of witnesses, unless the credibility of a witness is effectively destroyed, credibility and reliability are matters for the jury. Where the evidence is so weak that the prospect of conviction is minimal, it will not be of sufficient weight to commit.

Even if there was a reasonable hypothesis consistent with Pell's innocence, this would not have been sufficient reason to discharge him since there would be competing inferences of guilt and innocence. Moreover, the magistrate stated that it is the role of the jury to decide issues of fact. And the credibility and reliability of witnesses are matters for a jury – unless the credibility of a witness is effectively destroyed. To repeat, once charges are laid by Victoria Police, in all likelihood an accused will go to trial and their future will be decided by a jury – with all the unwarranted financial and reputational damage that this involves if they are found to be not guilty.

With so low a bar with respect to committing the accused to trial, it would be expected that a competent police force would see all – or nearly all – matters proceed beyond a committal hearing. Especially since the Senior Crown Prosecutor (on behalf of the Victorian DPP) appeared for Victoria Police at the committal proceedings and would be expected to engage in strong and effective advocacy. It was not to be the case in the matter of *The Police v George Pell.*

Victoria Police charged Pell with 26 offences involving nine persons. As Professor Gans has pointed out "that charging decision was ultimately shared with the then Director of Public Prosecutions John Champion (now a Supreme Court judge) and his successor, Kerri Judd, who could have stopped the prosecution if they disagreed with the police's call". They didn't. Here's the outcome of the committal proceedings in the Magistrates' Court.

• Charges 1-6 concerning one alleged victim, B.A., were withdrawn before the trial commenced. However, despite the lack of witnesses or forensic evidence and the inconsistencies in B.A.'s story, Victorian Police had believed the complainant and disbelieved Pell. The allegations had centered on Pell's time as a priest in Ballarat. The B.A. case is discussed in Chapter 8 – where B.A. is referred to as Bernie.

• Charges 7 to 14 involved offences alleged to have occurred against S.G. in Ballarat and its surrounds. They concerned two alleged sexual assaults by Pell in 1976 at the YMCA Pool in Ballarat – a public place. S.G. was around nine years old at the time. S.G. lived at Nazareth Boys' Home in Ballarat from the age of five until he went to high school. The Nazareth Boys' Home, sometimes termed the St Joseph Boys' Home, was run by a religious order – the Sisters of Nazareth.

Then, three years later in 1979, the charge was that – when S.G. was around 12 years of age – he was anally raped by Pell at The Regent cinema in Ballarat during the showing of *Close Encounters of the Third Kind* – another public place. The alleged rape took three minutes and S.G. screamed in pain but no one in the theatre noticed at the time. Later he bled heavily from the anus. The allegation was that S.G. was handed over to Pell by a nun at Nazareth Boys' Home and taken to the cinema.

Shortly after, a nun at Nazareth Boys' Home told S.G. again he was to go with Pell. The allegation here was that Pell anally raped S.G. on a slide at a playground in Warrenheip (a Ballarat suburb) – another public place. Not long after, it was alleged that Pell came to the dormitory where S.G. slept with others – another public place – and took him to the chapel where he was raped on the altar, which led to further bleeding. Later still, the Mother Superior told S.G. he was going out again – it was alleged that on this occasion S.G. was pack raped by three men (including Pell) at Mount Buninyong (15 kilometers south of Ballarat) – another public place. Once more bleeding was alleged to have occurred.

That was the case for the prosecution. Apart from the alleged incidents at the YMCA Pool, all the other matters involved S.G. being taken from Nazareth Boys' Home in 1979 – with the help of the nuns – to be sexually assaulted over a period of many months. The essential problem for the prosecution was that S.G. left the home on 20 January 1979. Victoria Police had not checked this. Nor, apparently, had the DPP counter-checked the allegation.

Moreover, *Close Encounters of The Third Kind* did not screen at The Regent in 1979. And S.G.'s foster mother said that, contrary to his claim, she did not recall him ever telling her of anal bleeding. He did see a specialist around that time. However the doctor, who had no memory of treating S.G., said that he would have recalled examining a child with anal injuries causing bleeding – but did not do so.

Magistrate Wallington found "there were inconsistencies both internally and within S.G.'s evidence and when matched against known facts". Also, S.G. could not reconcile the differences between his initial statement to Victoria Police and what he said to the police at a video re-enactment. Her Honour concluded:

> Inconsistencies as these are ordinarily within the province of a jury's assessment of a witness' credibility. In this case, the inconsistencies in S.G.'s evidence must be examined in the context of a fundamental defect in the evidence, that is the impossibility of S.G. being taken out of the boys' home in order to be raped over a 12 month period, although the allegations he made of offending at the YWCA[sic] change room have to be separately considered, the damage to S.G.'s reliability as a witness means it would be illogical to discharge only on those offences which cannot have happened as described. I find that the evidence as a whole is not of sufficient weight for a jury to convict. The accused is discharged on Charges 7 to 14.

So, despite the very low bar in getting charges committed to court, Victoria Police and the Crown prosecutor (who works for the DPP) failed completely with respect to Charges 7 to 14. Any professional investigation before the trial would have found that S.G. could not have been frequently taken from Nazareth Boys' Home and raped in 1979 – because he was not there for nearly all of that year. And he could not have been raped during *Close Encounters of the Third Kind* in 1979 – since the film was not shown that year in Ballarat. Moreover, S.G.'s inconsistency on these matters discredited his other recollections concerning the YMCA Pool. Victoria Police – with support in court of the DPP – had presented a witness whose credibility was effectively destroyed during the hearing.

Pell told Victoria Police in Rome that he had rarely visited the Nazareth Boys' Home when he was in Ballarat – and Victoria Police could not produce any evidence to refute this claim. He also disputed S.G.'s claim that he had been assaulted in the YMCA Pool on several Saturday mornings. Pell told Victoria Police that he never went to the pool on a Saturday morning. He also said that he rarely went to the cinema and had never seen *Close Encounters of the Third Kind*. And so it continued – with Victoria Police asking Pell about the location of places and churches which, as the investigator, it should have known. Despite a lack of evidence and the inconsistencies in S.G's story – Victoria Police believed S.G. and disbelieved Pell.

• <u>Charge 15</u> involved M.B. – who had watched Louise Milligan's report on the ABC TV *7.30* program 27 July 2016 in which two men, L.M. and D.D., claimed that they had been sexually assaulted by Pell in the Eureka Pool at Ballarat – a public place. After viewing *7.30* on 27 July 2016, M.B. went to Victoria Police and made similar allegations with respect to Pell throwing him in the pool.

It turned out that, under cross examination, M.B. had a woeful memory – not only with respect to two years earlier when he gave a statement to Victoria Police – but even concerning answers he had given previously in evidence in the Magistrates' Court. As Magistrate Wallington said in her finding:

> M.B.'s lack of recall was often a non-responsive way of avoiding answering the questions. When clarity was sought, he said variously, "Just whatever, mate, whatever. I'll leave it up to you. Whatever you think works", and "No comment". To the question, "Do you recall what you said a minute ago", he said, "I can't recall".
>
> M.B. was an unsatisfactory witness. It is difficult to see how a jury could convict on the evidence of a man who has said on his affirmation that he cannot recall what he said a minute ago. His evidence-in-chief provides evidence of an offence upon which a jury could convict and he did not resile from that allegation. Matters of credibility and reliability are generally matters for a jury to determine, but there is authority for the proposition that a committing magistrate may make some assessment of credibility in order to assess the strength of the Crown case. The test is not whether there is evidence but whether there is evidence of sufficient weight.
>
> Even allowing for the stresses of giving evidence, the overall effect of M.B.'s evidence is that the only matter upon which he is able to be certain is his allegation. His evidence is crucial to proof of

the charge. In my view this is one of those rare cases where the witness demonstrated such a cavalier attitude towards giving his evidence that a jury could put no weight upon it. After giving the matter serious consideration, I am not satisfied that the evidence is of sufficient weight to support a conviction and the accused is discharged on Charge 15.

Another total failure by Victoria Police and the DPP. Victoria Police charged Pell with assaulting M.B. despite the fact that its witness' memory was so poor that he could not recall what he had said only minutes earlier and had a cavalier attitude to giving evidence. Yes, the committal bar was set very low – even so, Victoria Police could not get over it. This case demonstrates the fallacy of those who, like Victorian Premier Daniel Andrews, believe that all complainants are victims who should be believed.

• Charge 16 was an indecent assault charge of Pell against P.C. who also lived in the Nazareth Boys' Home. He was drawn to the attention of Victoria Police by S.G. who, in turn, contacted P.C. The complainant claimed that on three separate occasions, when he was somewhere between the ages of seven and ten, Pell put his finger up his anus when throwing him up in the air at a pool at the Nazareth Boys' Home – another public place. P.C. said he had seen two friends, L.M. and D.D., talking to Louise Milligan on *7.30*. Before the Magistrates' Court, P.C. denied saying to Senior Detective Jason Rowles that he had been assaulted by Pell over a few years in the summer months, stating: "It would have been a lie and incorrect for me to have said that; so, no, I didn't." It is not clear why Detective Rowles would have misrepresented what P.C. told him – particularly since Victoria Police seemed keen to lay as many serious charges against Pell as possible. Also P.C. accepted that he had a substantial drug and alcohol problem.

Nevertheless, Magistrate Wallington found that the evidence of P.C. was of sufficient weight for a jury to convict. In this instance, Victoria Police got over a very low bar. However, the case did not go to trial – it was subsequently dropped by the DPP.

- **Charge 17** was of an alleged single assault by Pell against L.T. at the Eureka Pool. L.T. had also watched L.M., D.D. and one other on *7.30* and he got in touch with L.M. after the program. As Magistrate Wallington put it: "Charge 17 is a fleeting touch on a single occasion during boisterous activity". On the basis of tendency evidence – i.e. the alleged tendency of Pell to act this way with the likes of L.M. – she committed Pell to trial on this one count.

However, before doing so, Her Honour acknowledged the unfairness that had occurred to the accused since his counsel was deprived of the opportunity to cross examine P.C. or call other witnesses who might refute his evidence. Charge 17 never made it to trial – it, too, was subsequently dropped by the DPP.

- **Charge 18** was withdrawn – since D.D. had died before the hearing commenced. This involved an alleged incident in the Eureka Pool, a public place. Along with L.M., D.D. had spoken to Louise Milligan on *7.30* and given a similar account about Pell's alleged offending against them.

- **Charge 19** involved L.M. – one of the two men who spoke to Louise Milligan on *7.30* concerning Pell's alleged behavior at the Eureka Pool. He maintained that Pell molested him when throwing him in the pool. In Magistrate Wallington's findings, the following comment appears:

> In cross-examination L.M. was asked, "Did he ever touch you in the change room?", and he said, "No". L.M. was reminded of his signed statutory declaration in support of a VOCAT [Victims of Crime Assistance Tribunal] claim made in March 2016. In that declaration he said, "Father Pell used to play with my genitals and he's put his finger up my bottom at the swimming pool and in the showers". It was put, "He didn't touch you in the showers, did he?", and he said, "No, I can't remember saying that. I lodged a VOCAT claim to seek some financial help in getting into a rehab centre to try and stop my drug and alcohol use". "Is it true he penetrated your bottom?" "No, he didn't put his finger completely up my bottom. He was molesting my bottom."

[On] 9 June 2016 L.M. spoke with the journalist, Louise Milligan, who was working on the "7.30 Report". He told her that George Pell digitally put his finger in his anus. In cross-examination when asked about this he said, "That's what it felt like to me". It was put to him, "You said, 'He'd dry us and touch our genitals and vice versa sort of thing'". He said, "I don't remember saying that". "If you said it, it was a complete and utter lie?" "Well, it must be, yes." "How do you explain you said it?" "Obviously also at the time I was in a stage, as I said, where I'd asked to be put in a rehab centre. I had massive mental health issues. I was in the middle of a complete meltdown. I was going quite well until I was interviewed by SANO, then I spiralled out of control. It was basically drink, drugs, avoiding people, mass pressure. I told Louise Milligan I was in the middle of a meltdown." "When did the meltdown end?" "When I went to gaol."

Louise Milligan gave evidence and was asked whether L.M. had told her he was having a meltdown. She said she did not recall him saying that but he was under great duress at the time. There are a number of discrepancies in the versions L.M. has given in various contexts. Juries have to grapple with similar inconsistencies regularly. That is their role.

Despite L.M. giving different versions of his allegations against Pell in various contexts, Magistrate Wallington committed the defendant to stand trial. Once again, Victoria Police cleared a very low bar. And, once again, Charge 18 never made it to court – it was dropped by the DPP.

• <u>Charges 20-26</u> were the only ones to make it to the trial by jury. They involved alleged offences committed by Pell at St Patrick's Cathedral when he was Archbishop of Melbourne in 1996 and 1997 and led to his conviction in 2018 – which was eventually quashed by the High Court.

This is how Magistrate Wallington commenced her findings with respect to Charges 20-26:

The prosecution rely on the evidence of J.J. whose statements were tendered as his evidence-in-chief of sexual offences alleged to have been committed against himself and M.R. There is no statement from M.R., who died of a drug overdose in 2014, having never spoken to anyone of having been sexually assaulted and having specifically denied it when questioned by his mother. J.J. alleged a second incident where he was alone.

As discussed in Chapter 1, in the Victorian Court of Appeal and the High Court, "J" or "J.J." was described as "A". And "R" or "M.R." was described as "B". Her Honour's introductory comment made it clear that the prosecution relied solely on the evidence of A – there was no other witness and no forensic evidence.

Those sitting in the Magistrates' Court on 1 May 2018 might have got the impression that Magistrate Wallington was about to discharge the defendant on charges 20 to 26 as she assessed the evidence. Her Honour discussed the evidence given by John Mallinson (the choir master), Monsignor Charles Portelli (the master of ceremonies), Max Potter (sacristan), Geoffrey Cox (assistant organist and choir master) and Peter Finnigan (choir marshal) along with some eleven choristers.

None of what were called the "opportunity" witnesses – meaning those individuals who gave evidence as to Pell's opportunity to offend – supported the claims made by A with respect to himself and the late B. Even so, the accused was committed for trial on charges 20 to 26. Her Honour's conclusion was as follows:

> There was a preponderance of evidence that the archbishop spent time speaking with the congregants on the steps prior to returning to the sacristy. If a jury accepted the evidence of Monsignor Portelli and Mr Potter that the archbishop was never in the sacristy robed and alone, and that choirboys could never access the sacristy keys because they were always locked when unused, then a jury could not convict.
>
> Their evidence may not be as high as that, however even if it is that high, the submission that a properly instructed jury would have no

> ability to put their evidence or part thereof, to one side, cannot be accepted. The jury has the fundamental function of weighing the evidence and the unfettered ability to accept or reject it. A committing magistrate may not usurp that fundamental role.
>
> The evidence of J.J. is evidence capable, as a matter of law, of supporting a finding of guilt and it is not for this court to impose its own view, if held, that a jury would be unlikely to convict. Having found that there is evidence of sufficient weight that a properly instructed jury could convict, the accused is committed for trial on Charges 20 to 26.

Again, Victoria Police cleared a very low bar – relying, as it did, on the uncorroborated evidence of the complainant alone with respect to alleged assaults which occurred in a public place – St Patrick's Cathedral. The final charge even involved an alleged assault against A by Pell in the immediate presence of around at least 40 people. It was this charge which Justice Weinberg, in his dissent in the Victorian Court of Appeal, said should not have been prosecuted by the Victorian DPP.

The Magistrates' Court Outcome – 16 Down, 10 to Go

In the end, Pell went into the Magistrates' Court facing 26 charges and came out facing ten only. It was agreed that the media could report that approximately half of the charges were discharged – it was, in fact, closer to two thirds. Importantly, the most serious charges of anal rape were ruled out.

What was left were the St Patrick Cathedral allegations and various allegations about offences in three Ballarat swimming pools – the Eureka Pool, the YMCA Pool and the Nazareth Boys' Home pool. The swimming pool allegations were raised initially by ABC journalist Louise Milligan in her *7.30* program and in her book *Cardinal: The Rise and Fall of George Pell* (MUP, which was first published in May 2017). The St Patrick's Cathedral allegations were also initially raised, without detail, on *7.30* and in *Cardinal*.

Lucie Morris-Marr, a Pell-antagonist, described the scene at the end of *The Police v George Pell* in her book *Fallen:*

> As she [Belinda Wallington] left the bench, a group of advocates and survivors at the back of the courtroom clapped. Pell descended the steps outside through a wall of cadet police officers making a safe exit for him. "Three cheers for Mrs Wallington", shouted advocate Julie Cameron, clutching her mother's small, tattered missal in her hands and waving it in the air. There was something rather feudal and primitive about the spectacle of this powerful church leader being jeered and booed by angry onlookers less than a few kilometres from the cathedral where he once reigned as archbishop…

This was the example of the "mob-rule" or "witch hunt" mentality which Chief Judge Kidd referred to when sentencing Cardinal Pell after his conviction.

A fair reading of Magistrate Wallington's finding would indicate that the charges on which Pell was committed for trial were very weak. This was the time for the DPP to notice the problems involved in accepting the validity of A's claims about the alleged assaults at St Patrick's Cathedral. But the DPP pressed on until its case was demolished by Justice Weinberg in his Victorian Court of Appeal dissent and then fell apart before the High Court.

Moreover, the three charges with respect to what is best termed the Swimming Pool Case were withdrawn by the DPP – following its failed attempt to have tendency and coincidence evidence admitted as evidence before the County Court. In this instance, the DPP's case was mauled by Chief Judge Peter Kidd in the County Court of Victoria in *DPP v Pell (Evidential Ruling No. 1)*.

An Application for Discontinuance

It is a little known fact that on 22 May 2018 – three weeks after Magistrate Wallington handed down her decision – Robert Richter QC and

Ruth Shann lodged an Application for Discontinuance with the Victorian Director of Public Prosecutions. It was made pursuant to Section 177 of the Victorian *Criminal Procedure Act 2009*. This covers the policy of the DPP – which requires that a prosecution may only proceed if there is both a reasonable prospect of a conviction and the prosecution is in the public interest.

Mr Richter and Ms Shann submitted that there was no reasonable prospect of securing a conviction in relation to any of the charges and that it was not in the public interest to proceed with a costly trial in the busy County Court. They argued that A's uncorroborated allegations in the proposed Cathedral Trial were "fanciful and improbable" and contrary to both logic and sworn evidence of dozens of prosecution witnesses.

In relation to the proposed *Swimming Pool Case*, Richter and Shann argued that two of the 40 year old alleged offences were relatively minor and could be heard summarily (i.e. in the Magistrates' Court rather than in the County Court) with a substantial saving in costs. And that the third complainant had not been a credible witness at the committal proceedings. Moreover Richter/Shann submitted that all three had made prior inconsistent statements on the key matters alleged and had expressed anger towards the Catholic Church.

The Application for Discontinuance argued that the "no reasonable prospect of conviction test" which applies to the DPP, is a higher threshold than the test of whether the evidence is of "sufficient weight" to convict, which applies to a magistrate when committing for trial. Most of the document – 43 out of 66 pages – focused on the proposed Cathedral Trial.

The application advanced the very arguments which led the DPP eventually to drop the proposed Swimming Pool Case – and which convinced Justice Weinberg in the Victorian Court of Appeal and all seven judges in the High Court of Australia in the Cathedral Trial. Also, between two and ten members of the jury in the first trial came to a conclusion which was consistent with the case submitted by Robert Richter QC and Ruth Shann.

The confluence between the Application for Discontinuance and the High Court's unanimous decision in *Pell v The Queen* is readily demonstrated with respect to the alleged second incident in the *Cathedral Trial*.

Paragraph 70 of the Application for Discontinuance is as follows:

> J' [i.e. A's] description of this assault is, put simply, ludicrous. J claims that he was on his way to the choir room robed but had not snuck away from procession. That suggests that the choir were travelling through the sacristy corridor back to the choir room as occurred, at times, during inclement weather. That puts at least 40 people in this corridor. Indeed, J [i.e. A] himself says the corridor was fairly crowded at the time. Yet no one sees the most senior cleric in Victoria in full robes pin a choir boy against a wall and molest his genitals.

This comment is similar to what the High Court said about the second alleged incident at paragraphs 123 and 124 of its unanimous judgment. This is discussed in Chapter 1.

The DPP rejected the Richter/Shann application without providing any reasons. At the very least, the DPP could have instructed Victoria Police to provide evidence for the charge concerning the second incident in what became the Cathedral Trial. Especially since the DPP should have known that Victoria Police had not interviewed any of the at least 40 or so potential witnesses – which included altar servers, choristers and Fr Egan who said the Mass at which Pell presided on 23 February 1997. The DPP took no such action. The DPP continued with a charge against Pell which Victoria Police had not investigated. It would seem that, like Victoria Police, the DPP simply believed A. This is discussed in Chapter 10.

Cardinal Pell's defence team outside the County Court of Victoria

Cardinal George Pell's defence team outside the County Court of Victoria – barristers Ruth Shann, Robert Richter QC and solicitors Paul Galbally (at rear) and Kartya Gracer. Robert Richter (a non-Catholic) told author Melissa Davey that while he personally abhorred the politics of some of Pell's defenders, they were correct in their assessment that the offending was impossible. Richter believes that the media coverage of Pell's appearances before the Royal Commission turned the public against him. Photo by Michael Dodge via Getty Images.

Chief Judge Peter Kidd

On 15 October 2019, Chief Judge Peter Kidd of the County Court of Victoria sought and obtained an interview with Waleed Aly on Network 10's left-of-centre program The Project – he discussed the role of judges in jury trials. The Chief Judge made it clear that it was the role of the Court of Appeal to decide whether jury verdicts were unreasonable, having regard to the evidence.

3

THE TRIALS OF GEORGE PELL

"...why didn't Pell's prosecutors stop the trial because of the timing issue? And why didn't his jurors — the hold-outs in his first trial and all twelve in his second — acquit because of it? If the High Court is right about the timing evidence, then those things should have happened in one or both of Pell's trials in 2018. The best defence I can offer is speculative and uncomfortable: the prosecutors and jurors quite possibly didn't notice the issue. There is some compelling evidence behind this guess: two senior judges seemingly didn't notice it either and nor did any of the journalists who watched and described Pell's trials."

- Professor Jeremy Gans, "Pell in Purgatory", *Inside Story*, 13 April 2020

A Note of "Secrecy"

Many critics of George Pell delight in referring to the "secret trial" in which he was convicted. For example, the term "secret trial" is contained in the sub-title of Lucie Morris-Marr's book *Fallen*. Reference is also made by David Marr to "the secret trials of George Pell" in his endorsement of Melissa Davey's *The Case of George Pell: reckoning with child sexual abuse by clergy* (Scribe, 2020).

In fact, none of the hearings in the Magistrates' Court or the County Court were secret in the usual sense of the term. Members of the public – including journalists – were free to attend proceedings. The courts were open on all days – except when the evidence of the complainants was heard in the Magistrates' Court – and that of the complainant in both the Magistrates' Court and the County Court. In *DPP v Pell* this was done to protect the complainant – not the defendant – and it was obtained at the request of Senior Crown Prosecutor Mark Gibson QC.

Chief Judge Kidd made this clear in his opening remarks during Cardinal Pell's re-trial in the County Court:

> *His Honour:* …I also assume that the closed court is sought for this trial as it was for the last trial?
>
> *Mr Gibson:* It is.
>
> *His Honour:* No objections to that?
>
> *Mr Richter:* No objection.
>
> *His Honour:* Upon the same basis, to prevent distress and embarrassment to the complainant, Mr Gibson?
>
> *Mr Gibson:* Yes.

A transcript of A's evidence in the Magistrates' Court has not been released. The same is true of the County Court. The only accounts of what A said in the County Court can be found in statements by barristers when examining other witnesses or in their final addresses to the jury. There are also references to A's testimony in the Chief Judge's charge to the jury. And quotes from A's testimony can be found in the hearings and judgments at the Victorian Court of Appeal and the hearings before the High Court.

There was also no reporting of the County Court proceedings since the DPP was planning a second trial – the Swimming Pool Case – and there was concern that reportage of the Cathedral Trial would make it impossible for the defendant to receive a fair trial in the Swimming Pool Case. Once again, this suppression order was requested by the DPP – not the defendant.

These various orders assumed that jurors would not be aware of the Pell proceedings if they were not covered in the mainstream media. A naïve view, on any analysis.

The claim by Pell-antagonists, like Lucie Morris-Marr and David

Marr, that Pell enjoyed a secret trial and conviction is misleading. At a time of social media the trial was not really "secret". And it hindered, rather than helped, Pell's defence in the Cathedral Trial.

County Court of Victoria: *DPP v George Pell* – the First Trial

On 15 August 2018, *DPP v George Pell* – commonly referred to as the Cathedral Trial – commenced in the County Court of Victoria before Chief Judge Peter Kidd. Before the case commenced two charges of rape – on which the defendant was committed by Magistrate Wallington – were withdrawn by the DPP. Five charges remained.

Later, on 6 September 2018, His Honour decided that there was an "insufficient basis" for the charge to go to a jury that Pell had sexually penetrated B. It turned out that, when giving evidence, the complainant (A) said that he did not actually see the alleged incident – and had simply assumed that oral penetration took place.

Chief Judge Kidd said that, "at law" he had decided that "this is simply not enough". He formally directed that the entry of a not-guilty verdict be made on this charge. The Chief Judge advised, however, that the prosecution had substituted this charge with the alternative charge of committing an indecent act with a child under the age of 16.

A jury of 14 was empanelled – two to be excluded by ballot if there were still 14 jurors at the end of the trial. In fact, two jurors withdrew before the trial concluded. His Honour gave jury members the normal warning in trials of this kind. They were not to read anything on the internet or speak to anyone about the case. His Honour told the jurors: "Don't get on Google, don't do any searching". He added: "The trial must not make George Pell a scapegoat for the failures or the conduct of the Catholic Church more generally."

These instructions were proper and correct. But they rationalise a reality. These days most Australians own iPhones – which are not taken away from jurors. It is naïve to expect that no member of a jury will ever access a phone seeking information about a case or "get on Google". Also these days, the term "unconscious bias" is well understood

– meaning that someone can be prejudiced even if they do not believe themselves to be biased. There's no known test for unconscious bias.

When Cardinal Pell went on trial in August 2018, anti-Catholic sectarianism, which has been a feature of Australian society since European Settlement in 1788, was still present. It had altered over the decades but not gone away. This was a particular problem for the defendant since he is a theological conservative in a society which is increasingly secular. On account of this theological conservatism, Pell also had many opponents among theological liberal Catholics as well as disillusioned and former Catholics in addition to traditional anti-Catholic sectarians. And then there was the fact that Pell has one of the highest profiles in the land. The Chief Judge said all the right words – but there was no guarantee that all the jurors (consciously or unconsciously) would abide by his instructions.

In both trials Chief Judge Kidd also instructed the jury about what is termed the "forensic disadvantage" – meaning that the defendant had been denied advantages which they would have had if there had not been such a lapse of time between the alleged sexual assaults and the trial. In this case, some 22 years.

The forensic disadvantage was as follows. First, the delay in reporting the matter meant that Pell had been prevented from making inquiries about the alleged events which could have uncovered evidence at odds with A's allegations. Second, most of what were termed the opportunity witnesses could only give evidence about their recall of the practices, routines and traditions that applied to the cathedral in the mid-1990s. Whereas, had the allegations been made earlier, they might have had a specific recall of events. Third, the effluxion of time meant that some of the surviving witnesses did not have the recall or fluency of younger people. For example, Max Potter was 84 years of age. Fourth, the Dean of the Cathedral in 1996-97, Monsignor William McCarthy, who would have been a key witness about the archbishop's movements after Sunday mass, was in a nursing home and unable to give evidence in legal proceedings. Fifth, the passage of time made it difficult to test A's evidence given his inability to recall specific details. Sixth, B would have been a material witness if he had been alive and it was not known what he might have said.

The final point is important. It was accepted in the County Court that B had told his mother that he had not been sexually assaulted when a boy. B's father said much the same to Victoria Police. If B had been alive when Pell went to trial, it is possible that he could have given evidence in support of the defendant. In such an eventuality, even Victoria Police probably would not have been able to lay charges in the first instance since there would have been a discrepancy between the only witnesses to the alleged event.

It should be noted that, as the Chief Judge advised the jury, the only evidence against Pell was the testimony of A. There was no forensic or other testimony evidence. In addition to A, the DPP called a number of "opportunity witnesses" who were able to give evidence about church routine after a solemn mass and about the opportunity for any offending to occur. Some of the key witnesses called by the prosecution were individuals suggested by the defence – the defence itself did not call evidence. For example, the prosecution never thought to call anyone who had been an altar server who could explain what the altar servers routinely did in the sacristy after Solemn Mass when it was alleged by A that the sacristy was unoccupied.

Pell did not give evidence but his statement in Rome to Victoria Police was played at his committal proceeding and at both trials. A gave evidence by video-link before the Magistrates' Court and again at the first trial. The jury at the second trial saw a re-play of A's video-link evidence at the first trial. Under Victorian law, in sexual assault cases the complainant is only required to give evidence once if one or more re-trials are required.

In his directions to the jury, or charge, His Honour stressed the importance that a verdict of guilty had to be beyond reasonable doubt. He summarised the prosecution's case – namely that A's account should be accepted because he was a "powerful and persuasive witness". The Chief Judge summarised the defence's case that there was no evidence that could lead to a jury being convinced of the defendant's guilt beyond reasonable doubt.

The jury retired to consider its verdict on Thursday 13 September 2018. After deliberating for only 90 minutes it requested the video recording of A's evidence. On the Friday afternoon, the trial was adjourned for the weekend. On Wednesday 19 September the forewoman indicated that the jury had reached an impasse – the judge instructed jurors to continue their deliberations. The following morning, the forewoman indicated that the impasse had not been resolved.

At this stage Chief Judge Peter Kidd advised jurors that they could reach a majority decision – in Victorian law this is 11 out of 12 for conviction or acquittal. At 4 pm on Thursday 20 September 2018, the jury returned – this is how Morris-Marr reported the occasion in *The New Daily* later that day:

> Judge Kidd asked the jury if they had managed to reach a verdict with the majority direction. The forewoman shook her head and said they hadn't. Judge Kidd asked if one more night to "think things over" and come back fresh in the morning would help.
>
> The jurors departed briefly back into their room. Within a minute their buzzer rang loudly across the court. They filed back in. Many look devastated. The forewoman was red-eyed and tearful. The judge asked again whether one more night would help their impasse. The forewoman just shook her head and said "No", and then burst into tears.
>
> The judge then explained they would have to be dismissed and thanked them for their hard work in what had been a "challenging case". As he spoke, three more women began crying. It was a distressing scene... A man in his early 60s, sitting in the front of the jury box, also wiped away tears.

In her book *The Case of George Pell*, published after the trials, Melissa Davey had this to say:

> "In some cases, the burden is much greater than others," he [Chief Judge Kidd] told them, as they listened while in visible distress. By this point, five of the jurors were in tears. The burden had clearly been enormous, their deliberations and disagreements surely intense. "From the moment you were empanelled over a month ago,

the burden was going to be greater than most," Kidd continued. "It's obvious to all of us how much work you've done. I don't think you should be hard on yourself. I think you should be very proud of the effort you've put in. You go with our thanks and our best wishes." He excused them from performing jury duty for another 10 years, given the enormity and stress of what they had just been through together. He again told them not to speak to anyone about the case because, he warned them, "You cannot win. You will place yourself in an impossible position". As kind and as empathetic as Kidd had been, he also left them with a warning: "Whatever took place in that jury room must stay there."

The reports by such Pell-antagonists as Morris-Marr and Davey about the tension in the County Court following the announcement of the hung jury discredits the assertion that A was such a "compelling" witness.

George Pell remembers the occasion this way – as told to the author on 25 July 2020:

> I was a little naïve. I fully expected to be cleared at that stage. And so it wasn't the worst – but it wasn't good. The tip-staff was handing out tissues because there were four or five of the jurors crying. And I thought they were crying because they believed deeply that I was innocent. And I was. I think it's highly unlikely they would have been crying because I hadn't been convicted.

Correctly or otherwise, Pell's defence team seemed to believe that the first jury verdict was ten to two for acquittal – one short of what was necessary for a majority verdict. But one of his supporters thought it might have been nine to three for acquittal. We do not know this for certain – and in a sense it does not matter since juries can only give "guilty" or "not guilty" verdicts, whether of the unanimous or the majority kind.

What did matter is that between ten and two jurors believed that the defendant was not guilty. This should have warned commentators – and even some judges on appeal that it was unwise to consider A's evidence as "compelling", since not all jurors at the first trial believed this to be the case.

For her part Milligan, when speaking with Patricia Karvelas on ABC Radio National *Drive* on 13 March 2019, said that she would "defy anyone…not to believe what he's [A's] saying". Milligan contested the view that the jury in the first trial might have been 10 to 2 for acquittal. She claimed "that some of the court reporters have said that there were "four jurors crying and in the sense that they "were actually wanting a conviction". Milligan provided no evidence for her assertion and no such reports appeared in the media. Towards the end of the interview, Milligan said that she wondered how those who doubted Pell's guilt "can describe themselves as Christians".

According to Morris-Marr, in hearings while the jury was out of the court, Chief Judge Kidd had instructed the defence that it could not suggest to the jurors that Victoria Police had acted maliciously against the defendant as had been done in the committal hearing. Nor could the defence tell jurors that A had sought counselling in the past and been treated for depression in his early twenties. These rulings also applied in what turned out to be the re-trial. This decision prevented the defence running the line in the trials that Victoria Police were out to "Get Pell".

Another Application for Discontinuance

Following the hung jury in the first trial, Robert Richter QC and Ruth Shann forwarded to the DPP on 8 October 2018 an Application for Discontinuance of the Cathedral Trial. Paragraphs 4 and 5 are as follows:

> Evidence led from 22 prosecution witnesses other than Mr J [i.e. A] demonstrated that if the normal practice of Cardinal Pell, his Master of Ceremonies, the altar servers, the sacristan, and the choir were followed, the assaults could not have occurred for a series of reasons. Even on those rare occasions when Pell may have deviated from his practice to stay on the front steps to greet parishioners after Sunday Solemn Mass, the evidence demonstrated that he would not have been in the sacristy alone while robed at all let alone for the time required to have committed these offences undetected. The

> prosecution did not challenge this evidence. It came from numerous honest witnesses.
>
> The prosecution evidence also included a compelling record of interview of Cardinal Pell [in Rome]. He learns for the first time during that interview that the allegation is that he sexually assaulted choir boys immediately after Mass in the sacristies and expresses relief that the allegations, once investigated, will be so easily shown to be completely fanciful. Each exonerating point made by Cardinal Pell in that interview has been corroborated by unchallenged evidence. If she has not done so already, the Director [of Public Prosecutions Kerri Judd QC] should watch the record of interview in order to do justice to this application.

The reference to Pell's Rome interview turned on the fact that his legal team had been advised that A's allegations about the alleged attacks in the priests' sacristy occurred after choir (later Detective Reed said "after Mass"). Pell and his legal advisers had assumed that this meant after choir practice. Pell lived in the suburb of Kew – not near the Cathedral in East Melbourne. What's more, he rarely visited the Cathedral – so there was little prospect of him being in the presence of choir boys when they were practising. It was only when the Rome interview took place that Pell realised that the allegation had changed from after choir to after Sunday Solemn Mass – he believed that this was a change which strongly supported his case. Let's go to the transcript of the Rome interview:

> *Christopher Reed:* ...They found the wine and started to take a few swigs back and forwards.
>
> *George Pell:* This is after Mass?
>
> *Christopher Reed:* Yes, correct. Yes, after Mass on a Sunday morning. That's when, the information you have, as you were discussing a second ago, he [A] states that that's when Archbishop Pell came into the room.
>
> *George Pell:* No, that's not quite the – I never got the information that it was after a Mass.

> *Christopher Reed:* No?
>
> *George Pell:* It was after choir practice, it came through to me, I think. That's my recollection.
>
> *Michael do Rozario:* I think it is "after choir."
>
> *George Pell:* After choir.
>
> *Christopher Reed:* After choir.
>
> *Michael do Rozario:* That's the table you provided us.
>
> *Christopher Reed:* Sorry, yep, it's after singing in choir during Mass. After choir. After Mass....

Then Detective Reed moved to the alleged second incident:

> *Christopher Reed:* That's the extent of that allegation, that particular instance. There is a further instance that's been alleged, and this is only on behalf of A. It's some time after this, at least a month later and again after Church.
>
> *George Pell:* Now, this, now you've got "after choir."
>
> *Christopher Reed:* Yes.
>
> *George Pell:* Does that mean after the Mass or after the choir practice?
>
> *Christopher Reed:* No, it's –
>
> *George Pell:* I took it after the choir practice.
>
> *Christopher Reed:* This indication is "after Church," is how it's described, which is after Mass, after singing in the choir during Mass. These allegations, I can state to you, were not –
>
> *George Pell:* [interrupting]: We're about after Mass?
>
> *Christopher Reed:* After Mass, yes. Not in relation to –
>
> *George Pell:* Well, that's so much, that's good for me because it makes it even more fantastic and impossible.
>
> *Christopher Reed:* Neither of those were in relation to after choir practice.
>
> *George Pell:* Good.

Cardinal Pell and his legal team had been informed by Victoria Police that the alleged offences occurred "after choir" – which was interpreted as after choir practice in the Cathedral. This was an occasion in which the Archbishop of Melbourne was not involved. When Cardinal Pell found that Victoria Police was alleging that the offences occurred after Sunday Solemn Mass, he declared that it was "good for me" since St Patrick's Cathedral was what he termed "a hive of activity" after Sunday Solemn Mass. It seems that Detective Reed was unaware that, in a Solemn Mass, the choir is merely a part of the ceremony. The terms "after choir" and "after Mass" are not interchangeable – with respect to a Solemn Mass in a Catholic Church.

The Application for Discontinuance maintained that Cardinal Pell's shocked and emphatic response to Victoria Police's changed position on this issue when interviewed, was consistent with the evidence of some 20 opportunity witnesses at his trial – namely, that there was no evidence of such offences having occurred after Solemn Mass.

Early in the interview in Rome, Detective Reed volunteered the comment: "I'm not raised in the Catholic faith". He did so when asking Cardinal Pell about the Catholic sacrament of Confirmation – which is usually administered when children are about 11 years of age. Detective Reed had no idea of this – even though he was investigating a separate complaint against Pell which related to the timing of a Confirmation in the Catholic Church.

In some Christian denominations – the entire ceremony essentially consists of a sermon plus choir. Not in the Catholic Church, however, where the choir sings during Mass and Mass does not conclude with a choral performance.

Before concluding that there was "no rational way to explain how what Mr J [i.e. A] says occurred could have occurred", the Application for Discontinuance stated:

> ...the decision whether or not to prosecute must not be influenced by any public concern about Cardinal Pell's position in the Catholic Church, feelings towards him from some groups in the community,

the notoriety of this case, and/or any failings of the Church's response to sexual abuse exposed by the Royal Commission.

The reference here took a similar concern to that raised by Judge Ellis in *Wilson v R.*

Once again, the DPP, Kerri Judd QC, rejected the application and so the re-trial commenced in November 2018. This meant that the Swimming Pool Case – scheduled to go to trial in November 2018 – was postponed to March the following year. There was considerable doubt that the Swimming Pool Case would go ahead – so weak was the evidence.

County Court of Victoria: *DPP v George Pell* – Re-Trial

The re-trial commenced on Wednesday 7 November 2018. Senior Crown Prosecutor Mark Gibson QC with Angela Ellis appeared for the Crown and Robert Richter QC with Ruth Shann for the defence. Chief Judge Peter Kidd gave similar instructions to the 14 jurors as in the first trial about not researching the case and that they should dismiss any feelings of prejudice towards the accused. He also instructed the jury that they should not give too much weight as to how a witness gave evidence – since looks can be deceiving.

Once again, His Honour was unable to ensure that no member of the jury would go on the internet to check the case. Moreover, he could not eliminate the reality that some jurors might be hostile to the high-profile Cardinal Pell and that any such prejudice might manifest itself in conscious or unconscious bias.

First up, counsel for the prosecution, followed by counsel for the defence, addressed the jury. Then the video of A's evidence at the first trial was played. As mentioned earlier, under Victorian law, a complainant cannot be required to give evidence again if a re-trial takes place. This protects a complainant from the stress involved in giving evidence a second (or more) time. However, it is disadvantageous to the accused in that it prevents an examination of whether the complainant is consistent in their account. In this case, A altered some of his evidence between his appearance at the Magistrates' Court and his testimony at the first trial. We will never know whether there might have been additional inconsistencies if a third cross-examination had taken place.

The video recording of his testimony commenced on the Friday morning and concluded on the morning of the following Wednesday – over seven hours in all, with the court occasionally dealing with other matters in the absence of the jury. There followed the testimony – either live or by video link – of some opportunity witnesses, most of whom had given evidence in the first trial. The number of witnesses was cut in the trial with the agreement of the prosecution and the defence. Even so, the re-trial ran for 22 days – longer than the first trial.

On Friday 30 November 2018, Mark Gibson QC commenced his final address to the jury. It was much the same as the first trial – except that he went in even harder on the "interval of decorum" for private prayer time between the conclusion of Mass and the altar servers commencing to clean up after the conclusion of the ceremony – which, he submitted, made it possible for Pell to offend. Gibson insisted at the re-trial that there were five to six minutes available in this interval of decorum, during which the offending could have occurred. This reasoning was embraced by Chief Justice Ferguson and President Maxwell in the Court of Appeal – but fell apart during proceedings before the High Court.

As in the first trial, the Senior Crown Prosecutor's case was simple. Namely, believe the complainant. These extracts from Gibson QC's final address illustrate the point. It commenced as follows:

> Mr Foreman and members of the jury. As you know the critical issue in this trial is whether you accept beyond reasonable doubt that what J. J. [i.e. A] says occurred – during the first incident, and during the second incident – actually did occur. And in simple terms we have a young man who says that: "This is what happened to me and my friend when we were 13 years of age". The Crown says that that conduct that he has described, and he's observed, amounts to a number of offences.

Later, Gibson SC continued on this theme:

> You got to spend time observing him, indeed for an extended period of time, under pressure, being cross-examined and probed extensively by an experienced member of counsel in Mr Richter. So, what was the overall impression you were left with? Did he strike you as being an honest witness? An accurate historian? Was he being frank with you in his evidence? Did he appear to be recounting actual events and actual experiences that he'd had?

> You will remember there were a few occasions, two of which I recall specifically and you may recall it, where at p.160 of his transcript when asked in examination-in-chief, that's when I'm asking questions – how far he was from M.R. [i.e. B] when M.R. was offended against. You will remember he closed his eyes as though to think back to that time.

> He did again I recall, at p.305 of the transcript, when asked in cross-examination by my learned friend, Mr Richter, which hand Archbishop Pell used to push him against the wall, this is the second incident. And again he closed his eyes, thinking back in my submission to you, trying to recount the actual circumstance about which he was being asked. And in that case he said: "I'm not certain what hand" was his answer. But those things are cues, if you like, in terms of determining his honesty and reliability as a witness.

Later, still, Gibson QC saw essential truth in A's concession during the trial that he might have seen the priests' sacristy on an occasion before he was allegedly assaulted by Pell and that this might explain why he was able to describe aspects of the room:

> Now, of course, my learned friend cross-examined on this ability of J.J. to know that these features existed in the priests' sacristy because of a tour. Remember that the choristers were taken on when they first joined the choir. Remember that questioning at the very end of the cross-examination at p.362.

> Mr Richter asked, question: "Prior to the incidents, you have seen the inside of the sacristy?" Answer: "I can't recall". Question: "You were taken on a tour of the cathedral when you joined the choir?". Answer: "I would have, yes". Question: "And you were shown the

> sacristies?". Answer: "I have no recollection of that, no". Question: "Do you dispute it?". Answer: "No".
>
> I say two things about that. One, it gives a good insight into J [i.e. A].
>
> Remember at the outset I spoke about, is he a witness who's truthful or is he a witness who's dishonest and embellishing and making things up. And here he is, when he's given the perfect opportunity to say: "Yes, I do dispute it", he says: "No" – which you might think is a fair response to the question, as opposed to filling in gaps that are self-serving and suit his purpose....

Certainly the Senior Crown Prosecutor sought to cast doubt on the relevance of the evidence given by the opportunity witnesses. But his central point was: Believe A.

For his part, Richter QC commenced his address to the jury by querying A's credibility as a witness:

> Good morning ladies and gentlemen of the jury...The things I want you to bear in mind are these as you consider the evidence. No.1, that for about six minutes or so, and it is not possible to be precise about it, but for about six minutes or so of the episode that I'll describe as episode 1, the assaults alleged were committed on the word of J [i.e. A] and the sole evidence in this case is the word of J. Not a 13 year old, but of a 34 year old man who is able to deal with questions. And you've seen the video of the way he dealt with questions, evaded them, created new versions when faced with impossibilities and difficulties....
>
> For those six minutes, I want you to have it firmly in mind the question of where are Portelli, Potter, the altar servers, the other clergy including the Dean of the cathedral?... Where are the altar servers? Where are the other clergy? Where's Mr Mallinson, where's Mr Cox, where's Mr Finnigan, where are the choir boys, what are the choir boys doing for those six minutes? And those six minutes take place in a time span that has encompassed the procession that's going out and Archbishop Pell standing on the stairs or just down the bottom of the stairs greeting congregants. Where are they?[7]

During his address, in the absence of the jury, Richter QC was admonished by Chief Judge Peter Kidd for breaking a commitment he had given earlier to the court not to refer to the deficiencies of the Victoria Police investigation.

In particular, His Honour took exception to the fact that counsel for the defence had told jurors that Victoria Police put out a press release in December 2015 asking people to come forward who were aware of any sexual assault at St Patrick's Cathedral between the years 1996 and 2001. Richter QC said that there was no evidence that anyone had come forward alleging sexual assault during the time that Pell was Archbishop of Melbourne.

Initially Richter QC expressed surprise that he had broken such a commitment. After the Chief Judge insisted that he had – and stated that he was "furious" that this had been done – Richter QC apologised unreservedly and withdrew the comment. Later he delivered what he described as a "grovelling apology" before the jury. Richter QC, at the request of the Chief Judge, also withdrew his statement that Pell was innocent – when he should have said "presumed innocent".

Earlier, also in the absence of the jury, His Honour had suggested to Gibson QC that he had invited the jury to speculate that Monsignor Portelli, then a heavy smoker, had left Pell alone after Sunday Solemn Mass to go for a smoke. The point being that Portelli had denied this and there was no evidence to support the claim. When the jury returned, Gibson said that he had been speculating. Adding about the monsignor's purported smoko – "perhaps he did, his evidence is he didn't". The prosecution's case had been that Monsignor Portelli might have nicked off for a smoke, without anyone noticing, immediately after Mass – in spite of the fact that he was master of ceremonies to a newly installed archbishop in his first or second Solemn Mass at St Patrick's Cathedral.

The Senior Crown Prosecutor's treatment of Monsignor Portelli indicated how desperate the prosecution was to discredit what was, in effect, alibi evidence for George Pell.

In the first trial Portelli had admitted to being a smoker. Gibson QC suggested to Portelli that he might have been so desperate for a cigarette that he skipped off somewhere – in full monsignor kit – for a quick puff. Portelli rejected the suggestion out of hand. Even so, Gibson went ahead in his final address to the jury and put the smoke idea to the jury. Chief Judge Kidd, correctly, directed him to withdraw it.

In the second trial, Gibson gave the idea another go – asking Portelli whether he ducked out for a smoke after solemn Mass, leaving Archbishop Pell on his own. Portelli replied: "It would be as appropriate for instance, His Honour walking down William Street, dressed as he is, smoking a cigarette – which is not done."

Not to be deterred, Gibson raised the issue again in his address to the jury – as indicated above. Again Chief Judge Kidd ruled that Gibson should advise the jury that his comment was speculation. Gibson did so – but after putting the idea in the minds of the jurors.

Ruth Shann's PowerPoint Request Not Granted

Chief Judge Kidd's decision to prevent showing the jury a 19-minute PowerPoint presentation illustrating where everyone was during Sunday Solemn Mass on either 15 or 22 December 1996 was a blow to the defence. Ruth Shann argued that "we're in the 21st Century and this is communicating in a visual way". She made the pertinent point, with reference to the evidence of the sacristan Max Potter, that "when he's working at the end of Mass for five or six minutes – that's the start of the procession". That's a point which the High Court picked up – but which the defence was not able to put in visual form in its final address to the jury.

The Chief Judge's position was that "the evidence on no view establishes exactly where the protagonists were at any one time". He added that it was unusual to give directions to a jury on a matter of evidence that was not tendered during the trial.

Ruth Shann's point was that, in order to accept A's evidence that there was no one in or near the priests' sacristy when the alleged assaults took place, "you have to actually disappear a range of people". She added:

> Cardinal Pell shouldn't be deprived of an opportunity to make a visual argument because someone can't say: "I was here at this exact time". The jury will readily understand what is shown and not shown by the – it is not purporting to say: "Altar server one is exactly here at exactly this point in time." It is showing that the evidence is very strong. As soon as the procession ends, there is movement in and out of that [priests' sacristy] room the whole time, and that this sort of weaving of an opportunity that Mr Gibson presented where the altar servers would [be], he initially said stand, in the workers' sacristy. But in the end said: "Well, we don't know where they are".
>
> We want to be able to visually show there's nowhere for them to be. There's nowhere for Mr Potter to be. There's nowhere for Portelli to be. And you can say that a number of times. But it is something that we say is important in order to ensure a proper and fair defence of Cardinal Pell, is to be able to make our point, make our argument, that's all this is, in a visual way as well.

It was not to be. But, without question, showing the visual production to the jury would have assisted the defence's case. During both the first trial and the re-trial, the jury was taken on a tour of St Patrick's Cathedral. But both visits occurred on a weekday when the Cathedral was all but deserted – with rooms like the priests' sacristy remote hideaways. During the re-trial the visit took place on a Wednesday after lunch.

However, on a Sunday after Solemn Mass in 1996 and 1997, the Cathedral would be a very busy place with priests, altar servers, choristers, parishioners and visitors moving around – along with the archbishop, his master of ceremonies, the sacristan and so on. It was what Pell described to Victoria Police in Rome as "a hive of activity". A visual presentation would have demonstrated the reality of the alleged crime scene after Solemn Mass much more than the walk-through of a vast, deserted, Basilica-like church on a weekday afternoon.

Writing in the *Australian Financial Review* on 1 March 2019, shortly after Pell's conviction became public, Patrick Durkin and Michael Pelly quoted some anonymous barristers as saying that Chief Judge Kidd's decision had denied the defence an opportunity to put its "best case".

As Professor Gans wrote in *Inside Story* in his article titled "Pell in purgatory" on 13 April 2020:

> Even my generous take may seem quite damning of Pell's prosecutors and jurors (and others), but the true culprit could be the whole idea of resolving complex questions at a single "trial". Trials — and, especially, questioning dozens of witnesses in sequence and then summarising their evidence orally days later — are poorly suited to identifying crucial issues out of a mass of arguments, including fine issues of timing.
>
> That's why [Ruth] Shann wanted to show Pell's jurors her animation. She argued that illustrating the timing issues this way suits contemporary approaches to presenting information, which jurors would be familiar with from their own devices. Without it, she prophetically suggested, "it was possible that they might not understand the full force, cumulatively, of the defence argument in relation to opportunity." Weinberg's retort — that there is more risk of confusion from presenting such "material in this highly questionable form" — ought to be reconsidered now, as should trial prosecutor Mark Gibson's decision to object to the video in this case.

Justice Mark Weinberg's judgment in this instance – which was supported by the majority – did not matter since he was in a minority on the bigger issue in the Victorian Court of Appeal concerning Pell's guilt beyond reasonable doubt. But senior Crown Prosecutor Mark Gibson QC's opposition to the use of the video in the re-trial was significant – as was Chief Judge Kidd's decision to support the DPP's objection. As Ruth Shann argued again (unsuccessfully) before the Victorian Court of Appeal, the various priests, altar servers and choristers present at St Patrick's Cathedral during Sunday Solemn Mass could not simply be "disappeared". But, in effect, they were at the County Court and the Victorian Court of Appeal – until "located" by the High Court.

Kidd's Charge

As in the first trial, the Chief Judge Peter Kidd delivered his "charge" – the legal term for a judge's instructions to a jury before jurors commence their deliberations. Once again, he made a number of important points about memory:

> As I mentioned to you at the start of the trial, when you are assessing a witness' evidence, some matters, which may concern you, including credibility and reliability. Broadly speaking, credibility concerns honesty; is the witness telling the truth; and reliability is different. The witness may be honest, but have a poor memory, or indeed be mistaken, so there are those two aspects to a witness' evidence, and I am sure that corresponds with your day-to-day experience in life in judging people.

The Chief Judge added that, when assessing a given witnesses' evidence, "you should be careful not to overstate the significance of the manner in which the witness gave evidence". He delivered a direction not to make a witness's manner "the only factor or even the most important factor" in the jurors' assessment.

In summing up the defence's case, the Chief Judge pointed out that Robert Richter QC had argued that A had changed his dates when the offences occurred. His Honour pointed to the defence case that there were witnesses who placed Pell at the Main Door of the Cathedral after Solemn Sunday Mass on 15 and 22 December 1996. And he pointed to the defence's case that there were compounding impossibilities and improbabilities in A's allegations that proved that his claims were a mere fantasy.

The Chief Judge also drew attention to the common, albeit contested, ground which had been reached between the prosecution and the defence concerning A's different accounts of what happened. They concerned (i) A's account of how he and B left the procession; (ii) A's account of how Pell parted his robes – initially he said the robes were parted but later said that Pell reached under his robes and undid his trousers and belt and (iii) A initially said that both incidents occurred in 1997 before stating that the correct timing was late 1996 and early

1997 – with school holidays occurring in between. The prosecution and defence agreed that A's testimony on these matters was inconsistent – they had different explanations for these anomalies.

Towards the end of his charge, the Chief Judge directed the jury as to the forensic disadvantage that the defendant faced due to the complainant's delay in reporting the alleged crimes – along the lines he had done in the first trial. And he again raised the issue of memory:

> …because of the passage of time of so many years between the dates of the alleged offences and when the complainant made his complaint to the police I need to give you this direction about the reliability of the complainant's evidence in this respect. You will easily understand that the passage of time, as I think I mentioned before, with any witness will affect the witness's memory, and while in some cases people simply forget things in other cases their memory may become distorted, and that is they may come to remember things as honest recollections that did not really happen. Human recollection is frequently erroneous and liable to distortion in this way. The likelihood of this error increases with delay….

In his last direction to the jury, the Chief Judge stated:

> I direct you that you must carefully consider not only whether the complainant's evidence is honest in the sense that the complainant believes it to be true, but also whether it is in fact true. You must take this possibility into account in determining whether you accept the complainant's evidence on any particular matter and in deciding what weight to give to that evidence.

Soon after, the jury retired to consider its verdict. Neither the prosecution nor the defence could reasonably complain about the Chief Judge's charge to the jurors.[8]

DPP v George Pell: **The Jury Decides**

After almost four days, on 11 December 2018 the jury returned a verdict of guilty beyond reasonable doubt – as discussed in Chapter 1. This is the reaction of Pell-antagonist Lucie Morris-Marr who was present throughout the trial (except when A's evidence was shown on video) – as expressed in *Fallen:*

> Two female abuse advocates [in the courtroom] started crying. As I tried to write notes my own tears began falling on my laptop. My emotions stemmed from the fact the former choirboy [B] wasn't alive to know the verdict, but he and his family were getting their vindication. It felt like a voice from the grave. George Pell had been found guilty of an evil deed against an innocent young boy in his own holy cathedral. The betrayal of those who had trusted him – the victim, his parents, cathedral staff, the Catholic community – was immense. The hypocrisy of every sermon, every prayer and every word he'd written on faith, duty, homosexuality and celibacy was overwhelming….

Like so many media participants in the Pell pile-on, Morris-Marr accepted the line that A's evidence was compelling. What's more, she was a player or activist who barracked for the prosecution – like quite a few of her journalistic colleagues. She believed what she wanted to believe and took comfort that the conviction demonstrated the hypocrisy of Cardinal Pell's Catholic theological conservatism.

However, Morris-Marr also reported another reaction in the court. She wrote that when the foreman announced the first jury verdict "a collective gasp was heard around the room". Morris-Marr added: "Judge Kidd leaned forward, hands clasped together; even he looked startled". His Honour told jurors: "Thank you very much, members of the jury, for the work you have done in this case. I make no comment whatsoever about your verdicts; it wouldn't be appropriate for me to do so – that's your decision and yours alone."

Chief Judge Kidd then took the unusual action of stepping down from the bench and headed to his chambers for what turned out to be a break of ten minutes. When he returned to court, the Chief Judge granted Pell bail for medical reasons and advised the convicted man that when he returned to court he should be prepared to face a term of imprisonment.

The Swimming Pool Case

The suppression order imposed by the County Court in the first and second Cathedral Trial was put in place primarily to protect the identity of the complainant. It was agreed to by the DPP and the defence.

When Cardinal Pell was found guilty on 11 December 2018, another suppression order was put in place at the request of the DPP. This time to prevent any media coverage of Pell's conviction since it was believed that news coverage of this event could prevent a fair trial in the Swimming Pool Case. A proper decision – but somewhat irrelevant at a time of the internet, social media and so on. It was widely known in Australia and overseas that Pell had been found guilty – even though this "news" did not appear in the mainstream media until some two months later.

On 13 and 14 February 2019, Chief Judge Peter Kidd had presided over *DPP v Pell (Evidential Ruling No 1)*. At issue was whether the Crown could use tendency and coincidence evidence when, as the DPP intended, Cardinal Pell was put on trial for the matters on which he had been committed by Magistrate Wallington concerning alleged offences against boys in Ballarat swimming pools. Only two charges were continued – the third case was not pursued. In this instance the Crown relied on the evidence of someone who was referred to by the pseudonym "Timothy York" (this was the case that was not pursued). The others were referred to by the pseudonyms "Kole Novak" and "Ethan Osborne".

As defined by the *Lexus Nexis Butterworths Concise Australian Legal Dictionary,* tendency evidence is evidence adduced at trial to prove that the person had a tendency and acted in accordance with that tendency. For example, evidence that a defendant regularly runs red lights is adduced to prove that the defendant ran a red light on the occasion in question.

As defined by the *Lexus Nexis Butterworths Concise Australian Legal Dictionary,* coincidence evidence is evidence that two or more similar events occurred adduced on the basis that it is improbable that the events occurred coincidentally and that the explanation must be that a person did a particular act or had a particular state of mind. For example, evidence that a number of people with whom the defendant has had arguments have suffered food poisoning, adduced to prove that the defendant deliberately poisoned them.

Neither tendency nor coincidence evidence is admissible unless reasonable notice has been given by the party adducing the evidence and the evidence has significant probative value. With respect to a prosecution, tendency and coincidence evidence is not admissible unless its probative value substantially outweighs the prejudicial risk it poses to the defendant. The point being that tendency and coincidence evidence is a diminished form of evidence which is prejudicial to the accused.

In this case, Fran Dalziel SC assisted by Angela Ellis appeared for the DPP and Robert Richter QC assisted by Ruth Shann appeared for the accused. The defence denied that any of the alleged incidents took place. Early on in the hearing, His Honour was critical of the prosecution's argument. Later on, in a devastating judgment, Chief Judge Peter Kidd dismissed the DPP's case. The conclusion commenced as follows:

> By way of conclusion, two of the complaints by themselves are incapable of sustaining a conviction for a criminal charge – the Novak complaint is effectively missing an element (deliberateness) and the Crown has accepted that the York complaint remains uncharged, in part, because of the quality of the evidence (I have highlighted some of its deficiencies).
>
> The prosecution relies upon tendency and coincidence evidence (Osborne and York) to effectively supplant rather than merely support an element of the Novak charge: accepting that tendency and coincidence evidence can be used in such a novel way, this is a very high bar to jump and it has not been cleared in this case.
>
> Further, an isolated complaint which is not of deliberate touching (Novak) and a complaint which is equivocal on that point (York) do not strongly support the occurrence of a complaint of persistent overt deliberate touching (the Osborne charge).

Approaching the evidence more holistically in order to raise coincidence reasoning is no more convincing. This simply risks glossing over the depth of the evidential deficiencies in relation to two of the complaints (Novak and York), and invites a superficial overestimation of the unity between all three complaints. It does not raise, to the requisite degree, the improbability that these events all occurred by coincidence.

The function of tendency and coincidence evidence is undoubtedly to strengthen complaints and to make the whole stronger than the sum of its parts. However, in this instance, the whole has not been made greater than the sum of its parts, at least not to the extent necessary to justify the admission of the evidence.

There is a limit to what the law allows. Parliament recognises this limit through the imposition of admissibility restrictions via ss 97, 98 and 101 [of the Victorian Evidence Act]. It is one thing to strengthen or reinforce individual complaints through the lens of the collective weight of the complaints, it is quite another to seek to cure fundamental defects and weaknesses or to change or obscure a complaint's essential character. The tendency and coincidence applications seek to do the latter here. There is a limit to what can be saved.

For all of the reasons I have detailed above, the prosecution's applications to admit evidence of the complaints of Novak, Osborne and York as either tendency evidence pursuant to s 97(1) or coincidence evidence pursuant to s 98(1), or both, are refused.

On 26 February 2019, the DPP dropped the Swimming Pool Case charges – having failed before Chief Judge Kidd to have tendency and coincidence evidence raised in the case. The remaining evidence was deemed by the DPP to be not capable of obtaining a verdict of guilty beyond reasonable doubt. It was as weak as that – as the defence had maintained in the Magistrates' Court and in subsequent advocacy to the DPP, albeit without success.

The allegations that George Pell sexually assaulted young boys in public swimming pools got nowhere in the court. Yet this was the claim advanced by ABC reporter Louise Milligan in a full half hour on *7.30* on 27 July 2016 which fired up the campaign against George

Pell – and which formed the core of her best-selling book *Cardinal*.

Milligan has never commented on Chief Judge Kidd's decision. Nor has the ABC (including *7.30*) reported *DPP v Pell (Evidential Ruling No 1)*. All this appears to have gone down what George Orwell once referred to as "the memory hole".

Suppression Order Lifted

It was only when on 27 February 2019 Chief Judge Peter Kidd delivered his Reasons for Sentence, and the various suppression orders were lifted, that followers of the Cathedral Trial – including most of Pell's supporters – learned of the nature of the charges. To many they seemed just farcical – especially to those who understood the dress codes and rituals of the Catholic Church before, during and after solemn liturgical occasions.

Had there been no suppression order concerning the reporting of the Cathedral Trial – then it is possible that individuals who were present in St Patrick's Cathedral on 15 and/or 22 December 1996 could have come forward with evidence that could have assisted the defence. No such opportunity was provided. Clearly the media could not have reported the cross-examination of A. But there is no reason why – as in the Magistrates' Court – details could not have been reported concerning the evidence provided by the opportunity witnesses. But it was not to be.

The disadvantage to Pell can be illustrated with reference to two potential witnesses who could have assisted the defence had they been aware of the crimes with which Pell had been charged. Writing in *The Australian* on 30 September 2019, Pell biographer Tess Livingstone revealed that two women were only meters away from the priests' sacristy when the alleged crimes had taken place.

In 1996, Jean Cornish and Lil Sinozic were on duty at St Patrick's Cathedral every Sunday morning. Ms Cornish told Livingstone that she had a desk at the back of the cathedral. She was always active at the time of Sunday Mass – in part to make sure that tourists did not move into the area. She said that two boys drinking wine would have been noticed. Ms Cornish confirmed that Monsignor Portelli never left Pell's side during Sunday Mass. Portelli mentioned Cornish's role at the Cathedral when giving evidence at the Magistrates' Court on 20 March 2018. She was not interviewed by Victoria Police and not called by the DPP.

Lil Sinozic also confirmed that Portelli "never let him [Pell] alone for a second". Her office door was always open on Sunday mornings and she would patrol the corridor to check that tourists and others did not enter that part of the Cathedral behind the main altar. Victoria Police was aware of Lil Sinozic, who lives in Melbourne, but did not interview her.

Cardinal Pell Sentenced

Cardinal Pell, as the Chief Judge pointed out in his sentencing comments, had no history of sexual offending before or after the events of December 1996 to February 1997. Moreover, there had been no grooming of the complainant or of his companion who had died – neither of whom Pell had met.

The jury had accepted the DPP's case that Pell was an opportunistic offender who had assaulted young boys, whom he did not know, in a public place. And not just any public place – but St Patrick's Cathedral after Solemn Mass on a Sunday when there were between 350 to 500 people in the vicinity and Archbishop Pell was accompanied by a Master of Ceremonies, some other priests, altar servers and dozens of choir boys – and activities before and after mass was attended to by a sacristan. What's more, the first incident occurred during Archbishop Pell's first or second mass at St Patrick's Cathedral following his appointment by Pope John Paul II. It was an occasion where a Catholic religious celebration resembles a military parade, with the requisite discipline involved.

However, the jury accepted that, on his first or second time as the celebrant of Sunday Solemn Mass at St Patrick's Cathedral, the Archbishop of Melbourne had somehow nicked off without anyone knowing and fled to the priests' sacristy where, by chance, he came across and assaulted two boys whom he had never met and whom he had no reason to believe would be swigging wine in a place that was out of bounds and, according to Max Potter's evidence, always locked until he (Potter) opened it. Pell then assaulted the two boys in the priests' sacristy with the door open – while no one noticed that he had gone absent-without-leave.

The Melbourne barrister Matt Collins QC was reported in the *Australian Financial Review* (1 March 2019), as saying with respect to the late B, that "no one can recall a case where an accused person was convicted of an offence against a deceased person of this kind". But then, no accused had been the subject of such hostility in the media since the Lindy Chamberlain case.

Chief Judge Kidd invited television and radio to cover his sentencing judgment to a world-wide audience as, in his judicial robes, he condemned the defendant who had been found guilty by the jury – while making it clear that he was not second guessing the jury's decision. Nevertheless, His Honour's comments were extremely damaging to Pell in a situation in which, for the first time, the facts surrounding the crimes were revealed – and concerning which no one had any knowledge of Pell's defence, apart from the very few who had attended some of the trials.

George Pell was sentenced to a total effective sentence of 6 years imprisonment with a non-parole period of 3 years and 8 months – a reasonable sentence in view of the severity of the crimes on which he had been found guilty. Since Pell pleaded not guilty, he was not entitled to any discount in his sentence. In sentencing Cardinal Pell, the Chief Judge acknowledged that it was a real possibility that he "may not live to be released from prison". The Chief Judge summarised the prosecution's (successful) case – he did not give details of the defence's case.

Consistent with his strong plea of "not guilty", Cardinal Pell did not appeal against the length of his sentence. Nor did he request bail pending the outcome of an appeal which was lodged soon after the sentence – presumably because this would have led to howls of indignation from his many enemies, including those who belonged to the mob to which the Chief Judge had referred.

Freedom was a matter of living until November 2022 (when first eligible for parole). Or dying in prison. Or getting the conviction quashed on appeal.

Bret Walker SC and Ruth Shann

Defence barristers Bret Walker SC and Ruth Shann outside the Supreme Court of Victoria on 6 June 2019. They represented Cardinal Pell in his appeals to the Victorian Court of Appeal and the High Court of Australia. Ms Shann was also junior counsel to Robert Richter QC during the Pell committal proceedings at the Magistrates' Court and the two Pell trials at the County Court of Victoria. Photo: Erik Anderson,

The Victorian Court of Appeal, Supreme Court of Victoria

The bench of the Victorian Court of Appeal which sat on George Pell v The Queen – Chris Maxwell (President, Court of Appeal), Anne Ferguson (Chief Justice of Victoria) and Justice Mark Weinberg.

4

THE APPEALS OF GEORGE PELL

"I've said previously in judgments that juries almost always get it right, but the word is 'almost'".

-Justice Mark Weinberg, Victorian Court of Appeal, 6 June 2019

When the suppression order on Cardinal George Pell's conviction was lifted on 26 February 2019 – and the convicted man went to prison – the case caused huge international and national media interest. Pell was the most senior member of the Catholic Church anywhere in the world to be tried and found guilty of child sexual abuse.

Some years earlier, the Church of England removed from its institutions and buildings the name of George Bell (1883-1958), the Bishop of Chichester – whom the English writer Charles Moore has described as one of the heroes of the Anglican Church. As Andrew Chandler has documented in *George Bell, Bishop of Chichester: Church, State and Resistance in the Age of Dictatorship* (Eerdmans, 2016), Bell had his reputation destroyed following a complaint from a female concerning some form of sexual impropriety which took place six decades previously, when she was around five years of age. There was no supporting evidence of any kind – just one single complainant's memory of an alleged event, which was accepted as true without proper investigation.

John Silvester's Doubt

Cardinal Pell's many critics rejoiced – but his few defenders, including non-Catholics, were prepared to express their doubts in public about the jury's decision. Two of the most outspoken of Pell's supporters were News Corp columnist and Sky News presenter Andrew Bolt along with *Quadrant* editor Keith Windschuttle. Neither is a Catholic – the former an agnostic, the latter an atheist.

Soon after the news broke, concern about the verdict came from an unexpected source. The Melbourne-based John Silvester, one of Australia's most experienced crime reporters and commentators, is not a Catholic. Nor does he have any connections with the Catholic Church. Moreover *The Age* in Melbourne, for which he writes, was the repository of many members of the Pell media pile-on. So Silvester's response to the jury's verdict was telling and wise. He did not believe that the evidence against Pell was convincing.

Writing in *The Age* on 24 May 2017, before Pell was charged by Victoria Police, Silvester expressed doubt about whether the case should go to trial. Having described Pell as "cold and aloof…haughty, uncaring and egoistical" (the two have never met), Silvester doubted whether Pell was being treated fairly. He suggested that the DPP's decision not to prosecute itself but to leave the decision up to Victoria Police was – in Australian Rules Football terminology – a "hospital handball". Meaning that the DPP had got out of making a difficult situation by passing the decision to prosecute to Victoria Police.

Silvester concluded his article by suggesting that what was involved in this case amounted to kicking-the-can-down-the-road. That is, passing the buck by leaving the decision up to the courts. He added:

> The trouble is this case has dragged on for so long in such a public way there must be a strong desire to handball it to a court so there can be no suggestion of a cover-up. But if we are all equal in the eyes of the law then the decision on whether to prosecute Pell should be made on the evidence, for the case needs to satisfy a criminal court, not the court of public opinion.

After the jury's decision in the re-trial, which surprised many, John Silvester expressed a concern about the verdict in *The Age* on 28 February 2019:

> ...[Cardinal Pell] went to trial on allegations that he assaulted two boys in St Patrick's Cathedral in 1996. He denied the allegations, with the jury believing the testimony of one of the boys that he was molested in the crowded church. Pell was also convicted in relation to the second boy, although that alleged victim had previously denied ever being molested, did not make a complaint and was not interviewed by police or examined in court (he died in 2014). Which means Pell was found guilty beyond reasonable doubt on the uncorroborated evidence of one witness, without forensic evidence, a pattern of behaviour or a confession.
>
> If Pell did molest those two teenagers in the busy cathedral, it certainly does not fit the usual pattern of paedophile priests. Those in power identify vulnerable potential victims, groom and then isolate them, committing offences in private then pressuring the abused into silence. Most of the successful historical prosecutions come when police find multiple individual victims who testify about similar facts....
>
> In the Pell Case, although he had access to hundreds of boys over his career he did not groom the vulnerable. Instead he attacked two he did not know in broad daylight in a near public area. He could not have known if one of them was not the son of the chief commissioner, the premier or the chief justice who were waiting outside to collect them. He could not have known if one of them would walk straight out and blow the whistle on him, and with two kids in the room he would have been sunk. This is not the action of a cunning paedophile but of a random, opportunistic criminal who usually turns out to be a serial offender. Yet no one has alleged Pell had a history of this type of crime.

John Silvester's professional disinterest was not matched by the overwhelming majority of those who commented on the case. On the same day that his article appeared, *The Age* carried an opinion piece by Barney Zwartz – a Melbourne-based critic of Pell.

It was headed "What hideous hypocrisy". Early in his article, Zwartz wrote that "the dispenser of god's grace (through the sacraments) has surely reached the nadir of human disgrace". He highlighted the fact that Pell "was disliked by progressive Catholics and the many clergy whom he ruthlessly brought to heel when he thought them too liberal in their views or too flexible with the liturgy". Zwartz wrote that "Pell's guilty verdict by an independent jury" meant that his conviction would not be overturned as unsound. Clearly, in his anger and vindication, Zwartz overlooked the fact that, on occasions, appeal courts do overturn jury findings.

The leading critics of Pell found comfort in the jury's decision – and accepted the verdict without question. Those few who supported Pell expressed concern about how the jurors could have come to a verdict of guilt beyond reasonable doubt – and many were vilified for expressing doubt about the jury's verdict.

Frank Brennan and Greg Craven also Express Doubts about the Verdict

Writing in *The Australian* on 27 February 2019, the priest and lawyer Frank Brennan S.J. (who is a theological liberal, not a theological conservative like Pell) referred to "the inherent contradictions and improbabilities of A's narrative".

He focused on A's evidence that the alleged offences occurred when the priests' sacristy was "wide open" and maintained that "anyone familiar with the conduct of a solemn Cathedral Mass with full choir would find it most unlikely that a bishop would, without grave reason, leave a recessional procession and retreat to a sacristy unaccompanied". Frank Brennan focused on the (then) archbishop's liturgical vestments:

> Witnesses familiar with liturgical vestments had been called who gave compelling evidence that it was impossible to produce an erect penis through a seamless alb. An alb is a long robe, worn

under a heavier chasuble. It is secured and set in place by a cincture which is like a tightly drawn belt. An alb cannot be unbuttoned or unzipped, the only openings being small slits on the side to allow access to trouser pockets underneath. The complainant's initial claim to police was that Pell had parted his vestments, but an alb cannot be parted; it is like a seamless dress.

Later, the complainant said that Pell moved the vestments to the side. An alb secured with a cincture cannot be moved to the side. The police never inspected the vestments during their investigations, nor did the prosecution show that the vestments could be parted or moved to the side as the complainant had alleged.

In *The Australian* on 27 February 2019, the constitutional lawyer Greg Craven, then vice-chancellor of the Australian Catholic University, wrote that the Pell Case "has shown…that the justice system can be systematically assaulted from the outside in a conscious attempt to make a fair trial impossible". He expressed particular concern about the role of the media and Victoria Police:

> Parts of the media — notably the ABC and former Fairfax journalists [Fairfax Media was taken over by Nine in 2018] — have spent years attempting to ensure Pell is the most odious figure in Australia. They seemed to want him in the dock as an ogre, not a defendant. Worse, elements of Victoria Police, including Chief Commissioner Graham Ashton, co-operated in this. Ashton's repeated announcements of impending charges and references to "victims" rather than "alleged victims" were matched only by the coincidences in timing between police pronouncements and favoured media exclusives.
>
> The result was that when the trial judge imposed a blanket media order against reporting the trials themselves, it was like a ban on reporting that Vladimir Putin is a rather nasty chap. The damage had already been done in a conscious, timely and thorough way…. So what we have witnessed is a combined effort by much of the media, including the public broadcaster [the ABC] and elements of

Victoria's law enforcement agency, to blacken the name of someone before he went to trial. And remember, Victoria's prosecutorial authorities never determined to proceed. They returned the police brief three times, before the police forced the case to go forward.

This reputational blackening works in two ways. First, at the most human level, is there any Australian who does not now associate the word "Pell" with "child abuse"? Second, is there any public official in Australia who does not understand that any action, no matter how appropriate, that might tend towards Pell's acquittal, will meet swift, public retribution? This is not a story about whether a jury got it right or wrong, or about whether justice is seen to prevail. It's a story about whether a jury was ever given a fair chance to make a decision, and whether our justice system can be heard above a media mob.

Both Fr Brennan and Professor Craven were howled down. Brennan, who was scheduled to receive an honorary degree from the Melbourne University of Divinity, was advised that the occasion had been postponed. It never took place. And Leah Kaufmann, the Australian Catholic University branch president of the National Tertiary University, called on ACU chancellor John Fahey to "sanction" his vice-chancellor. Dr Kaufmann declared that Craven had shown a disregard for "survivors of child abuse" – the collective guilt argument which Chief Judge Kidd warned against – and called for Cardinal Pell's "portrait" to be removed from Tennison Woods House on the ACU's North Sydney campus. Neither request was met.

In time, the stances adopted by both Fr Brennan and Professor Craven were consistent with the unanimous decision of the High Court.

A Fundamental Problem – Whither did the Altar Servers "Disappear"?

In a sense the Crown's case against George Pell began to fall apart during the re-trial. The problem was that the DPP could not satisfactorily explain how the alleged crimes could have been committed. Just before the luncheon adjournment on 3 December 2018, Pell's counsel

Ruth Shann raised a crucial point about the Senior Crown Prosecutor's submission to the jury:

> *Ms Shann:* Your Honour.
>
> *His Honour:* Ms Shann?
>
> *Ms Shann:* Can we just raise one issue in particular which is really with the hope that our learned friend [Mark Gibson QC] might take the opportunity to either tell us where we've got this wrong or fix it up with the jury. The [Crown's] submission [to the jury] was put that the altar servers would go into the priests' sacristy to bow to the crucifix, and then go and wait in the workers' sacristy for the interval of decorum [of five to six minutes] to pass. That is not a concept which we can find anywhere in the evidence, nor was it put to McGlone [an altar server] who said: "We bow to the cross and then start going back and forth between the priests' sacristy and sanctuary"… or Mr Connor [an altar server] who says: "We bow to the cross and then start clearing in and out of the priests' sacristy for the next ten minutes".
>
> *His Honour:* All right. Mr Gibson, you've heard that. I won't ask him [Mr Gibson] to respond now, but it's a matter for him. Okay.

This was a clear direction from the Chief Judge for the Crown to support the claim or concede its error. The trial re-recommenced at 2.17 pm – and the following exchange took place:

> *His Honour:* Welcome back, members of the jury. Mr Gibson.
>
> *Mr Gibson:* Mr Foreman and members of the jury, before lunch I had spoken about there being this period of time after the altar servers had bowed to the crucifix in the priests' sacristy and before Mr Potter had started ferrying items from the sanctuary to the priests' sacristy. I think I might have said that the altar servers were in their workers' sacristy during this five to six minute time period. There is, of course, no evidence of that, and there's no evidence of where they were…. There is evidence of where they weren't from J [i.e. A, the complainant] and that is that they weren't in the priests' sacristy. So I was inviting you to conclude that it was during this

> period waiting for the green light from Mr Potter that, wherever the altar servers were, it was not in the priests' sacristy. I just wanted to make that clear.

Mark Gibson QC conceded that the Crown did not know where the altar servers were but noted that the complainant had said that they were not in the priests' sacristy (where the alleged offences took place). In this sense, a group of adult altar servers had "disappeared".

The Crown did not repeat the claim that the altar servers were in the workers' (or utility) sacristy for an interval of five to six minutes during the Victorian Court of Appeal hearing. However, this claim was made again when the matter went to the High Court – where it was dismissed by all judges. The Crown was never able to demonstrate how the alleged offending had occurred without anyone noticing.

George Pell v The Queen – in the Victorian Court of Appeal

On 21 February 2019, Paul Galbally (Cardinal Pell's solicitor) lodged a notification for leave to appeal against the conviction. The first, and main, contention was that: "The verdicts are unreasonable and cannot be supported having regard to the evidence, including unchallenged exculpatory evidence [i.e. evidence favourable to the accused] from more than 20 Crown witnesses, it would not be open to a jury to be satisfied beyond reasonable doubt on the word of the Complainant alone". This was Ground 1. The applicant also maintained that "the Trial Judge erred by preventing the defence from using a moving visual representation of its impossibility argument during the closing address" and that the accused was not arraigned in the presence of the jury panel as required under the *Criminal Procedure Act 2009*. These were known as Ground 2 and Ground 3 respectively.

All three judges granted special leave to appeal on the first ground – but, by two to one [Justice Weinberg dissenting], rejected the application. Leave to appeal on the other two grounds was refused, albeit after a hearing.

George Pell v The Queen was heard on 6 and 7 June 2019 before Chief Justice Anne Ferguson, President of the Court of Appeal Chris Maxwell and Acting Judge Mark Weinberg. Justice Weinberg had stepped down from the Court of Appeal on reaching the mandatory retiring age of 70 years of age. He was immediately appointed a reserve judge (to which this age limitation does not apply). On the occasion of Justice Weinberg's retirement, Paul Holdenson QC commented at his farewell address before the Supreme Court of Victoria: "Your Honour was undoubtedly the best criminal appellate advocate of your generation" and spoke of his success before the High Court.

Bret Walker SC with Ruth Shann appeared for the applicant and Christopher Boyce QC with Mark Gibson SC and Angela Ellis for the respondent.

Since the Crown could not state precisely how the defendant managed to assault two boys in the claimed five to six minutes without anyone noticing, it reverted to its fall-back position that the complainant should be believed. Here's how Christopher Boyce QC commenced the Crown's case before the Victorian Court of Appeal on the morning of 6 June 2019:

> *Ferguson CJ:* Could that applicant be brought in please. Yes, Mr Boyce.
>
> *Mr Boyce:* Thank you, your Honours. Your Honours, the complainant was a very compelling witness. He was clearly not a liar. He was not a fantasist. He was a witness of truth.
>
> *Maxwell P:* Mr Boyce, those are all conclusions.
>
> *Mr Boyce:* Yes.

So the Crown commenced its case with a conclusion. Namely, that A was very compelling and neither a fantasist nor a liar. He was a "witness of truth". It was as simple as that.

Kerri Judd QC was appointed Victorian Director of Public Prosecutions and commenced in this position on 6 March 2018. Ms Judd could have led for the Crown in George *Pell v The Queen* in the Victorian Court of Appeal. But the job was given to Christopher Boyce QC.

There was broad agreement after the event that Boyce had a difficult day in court. As Pell-antagonist David Marr wrote in *The Guardian* on 6 June 2019:

> On the surface, the day was a train wreck. Despite all that's at stake, after all these years of work by police and lawyers, after two difficult trials and a verdict that made news around the world, the barrister whose job was to defend the jury's verdict, Christopher Boyce SC, found himself lost for words. The judges peppered him with questions. As he struggled to answer, the cardinal's counsel, Bret Walker SC, played with his fountain pen. Pell wrote notes. At a certain point in the day the tone of the interrogation shifted: the judges began prompting Boyce, bringing him back to his own argument. By late morning, a little knot of victims and their supporters had gathered in one of the corridors. They looked shell shocked.

Later on, Marr quoted from one section of Boyce's advocacy:

> "It would…" Silence. "It would…" Silence. "Can I put this?" Silence. "I must say it is difficult." Pause. "It's not good enough for me to say what I said before." Pause. "Rehearsing the platitudes may not be all that helpful." Silence. Walker was staring at the ceiling. Pell was writing so much and so fast he seemed to be drafting his memoirs. The judges gave the lawyer a hand. He moved as quickly as he could to his next point … The transcript reads better than the experience in the room.

The Guardian's Melissa Davey – like Marr, a Pell-antagonist – reached a similar conclusion, writing on 6 June 2019:

> Prosecutor Christopher Boyce struggled through questions from three judges presiding over the appeal of Cardinal George Pell, finding it difficult to answer their inquiries about the victim's evidence and the case.

Boyce QC's position was that A was a witness of truth. It's just that the Crown found it difficult to explain precisely what the truth was.

Early on, Justice Weinberg asked Mr Boyce to explain why A had no proper explanation for his claim that, after the attacks, he had never spoken to B about the matter. This is an issue which President Maxwell later took up. Boyce's response was that the court should look to the manner in which A's explanation was delivered. He said that, at the end of listening, "one puts down one's pen and stares blankly at the [video] screen and is moved". He added: "At this point...any prima facie at least – any doubt that one might have about the account is removed". Weinberg was not convinced:

> *Weinberg JA:* Is there any significance at all, for the purposes of this application and the fact that the same evidence was played before a different jury in a first trial, and at least two members of that jury did not accept it beyond reasonable doubt?
>
> *Mr Boyce:* No.
>
> *Weinberg JA:* We simply ignore that?
>
> *Mr Boyce:* Yes.
>
> *Weinberg JA:* It's just that you make the point that this is so obviously compelling and so clearly reliable and truthful, I just wonder how that squares with the fact that another jury were not able to agree and we don't know the numbers, nor should we, having seen and heard exactly the same evidence.
>
> *Mr Boyce:* Well, I'm arguing about this case.
>
> *Weinberg JA:* This case concerns the same evidence.
>
> *Mr Boyce:* Yes.

In the two days hearing in the Court of Appeal, most of the exchanges took place between President Maxwell and Justice Weinberg on the bench and counsel. Chief Justice Anne Ferguson was not so prominent. Throughout the first day Christopher Boyce QC struggled. His comments included: "The point I'm making – and I don't think extremely well", "I wish I was of more assistance to your Honours" and "I apologise if I'm not being as helpful as I might".

It is widely acknowledged in Victorian legal circles that Christopher Boyce is a fine barrister. It's just that he had a difficult case to argue since the only evidence against the defendant was the statement of a complainant which was not supported by any of the opportunity witnesses. It turned out that Kerri Judd QC, who argued the Crown's case before the High Court, was to have similar difficulties – which is why she altered the Crown's case. Yet the decision to continue the prosecution of Cardinal Pell after the hung jury in the first trial was Ms Judd's alone.

The Judges Decide – 2 to 1

The Court of Appeal of the Supreme Court of Victoria delivered its judgment in Melbourne on Wednesday 21 August 2019 having read the transcript, visited St Patrick's Cathedral and viewed the evidence of the key witnesses on video – including that of A. The proceedings were live streamed. However, the feed from the court faltered temporarily as the Chief Justice read a summary of the decision. But it was soon evident that the Court of Appeal had dismissed the appeal. The Summary of Judgement released by the Supreme Court contained the following statements:

> Having reviewed the whole of the evidence, two of the judges of the Court of Appeal (Chief Justice Ferguson and Justice Maxwell, President of the Court of Appeal) decided that it was open to the jury to be satisfied beyond reasonable doubt that Cardinal Pell was guilty of the offences charged. In other words, those judges decided that there was nothing about the complainant's evidence, or about the opportunity evidence, which meant that the jury "must have had a doubt" about the truth of the complainant's account. They stated that it is not enough that one or more jurors "might have had a doubt". Rather, the jury "must have had a doubt". The Chief Justice and Justice Maxwell stated that they did not experience a doubt. The Chief Justice and Justice Maxwell accepted the prosecution's submission that the

complainant was a very compelling witness, was clearly not a liar, was not a fantasist and was a witness of truth.

Victoria's two most senior judges accepted the Crown's "Believe A" submission. The Summary of Judgement also contained the following statement:

> In his dissenting judgment, Justice Weinberg found that, at times, the complainant was inclined to embellish aspects of his account. He concluded that his evidence contained discrepancies, displayed inadequacies, and otherwise lacked probative value so as to cause him to have a doubt as to the applicant's guilt. He could not exclude as a reasonable possibility that some of what the complainant said was concocted, particularly in relation to the second incident. Justice Weinberg found that the complainant's account of the second incident was entirely implausible and quite unconvincing.
>
> Nevertheless, Justice Weinberg stated that in relation to the first incident, if the complainant's evidence was the only evidence, he might well have found it difficult to say that the jury, acting reasonably, were "bound" to have a reasonable doubt about the Cardinal's guilt. He went on to note, however, that there was more than just the complainant's evidence. In Justice Weinberg's view there was a significant body of cogent and, in some cases, impressive evidence suggesting that the complainant's account was, in a realistic sense, "impossible" to accept. To his mind, there is a significant possibility that the Cardinal may not have committed the offences. In those circumstances, Justice Weinberg stated that in his view the convictions could not stand. Nevertheless, the appeal on the unreasonableness ground was dismissed because the other two judges took a different view of the facts.

A Summary of Judgment is no more than that – it is not a substitute for the Court's reasons. The majority judgment, ran for 120 pages. Justice Weinberg's dissent ran for 200 pages.

The Majority Judgment

In Paragraph 87 of the 352 paragraph majority decision the following statement appears:

> On the appeal, senior counsel for the Crown singled out...passages as demonstrating why A should be viewed as "a very compelling witness". Both the content of the answers, and the manner of their delivery, were said to be such as to eliminate any doubt a juror might have had. In our view, this was a very significant part of A's evidence. It was rightly characterised as compelling, both because of the clarity and cogency of what A said and because of the complete absence of any indication of contrivance in the emotion which A conveyed when giving his answers.

Then at paragraph 91 the majority judgment reads as follows:

> Throughout his evidence, A came across as someone who was telling the truth. He did not seek to embellish his evidence or tailor it in a manner favourable to the prosecution. As might have been expected, there were some things which he could remember and many things which he could not. And his explanations of why that was so had the ring of truth.

Both these findings about the complainant's "compelling" evidence and "manner" – or demeanour – fell apart in the High Court.

Apart from Their Honours' acceptance of the Crown's case that A should be believed because he was a "compelling" witness, there were a number of problems with the majority judgment. Several instances illustrate the point.

- At Paragraphs 73 and 77 the following comments appear:

> 73. It is sufficient for present purposes to say that we saw nothing in A's answers under cross-examination to suggest that he had been caught out or had tripped himself up. And, where his responses involved any alteration of — or addition to — what he had said previously, the changes seemed to us to be typical of what occurs when a person is questioned on successive occasions, by different people,

about events from the distant past...

77. A further indication of A's credibility, in our view, was his admitted uncertainty about a number of matters which, if the story had been invented or was an entrenched fantasy, he might have been expected to describe with confidence. Striking examples of this were:

- his uncertainty about whether Cardinal Pell closed the door in the first incident;
- his lack of recall as to whether he had screamed or called out during the first incident; and
- his uncertainty about which hand Cardinal Pell had used in the second incident.

So Their Honours held that A's inconsistency and uncertainty in giving evidence increased, rather than diminished, his credibility. However, they also held that any uncertainty and imprecision on behalf of the opportunity witnesses weakened the defence's case. A contradiction that was never explained.

• At paragraph 95, Their Honours stated that the Crown's submission as to the credibility of A's evidence was enhanced by the accuracy of his description of the priests' sacristy in 1996. Their point was that, in 2016, A was able to correctly identify the layout of the priests' sacristy as it was in 1996. During his walk-through of the Cathedral with Victoria Police on 29 March 2016, A said that the priests' sacristy was "unchanged" from 1996. But the sacristan Max Potter gave unchallenged evidence at the trial that significant changes to the priests' sacristy had taken place in 2003 and 2004. It seems that the majority judges overlooked this point.

• Then at paragraph 96, the majority found it "striking" that A had identified the priests' sacristy as the setting for the offending since at "all other times Cardinal Pell would have robed – and disrobed – in the Archbishop's sacristy". However, there was no evidence that Pell had ever used the archbishop's sacristy – since the room had been out of use for robing/unrobing for around four years – well before Pell became Archbishop of Melbourne. This was the uncontested evidence of Monsignor Portelli. In this instance the majority's speculation was harmful to the accused. Contrary to the majority judgment, there were no "other times" when Pell would have used the archbishop's sacristy prior to December 1996.

• Then at paragraphs 112, 113 and 339, the majority accepted that the second incident – namely Pell's alleged groping of A in a corridor in the presence of some 40 people – could be "readily imagined". Their Honours stated: "Jurors would know from common experience that confined spaces, facilitate furtive sexual touching, even when others are in the same space" and maintained that it was "quite possible that this brief encounter was not noticed". They added: "At all events, the evidence once again falls well short of impossibility".

Justice Weinberg did not think so. Nor did all seven High Court justices. It is extremely difficult to imagine that – at a time of concern about clerical child abuse in the Catholic Church two decades ago – such offending would not be noticed. After all, there were around at least 40 individuals in the procession – including adults, some of whom had been put in charge of caring for children. Also, A's evidence was that Pell grabbed his testicles in such a way as to cause pain – this was not an occasion of "furtive sexual touching". Moreover the burden on the jury was to establish proof beyond reasonable doubt – not what falls well short of impossibility.

• Then at paragraph 300 the majority wrote that "taking the evidence as a whole, it was open to the jury to find that the assaults took place in the 5-6 minutes of private prayer time" and that this was before the "hive of activity described by the other witnesses began". In his uncontested evidence at the second trial, Max Potter said that the five or six minutes of prayer time started when the procession commenced at the end of the Mass and headed to the Main Door. There was no time for A and B, or for Pell himself, to break away from the procession and get to the priests' sacristy in time for any incident involving 5 to 6 minutes to have taken place in private in the priests' sacristy – since it would have taken A and B around that time to get to the priests' sacristy. There was no time for five to six minutes of criminality.

The judgment of Chief Justice Ferguson and President Maxwell in this case, Victoria's most senior judges was seriously flawed. It appears the President of the Court of Appeal Chris Maxwell wrote the first draft of the judgment since Chief Justice Ferguson took six weeks leave between the hearing and the announcement of the judgment.

Justice Weinberg's Dissent

Justice Mark Weinberg's minority judgment in *George Pell v The Queen* will go down as one of the most important judicial dissents in Australian legal history. It is a rare occasion indeed when all seven judges of the High Court of Australia reach a conclusion similar to that of an acting judge in dissent and overturn a majority judgment of a chief justice and a president of the appeal court in a State jurisdiction.

After an insightful and detailed examination of the evidence, His Honour summarised his findings, with respect to Ground 1, in the final ten paragraphs of his judgment. He maintained that the complainant's allegations fell short of the standard of proof required for conviction. Then, Justice Weinberg identified with Justice Deane's dissent in *Chamberlain v The Queen*. In particular, Justice Weinberg supported Justice Deane's argument that the "cause of the continued acceptance of trial by jury" was not likely to be served by treating a jury's verdict of guilty as unchallenged or unexaminable. Since to do so, quoting Deane, could "sap and undermine the institution of trial by jury".

This is an important point which runs counter to the views expressed by the likes of Barrie Cassidy, Fran Kelly, Jon Faine and Malcolm Knox quoted earlier. The Deane/Weinberg position is that the best way to preserve the community's trust in the jury system is to ensure that any errors of juries are corrected by appeal courts.

At Paragraphs 1111 and 1112, Justice Weinberg made the following telling points:

> 1111. I find myself in a position quite similar to that which confronted Deane J. To borrow his Honour's language, there is, to my mind, a "significant possibility" that the applicant in this case may not have committed these offences. That means that, in my respectful opinion, these convictions cannot be permitted to stand. The only order that can properly be made is that the applicant be acquitted on each charge.
>
> 1112. Mine is, of course, a minority view in relation to Ground 1. I am troubled by the fact that I find myself constrained to differ from two of my colleagues whose opinions I always respect greatly. That has caused me to reflect even more carefully upon the proper outcome of this application. Having done so, however, I cannot, in good conscience, do other than to maintain my dissent.

Justice Weinberg did not easily disagree with Chief Justice Ferguson and President Maxwell. But he did so in accordance with the demands of his conscience. Moreover, he would have known that his comparison of the Chamberlain and Pell Cases was bound to cause attention – not only in the public sphere but especially within legal circles.

In his judgment, His Honour consciously debunked the view of Chief Justice Ferguson and President Maxwell that courts should always give credence to the demeanour of a witness. All three judges had viewed A's video evidence at the trial but divided two to one on A's credibility. As Justice Weinberg put it:

> 917. Clearly, it is important to be aware of the risk of giving too much credence to matters such as demeanour, when evaluating the evidence of a witness. In the past, there has been a great deal of misplaced confidence in the capacity of a judge, or any other decision-maker, to discern the truth, on the basis of demeanour alone.
>
> 918. The High Court has observed that it can be dangerous to place too much reliance upon the appearance of a witness, rather than focusing, so far as possible, upon other, more objectively reliable matters. These might include, for example, contemporary docu-

ments, clearly established facts, scientifically approved tests, and the apparent logic of the events in question.

919. Empirical evidence has cast serious doubts upon the capacity of any human being to tell truth from falsehood merely from the observations of a witness giving evidence. That is particularly so in the artificial and stressful circumstances of a courtroom. There is today a substantial body of scholarly writing which cautions against giving too much weight to demeanour when assessing the probative value of evidence....

921. A witness who speaks hesitantly might simply be cautious, or taking the time to fabricate or embellish. An emphatic witness can be deceptive, or even convince himself or herself that what the witness is saying is true. A witness who looks the judge straight in the eye, rather than casting his or her eyes on the ground, can be telling the truth, or lying, with no way of knowing other than by relying on nothing more reliable than intuition.

This was a devastating critique of the decision of Chief Justice Ferguson and President Maxwell to place great store on their opinion that A was a "compelling" witness and, consequently, should be believed. Later on Justice Weinberg stated:

925. In the present case, the prosecution relied entirely upon the evidence of the complainant to establish guilt, and nothing more. There was no supporting evidence of any kind from any other witness. Indeed, there was no supporting evidence of any kind at all. These convictions were based upon the jury's assessment of the complainant as a witness, and nothing more.

Then, in another direct and telling comment, Justice Weinberg drew attention to the case of Carl Beech (aka "Nick") who – as mentioned in Chapter 1 – lied about being sexually assaulted by the one-time British prime minister Edward Heath and Lord Bramwell among others:

931. There are proven cases of "false memory"... including, in particular, in relation to sexual offending. The recent decision of this Court in Tyrrell provides a classic illustration of an apparently com-

pelling witness whose account had to involve a substantial measure of complete fantasy. In that case, the fact that the prosecution was brought more than 50 years after the alleged offending was, in itself, a portent of unreliability. Such a prosecution would never have been brought even as recently as 20 or so years ago, and if it had, it would have been stayed as an abuse of process.

932. Nor can it be doubted that some complainants in cases involving sexual abuse, including of children, have fabricated their allegations. Just within the past few weeks, a major scandal involving false allegations of that kind has erupted in England, and received enormous publicity [i.e. the Carl Beech case].

A Reflection on Demeanour

In an article in *Inside Story* on 28 August 2019 titled "A judge's doubts", Professor Jeremy Gans considered Justice Weinberg's dissent in *George Pell v The Queen* with reference to John Patrick Shanley's 2004 play *Doubt: A Parable* set in a Catholic parish in the Bronx. Sister Aloysius suspects that Father Flynn may be sexually abusing a young Afro-American altar boy. Gans cited that part in *Doubt: A Parable* where Aloysius confronts Flynn and refers to him "controlling the expression on your face right now".

The Melbourne Law School professor considered how three journalists had assessed Pell's demeanour when he learnt that his appeal had been dismissed by the Victorian Court of Appeal in a majority decision – and then reflected how the three judges had assessed the evidence of A.

> On learning his fate, "Pell slumped into his chair, looking frail. He appeared to grab onto the dock for support." At least, that's what Benjamin Ansell saw. Eliza Rugg saw his head bowed, "destroyed," his "poker face gone." But according to David Marr, "Pell displayed once more his Olympian detachment. Don't believe reports that he flinched. His lips pursed a little as he stared at the judges. That's all." These three were in the same room looking at the same man at the same time.

The 325 pages of the Court of Appeal's two judgements are replete with moments like that. "Throughout his evidence," the majority writes of the man who says Pell sexually abused him and another boy in 1996, "A came across as someone who was telling the truth. He did not seek to embellish his evidence or tailor it in a manner favourable to the prosecution." Not so, according to Weinberg. "On occasion, he seemed almost to 'clutch at straws' in an attempt to minimise, or overcome, the obvious inconsistencies between what he had said on earlier occasions, and what the objective evidence clearly showed." The judges watched the same video of Pell's accuser, the very one both juries saw, but it divided them nearly every time.

Doubt: The Parable is fiction; *George Pell v The Queen* is reality. But the message is the same. Judges, journalists and more besides should understand that an opinion about a person's demeanour is no more than an opinion.

John Francis Tyrrell v The Queen

What Justice Weinberg said in relation to the Tyrrell Case was particularly significant. In his view, if the Victorian DPP had taken a similar case as recently as 2000, it would have been discontinued by a court. However, Victoria Police charged Tyrrell and the DPP took the case. It obtained a jury verdict of guilty in the County Court of Victoria in April 2018 – on ten out of 14 charges. The conviction was overturned by the Victoria Court of Appeal on 15 March 2019 (shortly after Cardinal Pell's conviction) in a unanimous decision handed down by Justices Stephen Kaye, Richard Niall and Mark Weinberg.

The alleged incidents occurred in 1965 and 1966 at St Joseph's College in Geelong when John Francis Tyrrell was a Christian Brothers teacher at the school. At trial Tyrrell gave evidence for the defence as did a colorectal surgeon. Mr (the Victorian term for a surgeon) James Keck told the court that the anal assault which the complainant alleged could not have occurred without causing significant injury – of which there was no evidence. During the trial the complainant conceded that an erroneous recollection he had had was due to mistaking a vivid nightmare for a real event.

As with *DPP v Pell*, in *DPP v Tyrrell* the complainant's testimony was the only evidence against the accused. As with Pell, the complainant changed his account with respect to dates. As with Pell, there was no evidence that Tyrrell had committed any other criminal offences during his long career.

In view of the Court of Appeal's decision that Tyrrell should not have been found guilty beyond reasonable doubt, the court did not have to consider the applicant's second ground of appeal – namely that the half century delay in prosecuting Tyrrell resulted in an unfair trial. However, Justices Kaye, Niall and Weinberg felt the need to make this point:

> Without expressing a concluded view in relation to ground 2, it is sufficient to reiterate our observations under ground 1, that the delay, and the consequential unavailability of witnesses who might otherwise have been relevant, patently had a detrimental effect on the fairness of the trial, notwithstanding appropriate and thorough directions given by the judge to the jury in that respect.

The appeal court judges found no fault in the directions that Judge Trevor Wraight gave to the jury but considered the delay in prosecution, along with the fact that some persons who might have given evidence for the defence were dead, had a detrimental effect on Tyrrell receiving a fair trial. The appeal court judges made it clear that the delay was unfair to the accused.

The Court of Appeal ordered that the 80 year old Tyrrell – who was serving a minimum term of six and a half years and was in poor health – be released "quickly". The ABC did not report the outcome of *John Francis Tyrrell v The Queen*. However, many who were aware of the decision would not have been surprised by Justice Weinberg's dissent in *George Pell v The Queen*.

In spite of the strong unanimous judgment in *Tyrrell v The Queen*, the Victorian DPP applied to the High Court for special leave to appeal against the judgment. The application was dismissed on 9 August 2019. It turned out to be a bad day for the Victorian DPP.

Justice Weinberg's Reasoning Accepted by the High Court

Justice Weinberg in *George Pell v The Queen* was critical of the submission by Christopher Boyce QC, counsel for the DPP. He rejected the contention that the evidence provided by Monsignor Portelli, Max Potter and Daniel McGlone should be put aside. He found that Portelli was a "credible and reliable witness" and that, taking into account Potter's advanced age, he regarded him as an honest witness. His Honour also found the evidence of Daniel McGlone, who recalled a conversation between his mother and Pell outside St Patrick's Cathedral's Main Door in December 1996, as "credible".

Towards the end of his judgment, Justice Weinberg repeated his view that "the complainant's account could not possibly stand if the evidence given by Portelli, or Potter, were to be accepted". This was the essential finding when the Pell Case went on appeal to the High Court. It is worth remembering that Magistrate Wallington expressed a similar view at the committal proceedings – before committing Pell to trial on this matter.

Pell v The Queen – in the High Court of Australia

Four months after his release from prison, George Pell wrote an article for the journal *First Things* titled "My Time in Prison". It was published in *The Australian* on 14 July 2020. Towards the end of his piece, Cardinal Pell reflected on hearing the news that his appeal in the Supreme Court of Victoria had been unsuccessful.

> After I lost my appeal to the Victorian Supreme Court, I considered not appealing to the Australian High Court, reasoning that if the judges were simply going to close ranks, I need not cooperate in an expensive charade. The boss of the prison in Melbourne, a bigger man than I and a straight shooter, urged me to persevere. I was encouraged and remain grateful to him.

Another factor in the decision to appeal would have been the very strong dissent by Justice Weinberg. It's possible that if all three judges of the Victorian Court of Appeal had decided that the complainant must be believed and the jury decision must be upheld – then, maybe, the cardinal may have decided that the pack was stacked against him and that there was no option but to surrender and accept his fate. But the dissent was so strong – and Justice Weinberg so respected in legal circles – that the Pell camp decided to try again.

And so, on 17 September 2019, Bret Walker SC and Ruth Shann filed an Application for Special Leave to Appeal against the decision of the Victorian Court of Appeal with the High Court of Australia's Melbourne Office. The proposed grounds were as follows:

> 1. The majority erred by finding that their belief in the complainant required the applicant to establish that the offending was impossible in order to raise and leave a doubt.
>
> 2. The majority erred in their conclusion that the verdicts were not unreasonable as, in light of findings made by them, there did remain a reasonable doubt as to the existence of any opportunity for the offending to have occurred.

The whole process was undertaken via written submissions – without a hearing. This is not uncommon. Very few applications for special leave to appeal to the High Court are successful. Many a Pell-antagonist anticipated that his application would fail and that this would be the end of the case.

The ABC engaged Pell-antagonist Louise Milligan to preview the case just before the High Court handed down its decision on Wednesday 13 November 2019. Speaking on ABC Sydney Radio 702, she had this to say:

> *Louise Milligan:* It's been done "on the papers", as they say. So it means that there won't be a hearing about whether he can have a hearing.... A lot of lawyers are saying that because it is being done in this way, it tends to point to the fact that leave has probably been denied – but you never know, you know. You don't want to make

> predictions in these sorts of cases. It's a very high-profile case, and it may be that the High Court says – "we want to get involved in this". But the criminal lawyers that I've spoken to have said.... there doesn't seem to be a clear appeal point there.
>
> Apart from the mechanics you know, the thing about this is – every time this comes up it's just a little kick in the guts to a lot of people out there for whom this process has been extremely painful.

Ms Milligan's "criminal lawyers" got it wrong – there was an appeal point. But it's notable that – despite Chief Judge Kidd's clear warning in the County Court of Victoria – Louise Milligan as late as November 2019 still believed that Pell was somehow responsible for the crimes of others and the pain felt by the victims of others. The concept of collective guilt.

On Wednesday 13 November 2019 at 10 am, Justices Gordon and Edelman announced the results of the applications listed for determination that day. There were 22 applications. All but one was announced – via *Twitter* – as "dismissed". The only successful one was Case Number 16 *George Pell v The Queen:* "Application referred to a Full Court for argument as on an appeal". The full decision was announced by Justice Michelle Gordon at 9.34 am:

> *Gordon J:* In this application, Justice Edelman and I order that the application for special leave to appeal to this Court from the judgment and orders of the Court of Appeal of the Supreme Court of Victoria given and made on 21 August 2019 be referred to a Full Court of this Court for argument as on an appeal. The parties will be made aware of the directions necessary for undertaking that hearing.

That was it. Cardinal Pell heard the news soon after at the Melbourne Assessment Prison. It was not quite the granting of special leave to appeal. But it was much the same thing – since the case would be considered by the High Court. There, at any stage, the appeal could have been dismissed or the verdict overturned. All seven judges sat on *Pell v The Queen* – the hearings of which were held on 11 and 12 March 2020. It is unusual for all seven High Court judges to sit on an appeal in a criminal law case – usually five judges hear the case.

Bret Walker SC and Ruth Shann filed Cardinal Pell's initial submission on 3 January 2020. The Victorian DPP's initial submission was filed on 31 January 2020 and Walker/Shann filed further submissions on 19 February 2020, 20 February 2020, 11 March 2020 and 13 March 2020. The DPP also filed follow-up submissions.

In the Walker/Shann submission of 17 September 2019 seeking special leave to appeal, the following important – albeit sensitive – point was made:

> 21. Rigid application of the onus and standard of proof in 21st century sexual assault trials in Australia is of particular importance. Over the last two decades in each State and Territory the laws of evidence and procedure have been modified by Australian parliaments with the effect of making it more difficult to test allegations of sexual assault. Those who are accused, including by a complete stranger making decades old allegations, cannot, for example, investigate a complainant's psychological history in the hope of uncovering a reason why a seemingly credible person is accusing them of offending they say they did not commit. In such cases, an accused is heavily reliant on the presumption of innocence and the requirement for juries and appellate courts to apply processes of reasoning which accord with the onus and standard of proof. These reforms highlight the importance of the role of appellate courts in an unreasonableness appeal to ensure full compliance with the M test as applied in *SKA and Palmer* [the reference is to High Court cases].

The submission pointed out that the relevant Victorian legislation limits access to, and use of, any confidential communications with a medical practitioner or counsellor unless, inter alia, the applicant can establish (without having seen the material or having been permitted to ask questions about it) that it has substantive probative value and the public interest in preserving confidentiality is substantially outweighed by the public interest in admitting it. This is a very high bar indeed for any applicant. The courts determined that it was not met in Cardinal Pell's case.

In the final paragraph of the submission of 20 February 2020, Walker and Shann argued that the DPP (Kerri Judd QC) in her submission maintained that the alleged offences in the priests' sacristy occurred after the altar servers returned from the procession and bowed to the crucifix but before the post-Mass hive of activity commenced. But Walker/Shann pointed out that, at the trial, the Crown had conceded that there was no evidence of where the altar servers had gone.

Walker/Shann contended that the DPP had wrongly made "a submission to this Court that the majority [in the Court of Appeal] upheld an argument that was, in fact, withdrawn at trial as unsupportable" – namely, the claim that the altar servers had gone to the workers' sacristy. It was the continuing problem the Crown faced as to the "disappeared" altar servers.

Two (Almost) Pre-Pandemic Days in Canberra: Proceedings of the High Court, 11-12 March 2020

The hearings in *Pell v The Queen* were held in the High Court in Canberra on Wednesday 11 March and Thursday 12 March 2020. By then, Prime Minister Scott Morrison had already announced that COVID-19 would become a pandemic and the World Health Organisation declared it a pandemic on 11 March 2020. It was not until 13 March that the initial lockdowns were announced. So 11-12 March 2020 were some of the last days before Australia went into pandemic lockdown mode.

Bret Walker SC stated the applicant's case with few interruptions or interventions from the bench. Towards the end of his address, Justice Bell (the most experienced criminal jurist on the High Court) said that if Pell was standing on the steps of the Cathedral for 20 minutes or so following Sunday mass – "if that were the evidence, it would provide an alibi". Walker concurred.

Kerri Judd QC commenced her address to the High Court at 10 am on Thursday 12 March 2020. It was to be a difficult day – as the following exchanges demonstrate:

- **"A" as a Compelling Witness:**

  Bell J: Ms Judd, at a point in the closing address of the Crown Prosecutor, he invited the jury to remember two occasions when the complainant had been asked a question by defence counsel and the complainant had paused and he closed his eyes before responding, in the Crown Prosecutor's submission, one of those indications of a witness truthfully trying to reflect back and remember the subject matter that his attention was directed to.

  Now, the matter I am going to raise with you, Ms Judd, is this. It may be that watching and seeing the complainant close his eyes and think back impressed members of the jury as an evident sign of truthfulness. It may be that some people might look at that and say, "He's giving himself time to think up an answer". My point is it is such a subjective consideration that it is very difficult to see how the appellate court properly performing its function in accordance with the M test, can be assisted by its own subjective views about matters of that character. [The reference is to the High Court's 1994 decision in *M v The Queen.*]

  Ms Judd: Yes, but then we get to the real question about all of this, is that whether engaging in that viewing they have actually – and it can be demonstrated that they have improperly engaged in the assessment of the whole of the evidence, and that is the question that completes part of this cycle.

It was not much of an answer.

- **Practice As Powerful Evidence**

In Cardinal Pell's trials and appeals, the prosecution attempted to discredit the testimony of Monsignor Charles Portelli – since, in a sense, he provided alibi evidence for the defence. However, this began to fall apart in the High Court when it became evident that Kerri Judd QC failed to explain why it was open to the jury to find that Portelli was not with Pell at the time of the alleged offences:

  Keane J: Ms Judd, the jury would not have been entitled, would they, on the basis of the concessions and the uncertainties that you have taken us to in Monsignor Portelli's evidence to reject Monsignor Portelli's evidence that he actually was there at those two masses?

Ms Judd: I submit that they were entitled to

Keane J: They were entitled to reject his evidence that he was present at those masses?

Ms Judd: No, no – sorry, not that he was present at those masses, no.

Keane J: Okay. So in terms of the way the case was run, it was not open to the jury to take the view that Monsignor Portelli was not there. Monsignor Portelli gives evidence of a couple of practices that exist and says, it is possible they were not followed because of the exigencies of the particular day, but he cannot recall that there was any particular exigency that caused a departure from the practice. Is not the evidence of practice, where it is honestly given, usually regarded as powerful evidence?

Ms Judd: Yes, but

Keane J: I mean, I can say I shaved last Friday, not because I actually have a specific recollection of it, but because it was a workday and I shave on workdays.

Ms Judd: So, I think what I do need to do is go to some of the other material. So if I could take you to page 749

It was an important point – especially dealing with an organisation such as a church or an army which places emphasis on the importance of ceremony and routine. The continuity of practice or habit does make for powerful evidence.

- **Kerri Judd QC as a Prosecutor**

    Nettle J: Just before you pass to the next subject, you took us to 619 and [the chorister] Mr Thomas' evidence. Justice Gordon referred you to 617. At the top of that page Thomas talks about the other priests who processed at the back of the procession, around through the corridor and into the sacristy, with the altar boys – altar servers. There was also some evidence I think from the complainant that there were other priests in operation on the day, those days. Is one entitled to infer from that that other priests would have processed in with the altar boys into the priests' sacristy and have then begun to unchange, as Monsignor Portelli said that they did?

Ms Judd: I do not think it was ever definite that there were other priests on those days and

Nettle J: The complainant said that there were other priests on those two days.

Ms Judd: There would have been. McGlone said certainly for one of the days – there is a lot of material here.

Nettle J: There is a lot.

Kiefel CJ: You are not the only one who has a lot of material, Ms Judd, but you are supposed to be taking us through it efficiently.

Ms Judd: I am trying to take you through it efficiently.

Nettle J: Perhaps you can leave that to later, if it would suit you. You go ahead on your own pace.

Ms Judd: I have got a lot of helpers. I just have to know which one to go to....

To be fair to Ms Judd, she was not the only member of the prosecution team to have a problem in presenting the Crown's case. As previously pointed out, so did Mark Gibson SC in the County Court re-trial. And so did Christopher Boyce QC in the Victorian Court of Appeal. The problem continued into the High Court of Australia. All are able barristers. Clearly, they had a difficult case. But then, after Victoria Police took its initial 26 charges to the Magistrates' Court (only succeeding in ten instances) it was the Victorian DPP – Kerri Judd QC – who continued the case into the County Court for the first trial and, again, for the re-trial and who refused to discontinue the latter.

- **The Court of Appeal & Reversing the Onus of Proof**

Shortly before lunch, the hearing turned on the Victorian Court of Appeal's majority decision which found that:

> For the reasons we have given, the jury were entitled to view those answers [by Portelli], and the evidence more generally, as leaving open the realistic possibility that Cardinal Pell was "alone in the sacristies only a few minutes after the end of Mass".

The High Court judges focused on the issue of possibility and the onus of proof:

> *Bell J:* ...You have a conclusion that it was open to the jury to consider the realistic possibility that the offence could have occurred.
>
> *Ms Judd:* Yes.
>
> *Bell J:* Well, to some that seems awfully like a reversal of the onus of proof.... Coming back to paragraph 284, bearing in mind the requirement that the Crown eliminate the reasonable possibility that, no matter how impressive the complainant was, other evidence pointed to the fact that the offence could not have occurred in the way the complainant described because the Archbishop was somewhere else. Now, that is what their Honours are dealing with here and they are saying, well, it was open to the jury to consider as a realistic possibility that he was in the sacristy, which leaves rather open the realistic possibility that he was not, because he was on the steps outside the Western Door.

Justice Bell's point was convincing. If it was open for the jury to find that there was a reasonable possibility that Pell was in the priests' sacristy after Mass – then there was also a realistic possibility that Pell was on the Cathedral steps outside the Main Door.

• Problems as to When the Private Prayer Time Commenced

Kerri Judd QC had problems stating when the private prayer time of five to six minutes commenced. This was the period during which Pell is said to have left the procession and headed to the priests' sacristy unnoticed:

> *Bell J:* Ms Judd, the position is that - do you accept that the pri-

vate prayer time commenced as the procession was making its way down the nave?

Ms Judd: No.

Bell J: When did the private time commence – when the procession had fully exited the cathedral?

Ms Judd: I say there is no precise time as to when – the evidence does not indicate when that started.

Bell J: Well, when does the prosecution – in the way the case was run, did the prosecution put that the private time commenced. It is not a question of how long it was, but when did it commence?

Gordon J: What about Potter's evidence? Do you rely on him?

Ms Judd : Yes, of course. His evidence

Nettle J: Potter says that he did immediately – five to six minutes after it had commenced – that is to say, the procession.

Keane J: The evidence is of people coming up, to have their private time, as the others are leaving the cathedral. That is the natural reading of the evidence. They are not sitting there waiting for the procession to assemble or to set off, much less to leave the cathedral. They are moving up as the people in the procession are gathering and moving out.

Soon after, Kerri Judd QC said that she could not take the matter any further. No surprise there. This was the point that Victoria Police, the DPP, Magistrate Wallington and Justices Ferguson and Maxwell missed. There was no time for the offending to have occurred since the five to six minutes private prayer time commenced as the procession – containing both A and B as well as the (then) Archbishop of Melbourne – commenced at the sanctuary. This meant that neither the complainant nor the accused could have made it to the priests' sacristy in time for the offending (of five to six minutes) to have taken place.

- **Junking the 5 to 6 Minutes Offending Time**

As the afternoon wore on, Kerri Judd QC began to abandon the prosecution's case that the offending in the priests' sacristy took between five and six minutes and argued that it could have been longer. There were two problems here. First, the majority in the Victorian Court of Appeal had accepted that it was open for the jury to find that the offences took place in a five to six minutes period – and that it was reasonable for the jurors to have done so. Towards the end of their judgment, at paragraph 300, Chief Justice Ferguson and President Maxwell wrote:

> In our view, taking the evidence as a whole, it was open to the jury to find that the assaults took place in the 5-6 minutes of private prayer time and that this was before the "hive of activity" described by the other witnesses began. The jury were not bound to have reasonable doubt.

Second, when queried by the Chief Justice, Kerri Judd QC could not cite one witness who had stated that the offending may have taken place in a period longer than five to six minutes:

> *Kiefel CJ:* Ms Judd, was it put to any witness that it could be more than five to six minutes?
>
> *Ms Judd:* Well, it is put that going over to the
>
> *Kiefel CJ:* The question is not a difficult one, Ms Judd. Was it put to any witness that it could be more than five to six minutes?
>
> *Ms Judd:* It was put more in an open way to explore it rather than to put it
>
> *Kiefel CJ:* I take it the answer to my question is no?
>
> *Ms Judd:* No, but there was never any leave to cross-examine, so it was explored in an open –
>
> *Kiefel CJ:* But the Court of Appeal refers to five to six minutes. What we are concerned with is you seem to be saying that there is another view open.

• Kerri Judd QC Distances Herself from Mark Gibson QC

And then there was the problem with the "disappeared" altar servers. Before the High Court, the Victorian DPP threw her associate Mark

Gibson QC under the bus (to use a non-legal term) by stating that Gibson was wrong in conceding at the re-trial that that there was no evidence that the altar servers had gone to the workers' sacristy. Ms Judd claimed that Mr Gibson had been "very generous" to the accused:

> *Bell J:* On the evidence, once the altar servers bowed to the crucifix, on their account where did they go?
>
> *Ms Judd:* There was evidence that they left that room. There was evidence of McGlone that they went to what they called the "worker sacristy" to unrobe. That was a different sacristy. That was the workers' room or the candle room. Let me take you to McGlone,
>
> *Bell J:* Is this going back to the position that the prosecution disavowed at trial?
>
> *Ms Judd:* He [Gibson QC] incorrectly disavowed that there was no evidence, he was very generous in that....

Kerri Judd went on to explain that the prosecution did not have "a complete explanation" as to where the altar servers were at the time of the alleged offences. This was the problem which Ruth Shann had raised in the re-trial.

Ms Judd's submission concluded by stating that if it were held that the Victorian Court of Appeal should have found that there was reasonable doubt that the offence could have occurred – the latter should be remitted to the Victorian Court of Appeal for a new hearing. The High Court, as pointed out in Chapter 1, was to describe this argument as "specious" – a serious put-down indeed. To use a non-legal term, for Kerri Judd QC this was a bad day at the office.

Bret Walker's Final Pitch

Then it came to Bret Walker SC's final response. His position on the DPP's change of argument was devastating:

> We know that at trial, perceiving understandably a difficulty in proving beyond reasonable doubt the offending as alleged, the

Crown went to the jury initially, as I explained in-chief, namely, that there was a gap or hiatus constituted by a period when the servers went elsewhere after the bow to the crucifix.

There was objection at trial on the basis of there being no evidentiary foundation for that argument and the Crown accepted the propriety of the objection and to the jury withdrew it. That is now, startlingly, to us, described as an incorrect disavowal by a very generous prosecutor of that theory.

What we do not have, of course, is the second shoe dropping; so where is the evidence, the nonexistence of which, as understood by counsel on both sides at trial, led to the withdrawal by the prosecutor of such an argument and your Honours do not have it. In our submission, we should not have to deal with that kind of improvisation at this point. You will not find it in the exchange of written submissions, for example.

"Improvisation" is lawyer talk. To the layperson, "making-it-up-as-you-go" would be a more understandable term. Bret Walker SC also referred to an "improvised and rickety construction of a Crown case to make something fit that will not fit". And he objected to the Crown "cobbling together matters at this stage". He also objected to what he termed the Crown's "grotesque version of the reversal of proof". It was described this way – "that all the Crown has to do is to prove the possibility of something consistent with offending and you have got proof beyond reasonable doubt of offending". Walker QC described the Crown's claims that the Court of Appeal had not reversed the onus of proof as "wrong – simply wrong". It was a withering response to the DPP's case.

Mr Walker concluded his reply by stating: "This is an appeal from an appeal; it is not a first appeal from a trial" – meaning the case should not be sent back to another court for re-consideration. Chief Justice Kiefel then declared: "The Court reserves its decision in this matter."

Within a little over three weeks, the High Court of Australia, by unanimous judgment, quashed George Pell's conviction on 7 April 2020.

B.A. Santamaria and Cardinal Pell

The three famous Victorian Catholics – B.A. ("Bob") Santamaria (1915-1998), Archbishop Daniel Mannix (1864-1963) and (then) Archbishop George Pell. The photo was taken in early 1997 in front of Clifton Pugh's portrait of Dr Mannix at Newman College in Melbourne. (Photo Santamaria Collections: State Library of Victoria)

George Pell's Handwritten Journal

From the day he entered the Melbourne Assessment Prison on 27 February 2019 to the day he exited Barwon Prison on 7 April 2020, George Pell penned around 3 pages a day in what became his three volume Prison Journal (Ignatius Press). Cardinal Pell wrote by hand on a pad while sitting on a chair. His reflections, during his solitary confinement in prison, turn on the suffering, loneliness and humiliations of prison life and include spiritual thoughts and historical reflections, as well as musings on many codes of sport. Cardinal Pell appreciates his access to a kettle, a hot shower and meat pies and reports on watching television documentaries, films, sport (especially football, cricket and horseracing) and religious services of the various Christian faiths. He did this with limited access to books and no access to online search engines. Credit: Photo by Katrina Lee.

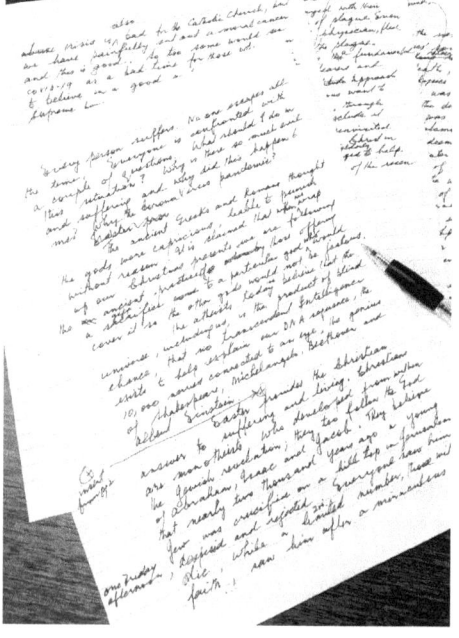

5

FROM BALLARAT TO ROME AND OXFORD, BACK TO BALLARAT AND ON TO MELBOURNE

> "If you regularly appear in the media in the areas of public contestation as a culture warrior – when the whole issue is very serious divisions over mightily important issues – it's not conducive to you being light-hearted. You can easily come across as being cynical. I still think there are considerable advantages in what is sometimes called a stiff-upper-lip and a little bit of stoicism. I don't resile from that in any particular way – I'd plead guilty. Of course, quite a number of people over the years have said to me, once they had to work with me or got to know me, how surprised they were that I didn't have two horns."
>
> - Cardinal George Pell, interviewed by Gerard Henderson, 25 July 2020

A Tale of Two Communions

George Pell was appointed the Catholic Archbishop of Melbourne by Pope John Paul II on 16 July 1996 and officially took over the position at a liturgical reception at the Melbourne Royal Exhibition Building on 16 August 1996 – St Patrick's Cathedral was closed and undergoing a major restoration at the time. It was not long before the new archbishop was involved in a public controversy.

What were called Rainbow Sash protests commenced in London's Westminster Cathedral on Thursday 29 May 1997 – the Feast of Corpus Christi. Nicholas Holloway had advised Cardinal Archbishop Basil Hume OSB that he was an "openly, publicly, actively homosexual person" who believed that God wanted him to have homosexual sex. Holloway requested that the cardinal give him communion.

Cardinal Hume replied that "no one has the right to demand that the Church should publicly endorse their private decisions in conscience, when that decision is not in accord with the teaching of the Church". Holloway advised Hume and the media that he would attend the Corpus Christi mass at the Cathedral wearing a Rainbow Sash. He presented for communion, which was refused by Cardinal Hume who spoke to Holloway before he returned to his seat. A statement by Westminster Cathedral was issued after the Mass which stated: "The normal rule whereby the Church offers Holy Communion to all who seek it does not apply if someone misuses the occasion of the sacrament to seek public endorsement of their private decisions in conscience."

According to the teaching of the Catholic Church, sex outside of heterosexual marriage is a sin. This includes homosexual and heterosexual sex alike. Same sex attraction in itself is not regarded as sinful. The Rainbow Sash Movement was engaged in by primarily Catholic men who were out and proud Catholic gays but who believed they were entitled to receive the sacraments of the Church – including communion – while proclaiming their support for what the Church regarded as an occasion of sin.

If the man who approached Cardinal Hume for communion had done so without a rainbow sash, he would have received the sacrament since no priest has an insight into whether anyone is in a state of sin – they may have gone to confession and been absolved of any sin. The problem the Cardinal Archbishop of Westminster faced was that he was approached by someone in a rainbow sash intent on making a statement against the Church's teaching.

It was only a matter of time before the Rainbow Sash Movement emerged in Australia. Its leader was the gay activist Michael B. Kelly, a former Franciscan seminarian who left the order before becoming a priest.

Cardinal Archbishop John O'Connor (1920-2000) was Pope John Paul II's delegate at the official re-opening of St Patrick's Cathedral which took place at 7.30 pm on Monday 27 October 1997 – on the hundredth anniversary of the blessing of the main altar which had been replaced by a new altar that conformed with the changes ushered in by Vatican II. Pell was an admirer of O'Connor, a fellow theological conservative, and personally asked the Pope to send him to Melbourne for the occasion.

What was termed the Centenary Mass was seen as an occasion for protest by the Rainbow Sash Movement in Australia. Originally protestors intended to interrupt the Solemn Mass but the Cathedral staff was tipped off by an anonymous phone call and security was increased. In the early part of the ceremony, Rainbow Sash members confined their demonstrating to standing, with their backs to Cardinal O'Connor, when he delivered the sermon. When it came to the Sacrament of the Eucharist, protestors joined the queues for communion – wearing a rainbow sash over their left shoulders. They were refused communion by Cardinal O'Connor and Cardinal Pell

The Rainbow Sash protests continued into 1998. On Pentecost Sunday 31 May 1998, George Pell said Solemn Sunday Mass at St Patrick's Cathedral. Kelly and around 70 supporters decided to confront the archbishop by presenting for communion in rainbow sashes. The Rainbow Sash Movement advised Pell in advance of its intentions and notified the media. As Tess Livingstone described the situation in her book *George Pell* (Duffy & Snellgrove, 2002):

> When the time for Holy Communion came, the sash-wearers approached the Archbishop, who refused them the Sacrament unless they took off their sashes. Instead, he proffered a blessing. Michael Kelly told the *Age* newspaper that Pentecost Sunday had been chosen because "that was when the Holy Spirit touched every tribe, nationality and tongue – but apparently not gay and lesbian people".

There were several subsequent such protests in Melbourne and one when Pell became Archbishop of Sydney in 2001. In a sense, Pell's future was defined at this time. He was depicted by gay activists – who had many friends in the Australian media, particularly at the ABC, *The Age* and the *Sydney Morning Herald* – as a bigoted theological conservative Catholic hardliner. In fact, Pell was just following the teachings and practices of the Catholic Church at the time and promoting what he regarded as Catholic orthodoxy. As had Cardinal Hume, the Benedictine monk, who was regarded as liberal – not a conservative – on social and theological issues.

Many Australian Catholics saw George Pell as a prince of the church – even before he was promoted to the rank of cardinal and, as such, eligible to become pope. He was tall, good-looking and presented well in archbishop robes – a colourful vestment with mitre on head and crosier in hand. Also, Pell spoke and wrote well. Agree with him or not, his voice was of authority.

Yet there was another side to Pell the man. The Christian Brother Ben Boonen, not a follower of Pell's conservative theology, happened to come across Archbishop Pell around this time when he was scheduled to speak at the Christian Brothers' Melbourne headquarters. Brother Boonen walked into the office and was surprised to see the archbishop doing his own photocopying – and recalls the event as follows:

> When I saw George that day I was rather surprised and said rather feebly: "Oh, hi George (not that I met him previously), how are things?" "Oh, fine", he said and went on with the copying.

This was around the time of the Rainbow Sash Movement's protests. Boonen recalls discussing the issue with one of his fellow Christian Brothers who helped to run a residential refuge for HIV-AIDS sufferers. The brother told Boonen that Archbishop Pell would visit the refuge most weeks and have a meal and spend some time with the men. It is likely that most of Pell's vehement critics in the mid-1990s would have never gone near an HIV-AIDS sufferer.

This is an example of the personal side to Pell which is rarely seen and of which he rarely speaks. During his time in Sydney, for example, he was willing to make representations to government with a view to obtaining visas for asylum seekers. Many who protested against the Howard government's tough line on unlawful arrivals on Australia's shores would not have known the names of individuals seeking asylum as refugees.

Also Pell is committed to social justice in the tradition of social teachings of Pope Leo XIII and Pope Pius XI who publicly advocated that workers should receive just wages so as to properly support their families. Pell was an opponent of the Howard government's WorkChoices legislation in the early 2000s since he believed that this industrial relations reform would make life more difficult for some employees. In time, the legislation was amended before the 2007 election which the Coalition lost.

George Pell is a follower of Church teachings but he is not of evangelical disposition – there is a lighter side to him. At a media conference soon after he took up duties as Archbishop of Sydney in March 2001, Pell was asked about the archdiocese's position on the Sydney Gay and Lesbian Mardi Gras. He replied: "Well, we're not going to sponsor a float – if that's what you mean."

As to the public persona, Pell saw himself as the Pope's man in Melbourne and later in Sydney and later still in Rome. John Paul II, who appointed him to the See of Melbourne, was the successor of Peter. As Matthew reported the words of Christ which were directed to Peter:

> And I say to thee that: Thou are Peter; and upon this rock I will build my church; and the gates of hell shall not prevail against it. And I will give to thee the keys of the kingdom of heaven. And whatsoever thou shalt bind upon earth, it shall be bound also in heaven; and whatsoever thou shalt loose on earth, it shall be loosed also in heaven. – Matthew Chapter 16: 18-19, *Holy Bible* (Douay Version)

Pell sees his role to back the Pope, as a kind of wing-man. This was especially the case with John Paul II and Benedict XVI – during which time Pell was made a bishop, archbishop and cardinal. Pell and Pope Francis, who promoted Pell to the position of the Vatican's Prefect of the Secretariat for the Economy, are not close when it comes to theology. But as Pell told Andrew Bolt on Sky News in early April 2020: "Francis is the successor of Peter, he's owed respect."

While Pell sees the popes as the successors of Peter, like Archbishop Mannix he admired John Henry Newman (the Anglican who converted to Catholicism and became a cardinal in 1879). Newman argued that the laity should have a greater role in the Church – his view was that the Church would look rather peculiar without the laity.

It is sometimes said that embracing the Christian faith, in particular Catholicism, is an onerous commitment. It's not easy to live by the teachings of Christ as interpreted by the Pope – or even to try to do so. But then, the Catholic Church is a voluntary organisation. Beyond the age of reason, no one is bound or forced to belong to the Church. Catholics exit the Church for all sorts of reasons – including the Vatican's teachings on sex. Moreover, some homosexuals readily adapt to the Church's teachings – and there are gay priests, brothers and nuns. Due to The Fall and the notion of Original Sin, the Catholic Church teaches that all of us are sinners – but that sin can be forgiven following confession and repentance along with a commitment not to sin again. Until the next time when the process can commence again.

In time, George Pell became one of the best known theological conservatives within the Catholic Church at home and abroad. The Rainbow Sash affair foreshadowed Pell's life as an archbishop, a cardinal and a high ranking official within the Holy See.

The fact that Pell is an "equal opportunity" defender of Church teachings and practices has been lost to history. In his March 2016 interview with Andrew Bolt in Rome, Pell was asked about opposition to his appointment as Archbishop of Melbourne by some Catholics. He responded:

> *George Pell*: …For many of the powers that be in the leadership of the church in Melbourne at that stage, that was the one thing they didn't want. First of all, I was theologically conservative. I was an academic. I came from the country, from Ballarat – and a lot of the Melbourne priests found that hard to take…. But all these things

were wrapped together. On top of all that, I was a supporter of Bob Santamaria.

Andrew Bolt: The "notorious conservative" –

George Pell: The "notorious conservative" – with very clear ideas of the way the Church should be going. And I think that the fact that, in many ways, the Church is going better in Australia than it was 20 to 25 years ago has much to do with the writings of Bob Santamaria – who spread the understanding, explained what John Paul II was trying to do. And then my basic thesis…that radical liberalism in faith and morals in Catholicism destroys the church.

Bartholomew Augustine (Bob) Santamaria died on Ash Wednesday 25 February 1998 at age 82. He received a State Funeral which was attended by, among others, Prime Minister John Howard, Deputy Prime Minister Tim Fischer, Labor MP Barry Jones (representing the leader of the Labor opposition Kim Beazley), Treasurer Peter Costello, former prime minister Malcolm Fraser, Victorian Premier Jeff Kennett and former governor-general Sir Zelman Cowen. Archbishop Pell was the principal celebrant at the Mass at St Patrick's Cathedral and delivered the panegyric.

In 1998, the practice of the Catholic Church was not to give Holy Communion (the Body and Blood of Christ – the Eucharist) to non-Catholics. However, around this time the tradition was breaking down and a few Protestants and other non-Catholics were presenting for communion at Catholic churches – especially at weddings, funerals and the like.

It was revealed by the *Herald Sun*, not long after Santamaria's State Funeral, that Pell had advised the non-Catholic Kennett not to attempt to receive Holy Communion at Santamaria's funeral. The Victorian premier complied with the request. But the Protestant Malcolm Fraser joined the queue for Holy Communion, perhaps unaware of Pell's practice.

In an interview in February 2001, Barry Jones vividly recalled communion time at the front of the Cathedral, where the official mourners, Catholic and non-Catholic alike, were gathered: "You had…George

Pell in the middle, Cardinal Edward Clancy [of Sydney] over there and Archbishop Frank Little [the retired archbishop of Melbourne] to the right. And so what happened was that Malcolm Fraser marched on George Pell whereas George Pell gave the sign of the cross and a flick-pass." [An Australian Rules Football term for hand-passing a ball on very quickly.]"[9]

This is an example of Pell, the observer of rules. He denied the Catholic Michael B. Kelly the sacrament because he went to communion wearing a rainbow sash. And he had denied Malcolm Fraser communion a few months earlier because he was not a baptised Catholic. Pell is a man of rules and rituals.

The Boy from Ballarat

George Pell was born in Ballarat, Victoria on Trinity Sunday – 8 June 1941. His father – George Arthur Pell (born 1906) – had been a first-rate swimmer and boxer. His mother (born 1904) was Margaret Lillian Pell (nee Burke). The former was a Protestant – a nominal member of the Church of England, now called the Anglican Church; the latter a Catholic of Irish background. When they met, he was manager at the Gordon gold mine near Ballarat and she worked at the Gribbles clothing factory in Ballarat.

The Pell-Burke union in those days was described in Australia as a "mixed marriage", between a Catholic and a non-Catholic. As such it could not take place at the main altar at St Alipius Church in Victoria Street, Ballarat East – but was held in the priests' sacristy at the side of the altar.

Margaret Lillian (Lil) Pell died in April 1980. Delivering the panegyric at her funeral mass, Fr (as he then was) Pell described his mother as "a woman of great strength and faith: a faith…that was very Irish and probably in particular a faith typical of the west of Ireland in its certainties and its impatience with theological subtleties". He added:

> She knew as well as St Paul and any of the gospel writers that any human achievement meant hard work, struggle and sometimes

sorrow. She and Dad worked enormously hard that their children would have opportunities not open to themselves. Mum was very proud that her children – through the grace of God, and luck and strong management direction from her and Dad – availed themselves to some extent of their opportunities.

George Pell also looked back in fondness and admiration for his aunt Molly Burke, a tuberculosis sufferer, who lived with the family. She gets a few mentions in his *Prison Journal*.

George Arthur Pell died in April 1985. At his requiem, Bishop (as he then was) Pell referred to his father as a strong man physically and personally: "He was sometimes gruff and always honest; he told it as he saw it; a private man in many ways he had high principles and he kept to them". He reflected on the quarter century the family ran the Royal Oak Hotel in Ballarat on the corner of South and Raglan Streets:

> For twenty-five years we had the Royal Oak Hotel here in Ballarat, where he dispensed hospitality, administered justice, kept the peace and incidentally built and maintained a sense of community which was as good as that in many of our parishes. I see some of these old friends here today. All who met him agreed that he was a great character, who regularly expressed himself colourfully and eloquently, sometimes with a pungent humour. I think he was a remarkable man.

While Margaret Lillian and George Arthur were not married at the altar of St Alipius in Ballarat East – both exited the world with a requiem mass said at the altar at the same church. The divisions between many Catholics and Protestants in the early 1940s diminished over the next four decades. Initially George Arthur was dismayed at his son's decision to train for the priesthood. But, over the years, he became openly supportive of many Catholic activities and teachings – especially with respect to his children and grandchildren. Certainly Bishop Pell felt it appropriate to celebrate the Eucharist for his father "and to commend his soul to the care of our loving God".

George Pell's reflections on his parents can be found towards the end of his book *Be Not Afraid: Collected Writing* (Duffy and Snellgrove, 2004). On his father's death, George Pell recalled "that as a child and an adult it never once crossed my mind that my parents did not love me" and he "never doubted for a moment that they would do anything they could to help us".

As a businessman with an English heritage who was nominally Church of England, it's not surprising that George Arthur voted for the non-Labor side of politics. After October 1944, the main non-Labor party was the Liberal Party led by Robert Menzies until his retirement in January 1966.

As a working woman of Irish heritage and a Catholic, Margaret Lillian initially voted for the Australian Labor Party (ALP). However, after the Labor Split in Victoria in 1955, she switched her political allegiance to the Democratic Labor Party (initially called the Australian Labor Party Anti-Communist) – which was formed by those who had been expelled from or left the ALP at the time of the Split. Bob Santamaria – as head of the Catholic Social Studies Movement (The Movement) – was involved in the formation of the DLP and it enjoyed the support of Archbishop Mannix in Melbourne and James O'Collins, the Catholic Bishop of Ballarat between December 1941 and May 1971. The DLP gave its preferences to the Liberal Party or the Country Party – i.e. the Coalition which governed Australia between December 1949 and December 1972 and again between December 1975 and March 1983 – for most of the final years of George's parents.

When a boy, George lived a life in Rowe Street, Ballarat – where Mannix's portrait hung on one of the walls and an image of the Sacred Heart of Jesus on another and the prayer of The Rosary (running for about 12 minutes) was said every evening. After George Arthur left the mining industry, he became a publican – initially at the Cattleyards Inn and then the Royal Oak Hotel where the family lived. George was the third-born child – baby twins, a boy and a girl, had died in 1940. His sister Margaret was born in 1944 and his brother David John in 1950. Margaret studied music at Melbourne University and later in

Rome with Angelo Stefanato and Remy Principe – and played in the first violin section of the Melbourne Symphony Orchestra for some 30 years. David studied at the Ballarat Institute of Advanced Education and became an accountant.

The young George was consistently unwell for a period – undergoing some 24 operations on his throat. Eventually a surgeon discovered the problem – the incorrect filling of a baby tooth had caused a benign growth. Once removed, there were no more problems. But young Pell suffered considerable pain between the ages of seven and nine. As Livingstone has reported, during these years he had to wear a poultice tied around his head which pressed up against his throat. Maybe this contributed to his resilience later in life.

Initially George Pell went to Loreto Convent and then to St Patrick's College. He was a star student at St Patrick's and partook widely in extra-curricula events. George performed in the school's Gilbert and Sullivan productions, was an under officer in the Cadet Corps and engaged in debating. At athletics he was good at sprinting, the long jump and the shot putt. He also played cricket and rowed. But, above all, George was a star at Australian Rules Football – so much so that, in his final year in 1959, he was invited to train in 1960 at the Richmond Football Club – an offer which he rejected in order to study for the priesthood. Writing in Ross Fitzgerald's edited collection *Heartfelt Moments in Australian Rules Football* (Connor Court, 2016), Pell had this to say about his prowess on the football field:

> After signing to play with Richmond in 1959 during my last school year at St Patrick's (St. Pat's) in Ballarat, I was promised a place on their training list and financial help to attend Melbourne University, to supplement a Commonwealth scholarship.
>
> While it was a hard decision for me to begin studying for the priesthood, and I loved my V.F.L., [the Victorian Football League later became the Australian Football League], I never had exaggerated notions of my football abilities. While I would have worked hard to make the grade, and was big, strong and fast, I never had the skills of other St. Pat's champions like Mick McGuane or Matt Rosa.

Professional careers, and not only my football, were the alternatives to studying for the priesthood. In those days (as today, if for different reasons) it was impossible to combine A grade football and seminary life.[10]

George Pell was also a very good student. He won a Commonwealth Government Scholarship in his first year of matriculation in 1958. He then did a second year matriculation – which was not uncommon at the time, an early version of a gap year. First time around, he concentrated on the humanities, next time the sciences. In 1959, his final year, George Pell was school captain. And then it was off to Corpus Christi College in Werribee.

At Corpus Christi College

According to Tess Livingstone, when at secondary school Pell and his St Patrick's friends "went to school dances and enjoyed mixing with girls" from the city's Catholic secondary colleges – Loreto Convent and Sacred Heart College. She added: "Like his class mates, George enjoyed the girls' company but there were no serious romances." This was not uncommon for a young man just completing school at an all-male college in 1959, the last year as a boarder. Also, Pell had to deal with what he told his biographer was a "small cloud" that had been "on the horizon for some time". Namely entering the priesthood.

All ordained Catholic priests take the vows of chastity and obedience. Those who belong to religious orders (i.e. the Benedictines, Josephites etc) also take a vow of poverty. In 1960 George Pell entered Corpus Christi College in Werribee Victoria, around 34 kilometres to the west of Melbourne, to study to become a diocesan priest. That is, he would train to be a priest working primarily in parishes – saying mass, hearing confessions, conducting confirmations, presiding over weddings and funerals and the like.

The possible path to promotion was assistant priest (or curate), parish priest, monsignor, bishop, archbishop, cardinal and (just possibly) pope. Pell was, in time, an assistant priest, parish priest, auxiliary bishop, archbishop and cardinal. This is not a rigid tradition. Some who became bishops and the like are recruited from religious orders – rather than from those who train to be diocesan priests. The current Archbishop of Sydney, Anthony Fisher OP, is a Dominican and Pope Francis is a Jesuit.

In December 1922, Archbishop Daniel Mannix announced that the Catholic Church had acquired Werribee Park from the Churnside family, including the mansion on the estate, to train priests for the archdiocese of Melbourne and the dioceses of Ballarat, Sale and Sandhurst (based in Bendigo). Later the archdiocese of Hobart (covering the whole of Tasmania) came on board. Corpus Christi College Werribee opened in 1923. Students did a first year in what was termed Rhetoric followed by three years of Philosophy and four years of Theology. Then they were ordained priests.

In late 1959 a second seminary was opened in the Melbourne suburb of Glen Waverley to cover the final Theology years. In his chapter in *Heartfelt Moments In Australian Rules Football*, Pell recalled his time at Werribee.

> Corpus Christi seminary was in Werribee and our community of 120 philosophy students (the first half of the eight year course) lived isolated from the world for nine months of the year. We had no access to television, radio and newspapers. Speaking was forbidden from 9 p.m. until after breakfast, which like nearly all other meals was taken in silence, and the textbooks were in Latin. While the buildings had no heating, much less air conditioning, the food was good, the showers were hot. The daily routine of prayer, study, recreation and exercise followed patterns decreed in the sixteenth century by the Council of Trent, a gathering of bishops to counter the Protestant Reformation. In those days most of us were happy most of the time and the atmosphere was generally good, but the daily-life routine was like that of a very strict boarding school. After the Second Vatican Council in Rome (1962-1965) the more repressive elements of this Tridentine model were abandoned.[11]

The seminarians went home for holidays – a break not extended to many studying to be priests or professed brothers and sisters in religious orders. But it must have been boring for many young adult men and women who were interested in politics, the arts, sport, business and the like. In his *Prison Journal* Pell wrote that "an old style pre-Vatican II seminary is not a bad preparation for prison life".

At Werribee, Pell excelled in football, took part in plays and showed an early interest in history and literature. At St Patrick's he had been taught by the Christian Brothers, many of whom had not undertaken advanced study. The academics at Werribee were Jesuits who, as a rule, were more focused on intellectual debate. At Corpus Christi College, he was introduced by Fr Jim McInerney S.J. to the great English Christian authors and poets – Hilaire Belloc, G.K. Chesterton, Graham Greene, Gerard Manley Hopkins, Ronald Knox, C.S. Lewis, John Henry Newman, Evelyn Waugh and more besides.

It was at Werribee that Pell met Denis Hart, formerly a student at Xavier College, Kew, in Melbourne. Hart was taught by the Jesuits and might have been expected to join the Jesuit seminary at Watsonia in Melbourne – but he chose the diocesan route to the priesthood. In 2001, Hart succeeded Pell as Archbishop of Melbourne. For those Victorians at the time whose commitment to God contained an element of clerical ambition, Werribee – not Watsonia or any other seminary of religious orders – was the place to be since it was the traditional route to promotion into the Australian Catholic hierarchy (a term used for all the archbishops, bishops and assistant bishops). Pell and Hart became close friends.

George Pell entered the seminary more than half a century ago. It was a less materialist time than today and Catholic boys and girls at school – from a young age – were encouraged by priests, brothers (i.e. those who entered male religious orders but were not ordained to be priests) and nuns (now commonly called sisters) to give up their life for God. It was called identifying and responding to a vocation to serve God in the way in which He wished.

The evidence suggests that Pell joined up to enter the priesthood because he believed that he should – not because he necessarily wanted to. This was not uncommon at the time, even if it sounds somewhat bizarre today. For all his positive and negative qualities, George Pell like the rest of us, has been afflicted by The Fall. But he is also a person of deep faith – which is spelt out at the end of *Be Not Afraid* in simple but unambiguous terms:

> Four Catholic Foundations
>
> 1. We believe in one God, Father, Son and Holy Spirit, who loves us.
>
> 2. We believe in one Redeemer, Jesus Christ, the only Son of God, born of the Virgin Mary, who died and rose from the dead to save us.
>
> 3. We believe in the Catholic Church, the Body of Christ, where we are led in service and worship by the Pope and Bishops.
>
> 4. We believe that Jesus, Our Lord, calls us to repent and believe; that is, to choose faith not doubt, love not hate, good not evil, and eternal life in heaven not hell.
>
> This is our faith.
>
> We are proud to profess it in
>
> Christ Jesus, Our Lord.

It is often overlooked that Catholicism, like other beliefs, is an act of faith. So, is atheism. Catholics believe there is a God. Atheists believe that god does not exist. Both are acts of faith – one religious, the other secular. Agnostics do not believe because they profess not to know.

John Molony, the one-time Catholic priest who became an academic historian and author, wrote about the young George Pell in his book *By Wendouree, Memories 1951-1963* (Connor Court, 2010). As a young priest, Molony would visit St Patrick's College in the capacity of chaplain and give lectures to the students. In *By Wendouree*, he wrote that "it would be perhaps easier to list the things in which George Pell was incompetent rather than those in which he excelled, but they do not readily spring to mind". Molony assisted young George in his decision to commit his life to God. In his book he recalls that:

> [George Pell] visited my study and is reported as having said that I greeted him with "I was waiting for you to come along". When he told me about his intentions, George asserts that he would have been

"quite relieved" if I had said, "No, you're not suited" because "it wasn't as though I was brimful of enthusiasm to become a priest". It is good that I never encouraged George to become a priest until he told me it was his own wish to do so. Had I encouraged him before he made up his own mind, his vocation could have been partly mine rather than his. He avers that he became convinced that God wanted him "to do His work" and that he "was never able to escape that conviction".

Louise Milligan, who led the media pile-on against Pell, interviewed some of his fellow Werribee students. In *Cardinal*, she wrote that "Pell's classmates say that he... seemed very happy in the seminary" and added that they were "convinced he was not, in the language they used at the time, 'a shirt lifter'" – i.e. an offensive contemporary word for a male homosexual. Like so many of his colleagues, Pell committed to a celibate life because he believed this was God's wish. It's easy for contemporary secularists and others to mock celibate Catholic priests, brothers and sisters. It's just that the same scorn is not directed at, say, the Dalai Lama or the late Australian nun, a liberal Catholic, Veronica Brady who once declared that she had no interest in sex.

The former Catholic priest and gay activist Julian Punch entered Corpus Christi in 1958 from Tasmania. He was there when Pell arrived in 1960 but was suspended in the early 1960s, when he was at the Glen Waverley campus, on account of what were termed "special friendships". In his book *Gay with God* (which was self-published in 2017), Punch wrote that he was involved in "a discreet affectionate physical relationship with one student in particular" and that this led to his suspension. Punch subsequently resumed his training and was ordained a priest in 1970. He worked in the Archdiocese of Hobart, having been invited there by Archbishop Guilford Young, and left the priesthood 11 years later.

Punch did not like Pell in the one year they were both on the Werribee campus – i.e. 1960. Punch described Pell as "deeply conservative even then" but acknowledged that he was a "very good footballer". In *Gay with God,* Punch criticised Pell and Hart for victimising gay priests when they subsequently held the position of archbishop – but provided no evidence in support of this claim. In a soft interview with Jane Hutcheon on the ABC TV program *One Plus One* in September 2017, shortly after his book was published, Punch accused Pell of ganging up against gay students at Werribee and reporting them to authorities. However, no such allegation is made in *Gay with God* and there is also no evidence to support this assertion.

Tess Livingstone's *George Pell* is a sympathetic biography – but it is not hagiography. She reports different views on Pell at Werribee. At Corpus Christi, the Jesuits mainly managed the college and did the teaching. Senior students were appointed prefects and were responsible for running much of college life. In the second half of 1962, Pell was appointed prefect of the first year students – responsible for discipline. Some students objected to what they considered his authoritarian style – but others held a different view.

Livingstone quoted Fr Martin Dixon as saying "George has always been a bully on and off the field; he's a tall, strong man and he loves a fight and will do anything to get his own way". But Livingstone also quoted Paul Bongiorno – who subsequently left the priesthood and became a high profile journalist – as saying that, in his first year, he got on well with his fellow St Patrick's alumnus:

> He was dominant, but very fair and I guess I was pretty compliant. George thought men had to be men and pansies belonged in the garden and no matter whether individuals wanted to play football or basketball at the prescribed times he'd push them out [on to the field or court]. But that was his job.

A decade or so later, Bongiorno became part of the Pell pile-on. But when he spoke to Livingstone around 2000, Bongiorno presented a picture of Pell as a man who was tough but fair. And, importantly, as someone who regarded himself as doing his job in a church which did not lay claim to be a democratic institution.

Corpus Christi College was like the rest of the Catholic Church then and now. No one had to be there. This applied to staff and students alike. Pell wanted to be at Corpus Christi. He remained there until the

Bishop of Ballarat, James O'Collins, decided that he would continue his studies at Rome's Pontifical Urban University – commencing in October 1963. It was an early promotion with many more to come. O'Collins also sent Bongiorno to study at the PUU – he left the priesthood in 1974, not long after returning from Rome.

As was the tradition at the time, Corpus Christi College students bound for study in Rome met with the Archbishop of Melbourne before departing. George Pell and two other seminarians visited Dr Daniel Mannix at his home in *Raheen* on Studley Park Road, Kew, in late 1963. Mannix's habit was to entertain visitors while sitting in his chair, invariably with a rug over his knees. *Raheen* was freezing cold in winter and cold in autumn, spring and even summer. Pell told Livingstone:

> Mannix had a rug over his knees and an Irish theological journal on a table next to him. He wondered who we were – we told him we were going to Rome to study and he courteously wished us well. There was certainly no sign of any confusion.

In September 1963, George Pell sailed for Europe on the *S.S. Stratheden* via the Suez Canal to Naples. Daniel Mannix died on 6 November 1963, after a sudden collapse, at 99 years of age. He was the third Archbishop of Melbourne – in three decades time Pell would become the seventh. George Pell did not return to Australia until 1971 – by which time the scandal of sexual abuse by Catholic priests and brothers had just become news.

Propaganda College during the Second Vatican Council

In late 1963 George Pell commenced his studies at the Pontifical Urban University which was associated with what was then called the Pontificio Collegio de Propaganda Fide or Propaganda College, on Janiculum Hill close to the Vatican. Propaganda College was established in 1627, at the time of Pope Urban, to train missionaries for the Catholic Church. It moved to its current site in Via Urbano VIII, 16 in 1926. Earlier generations of Australian Catholic seminarians were based at a site close to the Spanish Steps in the Piazza di Spagna.

The first Vatican Council was held in Rome in 1869-1870 when it ended prematurely due to the Franco Prussian War. This was a triumph for conservatives in the Church. In the Anglo-Celtic world, it saw the conservative Cardinal Manning (1808-1892), the Archbishop of Westminster, prevail over the liberal reformist John Henry Newman (1801-1890). The Council enhanced the authority of the Pope – then Pius IX – and took a stand against atheism and materialism in a revised constitution on faith titled *Dei Filius*.

In particular, Vatican I proclaimed the doctrine of papal infallibility. This entails that the Pope cannot be in error when speaking ex cathedra and binding the faithful on matters of faith and morals. An ex-cathedra pronouncement occurs when the Pope speaks in his capacity as the leader of all Christians by virtue of his apostolic authority which extends back to the apostle (and first Pope) Peter and through him to Jesus Christ. Or so the Catholic Church believes.

The concept of papal infallibility is widely misunderstood outside the Catholic Church and increasingly within it. It is a rare event indeed when a pope invokes infallibility. The last occasion this occurred was in 1950 when Pope Pius XII proclaimed the Assumption of the Blessed Virgin Mary – the mother of Christ – into heaven in his encyclical *Munificentissimus Deus*. Papal infallibility has nothing to do with national politics or foreign policy or the environment – and many theological teachings of the Church are not classified as the consequence of an infallible papal decree.

George Pell was 22 years of age when he arrived in Rome to continue his studies for the priesthood. The Second Vatican Council was in mid-term. Established by Pope John XXIII, it ran from October 1962 to December 1965 in four sessions. The essential task of Vatican II was *aggiornamento* which, in Italian, means renewal. Bishops, archbishops and cardinals – and their advisers – attended from around the world with a view to modernising the teaching and organisation of the Church.

Pope John XXIII died in June 1963 and was succeeded by Pope Paul

VI. The achievements of Vatican II involved (i) liturgical reform (including the use of the vernacular in Church services), (ii) a focus on ecumenism including improved relations with the Orthodox religions which had split with the Vatican some centuries earlier, (iii) reform of Church structures including the training of priests, (iv) increasing the role of the laity and (v) a declaration of religious freedom. Perhaps the major development of Vatican II was the doctrine of collegiality – namely that bishops share leadership of the Church with and under the Pope.

On 28 October 1965, Paul VI issued the papal statement *Nostra Aetate* (Declaration on the Relation of the Church to Non-Christian Believers). The aim was to improve relations between Catholicism and other religions – Buddhism, Hinduism, Islam and Judaism. However the prime focus of *Nostra Aetate* was to mend the division between Catholics and Jews which was particularly prevalent in parts of Europe – but not in Anglo-Celtic nations like Australia. For example, Mannix had very good relations with Melbourne Jewry. Paul VI declared that the death of Christ "cannot be charged against all the Jews, without distinction, then alive, or against the Jews of today". He condemned "displays of anti-Semitism, directed against Jews at any time and by anyone".

One impact of Vatican II was to relax the rules concerning the training of priests – which impacted on Propaganda College. As Livingstone points out, senior students were allowed to venture further afield than had previously been the case. In 1965, Pell won a scholarship from the French government to undertake a French language course at the Sorbonne and spent the summer in Paris living in a youth hostel. As Livingstone reported Pell's reflections:

> …Unlike many others in the same time and place, summer romances were out of the question. "We told people who we were and that provided some sort of protection. And also, it was still then, even in Paris, with mainly Americans, it still was a different world to what it is today. The sexual revolution hadn't run on to the extent it has now," Pell recalls.

That's correct. What's called in the West the sexual revolution of the 1960s was really a happening of the late 1960s and 1970s.

At Propaganda Fide College students from what were regarded as missionary countries – including Australia but primarily from nations of Africa and Asia – spoke in Italian and mixed socially in small groups. For someone with an interest in Catholic history, young George Pell would have found his years at Propaganda Fide College of considerable interest.

When Pell arrived in Rome, Paul VI was already pope. The Pontiff invited some trainee priests to the papal summer residence outside Rome, at Castel Gandolfo. There Pell met Paul VI (who visited Australia in late 1970) – he gave the young seminarian a statue of John the Baptist baptising Christ. Such a meeting between a pope and a trainee priest would not have occurred during the papacy of the somewhat remote Pius XII (1939-1958). Propaganda Fide had a summer residence at Castel Gandolfo, next to the Papal Gardens, where students spent some of the summer vacation. Pell loved his time there.

During his second year, Pell co-edited the English language annual journal *Cor Ad Cor Loquitur* – it was produced by the local Newman Society. Pell contributed a poem along with a critique of Australia's (then) White Australia Policy which prevailed until 1966. The following year he wrote a critique of the German playwright Rolf Hochhuth's *The Representative*. Hochhuth was a communist operative who set out – with some success – to blacken Pius XII's name by holding him substantially responsible for Adolf Hitler's genocide against the Jews. This is a myth. In fact, Pius XII did more than most in protecting the Jews of Europe.

While Vatican II was under way when Pell arrived, reform had yet to fully impact Propaganda College. Livingstone described college life in 1965, towards the end of Pell's studies:

> The students' days began at 5.30 am (6.00 am Sundays), with prayer, meditation and Mass before breakfast. Classes were held in the mornings, followed by lunch (the main meal of the day). After lunch there were times for a siesta (part of Roman life), recreation

and sport, study, evening prayer, supper at 8.00 pm, more study and Great Silence from 10.30 pm.

It was not unlike the routine at Corpus Christi. Except that on Thursday and Sunday afternoons students were allowed to discover Rome and there was the opportunity to travel in Europe during holidays. During his Propaganda days, Pell played on the college's basketball team. He travelled with his sister Margaret to East Germany and Czechoslovakia in 1966 and witnessed at first hand communist totalitarianism of the Stalinist East European variety.

This reinforced the anti-communism he had acquired at school and home which was a central tenet of the political teachings of Archbishop Mannix and the layman B.A. Santamaria (by then president of the National Civic Council). The NCC was formed in 1957 out of the Catholic Social Studies Movement which was an anti-communist organisation formed by Santamaria in the early 1940s. Archbishop Mannix and Bishop O'Collins were strong supporters of the CSSM/NCC.[12]

While at Propaganda College, Pell exhibited some of the social and political views he was to demonstrate in later life. In Australia, the Catholic Church and the DLP were among the first bodies to call for the end of White Australia. And George Pell understood that the communist regimes of Central and Eastern Europe – along with those in Asia and Latin America – supressed their citizens, including believers.

From his school days, Pell's heroes included Cardinals Josef Beran (Czechoslovakia), Jozsef Mindszenty (Hungary), Alojzije Stepinac (Croatia) and Stefan Wyszynski (Poland). Travellers to Budapest can examine the former prison where Mindszenty (who visited Australia in 1975) was incarcerated by the Nazi Iron Cross regime in 1945 and by the Stalinist regime in 1949. He was tortured and imprisoned by the communist totalitarian dictatorship until freed during the Hungarian Uprising in 1956, which was soon crushed by the Soviet Union. Granted asylum in the United States embassy in Budapest in 1956, Mindszenty remained there until sent into exile in 1971.

Livingstone reports that, when in Rome, Pell was a supporter of the

Vatican II reforms. As such, he was something of a young theological liberal – albeit of the tribal kind. At the time he was no fan of Pius IX who had established Vatican I. Pius IX was the most theologically conservative pope in the 19th or 20th centuries. However, in time, Pell became aware of how Pius IX had revived Catholicism. For example, Pius IX presided over the restoration of Catholicism in England and the Netherlands – some centuries after the Protestant Reformation – and concluded agreements with European and American governments. The empirical achievements of Pius IX appealed to Pell's tribal nature. For the record, Pell does not regard his loyalty to the Holy Roman Catholic Church as "tribal".

Yet Pell was not a rigid conservative. Like Mannix, Pell admired Cardinal John Henry Newman (1801-1890) – the Anglican priest who converted to Catholicism in 1845 and argued for a greater role of the laity in the Church. And he believed that the French Jesuit theologian Pierre Teilhard de Chardin (1881-1955) should have been allowed by the Church to publish freely during his lifetime. Pell had the advantage of reading Chardin's work in French.

George Pell was ordained a priest by the Armenian Cardinal Gregorio Pietro Agagianian in St Peter's Basilica on 16 December 1966 – some three and a half years since he commenced at Propaganda College. He graduated from the Pontifical Urban University with a Bachelor of Sacred Theology (STB) and a Licentiate of Sacred Theology (STL).

From Rome to Oxford

George Pell commenced studies at Campion Hall in Oxford in September 1967. He was to remain there for four years – graduating with a DPhil. His thesis, titled "The Exercise of Authority in Early Christianity from about 170 to about 270", was supervised by Stanley Lawrence Greenslade (1905-1977), the Regius Professor of Ecclesiastical Studies – an Anglican. Pell believes that he is the first Catholic priest to take a doctorate in the theology faculty at Oxford since the Reformation – a claim that has not been contested, even by his opponents.

As Tess Livingstone pointed out in her book, visitors to Oxford often come across the memorial to the members of the Church of England who were burnt at the stake for heresy in the 16th Century. Namely, Bishops Nicholas Ridley, Thomas Cranmer and Hugh Latimer during the time of the Catholic Queen Mary (1553 to 1558) – who attempted to turn back aspects of the Protestant Reformation. Livingstone reminded her readers that there was a Catholic Oxford around the same time which had its own martyrs.

As Gerard Kilroy documents in *Edmund Campion: A Scholarly Life* (Farnham: Ashgate, 2015), of the 116 Catholic priests executed under Elizabeth I, some 51 were Oxford graduates. Edmund Campion himself was hanged at Tyburn Tree on 1 December 1581 along with fellow Jesuit priests Ralph Sherwin and Alexander Briant. The trio had been imprisoned in the Tower of London. Campion's body was butchered after death and his bodily parts and possessions destroyed lest any relics remained around which English Catholics could rally. Campion said his last Mass and gave his last sermon at Oxford on his final day of freedom. One of the few relics that remain of Campion is the rope used for the hurdle on which his body was dragged through the streets – it is held at the Jesuits' Stonyhurst College in north west England.

Edmund Campion, along with 39 other English and Welsh Catholic martyrs, was canonised by Paul VI on 25 October 1970 when Pell was a student at Oxford. It was believed by Cardinal Archbishop John Heenan of Westminster that English Catholicism was losing its identity as a consequence of the ecumenism that had been embraced by many Catholics after Vatican II. The canonisation was designed to send a message to Catholics that their religion remained what is called the "One, True, Holy, Catholic and Apostolic Faith".

In October 1970 Pell addressed the Catholic boys of Eton College – a week before the canonisation of the Forty English and Welsh Martyrs took place in Rome, men and women alike. He had this to say, half a century ago:

> We cannot escape from our past; and there is no more certain sign of a superficiality of character than the tendency to despise all those

who went before us, in the Church, or in the history of our countries. They made mistakes, terrible mistakes, but they built on a scale quite beyond our capabilities. We should be proud of these man – as Englishmen, and as Catholics; but this pride must not degenerate into a tribal rejoicing, which despises others, rather than rests content in its own achievement.

No longer do we think (if we ever did) that Catholics are completely right, and others are completely wrong. We admit sorrowfully that Catholics also persecuted; and we admire the Anglican and other martyrs who died at our hands. But we firmly believe that the Catholic martyrs died for a fullness of faith, which is not found elsewhere and which was and is worth preserving.

Pell mentioned that Edmund Campion was "one who is better known" than the others. He described Campion as an Anglican who attended St John's College in Oxford and who had impressed Elizabeth I, when he spoke at Christ Church. Campion converted to Catholicism and fled England. Having been ordained a Catholic priest, he returned to England where he was arrested.

Martyrdom followed – embracing what Pell described as a seemingly lost cause, but one which survived the Reformation. Pell told the Eton students that Edmund Campion was no naïve ignoramus who was sucked into the Church:

> He was obviously no ignorant peasant, who had been brainwashed or bullied by his parish priest into believing all this superstition. Nor was he a religious fanatic, like some of the saints of pious memory who decided at the age of five and a half to be virgins and martyrs...Campion was intelligent, with a good job and excellent prospects. As we say, the world was at his feet.

George Pell admires Edmund Campion the man and the priest. Campion could have had a very successful career in the secular or non-Catholic religious world. But he believed it was his duty to convert to Catholicism and become a priest at a time when Catholic priests were being incarcerated and executed for (alleged) treason against Elizabeth I. Campion was no religious fanatic – nor was he overly pious. He did not complain about torture he suffered and, according to reports, died smiling. The inner calm was, no doubt, a product of Campion believing that he was doing God's work.

Pell's *Prison Journal* refers to his "Catholic prison heroes" – John Fisher (1469-1535), Thomas More (1478-1535), Maximilian Kolbe (1894-1941) and Francis Xavier Nguyen Van Thuan (1928-2002). Fisher and More were executed in Henry VIII's time for refusing to recognise the king as the supreme head of the Church in England. Fisher and More were canonised in 1935. Pell has been deeply influenced by the English Catholics who stood up for their church and their people during the reign of Henry VIII and Elizabeth I – especially John Fisher who was the only Catholic Bishop to oppose Henry VIII. Of Pell's "prison heroes" only one (Van Thuan) is a contemporary – he was incarcerated by the communist regime in Vietnam after the fall of Saigon in April 1975. Van Thuan served 18 years in prison, nine in solitary confinement. Pell and Van Thuan became friends.

Back to Ballarat

By the time Fr Pell left Oxford for Australia in April 1971, he was a fully mature man who did not change much over the next five decades. Pell supported the doctrinal and liturgical reforms of Vatican II but did not want to go further. During the papacy of Paul VI, between 1963 and 1978, tens of thousands of Catholic priests were laicised and returned to non-religious life. In the old-fashioned term, they lost their vocations. Pell told Livingstone that "as a young priest at Oxford once or twice" he wondered whether he was in "the right line of business". But Fr Pell's faith prevailed and he stuck it out – he remained on the Catholic priesthood team.

Livingstone reported that Pell did not believe that this exit from the priesthood had much to do with the Church's insistence on celibacy for priests, brothers and sisters. Rather, it followed a weakening of faith. Pell kept his belief in his Four Catholic Foundations. However, he concedes that – at times – he was tempted by the attraction of agnosticism. But not atheism which dismisses any belief in a divine presence.

Archbishop Pell addressed the issue of agnosticism when delivering the panegyric at Bob Santamaria's State Funeral on 3 March 1998:

> He [B.A. Santamaria] did believe strongly in the consequences of original sin, that flaw or fault-line that runs through every community and every human heart and that makes all improvement costly and difficult. But he also believed that our good and just God would implement in the next life the promises outlined in the beatitudes by his Son; and balance things up, even things out for the poor, oppressed and suffering.... These deep convictions of his were not retained without struggle. He knew the enticement to agnosticism, to set the great issue of God to one side as too difficult. He spoke of the silken thread which sustained personal faith, but for him it was a thread which never broke and which strengthened him magnificently in his last illness....

On his return to the Ballarat diocese in early April 1971, Pell was a pragmatic theological conservative of strong tribal disposition. Moreover, he was someone who accepted the authority of the Church enunciated by the Pope, the Vicar of Christ on Earth.

Pell did not want core Catholic beliefs to be watered down. As a student at Campion Hall Oxford he had exhibited the intellectual courage to challenge the views of the visiting Dutch Dominican Fr Edward Schillebeeckx (1914-2009), a theological liberal, who taught at the University of Netherlands. Michael Tate (who became a minister in the Bob Hawke and Paul Keating Labor governments in the early 1990s) attended the lecture. He told Livingstone that Pell's tone was "not belligerent but not deferential either". As Livingstone put it in 2002:

> This is a telling episode for what it says about the assurance of a young priest who dared to argue with one of the world's most renowned theologians in front of his college [Campion Hall] Master, senior Fellows and fellow students, at a time when Schillebeeckx was hailed as the voice of the future. Three decades on, Schillebeeckx is still revered by those who believe "relevance to the world" can improve on "divine revelation" – in other words, he is a favourite son of the radical left of the Church...

When Archbishop of Sydney, George Pell was wont to claim that, for all its difficulties, the Catholic Church in Australia had held its ground – unlike Netherlands Catholicism which went close to collapse. In his *Prison Journal,* Pell referred to the rout that afflicted the Church in Netherlands, Belgium and the Canadian province of Quebec.

After returning to Ballarat, Pell came under the authority of Bishop Ronald Mulkearns. During his appearance on the ABC TV *Revelation* program in March 2020, Pell critic David Marr told presenter Sarah Ferguson that Mulkearns was a "mentor" of Pell. This is not the case. The two men, a decade apart in age, were never close. Moreover, Mulkearns was a liberal Catholic – not a conservative like Pell. However, Pell recalls that Mulkearns always treated him professionally and did not attempt to thwart his career.

From 1971 to 1972, Pell was an assistant priest (or curate) at Swan Hill, on the Victorian side of the Murray River – some 280 kilometres north of Ballarat. It was not a great job for so qualified a priest. But Pell told Livingstone that, in hindsight, it was "one of the best things that ever happened" to him. It was as a humble assistant priest that Pell obtained pastoral experience – previously he had done some relief work in parishes in Baltimore (when visiting the United States) and near his Oxford base but had never worked full-time in a parish.

Dr Pell, one of the most educated priests in Australia, spent time doing the basic priestly duties – celebrating Mass, hearing confessions, conducting marriages, baptisms and funerals, anointing the dying and the like. He found time to write his first publication – a booklet titled *The Sisters of St Joseph in Swan Hill 1922 to 1972.* This is the Australian order (commonly known as the Josephites) founded by Mary MacKillop – now St Mary of the Cross, Australia's first saint. Pell has always had interest in, and respect for, the role of women in the Catholic Church.

When Archbishop of Sydney – with the particular help of Archbishops Denis Hart (Melbourne), Barry Hickey (Perth) and Bishop Geoffrey Jarrett (Lismore) – Pell established Domus Australia – a four star hotel (formerly a convent) near the centre of Rome. Opened by Pope

Benedict XVI in October 2011, the portraits on the chapel wall include St Mary of the Cross, St Brigid, Mother Mary John Cahill, Caroline Chisholm in addition to Our Lady of the Southern Cross. The male portraits include such Pell favourites as Cardinal Nguyen Van Thuan, St Patrick, St Thomas More and Cardinal John Henry Newman (who was canonised in 2019) – along with a painting of the first Catholics of Sydney circa 1818 – men, women and children alike. The commissioning of the art work was Pell's decision – since the Archdiocese of Sydney put up most of the money for Domus Australia.

In 1973, Pell was moved and became a junior assistant priest at St Alipius in Ballarat East – where his parents were married and where their requiem masses were said. There were four priests in the parish – including Gerald Ridsdale, who later came to be known as one of Australia's most notorious pedophiles with scores of sexual assaults on young boys. This is discussed in Chapter 9. At this time Pell also had a part-time academic position at the Sacred Heart Teachers College and a part-time chaplaincy at St Martin's in the Pines – the senior school of the Sacred Heart College which was run by the Sisters of Mercy.

When George Pell left Australia in late 1963, James Patrick O'Collins was the Catholic Bishop of Ballarat. In December 1968, Ronald A. Mulkearns, formerly a Melbourne archdiocese canon lawyer was appointed Coadjutor Bishop of Ballarat – meaning that he had a right of succession when O'Collins retired or died. O'Collins retired on 1 May 1971.

Pell did not remain in assistant priest status at St Alipius for long. From 1974 to 1984, he was full-time academic at the Aquinas College campus of the Institute of Catholic Education – a teachers' college. Between 1981 and 1984, while still based in Ballarat, Pell became principal of the Victoria-wide Institute of Catholic Education, in control of the various Catholic tertiary colleges of advanced education within the State. He was also the principal of Aquinas College during the time.

While Pell and Ridsdale shared accommodation for around a year in Ballarat East, they did not work together in the usual sense of the term. Moreover, unlike Ridsdale, Pell had no formal connection with the local St Alipius Primary School, which was run by the Christian Brothers religious order and which, for a time, contained a nest of clerical pedophiles.

In March 1973, Mulkearns had appointed Pell as Vicar for Education – a part-time position primarily focused on chairing the diocesan education board. Between 1974 and 1984, Pell travelled to Melbourne around two days a week. With the help of his friend and deputy, Sister Clare Forbes, Pell helped to save Aquinas College which was under financial pressure. It is now part of the Australian Catholic University.

After unsuccessfully petitioning the Whitlam Labor government (December 1972 to November 1975), Pell succeeded in convincing the Coalition government, led by Malcolm Fraser, to provide financial support for Aquinas College. Senator John Carrick, with whom Pell developed a close relationship, was Education Minister in the Fraser government which came to office in November 1975. In time, the Institute of Catholic Education became part of the State College of Victoria in spite of opposition from within the SCV to the entry of Catholic colleges into its ranks.

While all this was going on, Pell obtained a Master of Education at Monash University with a thesis on the American moral educator Lawrence Kohlberg. He also wrote two pamphlets on Catholic education titled *Bread, Stones or Fairy Floss: Religious Education Today* (ACTS, 1977) and *Are Our Secondary Schools Catholic?* (ACTS, 1979). Both works argued that Catholic school students should be instructed in the Church's traditional teaching – a contested view at the time in the wake of Vatican II. Then, in December 1979, Mulkearns made Pell editor of the monthly diocesan journal *Light*.

In 1980 Pell moved into the Bishop's House, where O'Collins remained living after his retirement, to help look after him since he was suffering from dementia. Fr Pell preached at O'Collins' Vigil Mass, following his death on 25 November 1983, commenting:

> It was the received wisdom that he was no expert theologian, no scholar. This is correct and he was not even an avid reader…. Yet

the same man, after working for some years with only primary education, passed his Leaving Honours [i.e. the final year of schooling] after twelve months study.[13]

Pell always regarded the bishop as highly intelligent and was impressed at how O'Collins had mastered the Italian language in his diaries.

When O'Collins died, Pell moved to Bungaree to work in the parish as a priest administrator – a somewhat lower rank than a parish priest. But his main duties remained elsewhere in various educational roles within and outside the Ballarat diocese.

And on to Melbourne

In 1984 Pell was appointed seminary rector of Corpus Christi College – by now located in Clayton near Monash University – and took up the position in January the following year. Corpus Christi College in Clayton was not a teaching agency – this was done at the nearby Catholic Theological College. It seems that Auxiliary Bishop John A Kelly along with the likes of Dr Eric D'Arcy, the Bishop of Sale, believed that the seminary had lost its way.

The decision to appoint Pell was made by the College Trustees who comprised the Province of Melbourne – namely Archbishop Little (Melbourne), Bishop Mulkearns (Ballarat), Bishop Noel Daly (Sandhurst) and Bishop Eric D'Arcy (Sale). Mulkearns conducted the negotiations with Pell and advised him of his appointment. D'Arcy, who later became Archbishop of Hobart, played a critical role in this appointment and in Pell's subsequent rise in the Catholic Church.

As Tess Livingstone reported, soon after his arrival, Pell posted a note titled "A Few Small Changes" on the college noticeboard. The changes included the introduction of the recitation of the Catholic prayer The Rosary, compulsory daily Mass along with a formal Sunday lunch with *Grace* to be said before and after all meals. Once again, Pell's focus was on the retention and propagation of the Catholic orthodoxy as he saw it. As Pell told Livingstone: "My focus in the seminary was on strengthening the spiritual life of the seminarians with a compulsory framework of daily Mass, meditation, the official prayer of the Church and public devotions."

By the time Pell arrived in Melbourne in 1985, he was well connected with political circles in Victoria and Canberra along with leading business figures – due to his involvement with promoting Catholic tertiary education. But, in this new position, he focused on reforming the Catholic seminary.

While embracing the reforms of Vatican II, Pell was of the view that some had used it to dismantle many of the teachings and practices of the Church. He was determined to hold the line – commencing with trainee priests. This led to open hostility towards the new rector by a majority of Corpus Christi staff and quite a few students, who had got used to a softer form of Catholicism. Pell wanted to restore what in the language of the day he called a "muscular Christianity" – which included placing an image of Our Lady, Christ's mother, in the seminary chapel. In his *Prison Journal* Pell described himself as a "Crucifixion Catholic".

As with most periods of Pell's life, his time at Corpus Christi College was controversial. Some students quit – although this was the case in other seminaries the world over at this time, including St Patrick's Seminary in the Sydney suburb of Manly. Others appreciated the fact that their life now focused on prayer, religious observance and study. Along with the fact that they were following the teachings of the Church as enunciated by the Pope. It would seem that this was noted by George Pell's supporters in Rome.

In March 1987, Pell was advised by the Apostolic Nuncio, the Vatican's ambassador in Canberra, that he was to be appointed by Pope John Paul II to the position of auxiliary bishop in the Melbourne archdiocese – led by Archbishop Frank Little. There were three other auxiliary bishops at the time. Pell told Livingstone that he was "partly surprised" by the promotion since his views at the time "were certainly not the flavour of the month" among the Australian Catholic hierarchy and within Australian theological circles. He added that he looked back in relative happiness on his time as rector:

> I had mixed feelings [about leaving Corpus Christi College]. Certainly I hadn't had long enough to do what I wanted to do at the seminary. But the other thing was that I was pleased to be out of the seminary because it was a difficult assignment. The majority of the staff and goodly percentage of the students felt that I was heading in the wrong direction.

George Pell was consecrated a bishop at St Patrick's Cathedral on 21 May 1987 – at 45 years of age, quite young for such an appointment. He was given responsibility for visiting parishes and conducting confirmations in Melbourne's south eastern suburbs and was parish priest of St Patrick's Church in Mentone on Port Phillip Bay.

In the Catholic Church, archbishops and bishops run their archdioceses and dioceses and report directly to the Pope in the Vatican. Based in Mentone, Pell was an auxiliary bishop. Archbishop Frank Little ran the Archdiocese of Melbourne. Pell had no power and little influence – the latter due to the fact that he was a theological conservative while Little was a theological liberal. Also the men never got on. In time Pell succeeded Little – after nine years as an auxiliary bishop.

* * * * *

During all his time in Ballarat, Rome, Baltimore, Oxford and suburban Melbourne there was never any suggestion that George Pell was involved in crimes against children (including grooming) – in private or in public places.

* * * *

Tim Minchin singing Come Home (Cardinal Pell)

Tim Minchin's song "Come Home (Cardinal Pell)" was released on YouTube and immediately run on Network 10's The Project and on the ABC. It contained the words "with all respect dude, I think you're scum". This is how ABC TV's The Drum invited viewers to comment on the case. Such anti-Pell publicity made a fair trial almost impossible.

Photo of Honi Soit

How Cardinal Pell was depicted on the cover of The University of Sydney student newspaper *Honi Soit* in March 2019.

6

THE MEDIA PILE-ON COMMENCES

"I'm a feminist. I'm a Democrat. I'm also the victim of both assault and rape. So I know what it feels like. And I know what it feels like to have somebody accuse you of lying. It's disgusting. Women, whether Democrats and Republicans, need to be women first…. Because I can speak from this experience myself, I always start off believing the women. But then I do my own investigation. And I do look at the facts that are there because, sadly Howie [Howard Kurtz], although the overwhelming majority of individuals out there are telling the truth when they come forward – there are times – a couple percentage of the time, two percent of the time – where somebody may not be telling the truth. And especially we see that in politics and I don't think investigations, left or right, are unwarranted."

- The American journalist and broadcaster Leslie Marshall, talking to presenter Howard Kurtz on Fox News' *Media Buzz,* 19 April 2020.

To fail to tell the truth is not necessarily to lie. Some individuals have clear recollections of events that never happened. Others are delusional – which may result from drug or alcohol abuse. Others still have false memories that lead to mistaken identity situations. And a few lie. As a professional journalist, Leslie Marshall stresses the importance, especially when high profile people are accused, of thoroughly investigating the allegations of complainants. Many areas of the Australian media failed to do so in the Pell Case.

Pell's Media Antagonists – A Roll Call led by Tim Minchin

When Cardinal George Pell was charged with historical child sexual abuse cases on 29 June 2017, no one in Australian criminal law history, before a trial was held, had been subjected to such unrelenting criticism in the media extending back some two decades. Especially concerning alleged crimes for which there were no independent witnesses or forensic evidence. The only evidence against the accused was the untested testimony of complainants. In the only matter that went to trial, there was but one complainant.

In mid-2017, Pell was one of the most hated Australians – despite the fact that he had a band of loyal supporters. He was accused of the heinous crime of pedophilia. But there was more. As one of the most senior Catholics in the world, and a theologically conservative one, Pell bore the added burden of alleged gross hypocrisy. He proclaimed the Church's teaching that sex should only occur in heterosexual marriage – and he was accused of sexually abusing two 13 year old boys in a vile manner inside the cathedral over which he presided.

And there was the timing. Victoria Police laid its charges against Pell when there had been a revival of anti-Catholic sectarianism – which had been extant in Australia, to a greater or lesser extent, since European settlement in 1788. This on top of a growing secularism in the wider society and deep divisions within the Catholic Church. Some of Pell's most vocal opponents were theologically liberal Catholics along with disillusioned Catholics and bitter ex-Catholics.

At the time Cardinal George Pell was charged and when he went to trial, few Australians would not have heard of him and the claims that had been made against him in the media – including at the Royal Commission into Institutional Responses to Child Sexual Abuse which ran from March 2013 to December 2017.

Many journalists and commentators who involved themselves in the Pell Case did so as activists. This is evident in the work of singer/song writer Tim Minchin whose *Come Home (Cardinal Pell)* was released online on 16 February 2016 and was taken up by Network 10's *The*

Project and shown on ABC TV programs among other places. On 17 February 2016, under the title *The People v George Pell*, ABC TV's *The Drum* asked viewers whether they approved of Minchin's song after placing it on the ABC's website. *Come Home (Cardinal Pell)* included the following words:

> I mean with all respect dude, I think you're scum
> And I reckon you should
> Come home, Cardinal Pell
> (Cardinal Pell)
> I know you're not feeling well…

Then there was the ditty of retired journalist – the late Mungo MacCallum whose anti-Pell rant titled "Pell and Damnation" was published in Morry Schwartz's *The Monthly* blog on 22 February 2016:

> I do not love thee, Cardinal Pell
> For child molesters burn in hell…

The immediate motivation for these rants turned on Pell's decision – on medical advice – not to return to give evidence at the Royal Commission's hearings in Ballarat. He had already appeared before the Royal Commission in person in Sydney in March 2014 and by video link from Rome in August 2014. Also he was to give evidence in Rome over four continuous nights between 29 February and 3 March 2016. In addition, in May 2013 Pell had appeared for some hours at a Victorian Parliamentary Inquiry. No one spent more time giving evidence before the Royal Commission than Pell – all of which was provided voluntarily since, as someone who was resident overseas, there was no requirement that he give evidence.

The Pell pile-on had already reached a level of considerable intensity when senior ABC journalist Louise Milligan launched a full-on assault on Pell on ABC TV's *7.30* which occupied the entire 30 minutes of the program on 17 July 2016. *7.30* is Australia's leading Monday to Thursday nightly current affairs television program. This was followed by Milligan's book *Cardinal: The Rise and Fall of George Pell* in June 2017 which received wide and sympathetic coverage –

especially on ABC TV and ABC Radio. The author was only ever subjected to soft media interviews by her work colleagues on the ABC – along with supportive panels and audiences at literary functions where few if any challenged her claims or disagreed with her analysis.

The ABC continued to engage Milligan as a reporter on the Pell Case even after she admitted that she was an activist in this instance – since she was advocating the cause of individuals who had made accusations against Pell. Interviewed by her friendly colleague Virginia Trioli on 16 May 2017 on ABC TV's *News Breakfast*, Louise Milligan had this to say:

> When I did the first story for *7.30* about the allegations, he [Cardinal Pell] came back the next day. And, you know, denied them all emphatically – you know, accused me of perverting the course of justice by collaborating with Victoria Police, which I have never done. And I stress that all of this [the case advanced in *Cardinal*] has come from the complainants' point of view.

And that's the point. In her TV reporting and her book *Cardinal*, Louise Milligan did not pretend to be an objective reporter. Rather she was an activist journalist presenting the case against Cardinal Pell "from the complainants' point of view". A media case for the prosecution.

Here's a list of journalists and commentators who took part in the Pell pile-on over around two decades. Some were more active than others – but all made clear their opposition to, and/or distrust of, Pell. For readers unfamiliar with the Australian media, all of those cited below are or were influential figures in the Australian media as academics, authors, cartoonists, clerics, columnists, comedians, commentators, journalists, lawyers, former police officers, politicians, presenters and publishers:

> Richard Ackland, Phillip Adams, Louise Adler, Emma Alberici, Waleed Aly, Wendy Bacon, Tom Ballard, John Barron, Steve Biddulph, Carrie Bickmore, Paul Bongiorno, Michael Bradley, Tara Brown, Scott Burchill, Kelly Burke, Julian Burnside, the late

Richard Carleton, Mike Carlton, Jane Caro, Barrie Cassidy, Philip Clark, Gorgi Coghlan, Richard Cooke, Rachel Corbet, Judy Courtin, Annabel Crabb, Stephen Crittenden, Melissa Davey, Quentin Dempster, Rafael Epstein, Jon Faine, Ellen Fanning, Elizabeth Farrelly, Sarah Ferguson, Peter FitzSimons, Peter Fox, Chris Geraghty, Richard Glover, Jonathan Green, Ray Hadley, Wendy Harmer, Peter Helliar, Derryn Hinch, Gael Jennings, Erik Jensen, Tony Jones (ABC), Tony Jones (3AW), Fran Kelly, Michael H. Kelly, Kristina Keneally, Paul Kennedy, Dom Knight, Meshel Laurie, John Lyons, Hamish Macdonald, Dee Madigan, Anne Manne, Russell Marks, David Marr, Ray Martin, Stephen Mayne, the late Mungo MacCallum, Joanne McCarthy, Kate McClymont, Phillipa McGuinness, Martin McKenzie-Murray. Alex McKinnon, Shaun Micallef, Karen Middleton, Lisa Millar, Louise Milligan, Tim Minchin, Lucie Morris-Marr, Julian Morrow, Linda Mottram, Chris Murphy, Paul Murray (up until Pell was charged), Tim Palmer, Janine Perrett, Kerryn Phelps, Charlie Pickering, Julian Punch, Craig Reucassel, Graham Richardson, Michael Rowland, Leigh Sales, Margot Saville, Russell Skelton, Chris Smith, Justin Smith, Tim Soutphommasane, Wendy Squires, Julie Szego, Josh Szeps, Magda Szubanski, the late Ron Tandberg, Chris Taylor, Virginia Trioli, Wendy Tuohy, Vivian Waller, Roz Ward, Ian Warden, Jack Waterford, John Westacott, Judith Whelan, Cathy Wilcox, Sue Williams, Tony Windsor and Barney Zwartz – among others.

No media organisation had more anti-Pell activist journalists and presenters than the ABC – Australia's taxpayer funded public broadcaster. The campaign against Pell was unrelenting across its main television (*7.30, Four Corners, Lateline, News Breakfast*) and radio (*AM, The World Today, PM,* Radio National *Breakfast*) outlets. The ABC also commissioned special programs which contained attacks on Pell – Geoff Thompson and Mary Ann Jolly's "Unholy Silence" *Four Corners* (2 July 2012), *7.30* (17 July 2016), Louise Milligan's "Guilty: The Conviction of Cardinal Pell" on *Four Corners* (4 March 2019) plus the third episode of Sarah Ferguson's *Revelation* documentary titled "Goliath" (2020).

Then there were the commercial TV networks – most notably Nine Network's *60 Minutes* and Network 10's *The Project*. And then there were the newspapers – most notably Nine Newspapers (formerly Fairfax Media) *The Age* and the *Sydney Morning Herald* plus *The Canberra Times* (once part of Fairfax Media), Schwartz Media's *The Saturday Paper* and *The Monthly* plus *The Guardian Australia* and *The New Daily*.

When Pell was in Melbourne, the media criticism of him was solid and consistent. But it exploded after his arrival in Sydney, during his time in Rome and on his return to Australia to face the charges against him.

Five Years as Melbourne's Eighth Archbishop

On 16 July 1996, it was announced that George Pell had been appointed by Pope John Paul II as Archbishop of Melbourne – succeeding Archbishop Frank Little who retired for health reasons at 70 years of age. This was five years earlier than the age at which archbishops and bishops are required to offer their resignation to the Pope – which may or may not be accepted. At normal times, the retirement of an archbishop or bishop is not followed by an immediate appointment of a successor. It was in this case.

It seems that the Pope and his advisers had grown tired of Archbishop Little's ineffectiveness and wanted to promote Bishop Pell. By mid-year 1996, child sexual abuse by male Catholic clergy was becoming a scandal in Australia. On 27 May 1996, ABC TV's *Four Corners* had broadcast a program titled "Twice Betrayed" by Sally Neighbour who documented clerical child sexual abuse in the Ballarat diocese and Melbourne archdiocese of the Catholic Church.

Tess Livingstone wrote in *George Pell* that "the program left viewers shocked, particularly by the evasive and indifferent responses of Ballarat Bishop Ronald Mulkearns and Monsignor Gerald Cudmore, the vicar-general of the archdiocese of Melbourne, to such serious allegations". At least Mulkearns fronted up – unlike Little who passed the task to Cudmore. While it is true that vicars-general invariably handle child protection issues in their respective archdioceses or dioceses, there was nothing to stop Archbishop Little taking control of the issue and addressing the media. As, later, Archbishop Pell did.

During "Twice Betrayed" the following exchanges took place:

> *Sally Neighbour:* Over a period of more than 20 years, Father Gerald Ridsdale sexually assaulted as many as 200 children – and his superiors did nothing to stop him.
>
> *Ronald Mulkearns:* I know that's the complaint. I have stated a couple of times to the people of the diocese that it's simply not true to say that I knew these things were happening and did nothing about them. The first time I received a complaint about Father Ridsdale, I immediately took him out of the parish he was in, put him under counselling and indicated that he would not be given another appointment until the counsellor said that that was an appropriate or responsible thing to do.

It is true that in the 1960s and 1970s sections of the medical and psychology professions took a different view on pedophilia from that which prevails today – and that attitudes changed in the 1980s and 1990s as the damage endured by victims became more evident. However, it was not true for Mulkearns to imply that he was unaware of Ridsdale's repeat offending in the 1980s and into the early 1990s. In fact, Mulkearns had referred Ridsdale for counselling in 1975 – a decision which, the evidence indicates, was supported at the time by Victoria Police.

Later in "Twice Betrayed", Gerald Cudmore found it impossible to defend the stance taken by Archbishop Frank Little towards a victim of the notorious pedophile priest Michael Glennon (1944-2014) who served a lengthy imprisonment before dying in jail.

> *Sally Neighbour:* The Archbishop [Frank Little], who is being sued for negligence, denies that Father Glennon was under his control or

supervision, or even in his jurisdiction. How can the church make that argument?

Gerald Cudmore: I'm not sure I understand what he said and why he said that – when he said it. Yes, I can't explain that.

Sally Neighbour: Doesn't make sense to you? And it's not a tenable argument, as you said?

Gerald Cudmore: I don't think so. And I think it's been misunderstood because clearly, a priest of the Archdiocese of Melbourne is under the jurisdiction of the Archbishop of Melbourne.

The *Four Corners* program went to air on 27 May 1996. Archbishop Little was replaced by George Pell on 16 July 1996. During "Twice Betrayed", Sally Neighbour made no reference whatsoever to Pell's time in Ballarat as a priest and consultor to Mulkearns or in Melbourne as auxiliary bishop to Little. Allegations about these matters occurred only after he became Archbishop of Sydney in March 2001.

During his five years as Archbishop of Melbourne, Pell did what his supporters and opponents alike would have expected. He attempted to ensure that Catholic orthodoxy was taught in churches, seminaries, Catholic tertiary institutions and schools alike. And he restored traditional practices – such as regular Sunday Solemn Mass at St Patrick's which he attended in his capacity as archbishop when in Melbourne.

Also, as a tribal Catholic, Pell oversaw the creation, outside the Cathedral, of statues to Archbishop Mannix, St Catherine of Siena and the Croatian Cardinal Aloysius Stepinac (who criticised the Nazi regime and was incarcerated by Tito's post-war communist dictatorship in Yugoslavia) along with a water feature containing four lines from James McAuley's poem *A Letter to John Dryden*. Pell came to admire the Sydney-born McAuley (1917-1976), a convert to Catholicism and one of Australia's finest poets who became a Professor of English at the University of Tasmania. He features on occasions in Pell's *Prison Journal.* McAuley was the inaugural editor of *Quadrant* magazine and became a close friend of Santamaria.

Perhaps Pell's most important initiative in Melbourne was the establishment of the Melbourne Response – which was described in Chapter 1. Yet it did nothing to absolve him of the subsequent charge – led by his critics and sections of the media – of failing to address the issue of clerical child sexual abuse.

Pell has been criticised by some for setting up the Melbourne Response in 1996 – before the national scheme titled Towards Healing was established in 1997 covering all the archdioceses (except Melbourne) and all the dioceses. Towards Healing was very much the work of Bishop Geoffrey Robinson (1937-2020) in Sydney who was a theologically liberal Catholic. Pell acted when he did to deal with an immediate crisis in the belief that the rest of the Catholic Church in Australia was moving too slowly.

The Archbishop of Sydney Meets the Sydney Media – including *Sunday's* John Lyons and *60 Minutes'* Richard Carleton

On 26 March 2001 it was announced that John Paul II had appointed George Pell to the position of Archbishop of Sydney following the resignation of Cardinal Edward Clancy who was aged 77. Pell took up the position on 10 May 2001.

The newly appointed Archbishop of Sydney soon got a taste of how the Sydney media would handle his appointment. On the Network Nine *Sunday* program on 12 May 2001, journalist John Lyons put to Pell a number of descriptions he said had been made about him and asked for a response. Namely, that Pell was (i) a bully, (ii) a right-wing fundamentalist, (ii) a homophobe, (iv) a careerist, (v) the Pope's man in Australia and (vi) a misogynist. Lyons' message was clear – his aim was to put Pell on the defensive and to imply that he was not a suitable figure to lead the Catholic Church in Sydney.

Pell pleaded innocent to all charges – except to the claim that he was John Paul II's man in Australia. But the *Sunday* interview gave an idea of what Pell might expect in Sydney, where most of the Australian media is based. However, it is worth noting that Lyons did not put it to

Pell that he was in the business of protecting pedophile priests – that came later.

The attacks continued. On Thursday 30 May 2002, Pell called a press conference ahead of allegations that were to be aired on Network Nine's *60 Minutes* program the following Sunday. The "scoop" was that, when an assistant bishop in Melbourne, Pell had attempted to cover up the abuse of David Ridsdale (when a boy) by his uncle – the Catholic priest Gerald Ridsdale. The unprofessional nature of Pell's ambush in this instance was analysed by the late Frank Devine in the September 2002 issue of *Quadrant*.

The pre-recorded interview was a set-up. Pell and his advisers maintain that Pell had been informed that he would only be involved in a pre-recorded interview with presenter Richard Carleton. The agreement was breached. David Ridsdale also appeared earlier on the pre-recorded program and Pell was asked to respond to his allegation when interviewed by Carleton. Part of the Carleton/Ridsdale interview, with which Pell was confronted, turned on David Ridsdale's claim that Pell had said to him in 1993, "I want to know what it will take to keep you quiet" – with a view to preventing David from reporting his uncle's abuse to Victoria Police:

> *Richard Carleton:* Are there any doubts in your mind that those were the specific words that he [Pell] used?
>
> *David Ridsdale:* "I want to know what it will take to keep you quiet"? None at all. Not those last two phrases, no… That one phone conversation is the reason that I went to the police and so on and everything that happened afterwards.

This allegation, effectively one of bribery so that David would not go to Victoria Police about the sexual assault by his uncle Gerald, did serious damage to Pell – despite the fact that he denied the claim. The allegation continued for years until, in its final report released in 2020, the Royal Commission – which for the most part had been hostile to Pell – came to the view that no such conversation took place. In fact, when David Ridsdale spoke to Pell in 1993, Victoria Police was already in the process of charging Gerald Ridsdale.

The David Ridsdale claim was not the only issue to which Pell was subjected to in the ambush by Richard Carleton and the *60 Minutes* production team. Carleton also interviewed Anthony and Chrissie Foster – two of whose three daughters had been sexually assaulted by the Catholic priest John Kevin O'Donnell in Melbourne. One of the Fosters' children committed suicide and another was traumatically injured when hit by a car while under the influence. The Foster family, after some time, received a substantial compensation payout from the Catholic Church. During the part of the interview that went to air, the identity of the Fosters was disguised.

When Archbishop of Melbourne, in February 1997, Pell met the Fosters. They believed that he was not empathetic when they discussed O'Donnell's attacks on their daughters. In August 1995, before Pell became archbishop, O'Donnell had pleaded guilty to the sexual assault of ten boys and two girls between 1946 and 1977. There were many other assaults – the evidence indicates that O'Donnell was an offender during most of his adult life. The first allegations against O'Donnell occurred in late 1993 and Victoria Police commenced investigations early the following year.

Also *60 Minutes* made much of the fact that in May 1993 Pell had walked with Gerald Ridsdale to the Melbourne Magistrates' Court where Ridsdale pleaded guilty to child sexual assault. This was the first occasion on which Ridsdale had been charged. There were subsequent charges and convictions – and the notorious pedophile has been in the Victorian prison system continually since 1994. Carleton told *60 Minutes* viewers: "They'd [Pell and Ridsdale] been at school together; they'd attended the seminary together and, as young priests they'd shared a house." The first two claims were wilfully false – the final one a gross exaggeration.

Pell has conceded on many occasions that accompanying Gerald Ridsdale to court was "a mistake" – even though he had declined to provide a character reference for Ridsdale that was compatible with the wishes of his defence counsel. Pell was asked by the Melbourne Curia, headed by Archbishop Little, to walk with Ridsdale to court.[14] Such actions at the time were commonly undertaken by Catholic priests, Salvation Army officers and so on. But Pell could have said "no". Even though, at the time, the extent of Ridsdale's offending over many decades was not known to Pell or most others. In spite of some claims to the contrary, Pell did not attend court during the sentencing after Ridsdale had pleaded guilty.

On Monday 3 June 2002 – in response to what he said had been his "ambush on *60 Minutes*" – in a written statement Pell corrected the program's errors concerning the Melbourne Response, denied emphatically that he had used the words attributed to him by David Ridsdale and said that when he met the Fosters "the perpetrator O'Donnell was already in gaol". Concerning Gerald Ridsdale, Pell has this to say:

> Gerald Ridsdale was born in 1934. I was born in 1941. We were never in any seminary together. I was training at Werribee 1960-63 and Rome 1963-67. He was training at Werribee 1954-58; Genoa 1958; Ireland 1960-61. I always strive to work amicably with my brother priests. This included Gerald Ridsdale. We were never close friends and overlapped at St Alipius for about a year.
>
> I accompanied him in mid-year 1993 to the Magistrates' Court. My sympathy was always with the victims and when I explained to his lawyer that I would insist on saying that Ridsdale had done great damage to his victims, the church and himself, he declined to call me as a witness and asked me to accompany Ridsdale to court. I had little idea of the full extent and gravity of his crimes. I did so in priestly solidarity. This was a mistake as it misled people about my basic sympathies for the victims, borne out by all my subsequent work to root out this evil.

The David Ridsdale allegation, the criticisms of Chrissie Foster and Anthony Foster (who died in May 2017) and Pell's walk with Gerald Ridsdale would appear constantly in the media over the next two decades.

Phillip Island Allegation Follows *60 Minutes'* Program

As a consequence of the *60 Minutes* interview and its aftermath, Pell had become a public figure at a national level. It was not long before he was accused of historical sexual assault. On 20 August 2002, Archbishop Pell called a media conference outside St Mary's Cathedral Presbytery in Sydney and made the following statement:

> Certain allegations have been made about my conduct when I was a seminarian over 40 years ago. These allegations against me are lies, and I deny them utterly and totally. The alleged events never happened. I repeat, emphatically, that the allegations are false. An independent inquiry to investigate these allegations has been set up by Archbishop Philip Wilson, Acting Co-Chairman of the National Committee for Professional Standards [NCPS], which supervises the Church's "Towards Healing" protocols. The inquiry will be conducted, I understand, by a retired Victorian Supreme Court judge.
>
> I will, of course, co-operate with this independent inquiry in every way possible, openly, frankly, unreservedly. For the good of the Church and to preserve the dignity of the office of Archbishop, I will take leave from today as Archbishop of Sydney until the inquiry is completed. I repeat that the allegations are lies, and that I am determined to refute them. I welcome the inquiry, and the chance to clear my name, recognising that I am not above civil law and Church law.
>
> I've taken a leading role in condemning and exposing sexual abuse within the Catholic Church in Australia. Six years ago in Melbourne, I set up Australia's first independent commission to inquire into sexual abuse by members of the Catholic clergy. To allege that I am now personally implicated in this evil is a smear of the most vindictive kind. I truly wish that I could say more right now. However, it is important that I do not say anything that could be seen to prejudice the inquiry. Therefore, I am unable to make further comment.

George Pell's denial in Sydney in 2002 was as emphatic as it was (on unrelated matters) in Rome in 2016. The allegation was that, at a camp for underprivileged children at Phillip Island in 1961 or 1962, Pell had groped a 11 or 12 year old boy and one other (who was deceased). At the time, Pell was a seminarian at Corpus Christi aged 19 or 20 years of age.

The complainant, "C", approached the Catholic Church's National Committee for Professional Standards in June 2002 – around a week after David Ridsdale and the Fosters appeared on *60 Minutes*. Earlier C had approached the Broken Rites organisation where he was advised that such a claim could earn a compensation payment of around $50,000. C had a criminal record and had served time in prison.

C maintained that he had first identified George Pell in May 2000 as the person who had assaulted him four decades previously, having seen him on the television news. But did nothing about it at the time – he took action in the wake of the *60 Minutes* program.

C was interviewed by the NCPS' Sister Angela Ryan in Melbourne who reported to Bishop Geoffrey Robinson in Sydney. Both urged C to go to Victoria Police, but he refused. Around this time, material highly damaging to Pell was posted on a website by an anonymous person or organisation claiming to be "Xavier O'Byrne, Parramatta". The cause was soon taken up by the Eros Foundation in Canberra, which was hostile to the Catholic Church – one of its operatives was a former member of the Rainbow Sash Movement.

Southwell QC Inquiry and Finding Re Alleged Phillip Island Incident

The Honourable Alec James Southwell QC, a retired judge of the Supreme Court of Victoria, was appointed by the NCPS to undertake an investigation similar to that of a royal commission or a statutory board of inquiry. He was not a Catholic and had been educated at Melbourne Grammar – a Church of England school. The hearings commenced on the last day of September and continued during the first four days of October 2002. Southwell QC's *Report of an Inquiry into an Allegation of Sexual Abuse Against Archbishop George Pell* was issued on 14 October 2002.

Among other matters, the complainant said that Pell told him he played football in the ruck for the Richmond Reserves. Pell denied this – and Southwell QC accepted that Pell had not said he played for Richmond at any level. Knowledge about Richmond's interest in Pell only became known in Melbourne after he moved there from Ballarat in 1985. There were many other errors and inconsistencies in C's testimony. Southwell QC's conclusion was as follows:

> I accept as correct the submission of Mr Tovey [for C] that the complainant, when giving evidence of molesting, gave the impression that he was speaking honestly from an actual recollection. However, the respondent [George Pell] also gave me the impression that he was speaking the truth.
>
> In the end, and notwithstanding that impression of the complainant, bearing in mind the forensic difficulties of the defence occasioned by the very long delay, some valid criticisms of the complainant's credibility, the lack of corroborative evidence and the sworn denial of the respondent, I find I was not "satisfied that the complaint has been established", to quote the words of the principal terms of reference. I so advise the appointers.

Southwell QC, in view of the seriousness of the allegations, adopted a standard of proof akin to beyond reasonable doubt. Adopting the legal notion of the presumption of innocence, Pell was cleared by the Southwell Inquiry. However, Stephen Crittenden – then presenting ABC Radio National's *The Religion Report* – argued on 18 December 2002 that Pell had not been exonerated by the Southwell Inquiry (a similar position was taken by the *Broken Rites Newsletter,* January 2003 issue).

Crittenden's evidence? Well, he said that this was the case since "the leading newspaper in the city where he's the archbishop says he has not been" cleared. This was a ridiculous comment – in view of the fact that the *Sydney Morning Herald* and its sister paper in Melbourne, *The Age,* were hostile to Pell. Not long after leaving the ABC, Stephen Crittenden took up a senior position with the Royal Commission where he worked from 2014 until it wound up in 2017. A Pell-antagonist within the Royal Commission.

Many of Pell's critics, like Crittenden, never conceded that he had been cleared by the Southwell inquiry – still less acknowledge that C's claim was not supported by any evidence and that he had changed his account on numerous occasions, including the year in which the alleged incident took place.

Others changed their minds. On 14 June 2010, Barney Zwartz had written that Pell "was accused of abusing a teenager at a church camp in the 1960s but an independent investigation by a retired non-Catholic judge cleared him". However, on 11 March 2013, Zwartz wrote in *The Age* that Pell was "tainted by sex scandals" and "long dogged" by allegations of sexual abuse against him. Like so many of Pell's critics, Zwartz came to believe what he wanted to believe.

The Phillip Island allegations were raised again when, following the setting up of "Operating Tethering", Victoria Police went looking for complainants who would make allegations against Pell. C declined to be interviewed by journalist Louise Milligan or by Victoria Police.

The Blame-Pell Campaign Commences

From the time of the *60 Minutes* ambush and the subsequent allegations by C about the alleged Phillip Island incident, George Pell became an on-going target for the media. The likes of Crittenden and Zwartz declined to accept that he had been cleared of the Phillip Island allegations. Meanwhile there were others who regarded Pell as somehow solely responsible for child sexual abuse in the Australian Catholic Church.

This became all the more so after Pope John Paul II elevated Pell to the Sacred College of Cardinals in October 2003. This meant that he became the Cardinal Archbishop of Sydney and entitled to participate in the election of the pope, should a vacancy fall due. Now Pell was certainly the most senior – and perhaps most influential – Catholic in Australia.

But, within Australia, Pell's authority, for the most part, did not extend beyond the boundaries of the Archdiocese of Sydney – which happened to be smaller in terms of the Catholic population than the Archdiocese of Melbourne. Separate dioceses were established in the greater Sydney region in Parramatta and Broken Bay in 1986. Similar changes were not made with respect to Melbourne and Brisbane.

As Pell well understood when first appointed a bishop in 1987, he had opponents within the Catholic hierarchy. Due to this reason, Pell was never appointed by his colleagues to the position of president of the Australian Catholic Bishops' Conference. This despite the fact that he was a resident Australian archbishop from 1996 until 2014. During this period, this position was held by Cardinal Edward Clancy of Sydney (1986-2000), Archbishop Francis Carroll of Canberra and Goulburn (2000-2006), Archbishop Philip Wilson of Adelaide (2006-12) and Archbishop Denis Hart of Melbourne (2012-18). In short, George Pell never had the numbers to head the Australian assembly of Catholic bishops. Yet many of his critics regarded him as responsible for all Catholicism's faults throughout Australia.

This belief was illustrated in Phillipa McGuinness' *The Year Everything Changed* (Vintage Books, 2018) which focused on the year 2001. She described noticing Pell in May 2001, while waiting for the traffic lights to change so that she could cross Elizabeth Street near Sydney's Hyde Park on a Sunday, in a chapter titled "Holy Shit":

> I felt agitated and a bit sick, feelings promoted by the church's unwillingness to reckon – *really* reckon – with the scourge of sexual abuse of children within its ranks. Pell's denial that he knew about any of it defied not only common sense but common decency. I knew I should say something; not as a woman, not as a mother, not as a lapsed Catholic, but as a person. As the green man [i.e. the traffic light] appeared I was so close to muttering, "You should be ashamed of yourself." But I said nothing. He walked off, ahead

of me. Pell, when I saw him, was head of the Catholic Church in Australia. He became Archbishop of Sydney – the Vatican's man in charge – in May 2001.

It's not clear to what extent that McGuinness' memory of her thought on this occasion was retro-fitted some two decades later. For, in 2001, there was little criticism that Pell had allegedly covered-up clerical child sexual abuse – that came later. The more important point is that, although presenting as a lapsed Catholic, McGuinness was simply wrong in maintaining that Pell was "head of the Catholic Church" or "the Vatican's man in charge" in Australia.

Even the Australian Catholic Bishops Conference has limited authority with respect to its members. All archbishops and bishops are autonomous in their own archdiocese or diocese and report directly to the Pope in Rome. This means that when Archbishop of Melbourne, Pell essentially only had authority for Melbourne. And when Archbishop of Sydney, he essentially only had authority for Sydney.

Also the religious orders (Christian Brothers, Jesuits, Josephites) report direct to their provincials in Australia who report to the international heads of the orders who report to the Pope. The structure of the Catholic Church was not well understood by most journalists and commentators who covered George Pell – even those who had been brought up in the Catholic faith.

Four Corners Blames the Archbishop of Sydney for what happened in the Diocese of Armidale and Parramatta

In the early years of the 21st Century, political and public pressure increased on the Catholic Church to do more about clerical child sexual abuse. This despite the fact that the Melbourne Response had been established in Melbourne in 1996 and Towards Healing (covering the rest of Australia) the following year.

The criticism intensified around 2012 following the *Four Corners* "Unholy Silence" program by Geoff Thompson. Mary Ann Jolley was the producer and Sue Spencer the executive producer. The program aired on 2 July 2012. Meanwhile around this time Joanne McCarthy was writing numerous articles and columns in the *Newcastle Herald* about child sexual abuse by Catholic male clerics in the Maitland-Newcastle diocese. "Unholy Silence" focused on the offending of Father F in the Armidale diocese in north east NSW.

Once again, Pell was unwise to do a pre-recorded interview with journalists – in this case Thompson. In the pre-recorded interview, Pell made it clear that he was only responsible for the Archdiocese of Sydney. *Four Corners* not only failed to run this comment in that part of the interview that went to air – but it also deleted Pell's words on his responsibility from the longer interview which it placed on the ABC website. A clear case of censorship. I took the matter up with Mark Scott, then the ABC's managing director and editor-in-chief at the time. He supported his journalists' decision to cut the pre-recorded Pell interview, from what was presented as the full interview, in the manner that they chose.[15]

In view of the fact that the media's pile-on against Pell surged from around 2010, I decided to become involved in the debate – primarily to provide some balance. I did so in my (then) weekly column in the *Sydney Morning Herald* (moving to *The Australian* in December 2013), in my *Media Watch Dog* blog (which commenced in March 2009 on The Sydney Institute website and which appeared in *The Australian Online* from December 2013) – as well as in my occasional appearances on the ABC TV *Insiders* program (where I was an occasional panellist between 2002 and 2019) and on *The Bolt Report* (which moved from Network 10 to Sky News in 2016).

Writing in the *Sydney Morning Herald* column on 14 November 2012, I criticised the *Four Corners'* "Unholy Silence" program:

> *Four Corners* raised two serious allegations of sex abuse by men against boys. One involved a Father F who moved from the diocese of Armidale to the diocese of Parramatta. Pell is not responsible for either diocese. Moreover, when the alleged offences occurred,

Pell was based in either Ballarat or Melbourne. The second allegation involved Father Julian Fox, a priest of the Salesian order, who is based in Rome. Pell said on *Four Corners* that if there is credible evidence against Fox, he should return to Australia to face his accusers. [Julian Fox was extradited to Victoria and jailed for historical child sexual abuse in 2015.]

I also made the point that F had been known as a child offender by NSW Police as far back as at least 1998. Moreover, F was sacked by the Bishop of Armidale in 1992. But *Four Corners* laid the blame at the feet of the Archbishop of Sydney despite the fact that Pell had no control over a priest of a non-Sydney diocese (F) or a priest of a religious order (Fox). Either Thompson and Jolley were ignorant of the structure of the Catholic Church or consciously set out to involve Pell in a matter for which he was not responsible.

At one stage, Fr F moved from the diocese of Armidale to the diocese of Parramatta. In July 2012, the Catholic bishops of Armidale and Parramatta (Bishop Michael Kennedy and Bishop Anthony Fisher OP respectively) commissioned a report on this matter by former Federal Court judge and former Labor Federal parliamentarian Antony Whitlam QC, a non-Catholic. The Commissioner was highly critical about the way in which the former bishop of Armidale, Bishop Henry Kennedy, handled complaints against F. However, the Whitlam Report made no findings critical of Cardinal Pell. In 2016, having been revealed as John Joseph Farrell, F was sentenced to a lengthy term of imprisonment.

On 17 January 2013, the bishops of Armidale and Parramatta released the Whitlam Report. This occurred around two months after Prime Minister Gillard announced the creation of the Royal Commission. In the final paragraph of his "Conclusions", Antony Whitlam QC made the following finding concerning Towards Healing (established 1997):

> I understand that the document [Towards Healing] setting out the principles and procedures in responding to complaints of abuse

against personnel of the Catholic Church in Australia will come under review in the foreshadowed royal commission. For my purposes it is only necessary to remark that, had the procedures for reporting child abuse laid down in that document been in force in 1984 and observed in Moree at the time, "F" would have been stopped in his tracks. Monsignor Usher's briefing paper usefully explains how the protocols work. They also include specific strategies designed to prevent the transfer of unsuitable priests from one diocese to another. If those procedures had been in place in 1989 and followed in "F"'s case, there is no chance that Bishop Heather would have agreed to take him on [in Parramatta].

What Whitlam wrote was that the Towards Healing process (which applied to all archdioceses and dioceses except Melbourne) had brought about a situation where the rampant crimes of Fr F in Armidale and Parramatta would not have continued once they had come to the notice of the Church authorities. It is reasonable to infer that the same applied to the Melbourne Response since both processes were similar.

In his report, Antony Whitlam QC pointed to an error in the *Four Corners* story – which had been repeated by *7.30*. ABC reporter Andy Park, in a follow-up story on *7.30*, interviewed Bernard Barrett of Broken Rites.[16] Barrett criticised Whitlam's report and, with hand gestures, mocked his conclusion.

In September 2016, Whitlam took legal action against the ABC for implying that his report was a cover-up with respect to Farrell's child sexual abuse. In his writ, Whitlam described the ABC as arrogant due to its refusal to correct, and apologise for, its errors. Whitlam sought damages and costs for personal and reputational harm. A settlement was reached before the Federal Court in early November 2016. This was yet another example of the taxpayer funded public broadcaster's unwillingness to admit to and correct errors – which was evident in its coverage of Pell.

The Victorian Parliamentary Inquiry

In March 2013 the Legislative Council in Victoria established the *Inquiry into the Handling of Child Abuse by Religious and Other Organisations* – subsequently known by the title *Betrayal of Trust*. Archbishop Pell of Sydney and Archbishop Hart of Melbourne gave evidence to the inquiry. They sometimes received a hostile reception from Victorian politicians – which was replicated in the media with hostile reports. *Betrayal of Trust* released its final report on 13 November 2013.

On Page 42 of *Betrayal of Trust's* first volume, the following comment is made:

> The Committee learnt that Archbishop Frank Little, who occupied the position of Archbishop of Melbourne from July 1974 to July 1996, a period in which abuse is known to have occurred, kept no records until 1993. He dealt with all complaints of abuse personally and in strict confidence. Bishop Mulkearns in Ballarat adopted a similar approach. It is clear on the basis of credible evidence that each was aware of reports of abuse by priests in their respective dioceses and that each tried to quarantine that information as far as possible. The Committee could not determine precisely what these two men knew about individual cases. Archbishop Little is now deceased and… Bishop Mulkearns was unable to give evidence to the Inquiry.

The Victorian Parliamentary Inquiry did not find that Pell had been aware of Gerald Ridsdale's crimes while in Ballarat or that he had failed to act on clerical child sexual abuse while an auxiliary bishop in Melbourne when Little was archbishop. However, the inquiry did put additional focus on child sexual assault in the Catholic Church since those with the highest profiles were Catholic archbishops – Pell of Sydney and Hart of Melbourne.

Peter Fox appears on *Lateline*

On 8 November 2012, Detective Chief Inspector Peter Fox appeared on the ABC TV *Lateline* program. At the time Fox was on leave from NSW Police for medical reasons. He did not return. Fox provided *Lateline* with a letter which he had written to NSW premier Barry O'Farrell alleging that NSW Police were covering up child sexual abuse in the Hunter Valley. On 15 November 2012, Fox again appeared on *Lateline* – this time interviewed by Emma Alberici. On this occasion, Fox effectively accused Cardinal Pell, whom he referred to as "Mr Pell", of covering-up child sexual abuse.

On 9 November 2012, Troy Grant, a Nationals member of the NSW Upper House and a former NSW policeman, went on ABC Radio and claimed that Pell was involved in thwarting a police investigation into clerical child abuse in the Hunter region. Grant provided no evidence for this assertion.

Later that day, New South Wales Liberal Party-Nationals Coalition Premier Barry O'Farrell announced the establishment of *Special Commission of Inquiry into matters relating to the police investigation of certain child sexual abuse allegations in the Catholic Diocese of Maitland-Newcastle* headed by Margaret Cunneen SC. This was to focus only on the Catholic Church in the diocese of Maitland-Newcastle – despite the fact that there was substantial offending against children by other religious and some secular institutions in the area.

On Saturday 10 November 2012, Troy Grant was interviewed on the ABC *AM* program and said:

> The behaviour of the Church has been consistent back in the '70s right through to the mid-2000s, which is why I've called for the leader of the Catholic Church, Cardinal Pell, to fall on his sword. He should've and could've done more and done better. I think he's lost the moral right to decide whether the Church's response is now appropriate. That should be left to a royal commission.

This comment showed significant ignorance about how the Catholic Church operates. As previously indicated, Pell has never been the "leader of the Catholic Church" in Australia. It provided an example about how the Pell pile-on had extended beyond the media and into the political debate.

On the morning of Monday 12 November 2012, Tony Windsor, the Independent member for New England, went on the ABC *AM* program and called for a royal commission. In doing so, he spoke specifically about the Catholic Church:

> I think when a senior policeman [Peter Fox] breaks ranks in a sense and actually articulates concern that there have been cover-ups within the Catholic Church – when a member of the New South Wales Parliament, Troy Grant, you know, a respected former policeman raises comments, not of a political or a religious nature but of a police nature – that to me says that there are a number of issues out there.

This comment indicated, that to Tony Windsor, the Catholic Church was regarded as a repository of virtually all child sexual assault in Australia – since he made no reference to other religious or secular institutions.

The Special Commission of Inquiry made no adverse findings concerning George Pell. Cunneen SC found that Peter Fox had used the term "Catholic police mafia" on multiple occasions concerning investigations into clerical child abuse but that there was no evidence to support his assertion that alleged offences regarding Catholic officials were not properly investigated by NSW Police. The Special Commission held that Peter Fox had an obsession about matters relating to the Catholic Church which had led to a loss of his capacity to approach the allegations of sexual abuse with the detachment required of an investigating officer in NSW Police.

In a soft interview with ABC Radio National's *Big Ideas* presenter Andrew Dodd on 26 June 2015, Fox accused Cunneen SC of acting as if she was running Guantanamo Bay. Dodd did not challenge Fox's hyperbolic assessment. Moreover, Joanne McCarthy – who was also a guest on the program – asserted that members of NSW Police who attended the Special Commission's hearings "wanted to disembowel" Fox. More hyperbole.

In late August 2019, Hachette published Peter Fox's *Walking Towards Thunder*. The front cover carries an endorsement by ABC TV journalist Paul Kennedy (who co-authored Chrissie Foster's *Hell on the Way to Heaven,* Bantam, 2010). Kennedy declared that Peter Fox's "courage and honesty will blow you away".

Walking Towards Thunder was withdrawn from sale in October 2020 and a grovelling apology was issued by Hachette and Fox to Detective Inspector Jeff Little concerning the allegations made about his conduct when "in charge of Strike Force Lantle investigating sexual abuse in the Newcastle/Maitland Diocese of the Catholic Church". It would seem that Hachette's management had not paid attention to Margaret Cunneen SC's warning about Fox's reliability as a witness before publishing his book. Pell antagonist Louise Adler, who at MUP published Louise Milligan's *Cardinal,* took up the managing director role at Hachette in September 2019, shortly after the publication of Fox's book.

The ABC did not report that *Walking Towards Thunder* had been withdrawn from sale – even though the ABC TV *News Breakfast* program had given the book publicity, including a soft interview with co-presenters Michael Rowland and Lisa Millar on 27 August 2019. Paul Kennedy (who appeared on News *Breakfast*) vouched for Fox's honesty on the cover of *Walking Towards Thunder*.

On a personal note, on 2 April 2018, Peter Fox tweeted that I had "jumped on Julia Gillard's head for announcing the RC". He just made this up – I supported the establishment of the Royal Commission – providing further evidence that Fox's state of mind was erratic at best.

In *Walking Towards Thunder*, Fox wrote that he was not involved in investigating alleged crimes by Catholic clerics in the Hunter region after December 2010 – having been accused of leaking material to the *Newcastle Herald's* Joanne McCarthy. He formally resigned from NSW Police in late 2014.

Julia Gillard's Royal Commission Announcement – The Media Response

On Monday 12 November 2012, Labor Prime Minister Julia Gillard announced that she would be "recommending to the Governor-General the establishment of a Royal Commission into institutional responses to instances and allegations of child sex abuse in Australia". At the conclusion of her written statement, the Prime Minister said: "I commend the victims involved for having the courage to speak out. I believe we must do everything we can to make sure that what has happened in the past is never allowed to happen again". Julia Gillard's statement implied that all complainants were "victims" – a not uncommon error but an unfortunate one since it indicated that the Prime Minister of Australia believed that everyone who spoke out as a victim was in fact a victim. The case of Carl Beech (aka "Nick") in Britain proved that this is not the case.

In view of the focus in the media on child sexual abuse in the Catholic Church, it came as no surprise that, when Julia Gillard announced the establishment of the Royal Commission, many thought that this was an inquiry into the Catholic Church alone. For example, this was the first question at the media conference in Sydney which followed the announcement:

> *Prime Minister:* I'll take some questions.
>
> *Journalist:* Prime Minister, is it right to say that this will look beyond the Catholic Church to all institutions?
>
> *Prime Minister:* Absolutely correct. It's institutional responses to instances and allegations of child abuse in Australia...

Technically, Julia Gillard was correct. However, the journalist had accurately interpreted the feeling in the community. The proposed royal commission, especially in view of the controversy concerning the Catholic Church in the lead-up to the announcement, appeared like it was to be an inquiry into the Catholic Church – which is why the journalist seemed surprised that it might look beyond Catholic institutions. This perception was confirmed when Prime Minister Gillard told the media that she had phoned Cardinal Pell as a courtesy prior to announcing the commission. This made it likely that complainants who were brought up in Catholic institutions were more likely to approach the Royal Commission than those who were not.

George Pell's Response – In the Face of ABC Hostility

On Sunday 11 November 2012, in his weekly *Sunday Telegraph* column, Cardinal George Pell had devoted his allocated space to assuring readers that the Catholic Church would cooperate fully with the Special Commission of Inquiry into the handling of sex abuse in the Catholic diocese of Maitland-Newcastle. He commented:

> My advice as archbishop to Catholic priests and people is the same as it always has been during my time as archbishop. Comply with the law; tell complainants to go to the police. In NSW, allegations of child sex abuse have to be reported; an obligation since the early 1990s. Much of the public discussion is about how the church dealt with cases 20 or so years ago. Critics talk as though earlier inadequacies are still prevalent. Major procedural changes in dealing with these matters have been implemented since 1996.

In response to Peter Fox's allegations, Pell said:

> It is ludicrous to suggest I was involved in some cover-up in the Hunter region. I am not bishop of the area and have only visited there a few times. I have never approached any politician or police official to speak of problems there, much less have I intervened to thwart justice. Although the Church started from well behind scratch, it is hard to name any other Australian organisation that has done more to produce a safe environment for young people. And I point out again (as I did in this column some time ago) that it is foolish and mistaken to assume these problems are confined to the churches or even simply to NGOs [i.e. non-government organisations].

When, the next day, the Royal Commission was announced – George

Pell decided that he should stand up for the Catholic Church. Few other senior Church leaders were prepared to do so at the time. A media conference was held at the Catholic Church's Sydney office in Pitt Street on Tuesday 13 November. It was a hostile event. The ABC sent along several cameras. One was focused on Pell, another on *7.30* presenter Leigh Sales and *Lateline* presenter Emma Alberici. Sales and Alberici in particular gave the impression that they were confronting the person most responsible for child abuse in Australia.

In fact, the two ABC presenters dominated the media conference – asking in total about half the questions and adopting the role of counsel for the (Pell) prosecution. Alberici's questions/comments focused on financial compensation to victims, the Catholic sacrament of confession and an allegation about a historical child sexual assault in Parramatta (which is not part of the Sydney archdiocese). Alberici later ran her contributions at the media conference in her *Lateline* report that night.

It was much the same with Sales. In her report on *7.30*, she focused on the questions/comments she had directed to Pell at the media conference (showing footage of the event). Namely Pell's walk to court with Gerald Ridsdale, the (alleged) inadequacy of the Melbourne Response, the Father F case in Armidale (despite the fact that this was not a matter for which Pell was responsible) and the confessional.

Later that day, *7.30* interviewed only critics of George Pell – (i) Stephen Woods who was presented as a victim called on Pell to resign, (ii) the Pell critic Helen Last (who was presented as a victims' advocate) and (iii) Andrew Morrison (of the Australian Lawyers Alliance – an organisation critical of the Catholic Church's handling of sexual assault). *7.30* did not report the views of anyone prepared to speak up for Pell. It was as one-sided as that.

In their reports for the ABC, Alberici and Sales adopted the role of journalist as activist. Many other journalists, within and outside the ABC, were to take a similar role.

The Only Cab on the Rank?

There was considerable criticism of George Pell's media conference including by *The Australian's* Paul Kelly, who was not part of the Pell pile-on. However, after re-viewing the event on *YouTube* and reading the transcript, it is reasonable to conclude that Pell put in a competent performance in view of the hostile environment. Moreover, Pell was the only leader to defend the record of the Catholic Church in recent decades with respect to clerical child abuse. The media conference was held so that Pell could get across this message – which he stated at the commencement of proceedings:

> *Cardinal Pell:* Well, ladies and gentlemen, thank you for coming so that we can talk about this enormously important topic and very painful topic. The Catholic Bishops of Australia welcomed the Royal Commission, which was announced by the Prime Minister last night. We think it's an opportunity to help the victims, it's an opportunity to clear the air and to separate fact from fiction.
>
> The first thing I would like to do is to repeat what I and the Church leadership have said for the last 16 years, which is that we are not interested in denying the extent of misdoing in the Catholic Church. We object to it being exaggerated. We object to being described as the only cab on the rank. We acknowledge, with shame, the extent of the problem. And I want to assure you that we have been serious in attempting to eradicate it and deal with it. And one of the reasons why we welcome the Royal Commission is that this commission will enable those claims to be validated, or found to be a significant exaggeration….

Pell's hopes came to naught. In the face of the evidence – see Chapter 9 – the Catholic Church was effectively seen by the Royal Commission as the main "cab on the rank" in so far as institutional child sexual abuse was concerned. And the allegations made against Pell in the Royal Commission made it impossible for him to receive a fair trial when charged by Victoria Police with historical child sexual assault some years later.

On Sunday 16 November 2012, I appeared on the ABC TV *Insiders* program. Barrie Cassidy was in the presenter's chair and my fellow panellists were Lenore Taylor (now editor of *The Guardian Australia*) and David Marr (now also with *The Guardian Australia*). The decision to establish what became the Royal Commission had just been announced by Prime Minister Julia Gillard. When discussion turned to this topic, I made the following comment:

> I'm not against it [the Royal Commission]. But it's going to be hugely expensive. No one knows where it will start and when it will stop. And what I'm concerned about is that it's not a distraction. If you look at the reports in *The Australian* this year, and on *Lateline* this year on the ABC, sexual abuse of children is rife among Indigenous communities in the APY Lands in South Australia, in parts of the Northern Territory, in parts of Western Australia and Queensland. As we understand it, there's widespread evidence for that. No one is focusing particularly on that, probably because no one quite knows how to handle it – including State and Territory police. But it's going on now. It's rife. And it probably went on last night….

Both Lenore Taylor and David Marr insisted that the matter had been handled by the John Howard led Coalition government's Northern Territory National Emergency Response in 2007. But, as I pointed out, this only covered the Northern Territory – and not the six States or the Australian Capital Territory. I continued:

> I'm not against a Royal Commission and I can see why both Julia Gillard and [Opposition leader] Tony Abbott supported it and I don't criticise that decision. But I'm not exactly sure what it's going to achieve to resolve current problems. Although I can see how it can achieve…the resolution of past problems.

It was at this stage that David Marr turned the discussion to references about "what's happening in Roman Catholic presbyteries this very day" but without providing evidence for the allegation that clerical child sexual abuse was a contemporary daily occurrence within the

Catholic Church. It was a baseless allegation made without any evidence. In return, I criticised my fellow panelist for his old fashioned anti-Catholic sectarianism – since, even over six years ago, it was evident that child sexual abuse by Catholic priests and brothers was essentially an historical crime.

Fuelled by the media in general, the Royal Commission in particular and by Victoria Police's decision to charge Pell – child abuse (real and alleged) by Catholic priests and brothers became a huge national story, led by the ABC. It remained so until diminished somewhat by the High Court's unanimous decision in *Pell v The Queen*.

Before Cardinal Pell walked from Barwon Prison on 7 April 2020 as a free man, the Catholic Church was considered by many to be the only cab on the rank concerning child abuse – with the Cardinal at the top of the rank. Due primarily to the Pell media pile-on.

Tweet by Lucie Morris-Marr

Lucie Morris-Marr's self-congratulatory tweet contains a photograph of her with the *Guardian* Australia's David Marr on the day that Cardinal Pell's conviction was announced. Lucie Morris-Marr reported the Pell hearings and trials for *The New Daily* and CNN and wrote the book Fallen.

Louse Milligan, Martin Foley and Louise Adler

How Melbourne University Press covered the launch of Louise Milligan's Cardinal: The Rise and Fall of Cardinal Pell on 17 May 2017. The Hon Martin Foley was a minister in Daniel Andrews' Victorian Labor government. Ms Adler was MUP's chief executive at the time.

7

THE LEADERS OF THE PELL-ANTAGONISTS' BAND

"...I feel a certain pariah sense in the ABC for never having said George [Pell] was guilty as charged."

- ABC religion reporter, Noel Debien, *Facebook* post, 10 October 2020. Noel Debien regarded himself as a "pariah" for failing to declare at any time he believed that George Pell was guilty – a position which he described as "unusual and unexpected" within the ABC.

Leaders of the (Media) Pack & the Silencing of Dissent

As pointed out in Chapter 6, over a hundred Australian journalists, commentators and the like took part in the Pell media pile-on. There were a few who spoke up for George Pell concerning allegations made against him at the Royal Commission into Institutional Responses to Child Sexual Abuse and in the media – but not many. Pell defenders were quickly labelled as pedophile defenders and so on. The likes of Janet Albrechtsen, Andrew Bolt, Frank Brennan, Greg Craven, Miranda Devine and Keith Windschuttle were not deterred – but there is no doubt that such verbal bullying played a part in all but shutting down the debate in the wider community with respect to those who believed that, at the very least, there was a reasonable doubt about Pell's guilt.

Noel Debien, the experienced ABC religion reporter, wrote on *Facebook* in October 2020 that he regarded himself as a "pariah" within the ABC – merely for failling to declare that he believed that Pell was guilty. Enormous psychological pressure was placed on journalists and commentators to join the intellectually fashionable Pell pile-on. Or at the very least remain silent, as Debien did.

Within the media pile-on, the most persistent players were those who had designated media outlets and who went on to write books. Namely David Marr (*The Guardian* and the ABC), Louise Milligan (ABC), Lucie Morris-Marr (*The New Daily*, CNN) and Melissa Davey (*The Guardian*). All members of this quartet exhibited hostility to Cardinal Pell before and after his conviction – and some even following his acquittal. There were many high-profile back-up members of the Pell-antagonists' band – who are discussed in Chapter 8. However, the leaders were David Marr, Louise Milligan, Lucie Morris-Marr and Melissa Davey.

● **David Marr**

During the Pell pile-on and earlier, David Marr and myself were panellists on the ABC TV Sunday morning program *Insiders*. Since there were a number of notable exchanges between us, many thought we were constantly on the program together. In fact, this was a relatively rare event – around twice a year. It was just that quite a few people remembered our disagreements – and there were quite a few on national and international issues.

On Saturday evening 17 August 2013, I caught the 8 pm Qantas flight to Melbourne (where *Insiders* was filmed). I passed David Marr on the way down the aisle to my seat – he must have noticed me. When I got off the plane, I realised that David had waited for me – and we walked together towards the exit. Shortly before reaching the departure gates, David commented about his forthcoming "Quarterly Essay" on George Pell. It was due to be published the following month by Schwartz Media.

I had declined an invitation to be interviewed for the 25,000 word essay. I was well aware of Marr's views and work and knew it would be a hatchet job on Pell – to a greater or lesser extent. Even though he had assured me – and, no doubt, others – that this would not be the case. My position was that if I spoke to Marr I would have given some authenticity to the essay – in that readers might believe that the author took seriously the views of people with whom he disagreed. This, in my experience, was unlikely to be the case.

Shortly before we entered the security gate, David said to me that Pell had declined to speak to him for the essay. In a matter of fact way, I merely responded that – from Pell's point of view – this was a wise decision. Whereupon Marr exploded. He started yelling and swearing and declared that he had never been so insulted in all his life. I could only assume that his life had been spared offence – since my comment was mild, if not mundane. Marr became especially angry at my suggestion that his work was likely to be a hatchet job on Pell.

In the resultant loud argument, I held my own – without swearing. I was conscious of the fact that some people do not like to hear bad language. The argument simmered for a moment but it soon re-ignited again when David and I were placed in neighbouring spots on the taxi-rank. He continued to complain about my alleged offensive comment – as somewhat bewildered taxi passengers passed us on their way to the designated pick-up rank and then home. In time we, too, headed off on our separate ways – only to meet again at the ABC Southbank studio the following morning. By then, I had learnt that if the Marr bear was provoked, albeit unintentionally, he was destined to explode.

David Marr is a well-regarded journalist, author and commentator with a large fan club among the left in Australia – which explains his ready access to the Australian Broadcasting Commission. The ABC is a Conservative Free Zone without one conservative presenter, producer or editor for any of its prominent television, radio or online outlets. So it's not surprising that Marr is a welcome guest on many of its programs. Between 2002 and 2004, he presented the *Media Watch* program on ABC TV and then wrote for Fairfax Media (now Nine Newspapers which publish the *Sydney Morning Herald* and the Melbourne *Age*) before moving to the leftist *Guardian Australia* in 2013. In the latter capacities, Marr has been invited regularly on ABC TV and Radio programs, particularly with reference to George Pell.

In his request for interviews, Marr presented his forthcoming work as a short biography of a high-profile Australian. The only existing book on Pell was Tess Livingstone's biography published in 2002. When Marr's essay was published, its title *The Prince: Faith, Abuse and George Pell* revealed the author's intention. It did so by linking the word "abuse" with the name George Pell. At the time I declined the interview request, I was not aware of the essay's title – but I was not surprised when it was revealed.

The Prince commenced with a reference to the "cardinal…floundering" and "falling apart in front of the cameras" in his media conference on 13 November 2012 – the day after Prime Minister Gillard's annoucement of the Royal Commission. It was a highly subjective view and somewhat hyperbolic. In spite of the hostile media pack and a difficult case to argue, Pell held his own.

In the first chapter of *The Prince,* there were references to Gerald Ridsdale, the Phillip Island incident, Peter Fox and Tony Windsor. And the essay concluded in mocking condecension about Pell's commitment to celibate life – which the author just could not understand:

> I have no reason to believe he is other than one of those rare priests who is totally celibate. But everything about him suggests he has paid a terrible price for this. He has had to gut himself to stay that way. All the rules he insists the world must follow are the rules he needs for his peculiar quest. As I read the man, listen to him and watch him in action, I wonder how much of the strange ordinariness of George Pell began fifty years ago when a robust schoolboy decided, as an act of heroic piety, to kill sex in himself. The gamble such men take is that they may live their whole lives

without learning the workings of an adult heart. Their world is the church. People are shadowy. Pell is one of these: a company man of uncertain empathy. He has the consolations of friendship, music and a good cellar. And he has what inspired him from the start: a place in the highest levels of his church and a voice in the nation. He has power....

Marr is wont to refer to Catholic prelates having good cellars, fine wines, being well-fed and the like. However, *The Prince* contained little that was fresh – just a rehash of the old allegations. Marr even supported the Stephen Crittenden/*Sydney Morning Herald*' interpretation of Southwell QC's inquiry – namely, that it had not cleared Pell. There was no way Pell was going to get a fair go in *The Prince* and he was wise not to speak with the author. Also, many hold strong views on Pell – for and against – but few share Marr's view that he is ordinary.

Soon after the publication of *The Prince,* Cardinal Pell put out the following statement concerning David Marr's essay:

> A predictable and selective rehash of old material. G.K. Chesterton said: "A good novel tells us the truth about its hero; a bad novel tells us the truth about its author." Marr has no idea what motivates a believing Christian.

It is the practice of Chris Feik, the *Quarterly Essay's* editor, to publish a Correspondence segment in the next issue about the previous essay. Sometimes individuals are invited to present their views – others submit them. The author is given a right of reply. The first letter published was from ABC presenter Geraldine Doogue who was brought up a Catholic. She was never part of the Pell pile-on but nor was she a Pell supporter. Doogue wrote that Pell's comment "did land some blows" and added:

> Unaccustomed as I am to find myself in easy agreement with Cardinal George Pell, I did approve of his response to David Marr's essay. It was published in the same week that I was to conduct a Gleebooks conversation with David in Sydney, and I was intrigued as to how the essay's subject would respond. Would he ignore Da-

vid altogether? Would he forensically rebut all the accusations and the terrible timeline of clerical malfeasance and church neglect in Victoria? Would he try loftily to contextualise his decisions?

As it turned out, he chose none of those options but did comment and land some blows, in my view. "Marr has no idea what motivates a believing Christian." That last statement especially rang true for me. My final sense was that for all David's writing's usual elegance and flair, it came with plenty of baggage, only some of it declared. And it didn't wrestle sufficiently with its own conclusion: that, above all, Pell simply could not contemplate a world without an operating Catholic Church. So yes, his best efforts would always, always be expended on its behalf, without apology, because he believed he was acting, by proxy, in the long-term interests of the wider society. I think this is a correct core judgment on the perplexing Pell, the man David ultimately found somewhat empty and hollow.

I was not asked, and did not offer, to contribute to the Correspondence segment. Nevertheless, in his response to Doogue and others, Marr took issue with a column I had written in the *Sydney Morning Herald* on 1 October 2013 about his essay. Wrote Marr:

> *The Prince* is an essay with a purpose. Henderson complained: "Marr had chosen to depict Pell almost solely with reference to the sex abuse scandal." But Gerard, that was the whole point of the exercise. It goes without saying that there is much, much more to be written about the man and the institution. There were those who regretted me not bringing a little sunlight to the text by giving some good news about the Catholic Church. This puzzles me. How can it be germane to the task at hand to record, say, the good work of St Vincent de Paul? Those who accuse me of writing a brief for the prosecution underestimate my ambition: I set out to deliver a judgment.

So, that's clear then. The whole point of Marr's essay was to focus on the child abuse scandal in the Catholic Church – as if Pell was primarily responsible for this. It's just that Marr declined to state, when seeking interviews, that his essay was not to be a balanced biography. Yet *The Prince* did not present the case for the prosecution – but rather handed down a judgment of guilt beyond reasonable doubt.

It so happened that Marr and I appeared on *Insiders* again on 31 May 2015. This time we met in the ABC's green room in the Melbourne Southbank studio before the program went to air. On arrival, I was greeted with an angry Marr who called me a "lying shit" and "a f---ing shit". His objection on this occasion was to my column in *The Weekend Australian* on 30 May 2015 in which I commented:

> In his book *The Prince*, *Guardian Australia* journalist David Marr wrote that Pell (born 1941) "noticed nothing" when he shared accommodation at the Ballarat East parish in 1973 with [Gerald] Ridsdale. The implication is that he should have noticed something.
>
> So far Marr has said nothing about left-wing journalist and former priest Paul Bongiorno (born 1944), who also said he noticed nothing when he shared a presbytery with Ridsdale at the Warrnambool parish at around the same time. Bongiorno received an empathetic hearing from ABC RN *Breakfast* presenter Fran Kelly on May 21 [2015] when he said: "Ridsdale never came into the presbytery in Warrnambool and said 'Guess how many boys I raped today?' They hide it. It was certainly hidden from me."
>
> Pell is entitled to the same understanding of his time in Ballarat as that which has been given to Bongiorno. But he won't receive it since, unlike his one-time fellow priest [Bongiorno], Pell is a social conservative who is the subject of a modern-day witch hunt.

In the ABC's Southbank green room, Marr loudly protested, while literally jumping up and down on one spot, that he had said on "hundreds of occasions" that he accepted that Pell did not know of Ridsdale's offending when they shared accommodation in Ballarat East for a year. On Monday 1 June 2015, Marr sent me an email in which he wrote:

> On Sunday before *Insiders*, while I was giving you a rich and full

account of what a weird shit I think you are, I told you I have defended Pell on this point for years. Your disbelief was total. You insisted I was attacking the man. You demanded proof. Well here I am, for instance, on *The World Today* on 23 September 2013...

It is true that on ABC Radio's *The World Today* on 23 September 2013, Marr said that he accepted "entirely that Pell was unaware of Ridsdale's activities at the time they shared the presbytery". Sure, Marr made one statement to this effect – but not "hundreds" as he later maintained. And he did not make this point in *The Prince* (published in October 2013) – which will live on in print. In contradiction to one interview on a low-ranking midday radio program which disappeared with little, if any, attention.

The line "I noticed nothing" is very similar to the line "I know nothing" of the Sergeant Schultz character in the *Hogan's Heroes* situation comedy. Readers of *The Prince,* as likely as not, would have taken Marr's reference to Pell having "noticed nothing" as a pointer to what is frequently termed the "Sergeant Schultz defence" – with the implication that Pell did know something about Ridsdale.

Moreover, Marr made no mention of Bongiorno in *The Prince* – despite the fact that Bongiorno was on the record as declaring that he did not know anything about the fact that Ridsdale was a pedophile when they shared accommodation in Warrnambool. Clearly Marr had one rule for the conservative Catholic Pell and another rule for the liberal Catholic Bongiorno. Whatever Marr believed when he appeared on *The World Today* in September 2013, this did not find its way into the original issue of *The Prince* or its reprints.

David Marr and myself were on *Insiders* once more on Sunday 9 July 2017 – shortly after Pell had been charged by Victoria Police with historical child sexual abuse. At the time Victoria Police had not advised as to how many charges Pell would face concerning an unspecified number of complainants. But Marr professed to know. Let's go to the transcript – which commences with one Pell-antagonist (presenter Barrie Cassidy) talking to another (Marr):

Barrie Cassidy: David, how do you understand that this will proceed from here?

David Marr: Well, um, there's a lot of rhetoric around about how difficult it will be for this man to have a fair trial. And, without paying sufficient attention to what's been done to protect his position—I mean, last week he was charged and in an almost unique move, Victorian Police did not say what the charges were.... [But we know they are] multiple historical sexual assault offences involving multiple complainants. Now the usual way in which trials of this kind then proceed is for there to be separate trials for each complaint. And in Victoria, the usual way for those series of trials to proceed is that none can be reported until the final one is resolved.

Barrie Cassidy: Because one might impact on the other?

David Marr: Because one *would* impact on the other. So, you could have a big trial which would be reported, or you would have a series of trials that could not be reported.

Gerard Henderson: Well they're now—

David Marr: No, just a second Gerard. So, it is highly likely that though these trials won't be called secret trials, they won't be held in camera. But it is highly likely that the public will know nothing of what he's accused of, or the results of any of these trials, for perhaps four or five years.

Gerard Henderson: Well David, you don't know that. You have no idea.

David: Marr: Well I'm, I'm only going— Gerard

Gerard Henderson: You don't know....

Marr was engaged in wish fulfilment during his *Insiders'* prophecy. Pell faced just one trial (which included a re-trial) – not a series of trials. And the whole case from the commencement of the first trial to the High Court decision took around 19 months – not four or five years.

Pell's conviction was made public on 26 February 2019. Soon after, Marr concluded an article in *The Guardian* titled "Brutal and dogmatic George Pell waged war on sex – even as he abused children" with this gloating comment: "The world can now know that a little over 20 years ago, in Pell's first months as archbishop of Melbourne, this scourge of sex was forcing choirboys to suck his penis."

At 6 pm that night, Marr appeared in a panel discussion on ABC TV's *The Drum*. In spite of the fact that Marr is a trained lawyer and well aware of a convicted person's right of appeal, he essentially told Pell's supporters to accept the verdict and be quiet. Having criticised Andrew Bolt, Frank Brennan and Greg Craven (none of whom were on the panel), Marr declared:

> ...a jury has decided that the highest ranking member of the Catholic Church ever has been guilty of these offences and he goes to jail tomorrow. And I think it is time, in looking at this horrible tragedy, to respect the victim, I think it is time, finally, to live up to the rhetoric of the Church about its great affection and respect for victims. This is the time.

There was a total of five panellists on the program – one of whom was *The Australian's* Greg Sheridan, a Catholic who would be regarded by many as a Pell supporter. In the wake of the jury verdict, Sheridan did not state that the convicted man had a right of appeal. Nor did any other panel member. Nor did the presenter Craig Reucassel.

After *The Drum*, Marr stayed in the ABC Sydney studio – since he was to appear on *7.30* later that evening. This time there was a panel of just two – both were Pell- antagonists – Joanne McCarthy (of the *Newcastle Herald*) and Marr. Leigh Sales, another Pell-antagonist, was the presenter. She fed Marr such leading questions as "David, the hypocrisy of George Pell, the leader of the Church's response in Australia to child sexual abuse, is very striking today".

This led to Marr bagging Pell's position on such issues as homosexuality, contraception, divorce, IVF for unmarried women – adding "he did the lot". This overlooked the fact that Pell's conviction had nothing to do with any of the above. Marr also sneered that Pell was "phenomenally eloquent on the subject of the benefits of priestly celibacy". Neither McCarthy nor Marr discussed the issue of whether, in view of the media's coverage of the case, a fair trial was possible. Nor did any of the Pell-antagonists draw attention to the fact that the jury in the re-trial was out for some four days before reaching its verdict. And no one mentioned Pell's right of appeal.

Writing in *The Guardian* on 27 February 2019, immediately after Pell had been sentenced, Marr acknowledged Pell's right to appeal but made the obvious point that he would be incarcerated before any appeal was heard:

> By then Pell will be in one of the prisons where Victoria houses paedophiles. He will know so many of the faces, so many priests and brothers who have done what he continues to deny having done himself. What reunions there will be. For the first time since they shared the St Alipius presbytery at Ballarat in the 1970s, George Pell will be back under the same roof as the worst of the worst. He and Gerald Ridsdale will have so much to catch up on.

Once again, another sneering reference. Once again, another reference to the fact that for one year half a century ago Pell lived with Gerald Ridsdale. Once again, no reference to Bongiorno also having shared accommodation with Ridsdale for about a year. And, once again, a false prophecy – Pell was never to spend time with Ridsdale in prison.

When Pell appealed to the Victorian Court of Appeal, Marr was again interviewed by Leigh Sales on *7.30* about the case – on 6 June 2019. He made one mistake when reporting the two day hearing – which *7.30* declined to correct.[17] He also suggested that if Pell's verdict was quashed by the Court of Appeal it would be re-instated by the High Court. Marr had run a similar line in *The Guardian* on 1 June 2019.

When Pell's appeal was dismissed by a majority decision in the Court of Appeal, *7.30* yet again went to Marr for "expert" comment. On 22 August 2019, Marr told the program's viewers that "it was by no means certain that the High Court will actually take the case and give it another review". Wrong – it did.

In this interview, Marr gratuitously advised those he termed "the most extreme barrackers for the Cardinal to at least admit that there is a basis on which he might be found guilty". The invitation was not taken up and, in time, the High Court's decision was welcomed by those whom Marr demeaned as Pell barrackers. Marr never criticised any of Pell's antagonists.

Then writing in *The Guardian* on 7 April 2020, immediately after the High Court's decision, Marr commented that the High Court had said that it was possible for Pell to have sexually assaulted A and B "but not reasonably possible". The High Court said no such thing. The test was not whether the accusations were possible or were reasonably possible – but whether they had been proven beyond reasonable doubt. Here, Marr made the same mistake as the majority judges in the Victorian Court of Appeal – in reversing the onus of proof.

David Marr was hopelessly wrong on the Pell Case from beginning to end. A not uncommon occurrence when a commentator allows feelings to influence judgment.

David Marr's "Quarterly Essay" *The Prince* was subsequently printed in book form by Black Inc. in May 2014 – and again in November 2019 (after the Victorian Court of Appeal's majority judgment) while the prisoner was in Melbourne Assessment Prison at the edge of the CBD awaiting the outcome of his appeal to the High Court. It concluded with a familiar Marr sneer:

> The cardinal will not be long in the city prison. He is bound for one of those jails in the bush where Victoria houses its pedophiles. He will know so many of the priests and brothers there.

More wish fulfillment. George Pell never served time in the Victorian countryside where many convicted pedophile priests are imprisoned – including Ararat Prison in central Victoria where Gerald Ridsdale is living out his final years along with other notorious Victorian pedophiles – clerics and laymen alike.

It is not clear whether David Marr will add a segment to another edition of *The Prince* following Pell's acquittal. But, in view of the High Court's emphatic unanimous decision, this is unlikely. In the meantime, Marr continues to publicise the work of such Pell-antagonists as fellow *Guardian* employee Melissa Davey – even launching her book *The Trial of George Pell* via Zoom (on account of the pandemic) in late September 2020. Marr has done appearances with Pell-antagonists such as Louise Milligan, Lucie Morris-Marr and Sarah Ferguson. It would seem that he is the go-to "in conversation" partner for Pell-antagonists – none of whom has had the intellectual courage to defend their written or broadcast work against an informed Pell supporter. It's a form of intellectual cowardice.

In his collected works *My Country: Stories, Essays and Speeches* (Black Inc, 2018), David Marr re-published an article originally printed in *The Guardian* on 13 December 2017. Marr (born 1947) wrote that when he "grew up on the sheltered Protestant North Shore of Sydney it was a given that when push came to shove the Catholic Church would obey Rome rather than the law". Marr acknowledged that he worked to get "that fear" out of his system because he saw it as "religious bigotry". The prejudice, he wrote, abated following the election of the Catholic John F Kennedy as president of the United States in 1960. Yet, by the end of 2017, Marr "could see evidence everywhere…that the only law that really counted" to the Catholic Church "was the law of Rome". It would seem that anti-Catholic religious bigotry, acquired in one's Protestant youth, can live into older age.

Reviewing *My Country* in *The Weekend Australian* (12 January 2019), writer Gerard Windsor suggested that Marr's youthful bigotry has not completely been shed, commenting:

> The Lord delivered George Pell into David Marr's hands, but his animus goes wider than that. A 2010 piece for *The Sydney Morning Herald* on Mary MacKillop's canonisation is done as a riff on the absurdity of miracles. It's very funny, and it's bigoted. Scorn

delights the partisan, but it's hardly the non-abusive debate whose absence Marr himself laments.

Earlier, in the review, Windsor wrote:

> Marr does not do doubt. Just once in these 562 pages does he admit to his mindset being challenged.... Otherwise Marr has the zealot's righteousness. Abuse of a civilised kind is what he does well. It's a patrician sniffiness that comes close to sneering without ever quite toppling in. Rather than argument, his weapon is a frequently ironic, pithy contempt.
>
> To his journalistic credit, he can also do a piece of seemingly calm, detailed reporting where his sympathies nevertheless are the bottom line. So he summarises the 2008 saga of Bill Henson's exhibition at the Roslyn Oxley Gallery as "the great press panic of my lifetime". No rational person could consider Henson's images pornographic, is his implied conclusion. Fair enough.
>
> Ten years later what we miss is any discussion of what now must be the central issue of this case: the acceptability of a middle-aged man taking photos of naked 12-year-old girls. Passing up this opportunity seems an odd omission for a writer so incensed by clerical sexual abusers. Marr's own moral code seems to be a selective libertarianism, but he never lays out any personal manifesto; we have to deduce it from what he is so bitterly opposed to.

Marr's book *The Henson Case* (Text, 2008) contains several colour images of the artist's photography of naked pre-pubescent girls. Which raises the point – what would David Marr have said in 2008 if a Catholic bishop, who was into photography, put on an exhibition including images of naked pre-pubescent boys? The evidence suggests – plenty. It's another example of Marr's prejudices leading to double standards.

Unlike many Pell-antagonists, following the High Court's decision in *Pell v The Queen,* David Marr has acknowledged that "Pell is innocent of these charges" (*The Guardian,* 7 April 2020). He understands the presumption of innocence which applies to all Australians. The likes of Louise Milligan, Lucie Morris-Marr, Melissa Davey and Sarah Ferguson – on the other hand – give the impression that they do not really accept the High Court decision. They are not alone.

• Louise Milligan's *Cardinal* – A Case for the Prosecution

Louise Milligan, one of Australia's best known journalists, joined the ABC in early 2013. On 20 February 2016, in a page one *Herald Sun* "exclusive", Lucie Morris-Marr broke the story that George Pell was under investigation by Victoria Police's SANO Taskforce. Morris-Marr wrote that "the allegations span four decades, with the Ballarat-born cardinal accused of abusing children – now adults in their late 20s to early 50s – between 1978 and 2001". It would seem that this was a leak from Victoria Police – either directly or indirectly.

The ABC immediately put Milligan, who was born in Ireland and brought up a Catholic, on the case. On 27 July 2016, ABC management made the extraordinary decision to devote the entire 30 minutes of its main current affairs TV program *7.30* to a report on George Pell by Louise Milligan which was produced by Andy Burns. *7.30's* executive producer at the time was Jo Puccini. The two women did some five months research in Ballarat and Melbourne. The program was introduced by presenter Sabra Lane, who made it very clear that *7.30* agreed with the complainants – since she implied that complainants were worried that the "full picture" of their situation would never be told without the likes of Milligan and Burns:

> *Sabra Lane:* In an investigation over several months, reporter Louise Milligan and producer Andy Burns spoke to scores of witnesses and other sources, piecing together the complaints being examined by the police. Many of those they spoke to are concerned that the full picture may never emerge and that's why they've decided to tell their story publicly…

7.30's claims against Pell turned primarily on his alleged offending in Ballarat's Eureka Pool in the late 1970s. L.M. and D.D. (who gave their full names) were both interviewed and made allegations against

Pell. Early in the program, Milligan told viewers that Pell "lived in the St Alipius Presbytery with Gerald Ridsdale earlier in the '70s". She made no mention of the fact that, when a priest, her fellow journalist Paul Bongiorno had also lived with Gerald Ridsdale. It was very much a case of guilt by association – but only as far as Pell was concerned, since both (then) young priests had lived with Ridsdale for about a year.

However, Milligan did acknowledge that the case against Pell was far from comprehensive:

> *Louise Milligan:* It's deserted here at the Eureka Pool this time of year, but in summer in the 1970s it was a hive of activity. The family who owned the pool at that time have confirmed to *7.30* that George Pell was a constant fixture and he was always surrounded by children. But they said they never saw anything untoward and if they had've, he would have been sent away and they would have called the police. When contacted by police, the pool manager's wife says she never saw any behaviour by George Pell that concerned her. He was very popular with the children. Her statement is one of many made to Victoria Police's Taskforce SANO, which investigates claims of sexual abuse coming out of the Royal Commission.

It is difficult to imagine how a tall man like Pell, who was very well known locally, could have touched-up young boys in a public pool without anyone noticing or talking about the matter. But Milligan believed what she wanted to believe – and that meant believing L.M. and D.D. She also reported that M had been abused by an unnamed male "vicious teacher" who "made him masturbate him and perform oral sex". And that D had been repeatedly abused by an unnamed "female relief teacher" – which had an "enormous psychological impact on him". Milligan failed to take up either matter – and Victoria Police did not investigate either case. The focus of Milligan and Victoria Police was on Pell.

In the second half of the program, Milligan extended her case beyond Ballarat to Melbourne in a piece to camera standing outside St Patrick's Cathedral:

Louise Milligan: 7.30 has now seen eight statements to the [SANO] Taskforce from complainants, witnesses and family members. The complaints range over several decades right into the 1990s when George Pell was Archbishop of Melbourne. At that time, he's accused of abusing two teenage choir boys here at St. Patrick's Cathedral.

Milligan told *7.30* viewers that L.M. had been jailed for eleven months for "assaulting his then girlfriend and another man over a drug debt in 2010". And that D.D. had "run foul of the law for assault". She then interviewed a psychologist who said that in the prison system "you see high numbers of men who've been severely abused during their childhood and are now simply labelled as bad". The psychologist was not queried about the fallibility of memory. And Milligan did not repeat what she had said earlier in the program – namely that both L.M. and D.D. claimed to have been abused by others in addition to Pell.

On 28 June 2017, George Pell was charged by Victoria Police with multiple offences of historical child sexual abuse against multiple individuals. Leaks about the likelihood of charges being laid appear to have led to Melbourne University Press bringing forward the publication of Louise Milligan's book *Cardinal* by two months to May 2017. Once Pell was charged, *Cardinal* was withdrawn from sale in Victoria. But it could still be purchased interstate (including at airports) as well as online (including Amazon Books whose website carried material from *Cardinal*.) Milligan's book was available from such sources before and during Pell's trial and re-trial.

Cardinal was launched in Melbourne by Martin Foley – the then Minister for Disability and Ageing, Mental Health, Equality and Creative Industries – at what Melbourne University Press described as "the intimate setting of *The Last Jar* in Melbourne". Foley, the member for Albert Park in Daniel Andrews' Victorian Labor government, was said by MUP to have delivered "a passionate, heartfelt speech about the culture of the Catholic Church and the stories of human suffering and endurance in the book".

In the speech which he released, Foley (who was brought up a Catholic) commenced by praising *Cardinal's* author:

> To the author, Louise Milligan – at a time when the death of journalism has been so regularly predicted, this work shows the best side of your noble calling. This work reflects the finest traditions and holds out hopes that well-researched, evidence-based journalism remains a pillar not only of our democratic system but of an accountable and decent civic culture, where the strong and powerful cannot automatically assume their position to be beyond reproach.

Martin Foley (who like Victorian premier Daniel Andrews and Victorian attorney-general Jill Hennessy is a member of Labor's socialist left faction) continued:

> This is a difficult book that deals with difficult issues. It makes challenging findings and levels grave allegations, whilst leaving the issues of guilt and innocence to the processes of the law and the rightly independent processes of the Director of Public Prosecutions and Victoria Police.
>
> As a member of the executive of the state of Victoria, it is not my role nor my intention to enter the space of guilt or innocence of those subject to allegations made here. Allegations, I note, that are strongly denied. That would be both inappropriate and counter to the efforts of those who seek justice for the events detailed in the book and would deny the presumption of innocence so central to our system.

However, by launching *Cardinal*, Foley did identify himself with a book which even some Pell-antagonists regarded as a case for the prosecution. This was an improper and unprofessional intervention by a senior Victorian government minister concerning what was at the time an on-going police investigation – and when Victoria Police was hinting that Pell would be charged. For example, the following comment by Foley was injudicious and a hindrance to Pell obtaining a fair trial:

> It is my role to launch this book that deals with the story of sexual abuse, cover-up and the culture and practice of a Church and society

that at best stood back and allowed it all to happen, or at worst was an active conspirator and perpetrator in its worst aspects – all highlighted through the career of the Prince of the Church, George Pell.

The use of "Prince of the Church" with respect to Pell was popularised by Pell-antagonist David Marr. Clearly, Foley was suggesting that, at least, Pell was into the cover-up of child sexual abuse in the Catholic Church – and that, at worst, he was "an active conspirator and perpetrator of its worst aspects". That was mid-May 2017. Pell was charged by Victoria Police in July 2017, faced a committal hearing commencing in March 2018 and a magistrates' hearing/trial/re-trial between May and December 2018.

There was a year between Milligan's *7.30* program and the publication of *Cardinal* followed by the decision of Victoria Police to charge George Pell. The enormous publicity created by both events – along with the ongoing hearings of the Royal Commission which focused primarily on the Catholic Church in general and Pell in particular – made it impossible for the accused to receive a fair trial. It's just that Victoria Police and the Victorian Director of Public Prosecutions came to a different view – to the acclaim of the likes of Milligan.

Cardinal became the media's case for the prosecution. This was acknowledged by various reviewers – none of whom were theological conservatives. The key Australian newspapers published reviews of *Cardinal* on the same day – 10 June 2017 – by well-qualified reviewers.

Writing in *The Age* and *The Sydney Morning Herald* (10 June 2017), Peter Craven described *Cardinal* as "a racketing case for the prosecution...a case being mounted for a witch-trial". He wrote that "Milligan does not give the impression of being very well versed either in questions of theology or law" and pointed to the book's "inaccuracies ranging from St Kevin's uniforms to clerical titles". Craven added:

> On questions of personal abuse she is relentless. She rehearses in vast detail the accusations of people who allege that as a young priest at a swimming pool in Ballarat, as he hurled boys over his

shoulder to their delight, he was in fact touching them intimately. She is utterly undeterred by the fact that some quantity of these people, damaged by other ghastly abuse, went on to lives of addiction and domestic violence.

Yes, she's right that this doesn't necessarily discredit their testimony but nor does it do much to authenticate it. Frank Costigan QC said to Geoffrey Robertson once on one of his *Hypotheticals* [TV programs] that he would not challenge someone because he was "one of life's unfortunates" but he would if he thought his testimony was coloured by drugs.

Writing in *The Weekend Australian* (10 June 2017), Gerard Windsor described *Cardinal* as "an attack" which exhibited an "animus" towards its subject. While praising the "enormity" of Milligan's work, Windsor doubted its key accusations:

> The jury, as they say, is still out on all these accusations. Individual stories have their puzzling, even questionable elements. Two boys at the same time in a room in his own cathedral? How easily does one "walk past the open door of the presbytery" and see "the aftermath of a rape"? If you're throwing boys into the air in a pool, is it easy to make sure your hands touch only non-private parts of their bodies?

In conclusion, Windsor asked: "Have we ever previously had such a damning character vivisection of a public figure?" It was a good question – but not one that troubled Victoria Police or the Victorian DPP before prosecuting Pell before a jury.

Writing in the *Australian Book Review* (October 2017), Pell-antagonist Barney Zwartz acknowledged that *Cardinal* "mounts a strong case for the prosecution". You can say that again.

I finished reading *Cardinal* in late May 2017. At 4.03 pm on Tuesday 30 May 2017, before writing about the book, I forwarded questions to the author – pointing out that "it has always been journalistic practice to send a list of questions to a person concerning whom you intend to write". There were eleven questions in all – which can be found in my *Media Watch Dog* blog for Friday 1 June 2017 and are reproduced in Appendix 1. My queries turned on several areas, including:

• The use of anonymous sources in a book which contains serious allegations. For example, *Cardinal* cites as evidence for the case against Pell (i) "one senior member of a religious order", (ii) "another Royal Commission source", (iii) "one of the most senior members on the curia of the Melbourne archdiocese of the time", (iv) "one church official", (v) "officials in the church", (vi) "a friend …who is a mother in the neighbourhood", (vii) "someone who works around the Royal Commission", (viii) "the father-in-law of an ABC journalist", (ix) "people who knew George Pell in his Ballarat days" and (x) "many" – cited on several occasions.

My concern was that Milligan had allowed anonymous individuals, none of whom claimed to be victims, to condemn Pell in a way that a reader had no chance of assessing their credibility or motives or of checking the accuracy of their allegations.

• The question of memory. At Page 101 Milligan wrote that "memory does strange things when it comes to visual description of people". Yet, elsewhere in the book, the author accepted the visual recollection of C – the man who made allegations about Pell at Phillip Island – despite the fact that he identified on a TV news report a person (Pell) he had not seen for around four decades and was reliant on his memory for faces to identify Pell as a young man who had allegedly attacked him four decades previously.

• The issue of direct quotation marks. At page 47 Milligan put in direct quotes the recollection of an elderly woman who claimed to have overheard Pell having a conversation some two decades previously. Yet the woman conceded that she was in the room next door and Pell was determined that his (alleged) conversation with her cousin in the other room could not be heard.

• The use of hearsay. On the basis of hearsay upon hearsay, in Chapter 6 of *Cardinal,* Milligan re-constructed in direct quotes the precise words which she alleged Pell had used some three decades previously. There was no independent evidence that Pell made any of the comments attributed to him in direct quotations by Milligan.

Milligan not only declined to answer my quite reasonable questions. She went so far as to seek the protection of her publisher Louise Adler, MUP's chief executive. At 5.10 pm on Tuesday 30 May 2017, I received the following email from Adler:

> Dear Gerard,
>
> Your correspondence has been forwarded to me as the book is not an ABC book, it is an MUP publication written in Louise Milligan's private time.
>
> MUP stands by the forensic and meticulous research that the author conducted to produce this important contribution to the community's understanding of the Catholic Church's response to child abuse.
>
> Best wishes,
>
> Louise

In response, the following day, I advised Louise Adler that I knew who was the publisher of *Cardinal* – but that my questions were directed to the author. I added:

> When MUP published my book *Santamaria: A Most Unusual Man* in 2015, I did not expect you – in your capacity as MUP's chief executive – to answer questions or criticisms about my work. Likewise, I expect that Louise Milligan will respond to my queries about her book *Cardinal* – and not attempt to avoid legitimate questions about her work by flicking the matter to her publisher. It's called a cop-out. A high profile ABC reporter should be able to do better….
>
> Sure, answering rigorous questions about *Cardinal* is more difficult than Ms Milligan doing soft interviews with her ABC "besties". But a Gold Quill winner should be up to the task.

Louise Milligan never answered any of my questions. Nor did she ever engage in discussion – on the ABC or at literary festivals – with an informed person who was critical, to a greater or lesser extent, of *Cardinal*. It would appear that she is super sensitive to criticism – or not able to take tough questions on her book. Probably both. But Milligan did correct one of the errors in the first edition of *Cardinal* to which I drew her attention. Milligan's sensitivity to criticism intensified after the High Court decided on 13 November 2019 that it would hear Pell's case in a sitting in early 2020.

On 16 November 2019, Pell-antagonist and journalist for the leftist online newspaper *The New Daily* Quentin Dempster put out this tweet – to which Milligan responded:

> Quentin Dempster @ Quentin Dempster Nov 16
> Dr Gerard Henderson attacks @Milliganreports and David Marr @GuardianAus over their George Pell case commentary. His Oz column 16/11/19. It seems every journalist is an "activist" except Dr Henderson – a self-appointed Pell Apologetic.
> Louise Milligan
> @Milliganreports
>
> Replying to @QuentinDempster and @GuardianAus
> Honestly, Quentin, don't copy me in on commentary from this vile bully. I don't want to hear about his paedophile-protecting nonsense.
> 3.53 PM . Nov 16, 2019

The intensity and anger of some Pell-antagonists was never more evident than in this exchange between Dempster and Milligan. Dempster responded to my column in *The Weekend Australian* on 16 November 2019 which was headed "Activist reporting to fore again in Pell appeal comment". This was a considered response to the reaction by some Pell-antagonists to the High Court's decision on 13 November 2019 that George Pell's case be referred to a Full Court of the High Court for argument as an appeal.

My column commenced with a comment about the increasing blur between the journalist as reporter and the journalist as activist – with special reference to Milligan and Marr. I pointed out that, shortly before the High Court's decision, Milligan had been asked to preview the case on the ABC Sydney Radio 702 *Breakfast* program by presenters Wendy Harmer and Robbie Buck. Milligan said that Pell's application "has probably been denied". She added that the criminal lawyers she had spoken to "have said there doesn't seem to be a clear appeal point here". Hopelessly wrong.

Immediately after the decision, Milligan appeared on ABC Radio on Melbourne 774's *Mornings with Virginia Trioli*. Asked if she was surprised by the decision, Milligan responded that "certainly a lot of media discussion in the past few days and people that I've been talking to, criminal barristers etc have been saying that they thought it would go the other way". This said a lot about Milligan's sources – since, in view of Justice Weinberg's very strong dissent in the Victorian Court of Appeal, there was always a significant chance that the matter would be considered by the High Court.

Trioli and Milligan seemed surprised that the case had been heard "on the papers" – that is without a hearing. They were apparently unaware that this is always an option with special leave to appeal applications. And both women believed that the High Court does not look at evidence but, as Trioli put it, "it can only look at very elevated aspects of the law". Clearly they were not aware of the High Court decision in *M v The Queen* where the judges assessed whether the jury should have had a reasonable doubt with respect to M's guilt. This had nothing to do with "very elevated aspects of the law".

Milligan's lack of objectivity towards the defence was evident when she told Trioli that "from the point of view of a lot of people who are affected by this case, it certainly prolongs the process…it's just sad". Milligan added: "It's that feeling in the pit of the stomach that just won't go away". Clearly Milligan was too emotionally involved in the case to report dispassionately on the views of both parties. The key issue here was that the ABC was engaging a Pell-antagonist to comment on a news event about Pell. Moreover, the only people directly affected by the case were the complainant (and his family) and the defendant (and his family). Here Milligan was implying that Pell was responsible for the crimes of others.

In my *Weekend Australian* column of 16 November 2019, I also criticised the fact that ABC TV's *The Drum* had asked David Marr to provide the only expert comment on the Pell Case after the High Court decision of 13 November 2019. Marr had previously predicted that the High Court would uphold the jury verdict and had not foreseen that an appeal had any prospect of success. Marr did not explain away his earlier false prediction but proceeded to prosecute the case against Pell by stating that "properly instructed juries can deal with famous people".

Presenter Ellen Fanning did not ask why, then, had all mainland States except Victoria introduced trial by judge alone. In his comments on *The Drum*, Marr made it clear that he believed that the High Court should uphold the jury's verdict that Pell was guilty beyond reasonable doubt. No other view was heard as yet another Pell- antagonist was engaged by the ABC to comment on the Pell Case as a news event.

My *Weekend Australian* column – to which Dempster objected – also quoted Chief Judge Kidd's sentencing judgment that Pell was not to be made a scapegoat for "other victims of clerical or institutional abuse". And I quoted Justice Weinberg's comment in his Victorian Court of Appeal dissent that "juries almost always get it right" and his clarification that "the word is almost". The column concluded:

> The fact is the media pile-on against Pell, in which Milligan and Marr played prominent roles, contributed to the lynch mob mentality that Kidd condemned [in his sentencing judgment]. But they were the go-to commentators when the ABC was seeking comment on the High Court decision on Wednesday. Their views were contestable — but were not contested.

Contrary to Dempster's assertion, my column was not an "attack" on Milligan and Marr. It accurately reflected their position on Pell. Also, it was essentially a criticism of the ABC for its one-sided commentary on the case. But Milligan used the occasion to describe me as a "vile bully" who engaged in "pedophile protecting". I emailed David Anderson, the ABC's managing director and editor-in-chief on 16 November 2019, and asked whether he thought that it was appropriate for one of his senior journalists to describe a columnist as a "vile bully" who was into "pedophile protecting" – without any evidence. Anderson responded the following day: "I will look into it and get back to you." He never did.

Not long after Milligan's outburst, she tweeted that I was "pathologically weird and creepy" and agreed with Pell-antagonist Ray Martin that my comments on her coverage of the Pell Case had been "defamatory" (2 December 2019) – but cited not one (alleged) defamation. This seems to have been an example of the psychological phenomenon known as projection – Milligan had defamed me but she alleged that I had defamed her. She bullied me by publicly stating that I was into "pedophile protecting" – but alleged that I was bullying her without stating any evidence to support the claim.

The point is that Louise Milligan was always a player in the Pell Case. Despite this, the ABC encouraged her to both report and comment on the matter. In December 2019, while Pell's appeal to the High Court against the Victorian Court of Appeal's decision to uphold the jury verdict was underway, Milligan bought into a Twitter debate about Justice Mark Weinberg – who had dissented in the Victorian Court of Appeal and come to a different opinion to Chief Justice Ferguson and President Maxwell. It led to this exchange involving Hobart-based barrister Greg Barns SC and Melbourne journalist Gay Alcorn:

> *Louise Milligan:* This convicted paedophile's mates in the media have insulted and patronised Maxwell P and Ferguson CJ uphill and down dale and implied that Weinberg someone [sic] knew more than them. I am simply subjecting the evidence of that to the scrutiny it deserves.
> Dec 6, 2019

Greg Barns SC: You are not. Louise you are a player in this case from the get go. You have no objectivity on #pell
Dec 7, 2019

Earlier, on 3 December 2019, Milligan made angry criticisms of Justice Weinberg – as the following *Twitter* exchange demonstrates:

Catholic Watcher: A whole slab of public discourse is also devoted to asking if the Pell verdicts should be upheld, including from people who haven't any allegiance to the Cardinal and/or the Church but an interest in the justice system
Dec 3, 2019

Gay Alcorn: Indeed, given dissenting judge [Weinberg] is highly respected and the most experienced of the 3 in criminal matters (and as a former prosecutor not instinctively disposed towards defence), it remains a fraught case. You don't have to be a one-eyed Pell supporter to acknowledge that.
Dec 3, 2019

Louise Milligan: His [Weinberg's] experience is Commonwealth jurisdiction. Not sexual matters. Perhaps why he thought grabbing boy's genitals in busy corridor implausibly brazen. I'd invite his Honour to speak to women. Not sure about you, Gay, but happened to me, many times. & my friends. Men do that stuff.
Dec 3, 2019

Greg Barns SC: Wrong Weinberg JA has extensive experience in criminal law both state and federal. He is regarded as the top criminal appeal judge in Australia.
Dec 4, 2019

Milligan's activism is evident in her assertion that, because she and some female friends had been groped by men, Justice Weinberg was naïve to query whether Pell would have groped a young boy in the midst of a procession at St Patrick's Cathedral in the presence of some

40 to 50 others without anyone noticing. As it turned out, all three female High Court judges came to a judgment on this matter similar to that of Justice Weinberg – clearly Milligan's reference to Weinberg's need to speak to women on this matter was a sneer.

For the record, at the time Gay Alcorn was the Melbourne editor of *The Guardian*. She was one of the few left-wing journalists who commented on the case dispassionately. In this Twitter exchange, Alcorn later wrote that, while not a Pell supporter, she was "married to a criminal barrister and knew many" who regarded Weinberg's dissent as "important". It would seem, from her 13 November 2019 conversation with Trioli, that Milligan took her legal advice from different sources.

Greg Barns SC was one of the few civil libertarian lawyers in Australia to speak out that Pell should be treated with justice. His comments were consistent with the position reached later by the High Court - unlike Milligan's legal sources.

When Pell was convicted, and some weeks before the verdict was publicly released, Milligan put a red heart on her *Twitter* feed. When the conviction was quashed by the High Court, she tweeted "Hug your children". An activist, to be sure.

Once again, the problem was that the ABC engaged this activist journalist to both report and comment on George Pell. Even after Pell was convicted, and he had lodged an appeal to the Victorian Court of Appeal, ABC management allowed Milligan to present a *Four Corners* program on the case on 4 March 2019. It was titled "Guilty: The Conviction of Cardinal Pell". Sarah Curnow and Jeanavive McGregor were the producers and Sally Neighbour the executive producer.

Pell's appeal against the jury verdict had been lodged a couple of weeks earlier – on 21 February 2019. This was only mentioned at the end of the program. Before then, Milligan only interviewed individuals who were either hostile to or highly critical of Pell – including Doug Smith (former SANO Taskforce sergeant), Bernard Barrett (Broken Rites) and Vivian Waller (the complainant's lawyer). Also interviewed was Les Tyack – who featured prominently on Milligan's

7.30 program and in her book *Cardinal*. On *Four Corners*, Tyack claimed to have called Pell a "dirty, rotten, sneaking, conniving bastard" in the mid-1980s. There is no independent evidence that such a comment was ever made or that Tyack ever spoke to Pell.

After following hearings of the Royal Commission, Tyack went to Victoria Police and reported that he had seen Pell standing naked in a change room in such a manner that his private parts could be seen by young boys. Tyack was not brought up a Catholic and had no special knowledge of Catholic clerics. Still he claimed in February 2016 that he had seen Pell naked in the Torquay Surf Club during what he estimated to be the summer of 1986-87 – that is, some three decades earlier. By the mid-1980s to then, Fr Pell had only resided in Melbourne for a couple of years and was not well known, especially to non-Catholics.

There were no witnesses to this alleged event. Moreover, while acknowledging that he spent time at Torquay over the Christmas/New Year holiday period around this time, Pell said he always changed at the house in which he stayed – and never at the Torquay Surf Club. Milligan did not tell *Four Corners* viewers this. This is how "Guilty" concluded:

> *Louise Milligan:* County Court Chief Judge Peter Kidd described Pell's crimes as "...callous, brazen offending... He exploited two vulnerable boys and there was an element of force... There was an element of brutality to this assault. It was an attack." George Pell maintains his innocence and is appealing. A 77-year-old man, who once cast an enormous shadow over the Australian Church and culture, is now in jail awaiting sentence.
>
> *Doug Smith Former Sergeant, Taskforce SANO:* There'd probably be millions of people out there who will look at it and think how important it is. That no-one's above the law. The Catholic Church isn't above the law. A lot of times the system doesn't work. But this time, the system has worked and there's going to be a lot of people who are going to benefit from that.

Milligan did not tell viewers that Chief Judge Kidd said in his sentencing remarks that he was not second-guessing the jury's decision and that he was required by law to accept the veracity of its findings. Also Doug Smith's comment was disingenuous in that the Catholic Church has never said it is above the law – evident by the fact that, before Pell's conviction, there were a number of male Catholic clergy in prison for child sexual assault, including Ridsdale.

Milligan's "Guilty" was just a re-statement of the case for the prosecution she had originally broadcast on *7.30* in 2016 and re-run in *Cardinal* the following year. Milligan even said again that "George Pell lived in St Alipius presbytery at the same time as the notorious child abuser Gerald Ridsdale" – without mentioning that this was for around one year and that her journalist colleague Paul Bongiorno had once lived in the same presbytery as Ridsdale for about a year.

Nevertheless "Guilty" had an impact on Sydney Radio 2GB presenter and Pell- antagonist Ray Hadley who told his listeners on Tuesday 5 March 2019 that he had watched the program three times and had become absolutely convinced of Pell's guilt. Like Milligan, Hadley believed what he wanted to believe.

This decision by ABC management to provide Milligan with the opportunity to do an entire *Four Corners* program on Pell, after his conviction but before his appeal, was criticised – following Pell's acquittal – by ABC TV *Media Watch* presenter Paul Barry.

Barry is not a Pell supporter and he is not frequently critical of his ABC colleagues. On *Media Watch* (20 April 2020), Barry argued that while the ABC "probably" did not get "their judgments on Pell 100 per cent right" nevertheless he did not think that the Pell Case was a "dark day for journalism". A controversial conclusion, in view of the media pile-on which was led by the ABC. However, concerning Louise Milligan's "Guilty", Barry had this to say:

> *Media Watch* pointed out at the time that Pell might appeal…And we warned that all the week's screaming headlines, quote, "may need scrubbing out". There was, however, no such caution from Louise Milligan and *Four Corners*, which did not canvass any of

Pell's defence from the trial — in my view it should have done….

Milligan held the view that Pell's appeal would not succeed in the Victorian Court of Appeal — she was correct, following the two to one majority decision. Then she maintained that Pell would not get leave to appeal (or something similar) to the High Court. Wrong. Then she believed that Pell's appeal would not succeed before the full court of the High Court. Wrong again — this time by a seven to zero unanimous decision.

Now it is clear that Milligan does not accept the High Court's decision — as is evident in her book *Witness: An Investigation into the Brutal Cost of Seeking Justice* (Hachette Australia), published in late October 2020. Also on 15 November 2020, in response to a comment by Senator Jim Molan, Milligan drew his attention to the "findings of the two most senior judges in Victoria" plus the jury in the re-trial. She simply ignored the High Court's unanimous decision.

Since Milligan was a player in the Pell Case, it came as no surprise that she was called to appear during the committal hearings before the Victorian Magistrates' Court. She spent a whole day in the witness box on Tuesday 27 March 2018 under cross-examination by Robert Richter QC. Earlier, on 11 July 2017, Milligan had made a statement to Victoria Police concerning the complainants against Pell with whom she had been in touch — which made her a player in the case.

It was not clear that the Richter/Milligan cross-examination was a wise decision. In March 2018, the pugnacious barrister was 72 years of age. Whereas the pugnacious journalist was 43 years old. In the modern era, it's probably best to avoid an older man cross-examining a younger woman — especially in a sexual assault case. Ruth Shann, Richter's extremely able assistant, would probably have been a better choice to lead in this point of the committal hearings. Nevertheless, optics aside, Richter cut through Milligan's case a number of times.

It turned out to be a testy exchange. On no fewer than 50 occasions, Milligan responded to Richter's questions with a "can't recall", "can't remember" or "don't remember" response. She also evoked journalistic privilege not to reveal what her sources had told her on several occasions. Magistrate Wallington declined to agree with Richter's request that the witness be compelled to answer some of his questions. Milligan was handled gently by the magistrate. Richter, on the other hand, was treated harshly by Wallington.

Moreover, on a number of occasions, Milligan answered "I just didn't" to questions as to why she had not asked M and D how Pell managed to fondle their genitals with one hand while his other hand was holding their feet under the water before propelling them into the air – without anyone noticing.

There was a similar "I just didn't" answer to the question as to why Milligan had not checked when Pell might have said Solemn Mass in the Cathedral in 1996 or 1997 – in view of the fact that A was in doubt about the dates of the alleged offending. And when asked why she had not asked any one-time choirboys whether they had even seen Pell at St Patrick's Cathedral alone when in full robes – she replied "I asked them other things".

However, the most surprising testimony came near the end of the hearing when the following exchange took place:

> *Robert Richter:* ...your book was a pre-judgment of [Pell's] guilt, was it not?
>
> *Louise Milligan:* I don't agree with that.
>
> *Robert Richter:* You don't? Anyone sensibly reading that book – with you expressing belief in certain people [i.e. the complainant] – would be justified in concluding that it was a pre-judgment of guilt before charges were laid? –
>
> *Louise Milligan:* I don't agree with that.
>
> *Robert Richter*: You do not?
>
> Louise Milligan: No.
>
> *Robert Richter:* Why not?
>
> *Louise Milligan:* Because I was very fair to the Cardinal in the book.
>
> *Robert Richter:* Were you?
>
> *Louise Milligan:* M'hmm.

Robert Richter: Okay. All right. So you didn't pre-judge him in the book? That's your evidence?

Louise Milligan: Yes.

Robert Richter: You did not in any way suggest that his accusers were to be believed?

Louise Milligan: I thought his accusers were believable.

Robert Richter: No, no, no. Did you suggest that they were to be believed?

Mr Gibson [Crown Prosecutor]: Asked and answered Your Honour.

Mr Richter: No.

Mr Gibson: We had this question before, today.

Mr Richter: I don't think so. Can't recall it.

Her Honour [Belinda Wallington]: I remember some fairly lengthy cross-examination on that topic hours ago.

Mr Richter: That wasn't asked.

Her Honour: I think it was.

At this point, following the intervention of Crown Prosecutor Gibson and Magistrate Wallington, Milligan was able to avoid answering the question as to whether when writing *Cardinal* she held the view that the complainants in the case were to be believed. A reading of the transcript does not indicate that Richter's question – as to whether the complaints were to be believed – was in fact answered earlier. However, Richter did raise questions about Milligan's view on the accusers' credibility. The cross examination continued:

Mr Richter: No. Well, in which case the answer will be evident. (To witness) And having pre-judged the Cardinal?

Louise Milligan: I don't accept that that's the case.

Mr Richter: Well, I'm putting it to you as an accusation and you don't accept it?

Louise Milligan: I don't accept it.

Mr Richter: I'm putting it to you as an accusation that you came to know that charges were imminent in June 2017, and that as a consequence the publication [of *Cardinal*] was rushed so you could beat them?

Louise Milligan: That's your opinion, Mr Richter, and I disagree with it emphatically.

Mr Richter: I'm putting it to you and you can disagree, which you do?

Louise Milligan: I just did....

It was an interesting response. Louise Milligan gave sworn evidence on 27 March 2018 that *Cardinal* was "very fair" to George Pell and did not pre-judge him. But she had told Virginia Trioli on 16 May 2017 that *Cardinal* was written "from the complainants' point of view". It's difficult to see how a book written from the point of view of Pell's accusers can be "very fair" to Pell. Likewise it's difficult to accept Milligan's account that she thought the likes of A were merely "believable" – in view of the fact that, shortly after news of Pell's conviction was announced, she told ABC TV News: "I defy anyone to meet this man [A] and to think he is not telling the truth".

Louise Milligan declined to answer questions about *Cardinal* and never willingly engaged with critics of her work. Indeed, the only exposure of her book occurred before the Magistrates' Court where she failed to recall many instances relating to the matter. This means that Milligan's case against Pell has never been subjected to critical analysis – especially with respect to her claims concerning A and B, which played a key role in Pell becoming the defendant in the *Cathedral Trial*.

A reading of *Cardinal* makes it clear that A never spoke to Milligan about his alleged assault by Pell in St Patrick's Cathedral. Milligan did talk to B's mother about A and B (who died in 2014). B told both his parents that he had never been sexually assaulted. Assuming that Milligan is an accurate reporter, what we learn in *Cardinal* about A's case is what B allegedly told his mother about what A had allegedly told him – as told to Milligan by B's mother. This is hearsay upon hearsay.

According to Mrs B (i.e. B's mother), A and B "used to play in the back of the Cathedral in the closed-off rooms". This could not have been immediately after Solemn Mass on Sunday when such behaviour would have been impossible. But it could relate to a time before or after choir practice in the Cathedral which was sometimes held on weekdays.

This is what Victoria Police had told Pell before the interview in Rome – namely that the alleged assaults had occurred "after choir" – which, presumably, meant after choir practice. It seems that Victoria Police at the time were unaware that Pell did not live in the Cathedral and only attended there for Mass. Mrs B gave Milligan the impression that A and B were encountered by Pell in a room which they had frequented on a number of occasions "after choir".

In the first edition of *Cardinal*, Mrs B is said to have told Milligan that A had told her that Pell had locked the door of the room. But in the second edition, Milligan changes this – saying that A had said that Pell blocked, not locked, the door – in other words the alleged offences took place in a room with an open door. This is what A said in court. But it was not clear whether Milligan's report of her conversation with Mrs B was faulty or whether Mrs B's recollection was wrong or whether A changed his position. Also it is not clear whether Milligan re-checked with Mrs B about the locked/blocked door contradiction.

There are other inconsistencies. In the first edition of *Cardinal*, the author reported that B had told his mother (Mrs B) that A had been picked up after the incident by his parents. In the second edition of *Cardinal*, there was no reference at all to "parents" having picked up A. Again, it is not clear whether the error was caused by a Milligan inaccurate report or by Mrs B's account of what A had told the late B or whether A just changed his mind. When A gave evidence at the trial it appears that he was not aware of which adult had picked him up – according to the case put by both the prosecution and the defence.

However, neither the first nor subsequent editions of *Cardinal* changes the author's report that Mrs B told her that A and B were assaulted by Pell when "playing in the back of the Church in closed-off rooms".

But A subsequently claimed that the assaults took place in the priests' sacristy after Solemn Mass on a Sunday. The issue is this – if Mrs B's account is incorrect about this matter, why should it be accepted by Milligan concerning related matters? Like many an activist journalist, *Cardinal* demonstrates that Louise Milligan believes what she wants to believe.

On 30 January 2019, Louise Adler stepped down as MUP's chief executive officer after 15 years in that position. Su Baker, Melbourne University's Pro Vice-Chancellor (Engagement), paid tribute to Adler's "remarkable service to Melbourne University Publishing". The following day Robert Bolton reported in the *Australian Financial Review* that MUP was costing Melbourne University $1.25 million a year to operate and had run deficits for over 15 years – which was why it had been restructured.

Adler took up the position as chief executive officer of Hachette Australia in early September 2019 and became the go-to publisher for Pell-antagonists. In 2020, Hachette published Louise Milligan's *Witness: An Investigation into the Brutal Cost of Seeking Justice* with *Revelation* by Sarah Ferguson and Tony Jones to follow.

Early in *Witness,* Milligan declared "this book…is not about me". But it is. Later, she wrote "this is not a book about Pell". But it is. Around a third of the chapters in *Witness* focus on Pell and he is covered elsewhere in the book.

A significant part of *Witness* turns on the trauma Milligan experienced when called to give evidence at Pell's committal proceedings in the Victorian Magistrates' Court and when Pell's defence team tried to obtain documents from her before the County Court. The latter action was dropped because Pell did not want his trial delayed by protracted proceedings about access to documents.

As *Witness* attests, Milligan could not sleep before the Magistrates' Court hearing, experienced a sick feeling that continued for months such that she felt suspended from the ceiling. After her day in court, Milligan was "unable to get out of bed" – indeed she "could not move".

There's no reason to disbelieve any of the above – but it is appropriate to point out that Milligan was only a witness – not the accused or a complainant or a victim. Moreover, Milligan held her own in the witness box and was lawyered-up with her own legal team assisted by the ABC's legal department.

Witness makes some strong points about how defence counsel deal with the evidence of complainants/victims. But the author barely considers that not all accused individuals are guilty – although many are – and that the accused are entitled to be defended.

Milligan emerges as the hero of her own book for standing up to the likes of Robert Richter QC in the Magistrates' Court and for fighting Pell's defence which was trying to get access to her material that had played an important part in the decision by Victoria Police to prosecute Pell in the Country Court.

Milligan's emotive involvement in the anti-Pell Case is evident in *Witness* when she recounts an occasion when she was interviewed by fellow ABC colleague Margaret Throsby at the fashionable leftist Byron Bay Literary Festival in August 2018:

> I had two sessions at the festival. The last one was with legendary ABC broadcaster Margaret Throsby. I wasn't permitted to discuss anything to do with the allegations about Pell. I talked about the damning history of sexual abuse in the Catholic Church.
>
> Throsby asked in a careful way about the impact of my journalism. I told her and the crowd that, the next day, I was going to have to go to a court to protect my confidential sources… All I said was that "my sources came from a community of people that have been profoundly betrayed by an institution. And I will not betray them".
>
> There was a standing ovation. I looked out, bleary-eyed, at the crowed, trying to stop my hands from shaking. People were weeping. I walked off the stage, people gripped my hands and hugged me and told me to be strong, they'd be thinking of me.

At the time virtually no one in the audience knew anything about the details of the charges against Pell. But their enthusiasm suggested that they disliked Pell and the Catholic Church. And they found their own saviour in Milligan.

After her years of activist-campaigning against Pell, Milligan found it hard to accept the High Court's unanimous decision in *Pell v The Queen*. On 14 April 2020, a week after Pell's conviction was quashed, Channel 9 News put out this tweet:

> #BREAKING: Police have visited the Sydney seminary where George Pell is currently staying.
>
> It follows reports by NewsCorp the Cardinal is being investigated over fresh child abuse allegations. @Eliza_Rugg9 #9News

Louise Milligan re-tweeted the 9 News breaking story, with her own interpretation attached:

> *Louise Milligan:* I am told there are complaints in more than one jurisdiction. That is, not just Victoria. And they are more recent. #Pell

In fact, NSW Police visited the seminary in Homebush in response to a possible security incident with respect to Pell. Despite Eliza Rugg's Channel 9 report and Milligan's initial statement, there was no evidence that police in any jurisdiction were investigating new complaints against Pell.

In December 2020, Milligan was interviewed by Astrid Edwards for *The Garrett* podcast. It was another soft interview – this time about *Witness* and related matters. At the conclusion of the discussion, Edwards commented: "I adore your honesty – and I have to say I respect your compassion, your integrity and your intellect as well." Towards the end of the interview, Milligan had this to say:

> …the High Court ultimately found that there must have been a reasonable doubt in the jury. It decided in its wisdom, that it knew better than the jury who sat and watched every single day of evidence. I don't understand why they can just push away everything else that has been exposed about this person [Pell], but it just tells you a lot about the way that some people in the community are really fixed in their views, and they just don't want to know anything that might

tear down people that align with them.

This is an unprofessional criticism of the High Court. Any considered person who read the transcript of the two days hearings in *Pell v The Queen*, or watched the video, would know that all seven judges were completely across all the evidence. One of the roles of appeal courts is to scrutinise jury verdicts. Milligan does not appear to understand this. And the idea that High Court judges "don't want to know anything that might tear down people that align with them" is meaningless jargon. The interview demonstrated that Louise Milligan did not approach the Pell Case with the necessary impartiality and detachment expected of a professional journalist.

• Lucie Morris-Marr Fails to Anticipate High Court Judgment

On 5 October 2020, Lucie Morris-Marr tweeted that she "had attended every minute of the Pell mistrial and re-trial". This was not the case. In fact, no journalist saw the complainant give evidence in the committal hearing or at the first trial – since this is not allowed by Victorian law. In the re-trial, the video of the complainant's evidence at the first trial was re-played as required by Victorian law – and, again, reporters were not allowed to witness the occasion.

Yet it is true that Morris-Marr was present at all times that she was allowed to attend – at the committal proceedings and the subsequent trials. She did so as a reporter for *The New Daily* – an online, non-paywalled Australian newspaper which is owned by Industry Super Holdings, a superannuation fund comprised primarily of individual trade union superannuation funds. Morris-Marr also covered the Pell Case for CNN.

Morris-Marr, along with *The Guardian's* Melissa Davey, were the two journalists to report every day of Pell's hearings/trials when the courts were open. As such, their work is a valuable source of material. Provided it is borne in mind that both journalists were, and remain, Pell-antagonists.

On 2 November 2016, Morris-Marr tweeted in response to a claim by

Herald Sun columnist Andrew Bolt that Pell was the victim of a witch hunt – commenting: "When it comes to child abuse, I'm happy to be the witch leading the hunt." It follows that Morris-Marr acted in this manner not just as a reporter but also as an activist. So much so that, on 27 September 2020 – around six months after Pell's acquittal by the High Court – Morris-Marr referred to him in a tweet as a "former convicted pedophile". He was, in fact, by then an innocent man.

Like many journalists, Morris-Marr criticises others but is very sensitive to criticism. On 3 March 2019, she put out the following tweet:

> *Lucie Morris-Marr:* What Pell and his media mates have done to me since 2016 – 1: Pell wrote to Vic Police and the government demanding enquiries into my original scoop. 2: Bolt @theheraldsun said my story was a smear and demanded to know sources. 3: Gerard Henderson @australian defamed and attacked me.

All George Pell had done was to object to Victoria Police that it had leaked to the media that there was an investigation into his case – something Pell was perfectly entitled to do, irrespective of the journalist who had reported the story. That's all. Andrew Bolt had engaged in criticism about the nature of Morris-Marr's story which, as a journalist and commentator, he was perfectly entitled to do. And then there was her final objection about the author of this book.

Sure, I criticised some of Morris-Marr's reporting of the Pell Case. After all, I am a commentator with a weekly column and a weekly blog. But I never defamed her – and she never initiated defamation proceedings against me. In her book *Fallen,* Morris-Marr reflected that I might have been instructed by News Corp proprietor Rupert Murdoch "to help out Australia's most senior Catholic". She added: "I had no proof at all that the chairman [Murdoch] was involved, but it was little wonder my bewildered, sleepless brain was starting to liquefy as I tried to make sense of the turmoil." In short, Morris-Marr is willing to make allegations concerning which she admits to having "no proof".

Having described my criticism of her in *The Weekend Australian* of

26 February 2016 as "the last straw", Morris-Marr wrote in *Fallen*:

> ...at home in Melbourne the complex ramifications of my scoop were finally pushing me over the edge. I had given my heart and soul in my search for the truth; I'd listened to the most horrific stories in Ballarat to try to help and understand those haunted victims without a voice; I'd worked with sensitive sources to uncover the news of the secret Pell police operation; and now I was lost at sea and had nothing firm to hold on to amid the mayhem. I was now paying a very personal price for my passionate defence of the story; I no longer knew who to trust at News Corp and I was mentally and physically exhausted. A sleeping tablet hadn't helped. An ambulance was called.

It's appropriate to sympathise with the stress Morris-Marr felt in response to criticism. But it's also appropriate to sympathise with Pell who was under investigation by Victoria Police, news of which had found its way to Morris-Marr who was then working at the *Herald Sun* in Melbourne. The fact is that, as it happened, Pell never went on trial for alleged offences committed when he was in Ballarat to which the author refers to in *Fallen*. For the record, I have never communicated with Rupert Murdoch about the Pell Case. At the time, Morris-Marr, Bolt and myself all wrote for News Corp newspapers – the *Herald Sun* (Morris-Marr, Bolt) or *The Australian* (myself). What took place was a debate within News Corp papers about what was to become one of the most important criminal cases in Australian history.

The fact is that Morris-Marr received a leak that Pell was being investigated by Victoria Police shortly before the opening of the Royal Commission's case study concerning historical child sexual abuse in the Catholic Church's Ballarat diocese. In view of this, it stood to reason that at least some commentators would query Morris-Marr's sources and the timing involved.

Like many members of the media's Pell pile-on, Morris-Marr was a player in the case. This is evident from her interventions in the matter. The first chapter of Morris-Marr's *Fallen* focuses on a trip which the author made to visit a woman in the Gippsland area of Victoria "who may have some essential information about Cardinal George Pell"- given the name "Margaret". As the author put it:

> It was believed that the woman had named a mystery priest who saw her getting abused [by Gerald Ridsdale] in either 1972 or 1973 in her private victim's impact statement tendered to the court. He'd failed to intervene. He [Pell] simply walked past and did nothing. The victim was ten or eleven at the time. In 1972 Pell would visit his family in the area [Ballarat] while he was working in his first role as an assistant priest a few hours away in Swan Hill. He has confirmed in the past that he then lived as a resident at the presbytery in 1973. The dates potentially matched.

And so it went on. "Margaret" declined to give any details to Morris-Marr. There is no evidence as to the identity of the priest who allegedly walked past the room where the alleged rape was taking place. But, without a shred of evidence, Morris-Marr came to the conclusion that it was Pell. As she said to "Margaret", as reported in *Fallen*:

> ...if Pell saw anything happen to you and did nothing to help, he deserves to be brought to justice. That's what I care about and why I came here to see you, to see if you'd help me. When I read details of what happened to you, I cried. I think it's a disgrace because you weren't helped by Pell....well, he's right up there in Rome, he's number three, and if he's possibly witnessed anything that happened to you then he deserves to be held accountable.

That was on Page 19. "Margaret" does not appear in *Fallen* again until Page 328 where the following comment is made concerning the situation after Pell's conviction but before his acquittal:

> He [the complainant A] may also have brought courage to a woman in Gippsland who should have been saved, not ignored as a tiny girl trapped in Ridsdale's ruthless grip. For those many legacies, his [A's] voice will never be forgotten. He'd proved to the world the meek really can inherit the earth.

Morris-Marr produced no evidence whatsoever that Pell saw Ridsdale do anything to "Margaret". Like Milligan, she simply believes what she wants to believe. It's possible that Ridsdale raped "Margaret" –

even though he mainly targeted boys – but there is not a skerrick of evidence that any such incident was observed by Pell.

The problem with activist journalists is that they are so involved in a case that it affects their judgment. On 26 February 2019, Morris-Marr published a piece in *The New Daily* titled, "Tantrum and tears: The moment the George Pell verdict was delivered". It purported to be an eye witness account of the events in the court room on the afternoon of Tuesday 11 December 2018 when the jury delivered its guilty verdict. She wrote:

> Pell's most high-profile supporter, former deputy prime minister Tim Fischer, had been at court to support Pell in the final days of the trial despite suffering from leukaemia. On that day he was absent. But loyal supporters Katrina Lee, executive advisor from the Archdiocese of Sydney and human rights lawyer Father Frank Brennan remained poker-faced in their seats.

Brennan, may, or may not, have been poker faced on that day. But he was not in court – nor, indeed, in Victoria. Rather Brennan was driving from Canberra to Bathurst – a thousand kilometres from Melbourne. When I pointed this out in my *Weekend Australian* column of 9 March 2019, Morris-Marr put out a tweet which concluded: "Brennan…says he wasn't at the verdict. So what. Maybe it was his twin." It seems to Morris-Marr, facts don't really matter. A loyal supporter here, his twin there, who cares? By the way, Morris-Marr deleted her reference to Brennan from the *Daily Mail* website – without acknowledging her gross factual error. Being an activist journalist means never have to say you're sorry for howlers.

It would seem that, to Morris-Marr, facts do not matter all that much when it comes to writing about a Pell supporter from the perspective of a Pell-antagonist. Also, in her response to me, Morris-Marr lacked the self-awareness to recognise that her own example of mistaken identity, which occurred immediately after an event, could well apply to the likes of "Margaret" some four decades after an event. Sure, Morris-Marr's account of Brennan's alleged demeanour in court painted a compelling journalistic picture – it's just that it wasn't true.

On 7 April 2020, the day of Pell's acquittal, I appeared in my regular slot on Sky News' *The Bolt Report*. I had prepared a "little list" of the leading figures in the Pell media pile-on, which Andrew Bolt and I discussed. Morris-Marr was named among the leading Pell-antagonists. I also wrote about this in my *Weekend Australian* column the following Saturday (12 April 2021). It is not bullying to describe a Pell- antagonist as a Pell-antagonist. Lucie Morris-Marr thought otherwise and tweeted on 11 April 2020:

> *Lucie Morris-Marr:* The bullying by the powerful media commentators towards those of us who dared to investigate #pell is getting sinister and ugly. Gerard Henderson has today published a list of us in @theaustralian saying we were part of a "pile on" and also read out our names @SkyNews

Soon after on 12 April 2020, she added:

> *Lucie Morris-Marr:* Update; I filed a complaint against Gerard Henderson @australian to the Australian Press Council.

As it turned out, nothing happened – in so far as I am aware. It seems that Morris-Marr believed that she was entitled to make the most outrageous claims about Cardinal Pell but was offended by being cited as a Pell-antagonist. Just another hyper-sensitive journalist, it would seem. Morris-Marr tweeted on 15 May 2018 that I had "defamed" her and that she was "considering her "legal position". The tweet was soon deleted, and nothing happened. It would appear that Morris-Marr on occasions equates intellectual criticism with libel.

In November 2020, it was announced that Lucie Morris-Marr had won the Wakeley Book Award for *Fallen* – part of The Walkley Foundation's Walkley Awards for Excellence in Journalism which is supported by the Media Entertainment and Arts Alliance (MEAA). This despite the fact that *Fallen* commences with an unproven allegation about Pell having witnessed a rape of a young girl (see above). It also contains a new allegation, which even Victoria Police did not investigate, that Pell sexually assaulted a young boy whom she names. It appears that when the alleged crime took place, Pell was not in Australia. Morris-Marr did not properly investigate the allegations.

In his influential media column in *The Australian* on 30 November 2020, Chris Mitchell (a former editor-in-chief of the paper) had this to say:

> Morris-Marr's personal observations may have seemed fine at the time of writing but are odd in light of the High Court's ruling. Many journalists she criticises have been proven correct about the Pell charges. Here's the rub for the Walkley judges. *Fallen* was published in September 2019, but Walkley 2020 nominations did not open until July 1, 2020, three months after the High Court decision. Both *Fallen* and the third episode of ABC TV's *Revelation* — before re-editing — are presented without the full facts: the High Court ruling. They are like halftime match reports without a full-time score. [Re *Revelation* see Chapter 8.]
>
> Walkley judges board chair Lenore Taylor, editor-in-chief of *Guardian Australia*, should have stepped in. The MEAA would not comment on specifics but offered this column a general statement of judging principles. That is not good enough. A Walkley is the profession's endorsement of a story. And Taylor also publishes the work of another Pell trial author and critic Melissa Davey. *Guardian Australia* has been Pell's fiercest media critic.

This is what the Walkley Awards Judges, chaired by Lenore Taylor, had to say about *Fallen* in November 2020:

> This compelling analysis of the trial of George Pell stood out for the sheer quality of the writing, the momentum of the story and new insights on how power operates in Australia. Morris-Marr adeptly builds context around a complex trial that grabbed global attention with a clear dissection of the legal process, media machinations and the legacy for a besieged Catholic Church, while weaving in her personal and often harrowing experience. Her tenacity and insight has produced a brilliant and eye-opening book.

The judges made no reference to the fact that the thesis of *Fallen* was discredited by the High Court of Australia's unanimous decision in *Pell v The Queen*.

- **Melissa Davey's Change of Book Title**

Along with Lucie Morris-Marr, *The Guardian's* bureau chief Melissa Davey was the only journalist who covered Pell's legal proceedings on a daily basis – in the Victorian Magistrates' Court, the trial and re-trial in the County Court of Victoria and the appeal to the Victorian Court of Appeal and the High Court hearings. Along with Morris-Marr, Davey was a Pell-antagonist.

On 8 April 2019 – not long after Pell was convicted – Melissa Davey sent out this tweet:

> *Melissa Davey:* I have some news; my book "A FAIR TRIAL: Cardinal George Pell and society's struggle to grasp child sexual abuse by clergy" – will be published by Scribe @scribepub next year. Thanks to @GuardianAus and @lenoretaylor for being supportive, and @literaryagent1 at Zeitgeist Media.

Before Pell had exercised his right of appeal with respect to his conviction in the re-trial, Davey was convinced that Pell had received a fair trial. A year later, on 23 May 2020, Davey put out another tweet concerning the publication of her book:

> *Melissa Davey:* My book, "The Case of George Pell: reckoning with child sexual abuse by clergy" now has a front cover. I have been working hard the past week on a final read and edit, and all things going to plan, it will be released by August/September. Pre-order it here: scribepublications.com.au/books-authors/…

So Davey changed the name of her book from "A Fair Trial" to *The Case of George Pell* – without acknowledging that she had done so. Like virtually all Pell-antagonists, she was convinced that the Victorian Court of Appeal and/or High Court would uphold the jury's verdict in the re-trial. Writing in *The Guardian* on 24 August 2019, after the Victorian Court of Appeal's majority decision, Davey concluded her piece as follows:

> Pell supporters will hope [Justice] Weinberg's comprehensive dissenting judgment will see Pell through an appeal to the High Court. Few defence barristers in Victoria will weigh-in publicly on the case or the prospects for High Court success, so heated and divisive

are opinions on the trial. The founder of O'Brien Solicitors and criminal defence lawyer Peter O'Brien, who practises in NSW, says those relying on Weinberg's dissent for the case to be heard in the High Court may be disappointed. "The High Court is not generally interested in questions of fact but matters of law," O'Brien says. "They are also interested in issues of high public interest.

The fact Cardinal Pell is a very public figure who has been convicted doesn't mean it's a matter of public interest, it has to be a matter of public interest so far as law is concerned. Very rarely will the High Court descend into matters associated with facts of a case. If I had a client in this situation, I would be advising them that their chances of High Court success are very slim."

There were lawyers within and outside of Victoria who did not share Peter O'Brien's view – but Davey did not approach them. O'Brien's view was wrong. The High Court did not just focus on "matters of law". Rather it followed the precedent set in *M v The Queen* and looked at the weight of evidence – with devastating effect on the Victorian Director of Prosecution's case.

In the "author's note" to *The Case of George Pell*, Davey wrote:

> I believe I am the only journalist to have covered Cardinal Pell's appearances at the child sexual abuse royal commission, as well as the entirety of his committal hearing.

As with Morris-Marr, this statement is not correct. Davey did not watch or hear the complainant's testimony. In the text of *The Case of George Pell*, however, the author claimed that she learnt about the complainant's demeanour from lawyers – with the implication that this convinced her of Pell's guilt beyond reasonable doubt:

> Jesuit priest and human-rights lawyer Frank Brennan, who attended a few days of the re-trial, described the complainant's evidence as "confused", even though he had not seen or heard the complainant testify. By contrast, in the conversations that occurred between journalists and lawyers in the corridors of the courthouse, I never heard anyone who'd been present during the complainant's testimony say that he had performed badly. Instead, the complainant was described as "compelling" and "honest".

In fact, Brennan had read those parts of the transcript of the complainant's evidence which were cited in the appeal process before he made this claim. Moreover, it is unlawful under Victorian law for a lawyer for the prosecution or defence to discuss the evidence of a complainant in a sexual assault case with anyone, including journalists like Davey. What's more, Davey has an inconsistent position on demeanour. She accepted the alleged advice of unnamed lawyers that the complainant was "compelling" and "honest". Yet, elsewhere in her book, Davey wrote that "demeanour is not always a good indication of truth" – the latter, not surprisingly, pertaining to a witness giving evidence consistent with Pell's innocence. Once again, an unpleasant double standard, perpetrated by an activist journalist.

In her book Davey is interested in the case of George Pell up until the time he was acquitted by the High Court. *The Case of George Pell* is extremely weak in its coverage of one of Australia's most significant court cases. A reading of the chapter titled "Acquittal" makes it clear that the author does not agree with the High Court decision. She found one lawyer, La Trobe academic Professor Gideon Boas who is also a barrister, to throw doubt on the High Court decision:

> "Victoria's Court of Appeal upheld the jury decision by a majority, and the High Court went the other way," Boas said. "I've heard it said a lot of this case, "How could the jury get it so wrong when the High Court decided unanimously it was an unreasonable verdict?" My response is: "What's to say the High Court got it right?"

The Pell-antagonist Davey did not seek out one alternative view to that of Boas. Also she neglected to point out in this instance that the Victorian Court of Appeal went two to one against Pell – whereas the High Court went seven to zero in his favour.

David Marr launched *The Case for George Pell* as an "in conversation event" with Melissa Davey in a Gleebooks Sydney Zoom meeting, due to COVID-19 and all that, on 24 September 2020. Early on, the following exchange took place in which Davey appeared to express satisfaction that Pell had served over a year in prison – even though his conviction had been quashed on appeal:

David Marr: After all these years now, and after all those investigations and all those trials, George Pell was acquitted unanimously by the High Court. So was it all just a mistake – just a terrible waste of time and a mistake?

Melissa Davey: Ultimately a cardinal sat in prison for almost a year now. Now, yes, he was ultimately acquitted and the decision was overturned. But that's extraordinary to think that a cardinal did time in jail, from the Vatican. You know, it comes back to this idea of justice and what does justice look like? And I suppose what this case really highlighted is that it's very difficult to ever have a perfect case with a perfect set of facts and where the entire case is clearly laid out. And this case really highlighted that –

David Marr: He sat in prison for a year, but he was declared an innocent man, and that's –

Melissa Davey: Well, he wasn't declared innocent though…. All up it was, it was months. Each trial took five weeks. And I just want to point out, he was never declared an innocent man by the High Court….

In her Pell-antagonist mode, Davey declined to accept the presumption of innocence that applies to all Australians – including cardinals of the Catholic Church. Everyone is innocent until proven guilty. Marr understands this, albeit reluctantly. Not so Davey.

Like Morris-Marr, Davey found the task of reporting the Pell Case stressful. Early in *The Case of George Pell*, she related that her "mental health and stamina began to seriously deteriorate". Towards the end of the book, Davey writes that, after the Pell Case, she travelled to New Zealand to report on the Christchurch terrorist attack on two mosques by a right-wing extremist. On returning to Australia, she was "exhausted and broken". Davey added:

> I had a mental breakdown. I felt ashamed. I learned it is not the stories you cover that will break you, but the lack of support that will. The criticism of the reporters covering the [Pell] trial still did not stop.

Like Marr, Milligan and Morris-Marr, Davey fails to appreciate that if journalists become activists they should expect to be criticised. Otherwise the targets of their activism – in this case Pell – have no right to defend themselves.

The need for someone to speak for the defendant is illustrated by *The Case of George Pell*. At Pages 263-264, Davey cites the Crown Prosecutor Mark Gibson SC as saying that there was an interval "in the order of half [a minute] to two minutes" before the sacristan would unlock the priests' sacristy and commence clearing up the sacristy (i.e. the altar). But in *The Queen v Pell* in the County Court, it was agreed that there was a period of between five or six minutes when the offending acts could have occurred. Davey does not state how the offences for which Pell was convicted could have occurred – since she identified no interval in which the assaults could have taken place in five minutes or even six minutes after Solemn Mass and the procession out of the Cathedral commenced. Davey simply accepts that six minutes of alleged offending could have occurred in two minutes or less.

A problem with *The Case of George Pell* is that it required a complete re-write before publication – since the initial draft was based on a false premise. The confusion in Davey's account turns on her willingness to believe what she wants to believe – rather than assess how the alleged crimes could have been committed in view of the existing evidence. Davey completely underestimates the significance of a seven to zero quashing of a verdict in a criminal trial by the High Court. So, apparently, does her publisher, the left-wing activist Henry Rosenbloom at Scribe.

As Gerard Windsor wrote when reviewing Davey's book in *The Weekend Australian* (20 August 2020), *The Case of George Pell: Reckoning with child sexual abuse by clergy* contains a contradiction between its title and sub-title: "Reckoning with child sexual abuse by clergy is not done by lengthy examination of one case where a clergyman is not proven to be an abuser."

As late as June 2020 – two months after Pell's acquittal – Scribe advertised Davey's book as follows:

The Case of George Pell is not just about one alleged offender, and one complainant. It is also about how the sexual abuse of children occurs – and has been allowed to continue.

By June 2020, Pell was not an alleged offender – he was an innocent man. And *The Case of George Pell* said nothing whatsoever about how or where the sexual abuse of children occurs or how it has been allowed to continue. Nothing whatsoever.

* * * * *

The likes of David Marr, Louise Milligan, Lucie Morris-Marr and Melissa Davey were highly critical of Pell and his supporters. But all four acted with considerable sensitivity when they were subjected to criticism, however considered. Moreover, as leaders of the Pell-Antagonists Band, they helped create the climate whereby the likes of Noel Debien at the ABC felt that he felt unable to tell his colleagues that he believed that Cardinal Pell was not guilty.

Miles Martignoni, Melissa Davey and David Marr

The *Guardian Australia* was one of the leaders of the Pell pile-on. Here's how it celebrated two New York Festival International Radio Awards received for *The Reckoning* podcast on the Pell Case. *The Reckoning* was presented by David Marr and Melissa Davey (both *Guardian* journalists) and produced by Miles Martignoni. Photo credit: Jonny Weeks/*The Guardian*/Australscope

ABC TV's Sarah Ferguson appearing in her Revelation documentary outside St Mary's Cathedral in Sydney

ABC management moved Episode 3, titled "Goliath", of the Revelation documentary forward (from the scheduled Tuesday 7 April) to Thursday 2 April 2020 to place it before the High Court's decision in Pell v The Queen. "Goliath" – presented by Sarah Ferguson and written by Tony Jones – contained vile allegations against Cardinal Pell by Bernie, whom Ferguson described as "an extraordinarily compelling witness". The High Court of Australia has held that, in both criminal and civil cases, it is unwise to place emphasis on the demeanor of litigants or complainants. Bernie declined to give evidence at the committal proceedings of The Police v Pell. The fact that Cardinal Pell comprehensively refuted all of Bernie's allegations when interviewed by Victoria Police in Rome was not mentioned in the body of either the original showing of "Goliath" or in the re-cut version which is on the ABC's Iview.

Tony Abbott and Cardinal Pell as seen by artist Tony Sowersby

The front cover of Tony Sowersby's The Political Landscape depicts his portrait of Cardinal Pell as puppeteer with a puppet (Tony Abbott). Tony Sowersby's work, titled "The Cardinal with his Abbott" won the People's Choice for the Bald Archy Prize in 2005. The prize is awarded for the best comic or satire portrait of an Australian distinguished in arts, sciences, letters, politics, sport and the media. The prize winners invariably target conservatives – in 2005 Pell was Archbishop of Sydney and Tony Abbott (a Catholic) was a minister in the John Howard-led Liberal Party-Nationals Coalition government.

8

STACKS ON THE PELL MILL – AND MORE ON STILL

> "Speaking as a lawyer, I know we have few appealing qualities. But we do believe in our own justice system. All my life, I have joined in the chorus that our justice system is the best in the world. With the case of Cardinal George Pell, I am not singing quite so loud.... So what we have witnessed is a combined effort by much of the media, including the public broadcaster [the ABC], and elements of Victoria's law enforcement agency, to blacken the name of someone before he went to trial....
>
> This is not a story about whether a jury got it right or wrong, or about whether justice is seen to prevail. It's a story about whether a jury was ever given a fair chance to make a decision, and whether our justice system can be heard above a media mob."
>
> - Greg Craven, "George Pell: a case in which justice never had a fair chance", *The Australian*, 27 February 2019.

Writing in *The Australian* on 27 February 2019, the day after the Director of Public Prosecutions in Victoria lifted the suppression order on the Pell Case and news of Cardinal Pell's conviction was announced, Professor Greg Craven expressed concern about how the accused could have obtained a fair trial. As previously discussed, this led to a demand by Dr Leah Kaufmann, the Australian Catholic University branch president of the National Tertiary Education Union, that the ACU rename the Pell Centre on the university's Ballarat campus and remove Pell's portrait from the North Sydney campus.

In his response to Dr Kaufmann (a senior lecturer in psychology at the ACU's Melbourne campus), the late John Fahey AC – the ACU's chancellor – made the following comment:

> ...you stated that Professor Craven authored an article commenting on Cardinal Pell's conviction. He did not. He wrote an article which questioned the capacity of Cardinal Pell to obtain a fair trial in Victoria due to the climate and atmosphere fuelled by police leaks and left leaning journalists in the time leading up to the hearing. He did not criticise the judge. He did not criticise the jury. His argument was based on a well that had been poisoned, which is not in the interest of anyone including our system of justice.

This is the issue that those engaged in the stacks-on-the-mill campaign against Pell did not want to discuss. Ignoring the fact that the jury in the first trial was split, they demanded that everyone accept the unanimous verdict in the re-trial. This led to an insistence that those who had doubts about the safety of the verdict – that is, those who at the very least believed that there was a reasonable doubt about Pell's guilt – should be silenced. Then there was a demand that Pell should accept his fate and not take a case to the Victorian Court of Appeal. When Pell went down in a majority decision, there was a demand that he not appeal to the High Court while the High Court was advised by some not to overturn Pell's conviction.

The Project's Anti-Pell Project

The controversial politician Craig Kelly – formerly a Liberal Party member (now a member of a minority party which had one seat in the House of Representatives), who is not a Catholic – had doubts about the jury's verdict in *The Queen v Pell*. In a series of *Facebook* posts, Kelly condemned pedophilia and said that the Catholic Church had covered up this crime for "many, many decades". However, he went on to state that Pell's conviction was "a grave miscarriage of justice" and expressed the view that "a lot of Australians would have made up their minds about Cardinal Pell even before they heard any evidence".

The Project on Network Ten is a news and current affairs program aimed at a younger audience. It is unashamedly left-of-centre. It was on *The Project* on 16 February 2016 that Tim Minchin launched his *(Come Home) Cardinal Pell* musical rant. *The Project* invited Craig Kelly to appear on the program on 28 February 2019. After Kelly stated that he doubted that Pell was guilty, the following exchange took place:[18]

> *Hamish Macdonald:* How are you qualified to make a judgment?
>
> *Craig Kelly:* Well, this is the thing. There were two trials in this case. The first trial, there was a substantial number of jurors, and we don't know how many they were, that actually found Cardinal Pell innocent.
>
> *Hamish Macdonald:* This is completely irrelevant. You're coming on national television saying that there's been a miscarriage of justice – that the court, the jury got it wrong. And you have not heard the evidence that they heard.
>
> *Peter Hellier:* If this fails on appeal, will you come back on our show and denounce George Pell as a convicted pedophile?
>
> *Rachel Corbett:* Craig, he has been found guilty. I think there'd be barely a criminal alive who hasn't tried to go through the appeals system and get their conviction quashed. So I'm not sure how you can say that just because he said "I didn't do it" that that somehow absolves him of all - he has been convicted.
>
> *Craig Kelly:* Balance of probabilities –
>
> *Gorgi Coghlan:* Please answer the question. How do you think your comments tonight on our show, and on your *Facebook* posts, affect victims of child sexual abuse?
>
> *Craig Kelly:* No no, hang on –
>
> *Peter Hellier:* You are defending a convicted pedophile –
>
> *Craig Kelly:* No no not at all –
>
> *Gorgi Coghlan:* Despite a jury, finding him guilty, You're still defending him Craig. So like it or not, you are defending on national TV –
>
> *Craig Kelly:* No, no –
>
> *Gorgi Coghlan*: You are defending a convicted pedophile.

Talk about a pile-on. Kelly was invited on *The Project* to discuss his position on Pell. Then all four presenters – Hamish Macdonald (who also presents for the ABC), Peter Hellier, Rachel Corbett and Gorgi Coghlan howled Kelly down by suggesting that he was a pedophile defender. Not one acknowledged that the convicted man had a right to appeal. On *The Project* it was four to zip against Kelly. But in the High Court, just over a year later, it was seven to zip against *The Project* team.

ABC TV's Barrie Cassidy and Friends Criticise John Howard and Tony Abbott Over George Pell

On 1 March 2019, the morning after Pell's guilty verdict was announced, ABC TV *Insiders'* presenter Barrie Cassidy made his regular Friday appearance on the ABC TV *News Breakfast* program. Cassidy, a Pell-antagonist, had this to say, with Pell-antagonists Paul Kennedy and Lisa Millar on the presenters' couch, concerning the reference which former prime minister John Howard provided to the court after Pell was convicted:

> *Barrie Cassidy:* John Howard said that in all his dealings with him, he found George Pell to be of exemplary character. Now that's fine as far as it goes. But then he went on to say that he hasn't changed his view as a result of the conviction on child abuse.
>
> *Paul Kennedy:* Because he wrote it after the conviction.
>
> *Lisa Millar:* And he was asked about it again yesterday.
>
> *Barrie Cassidy:* And to say that it hasn't changed your view. Then what would change your view about somebody's character if child abuse does not? And even the conservative commentator Ray Hadley has had a go at him and said: "Well hang on, what you're implying here is not only that you believe George Pell but by extension you're calling the survivors liars."

This was a statement born of ignorance. John Howard was providing a character reference to Chief Judge Peter Kidd to be considered in the sentencing of Pell. That's all. It was a reference concerning one man who had been convicted of a crime against two men (one of whom was deceased) when they were boys. Howard did not call anyone a liar – and certainly not "the survivors" of child sexual abuse. In any event, in normal times Cassidy would have taken little notice of the view of Radio 2GB presenter Ray Hadley whom he would have regarded as right-wing "shock jock". It's just that times were not normal since both Cassidy and Hadley were part of the Pell pile-on. Cassidy continued:

> *Barrie Cassidy:* …but the feeling around the country on this issue is absolutely white hot. And it does make it difficult for John Howard because, as of now, he'll need to be involved in some way or another in the NSW State election. And then within four or five weeks he'll be invited, I'm sure, to participate in the Federal election.
>
> *Lisa Millar:* So you think it has political ramifications?
>
> *Barrie Cassidy:* Well it might limit his ability to campaign because of the strong feelings that you see expressed every day on this issue.
>
> *Paul Kennedy:* Damaging his credibility to talk on any issue?
>
> *Barrie Cassidy:* Yeah, damage his credibility, but also he might be confronted by people as he makes public appearances….

In fact, John Howard supported the Coalition in both the NSW State election (23 March 2019) and the Federal election (18 May 2019). The former prime minister's credibility was not damaged, and the Coalition won both elections – contrary to the expectations of many commentators, including Cassidy. And Howard was not confronted by anti-Pell demonstrators.

Pell's conviction was discussed at length again on the ABC TV *Insiders* program on Sunday 3 March 2019. This time Cassidy was in the presenter's chair – and the panel comprised Pell-antagonists Fran Kelly (ABC Radio National) and Karen Middleton (*The Saturday Paper*) as well as Mark Riley (Network Seven). Cassidy referred to "the intervention of two former prime ministers John Howard and Tony Abbott" – concerning the former's character reference and the latter's phone call to Pell after his conviction was revealed.

Cassidy threw to Fran Kelly who declared that "former prime ministers should think very carefully about offering them [character references] in a situation like this". Karen Middleton concurred saying that "it's hard to reach a conclusion other than he's not believing the victims or he's dismissing the severity of offence". In fact, there was only one complainant in this case. Mark Riley proffered the opinion that if Howard "were given the opportunity to write that again he might think about playing some courtesies towards…the victims". The reference was to Howard's comment that Pell's conviction did not change his view of the man.

Then it was time to focus on Abbott – who had told Sydney Radio 2GB presenter Ben Fordham that Pell had a right of appeal. Cassidy played footage of Pell-antagonist Ray Hadley bagging both Howard and Abbott on his 2GB program – he referred to Cardinal Pell as "Mr Pell". Hadley maintained that both Howard and Abbott had "shown a complete lack of understanding of victims of pedophiles" – overlooking the fact that they did not believe that Pell was guilty of this crime. The panel members did not have a fundamental problem with the Abbott/Pell phone call.

The session concluded with an unchallenged claim by Middleton that an appeal court would only look at "matters of law, not matters of fact". This hopelessly wrong statement was not corrected by Cassidy in his capacity as presenter. In time, both the Victorian Court of Appeal and the High Court considered the facts of the case which had led the jury in the re-trial to its conclusion.

Q&A Host Tony Jones and Labor Senator Kristina Keneally concur with Francis Sullivan's Demand that Pell Supporters "Just Shut Up"

The ABC TV *Q&A* program, which in 2019 aired on Mondays, devoted most of its time on Monday 4 March 2019 to the Pell Case – in a program titled "A Church in Crisis". The presenter was Pell-antagonist Tony Jones. There were four Australians on the panel – Francis Sullivan (the former head of the Catholic Church's Truth, Justice and Healing Council), Viv Waller (a lawyer for A – the complainant in *The Queen v Pell*), Jim Molan (a Liberal Party senator who was brought up a Catholic) and Kristina Keneally (a Labor Party senator who was brought up a Catholic and who worked for some years as a Sky News presenter). All were critical of the Catholic Church to a greater or lesser extent. Moreover, all but Molan were Pell-antagonists. Also two of the audience members called by Jones to ask pre-arranged questions were high-profile Pell-antagonists. Namely, Peter Fox and Chrissie Foster. The fifth panellist was a visiting American rabbi.

The first question was from Fox to Keneally. In reply, the Labor Party senator criticised John Howard (for having provided a court reference for the convicted man) and Tony Abbott (for having phoned Pell when news of his conviction was announced). She maintained that such actions were "disrespectful of the jury verdict" and "quite disrespectful of victims". However, Keneally did acknowledge that Pell had a right to appeal. Then Jones called on Sullivan:

> *Tony Jones:* …Francis Sullivan, what do you think about the question, first of all? Stick to that. And Kristina Keneally raised the point, it's disrespectful both of the jury and of the victim witness.
>
> *Francis Sullivan*: Yeah, thanks for the question, Peter [Fox]. I mean, I think it's a question that a lot of people have in their minds. I think they're worried about the process from here. Because, let's face it, George Pell is a very divisive character and people had a view about him a long time before this trial. I think that's in the swirl of things. But I agree with everybody at this point – we don't want to put the victim now on trial by suggesting that somehow, maybe, what they said was wrong. And that's what this debate's doing. And I don't want to be part of any cheer squad that tries to do that…So, as far as I'm concerned, everyone should just shut up.
>
> *Kristina Keneally:* Yep.
>
> *Tony Jones:* Yeah.

Senator Keneally was not the only senior Labor Party figure to bag John Howard for his decision to provide a court reference. So did (then) Labor leader Bill Shorten and Senator Penny Wong along with (then) Greens leader Richard Di Natale. The fact is that Howard did not run a public commentary on the Pell Case. He just did something which is part of Australia's legal system – namely, provide a reference for a convicted person which a judge might take into account when deciding on the term of sentence that may be imposed. So did others including Greg Craven, Sue Buckingham and Delsie Heiss. That's all. Labor's shadow attorney general Mark Dreyfus QC, no supporter of Pell, made this clear when he commented on 28 February 2019 that court references were part of the legal system and could be of assistance to a sentencing judge. And Abbott merely made a private phone call to a friend. But Sullivan just wanted silence – as did Keneally and Jones.

Steve Biddulph, Tim Soutphommasane & Jack Waterford Oppose Pell's Decision to Appeal

As discussed in Chapter 4, George Pell's appeal against the decision of the jury in the re-trial was rejected by a two to one majority in the Victorian Court of Appeal in August 2019. Yet in the lead up to, and after, the decision some commentators held the view that Pell should not exercise his right to appeal the conviction.

On 20 August 2019, Nine Newspapers (*Sydney Morning Herald* and *The* Age) carried an opinion piece by child psychologist Steve Biddulph titled "Should Cardinal Pell have appealed his conviction?". His article, which focused on the forthcoming decision by the Court of Appeal, commenced as follows:

> Judgement Day: The decision on Cardinal George Pell's appeal will be handed down on Wednesday. On Wednesday morning, a judgement will be made on Cardinal George Pell's appeal against his child sexual assault conviction. The judges in the case have deemed it so important that, like the original [sentencing] judgement, it will be broadcast live on TV. But as the world holds its breath for the result, a larger question than his innocence or guilt is being ignored. What will be the effect on sufferers of child sexual abuse, past and present, if his conviction is overturned, and he walks free?

How about that? Biddulph claimed that there was a more important issue involved in this case than Pell's innocence or guilt – an extraordinary statement. In a criminal trial there is only one issue – whether the accused is guilty beyond reasonable doubt. But not to this psychologist. Biddulph raised the issue as to "whether in even initiating an appeal and the possibility of walking free, Pell is committing the most harmful action in a long life of moral ambiguity".

Leaving aside Biddulph's assertion about Pell's "long life of moral ambiguity" – a diagnosis by a psychologist who had not met the person concerning whom he was making a clinical assessment – this was a claim that Pell should serve out his time in prison irrespective of whether he was innocent or guilty. This, according to Biddulph, "would send a message of atonement and assurance to every terrified young person or older victim that they are safe to speak up, and be listened to".

Biddulph concluded his article by asking a self-serving question. "And would not his walking free, as a result of a well-funded appeal, lead to more deaths and despair, and even more abuse? I don't know the answer but I think it ought to be asked."

This was an appeal to emotion. The successful appeals by John Francis Tyrrell in the Victorian Court of Appeal (15 March 2019) and Steven Fennell in the High Court of Australia (11 September 2019) demonstrated that an applicant does not need to have "a well-funded appeal" to succeed before a court of appeal or even the High Court. Moreover, Biddulph produced no evidence that an acquittal in a high-profile case of alleged historical child sexual abuse "leads to more deaths, despair and abuse" – as he himself acknowledged.

On 23 August 2019, soon after the majority decision in the Victorian Court of Appeal dismissing Pell's appeal, Nine Newspapers published a piece by political philosopher Tim Soutphommasane titled "Pell and the twisted inversion of victimhood". Apparently unaware of the recent Tyrrell acquittal, Soutphommasane made this assertion:

> Justice has been served. Or has it? The saga of George Pell is not yet over. The Victorian Court of Appeal's decision to uphold the cardinal's conviction for child sex abuse may yet reach the High Court. We will find out soon enough. Our response to the case has revealed much about us as Australians. For all our national myth-making

about egalitarianism, it's clear that power still goes a long way in this place. The powerful will always have their friends, who will always defend them. No matter what their crime.

Soutphommasane, who wrote in his capacity as a political theorist and professor at the University of Sydney, cited not a skerrick of evidence for his assertion that "the powerful will always have their friends who will defend them". He went on to argue that "conservatives are supposed to champion the rule of law; not this time". This overlooked the fact that a genuine conservative would be expected to accept that both the poorest and the richest in our midst have a right to appeal to the High Court of Australia.

According to Soutphommasane, in the Pell case the "perpetrator is now the victim". At the time he wrote this, the appeal process had not been extinguished and it was still possible that Pell would not be held to be a "perpetrator" following a hearing in the High Court. Soutphommasane went on to claim that "the surviving victim himself, known as 'J' [i.e. A] has been rendered invisible and silent within much of the debate". This is misleading. The process adopted in the Pell Case was no different to that which applied to individuals charged with similar crimes at the time. Moreover, A could have given evidence and spoken in public had be wished to do so.

There was no mention of Justice Weinberg's dissent in Soutphommasane's article and it is not clear that he had read the 200 page dissenting judgment. Soutphommasane finished his piece as follows:

> Our society's functioning depends, in part, on our collective temper and spirit as citizens. It depends on us accepting the rule of law, whether we may like the results or not. Our institutions can't survive if substantial factions of our society treat law courts with moral contempt. The response this week by some conservatives does make you wonder. Will some only accept the rule of law when they win? What will happen the next time the result doesn't go their way? And what does that mean for the rest of us?

In fact, when the High Court brought down its verdict it was the Pell-antagonists, many of whom were on the left, who refused to accept the decision. Moreover, there is no evidence that Soutphommasane ever corrected the views he expressed in August 2019 that Pell was a "perpetrator" of historical child sexual abuse.

Between 2013 and 2018, Soutphommasane held a senior position at the Australian Human Rights Commission. However, by mid-2019, he was expressing the view that a convicted man should not exercise his human right to appeal a conviction.

Writing in the *Canberra Times* on 24 August 2019, the trained lawyer Jack Waterford – who was a former editor of the newspaper – all but told the High Court what to do. Towards the end of his article titled "High Court should leave Pell alone", Waterford wrote:

> It is, of course, for the High Court to decide whether it would hear an appeal. But it is quite unlikely that it would be affected much, one way or another, by the notoriety of the appellant, or the fact that his highly expensive lawyers are seeking a third bite of the cherry with arguments that have so far been considered at length, and rejected by three judges and a jury, and which have not improved much in the repetition.
>
> They would also be very sensitive to suggestions that the court was giving audience to a well-heeled, well represented and well-connected defendant who would almost certainly have failed to get a hearing if he were merely a common or garden-variety sexual molester.

This comment contained an error. There were two judges who found against Pell – not three. Chief Judge Kidd in the County Court made it emphatically clear that it was not his role to second guess the jury. What's more, Waterford produced no evidence to support his claim that Pell's case only got to the High Court because he was "well heeled" and "well connected". The fact is that it is most unlikely that Pell would have been charged by Victoria Police on such evidence if he were not a high-profile Catholic prelate – a "prince" of the Church, no less. This is discussed in Chapter 10.

Jack Waterford went on to assert that "there will be some who for political, ecclesiastical or personal reasons would deny Pell's guilt even if there were 1000 witnesses". This overlooked the fact that there were no witnesses against Pell (apart from a single complainant) and that Pell had an alibi supported by at least two (Portelli, Potter) witnesses – four in total if the testimony of altar servers Daniel McGlone and Jeffrey Connor is taken into account. It is a matter of record that seven judges of the High Court did not do what Waterford believed they should do.

Waterford returned to the topic after the High Court decision. Writing in the *Canberra Times* on 11 April 2020, he conceded that "Pell must be regarded as innocent" and he acknowledged that he was wrong in predicting that the High Court would not "grant special leave to appeal, let alone hear the case". Moreover, Waterford recognised correctly that the judgment "essentially turned on the facts".

We do not know why the second jury came to its unanimous decision – which was expressed in one word "Guilty". But we do know why Justice Weinberg in the Court of Appeal and all seven High Court judges came to their decision – since they gave reasons. And we know that they were not affected by the media pile-on.

And There's More Still

The attacks on George Pell in the media were so extensive over so long a time leading up to his charging, trial and conviction that it would take a very large book to cover the issue extensively. The following examples illustrate the intensity of the hostility to Pell by some influential commentators who felt the need to express themselves as Pell-antagonists.

- **Julian Burnside AO, QC** (Melbourne barrister who unsuccessfully ran in the 2019 Federal election for the Greens party).

In July 2016, Julian Burnside responded to a tweet with the following words: "Actually it would not surprise me if Pell did that". The "that" in question was the suggestion as to what would be the response if Cardinal Pell had openly encouraged a "mandate to murder and burn gays". The question had been raised as to whether, in such a circumstance, Pell would be treated the same as a radical imam who said the same thing.

Burnside missed the point – and said that he would not be surprised if Pell encouraged others to "murder and burn gays". When I asked Burnside what was his evidence that Pell was not opposed to the murder of gays, he responded:

> Dear Gerard
>
> I did not assert that he [Pell] had said it. I said it would not surprise me if he said it. I stand by that. I regard him as a person who has no discernible ethics. Nothing he says would surprise me.
>
> Very best wishes
>
> Julian
>
> Julian Burnside AO QC

At the time he wrote to me, Julian Burnside was one of the most influential barristers at the Victorian Bar. He is a past president of Liberty Victoria (formerly the Victorian Council for Civil Liberties). Chris Maxwell QC, the President of the Victorian Court of Appeal, was once a Liberty Victoria president and board member. It's an important body.

It shows the intensity of hatred towards Pell among influential sections of the Melbourne legal fraternity that Burnside could write in July 2016 that he would not be surprised if the Cardinal had urged that gays be torched and murdered.

- **Richard Glover** (ABC broadcaster/*Sydney Morning Herald* columnist)

This is how Richard Glover commenced his article in *The Washington Post* on 26 February 2019, shortly after Pell's conviction had become international news:

> As a Sydney radio host, I've known Cardinal George Pell for years — even before he became one of the most senior Catholic officials in

the world, selected by Pope Francis to reform the Vatican's finances. I never warmed to him. He was always cold and imperious, suspicious of whatever question might be asked. Trivial, I know, but I recall the dandruff on his clerical collar whenever he came into our radio studio. It was as if he didn't care what people made of him…

Strange that Glover decided, first up, to tell his American readers that Pell had dandruff on his clerical collar. Then Glover attacked Pell's "hard-line, unbending, unfeeling attitude to every issue – homosexuality, divorce, abortion, contraception, sex more generally". But Glover did not state that the man who he admitted to "dislike" was espousing the official teachings of the Catholic Church. It was only in his third paragraph that Glover got around to stating that Pell had been convicted of pedophilia.

On 26 February 2019, in his *Drive* program on ABC Radio 702 Sydney, Glover volunteered the information that it had been said by bodies like the Victoria Police that they were worried by the way the Melbourne Response had operated – in particular "the way it might have shut down victims". The following day, I emailed Glover advising that his assertion was wrong and told him that the Melbourne Response had been established in co-operation with Victoria Police.

I concluded my email by stating that if he was going to make comments outside his "area of competence" he should "engage a fact-checker". Glover replied "I took that from the Marr *Quarterly Essay* where he directly quotes a statement from Victoria Police". In response, I reminded him that David Marr was a Pell-antagonist and advised that Victoria Police had changed its attitude to the Melbourne Response. I also pointed out that the Victorian Parliamentary Inquiry had found that some of the evidence provided to it by Victoria Police was inaccurate. See Chapter 10.

Glover ignored the evidence which I had provided to him and sent me a copy of his *Washington Post* article which he maintained was "balanced". In response I noted that the only source quoted in his "balanced" account was a Pell-antagonist, Chrissie Foster.

When Pell was sentenced on 13 March 2019, Glover put out this tweet which was supported by his ABC Radio Sydney colleague Wendy Harmer:

> *Richard Glover:* I know some victims thought the #pell verdict inadequate. My focus was on the empowering way Judge Kidd accepted the victim's evidence, his tender empathy in describing the impact of the crimes. These are the deeper victories. His verdict, the manner of it, made my heart sing.
>
> *Wendy Harmer:* Hearing that your dear heart is singing is everything.

If Glover had studied Chief Judge Kidd's comments carefully, he would have understood that the judge had not delivered a "verdict". Judges do not do that in trial by jury cases. He was acting on the jury's verdict – as he was bound to do by law. That's all.

- **Derryn Hinch** (Journalist and author; Senator for Victoria 2016-19 – Derryn Hinch's Justice Party)

Derryn Hinch is a long-time Pell-antagonist. Before entering the Senate in July 2016 and remaining there until June 2019, he presented *Hinch Live* on Sky News and appeared regularly on Sky News' *Paul Murray Live*. Hinch returned briefly to Sky News after he lost his Senate seat. Hinch frequently used his television platform to criticise Pell and anyone who spoke up for him in the face of the media pile-on, including myself. Yet neither Hinch nor Murray ever invited me into the Sky News studio to state my case in response to constant verbal attacks on me by themselves and their chosen panel members.

I complained to Sky News' management that it was somewhat unfair that I was targeted on Sky News by Murray and Hinch and their guests, but never given a right-of-reply. In time, Sky News' (then) managing director Angelos Frangopoulos apologised in person for Sky News having treated me unfairly – but I never appeared on *Hinch Live* or *Paul Murray Live*.

Needless to say, Hinch was delighted when Pell was found guilty. When sentencing took place on 13 March 2019, he put out this tweet:

> *Derryn Hinch:* Judge Kidd. Demolition of Pell in 69 minutes. Erudite, forensic, dispassionate, clinical. Especially on trust/duty of care. Six years with 3.8 minimum. Judge saw right through him. And Pell is on the child sex offender register for life. Passport ban applies. No more Rome.

If Hinch had paid attention when watching or reading Chief Judge Kidd's sentencing comments, he would have known that – on two occasions – the judge made clear that it was his duty to accept the jury's verdict. So Hinch's claim that Kidd "saw right through" Pell was misleading.

Editorialising on *Hinch Live* on 4 July 2019, the presenter looked back on the case and rejoiced that "the last thing disgraced pedophile Cardinal Pell did before stepping out of the dock was to sign the sex offenders register – which means he can't go back to Rome or London for a steak or a glass of red".

As a senator, Hinch had campaigned successfully to establish a national public register of child sex-offenders. Anyone on the list is prevented from travelling overseas – since it is deemed possible that they might engage in under-age sex outside of Australia. Hinch's claims that Pell would be on the sex offenders register for life and would never see Rome or London again was just wish-fulfillment. But it spoke volumes of his bitterness.

When the Victorian Court of Appeal was about to hand down its judgment, Hinch indicated on Sky News that he knew what the decision would be – and implied that he would not be unhappy with the result.

Later, Hinch was extremely confident that the High Court would not consider an appeal by Pell – and tweeted this on 25 August 2019:

> *Derryn Hinch:* Hinch's Hunch: The High Court will deny Pell's application for special leave. There are no specific legal grounds for this to be approved.

Here Hinch made the error of maintaining that the High Court only considered criminal court appeals with respect to "specific legal grounds". A statement lacking legal knowledge, which should have been familiar to an experienced journalist.

On *Hinch Live* on 31 May 2015 – two years before Pell was charged – the presenter was asked what he thought about when he was swimming for exercise. His response demonstrated an anti-Pell obsession which went back to around 1996 when Pell became Archbishop of Melbourne:

> *Derryn Hinch:* I think about what I'm gonna talk about on the program tonight. I'm thinking: what am I gonna write for my blog? I don't relax in there and think Dalai-Lama-sort-of-thoughts. I think – what am I gonna write on my blog today? And am I going to go George Pell again? Will Gerard Henderson work me over again or complain to my boss? That's the sort of things that I think about.

It was no surprise, then, that like many a Pell-antagonist, Hinch refused to accept the High Court's unanimous decision. In response to a tweet by Greg Barns SC that "all those who passed judgment on Pell before waiting for the final appeal have learned something about the rule of law and fairness to all defendants", Hinch declared in a tweet on 7 April 2020:

> *Derryn Hinch:* Jeez…a jury and an appellate court confirmed his guilt. What planet are you on. The High Court did not find Pell innocent.

In fact, Barns was on the "planet" of the common law. No court in Australia, including the High Court, can find anyone "innocent". The High Court did all that any court can do in quashing a conviction – it ruled that Pell was not guilty beyond reasonable doubt. However, in this case, all seven judges declared that it was possible that an innocent man had been convicted – a finding that they did not have to make.

The tweet indicated not only that Hinch was ignorant of the law but also revealed his prejudice. Hinch was willing to accept the two-to-one majority decision of the Victorian Court of Appeal. But not the seven-zip unanimous decision of the High Court of Australia.

2004 had seen the publication of Derryn Hinch's *The Fall and Rise of Derryn Hinch: How I Hit the Wall and Didn't Bleed* (Hardie Grant). In his memoir, Hinch regretted that he "did not get this exquisite Swiss woman" at a party hosted by Molly Meldrum in Melbourne in the late 1970s. However, they met for dinner "days later". He reported in his memoir that the "stupendously beautiful model" had told him she "was fifteen years and five months old".

The story is ambiguous, but was clarified in Hinch's blog on 1 November 2013 where the following comment appeared (it has now been deleted): "About ten years ago, in my book, *The Rise and Fall of Derryn Hinch*, I admitted that in my thirties I had sex with a 15 year old girl". He placed the Meldrum party as having occurred in 1979 and said that the girl in question, now a woman, had told him recently that she was 18 years old at the time. The implication was – no problem here.

In 1979 the age of consent in Victoria was 16 – it still is. The point here is that Hinch had no qualms about writing what he wrote in 2004 about (unintentional) underage sex. Until 2013 – the year in which the Royal Commission commenced its operations – when he saw fit to issue a clarification by stating that the female in question was 18 years old.

• **Chris Geraghty** (former Catholic priest, former judge NSW District Court, author)

Chris Geraghty was one of a number of former or current Catholic priests who willingly joined the Pell pile-on. On 12 May 2020, not long after the High Court quashed Pell's conviction, Geraghty wrote a mocking piece which was published on John Menadue's *Pearls and Irritations* blog. It took the form of an open letter which commenced: "Dear George, More bad news. When will it cease?"

Not surprisingly, Geraghty gleefully accepted all the findings of the Royal Commission concerning Pell which had just been released – yet none were supported by witness or forensic evidence. See Chapter 9. In sneering style, the letter concluded:

> Look, George, in the circumstances, it's probably best, for you and all of us, especially for the traumatized members of your Church, if you take off the robes and rings, put on some sack-cloth, accept the findings of the Commission with all the dignity you can muster, and disappear into a retirement village. I suppose you are aware that I have never been a fan of yours. However, truly, I have never, and now do not wish that any harm come to you in your twilight years. And I hope we can together wish the victims of institutional abuse healing, justice and peace.
>
> I remain,
>
> Yours ontologically,
>
> Chris Geraghty.

2012 had seen the publication of Christopher Geraghty's *A Journey from the Pulpit to the Bench* (Spectrum Publications). Linda Morris interviewed the author for the *Sydney Morning Herald* (14 July 2012) and filed the following report – about Geraghty's time on the staff of the St Columba's Seminary at Springwood in the NSW Blue Mountains:

> Geraghty has his own confession to make, admitting he never passed on to police or to his superiors information about a sexual relationship between a well-known priest and one of the seminarians in his care. There were extenuating circumstances.
>
> Geraghty was sexually naive and the student spoke to him on condition of silence. Geraghty advised him to confront the priest, Father Vince Kiss, and to end the relationship, which had been going on since he had been about 12, and assisted him in "his search for a new life". The two later renewed their friendship when the victim, a headmaster at a state school, came forward to testify against Kiss. [At the time some students for the priesthood entered St Columba's Seminary at about 12 years of age.]
>
> "I don't feel remorseful about it, I don't feel guilty, but I do feel diminished. I'm regretful I was not more worldly wise, I wasn't more informed, I wasn't more educated; that I was never aware of the

possibility that priests could be paedophiles as they were; and how to deal with it. If I'd known then what I know now and dealt with it aggressively, Vince [Kiss] maybe would not have interfered with a number of other boys and caused them untold trauma."

Geraghty was born in 1938 – he left the priesthood in late 1976. Pell was born in 1941. Vince Kiss was a notorious pedophile Catholic priest with a record of offending not far off that of Gerald Ridsdale. Geraghty has admitted that, when on the staff of St Columba's between 1968 and 1972, he knew that Kiss was a sexual offender but did nothing about it. Yet he is critical of Pell for not acting on clerical pedophilia at around the same time. However, there is no evidence that in the 1960s and 1970s Pell had special knowledge about the sexual assaults by clergy against boys.

• **Peter Saunders** (British-born advocate for child-sexual abuse survivors)

In late 2017, Peter Saunders announced his resignation from the Pontifical Commission for the Protection of Minors to which he had been appointed by Pope Francis three years earlier. He had taken leave from the body in early 2016. Saunders was the British founder of the National Association for People Abused in Childhood (NAPAC).

Saunders became well known in Australia, and to some extent internationally, for his withering criticisms of Pell on Network Nine's *60 Minutes* program. On Sunday 31 May 2015, *60 Minutes* ran extracts from an interview which Tara Brown had conducted with Saunders in Rome. It was a hatchet job on Pell – in which Saunders was the "star" of the evening with the comment:

> Personally I think that his position is untenable, because he has now a catalogue of denials. He has a catalogue of denigrating people, of acting with callousness, cold-heartedness. Almost sociopathic – I would go as far as to say – this lack of care. Given the position of George Pell as a cardinal of the church and a position of huge authority within the Vatican, I think he is a massive, massive thorn in the side of Pope Francis's papacy if he is allowed to remain. And

> I think it's critical that he is moved aside, that he is sent back to Australia, and that the Pope takes the strongest action against him.

The program implied that Saunders had some authority from the Pope to speak about Pell – this was not the case. Moreover, the indication was given that Saunders and Pell had at least met. Not so. Pell had not spoken to Saunders and Saunders had no personal knowledge of Pell. The reference to Pell being "almost sociopathic" was taken from a criticism of him by Pell-antagonist Anthony Foster and re-run by Saunders. Moreover, Pope Francis was always supportive of Pell. Not because the two men agreed on all issues. But because virtually no one in the Vatican – supporters and opponents alike – believed that Pell was a pedophile.

Tara Brown ran Saunders and the Fosters again on *60 Minutes* later in the year – 6 December 2015. Brown specifically called Pell "a liar" and Saunders alleged that the "Melbourne Response was, and is, a cynical attempt again to denigrate, to silence, families who are grieving – and families who are hurting". No other view was heard.

Saunders did not remain for long in the Vatican position. In August 2019, Saunders was forced to step down from the Victims and Survivors Panel of the Independent Inquiry Into Childhood Sexual Abuse (IICSA), which was set up in Britain to investigate systematic sexual abuse in institutions.

When appointed to the IICSA in 2015, Saunders failed to declare that he had been arrested in 2008 in Manchester, following a sexual encounter with a woman in the toilet cubicle of a restaurant. The woman, who had been abused as a child, was invited to the lunch by Saunders. He said the encounter was consensual – she denied this. Police did not press charges due to insufficient evidence.

Saunders made no further appearances on *60 Minutes* or on *7.30* (where he had been given a soft interview by Leigh Sales on 29 June 2017 after Pell had been charged by Victoria Police). Neither program reported the circumstances surrounding Saunders' forced resignation from IICSA.

• **Michael H Kelly** (Jesuit priest, editor)

On the morning of 3 March 2016, the Jesuit priest Michael H Kelly, a Pell-antagonist, phoned ABC Radio Sydney 702 and spoke to presenter Wendy Harmer. In the wake of Pell's 19 hours testimony before the Royal Commission, Kelly wanted listeners to know what he thought of the Cardinal. It wasn't positive, as the transcript indicates:

> I've known Cardinal Pell for over 30 years. And I really think he's one of the best developed narcissists I've ever met in my life. He's astonishing at the way in which he can deploy his insensitivity. He seems just impervious to human experience… He's a bully, he's just a bully. He gets exactly what he wants by standing over people. As one priest in Melbourne said to me recently – he's lived by the sword, he's gonna die by the sword.

When Kelly told Harmer that clerical child sex abuse was "clearly well known and much discussed in clerical circles", Harmer responded: "If you all heard it… then you must have all colluded in hiding this". Not surprisingly, Kelly did not address the issue.

Soon after the news of Pell's conviction was announced in February 2019, Kelly wrote an article for *La Croix International*. Published on 18 March 2019, it contained the following comment:

> Pell as a local bishop and in his actions and influence in Rome is the embodiment of the firm wall of religion that passed for Catholicism in its unsuccessful attempts since Vatican II to say "carry on as usual" — as if the Council really didn't matter much at all. It's no exaggeration to say that the Church in Australia and in many parts of the world has needed a cataclysm of earth-shaking proportions if change is really to occur.
>
> The defense teams in the public square – right-wing newspaper columnists, various culture warriors, a leading Jesuit commentator and two former Prime Ministers – have all rushed into print to say how implausible the [Pell] conviction was. As has been pointed out by some observers, these leading figures in the conservative establishment have together done something conservatives should abhor: by their criticisms they are undermining the rule of law one of whose

primary foundations is trial by jury and acceptance of the outcome, however unpalatable.

The right-wing newspaper columnists referred to appear to be Piers Akerman, Janet Albrechtsen, Andrew Bolt, Miranda Devine and Gerard Henderson. Only Devine and Henderson were brought up Catholics. The leading Jesuit commentator is clearly Fr Frank Brennan S.J. – who is no conservative and who disagrees with Pell on some theological issues. The former prime ministers are John Howard and Tony Abbott – of whom Abbott was brought up Catholic. Clearly this group was not collectively involved in building a "firm wall" to resist the path of Vatican II reforms.

Then on 23 August 2019, following the majority Victorian Court of Appeal decision in *George Pell v The Queen*, Kelly – writing again in *La Croix International* – declared that it was unlikely that the High Court would hear Pell's appeal. He also predicted that Pell would face "further civil charges related to sex abuse and possibly other criminal charges arising from his testimony to the Royal Commission into sexual abuse". More false prophesy.

- **Dee Madigan** (creative director of Campaign Edge, regular guest ABC TV)

Dee Madigan used to appear regularly on Sky News' *Paul Murray Live* where, on occasions, she joined the (then) regular Pell pile-on, which included Derryn Hinch and Paul Murray. On 17 February 2016, soon after the release of Tim Minchin's song *Come Home (Cardinal Pell)*, the following exchange took place:

> *Paul Murray:* …Dee, we know there's someone writing down every word that we say, so let's do it.
>
> *Dee Madigan:* Hello, Gerard [Henderson].
>
> *Paul Murray:* Yeah, hello Gerard. What do you think [about Tim Minchin's song]?
>
> *Dee Madigan:* …You know, as a daughter of a Catholic priest, I knew what they were like in Melbourne. I grew up in Melbourne.

I knew these guys gossiped about everything. There was simply no way on earth that Pell did not hear those stories. I'm a huge Tim Minchin fan anyway. This isn't quite *White Wine in the Sun* – but I bought it straight up. Having said that – Kristina Keneally, I thought, wrote the best thing on it today. It was a searing piece against Pell that was just fantastic.

Paul Murray: Yeah it's a piece up on *The Guardian* she mentioned it today as well [as on Sky News]....

In her *Guardian* article titled "When I first heard Tim Minchin's song about Cardinal Pell, I laughed; Then I started crying", Kristina Keneally (who was at the time a Sky News contributor) declared that she was a Catholic and a "public critic of Cardinal Pell". The article contained few facts and lacked an empirical criticism of the Australian Catholic Church's handling of clerical child sexual assault since the mid-1990s. But it sure impressed Murray and Madigan – no doubt because Keneally expressed her "deep fury" at Pell.

On 18 February 2016, I emailed Madigan as follows – after thanking her for the "Hello Gerard" shout-out:

If, as you assert, George Pell should have known about pedophile priests because "these guys gossiped about everything" – then your father should have known about clerical child sexual abuse when he was a priest. So my questions are: What did your father do about clerical child sexual abuse by priests? Did he report it to the police? Did he report it to a bishop or an archbishop? Did he do nothing but enjoy the gossip? I ask these questions because – according to you – "there was simply no way on earth" that your father did not hear stories about the sexual crimes of priests.

The reply was short: "Unfortunately he [Dee Madigan's father] died in 1989 so I'm unable to ask him what he knew." This should not have been necessary, since Dee Madigan had told *Paul Murray Live* viewers the previous night that all Catholic priests – including, she claimed, Pell and by implication her late father – gossiped about everything and heard stories of clerical child sexual abuse.

- **Peter FitzSimons** (*Sun-Herald* and *Sydney Morning Herald* columnist)

Peter FitzSimons is one of Australia's best known commentators. His work is published in the *Sydney Morning Herald* and its Sunday offshoot the *Sun-Herald*. And he appears regularly on ABC radio and television as well as on Network 10's *The Project*.

For years FitzSimons maintained that George Pell lived in a "$30 million mansion in Rome". It wasn't true. When news came out that Pell had been charged by Victoria Police with historical child sexual abuse, FitzSimons put out the following tweet on 29 June 2017:

> *Peter FitzSimons:* Will Cardinal Pell step down from his roles, until such times as he proves innocence?

Naturally, Cardinal Pell stepped down from his role in the Vatican when charged and voluntarily returned to Australia. As a resident of the Vatican, with a diplomatic passport, he was not required to do so. Indeed, Graham Ashton, the head of Victoria Police, had publicly flagged the possibility of applying for an extradition order if Pell was charged.

The point about FitzSimons' tweet is its invincible ignorance. He was of the impression that defendants in the criminal jurisdiction are required to prove their innocence. This suggests that he is – or was – totally ignorant of the criminal law and has – or had – no comprehension of the requirement of proof beyond reasonable doubt.

When news emerged of Pell's conviction, FitzSimons wrote in the *Sun-Herald* (3 March 2019) that anyone who queried the verdict was "disrespectful to the jury who, after weighing all the testimony, came to the conclusion that he was guilty". FitzSimons maintained that, in writing his reference for Pell, John Howard was "basically saying he [the complainant] may well have been lying". It appears that the columnist has also no understanding of the concept of false memory. FitzSimons concluded his column:

> Our justice system, a pillar of our democracy, turns on respecting the decisions reached by a jury of peers. They have reached that de-

cision in the case of Pell, and I respect that decision, just as I respect the work of the Victorian Police and DPP who pursued this case, despite knowing the colossal forces that would be arrayed against them. They went after justice, come what may, they got it, and they were not just supported by the jury, but also Judge Kidd who presided over the case and was strong in his support of the jury decision.

It would seem that FitzSimons was unaware that it is not uncommon for an appeal court to overturn a jury verdict. Also he made a familiar error of many a Pell- antagonist in believing that Chief Judge Kidd "strongly supported the jury decision". In fact, no one knows what the judge thought about the validity of the verdict – but his demeanour when the verdict was handed down and his subsequent appearance on *The Project* does not lead to the automatic conclusion that he was "strong in his support of the jury decision".

FitzSimons did not even understand the function of the Royal Commission. Writing in the *Sun-Herald* on 2 July 2017, he claimed that its role was to inquire into "child sexual abuse". Not so – the remit was to examine institutional responses to child sexual abuse. FitzSimons then wrote that the Royal Commission "has accomplished so much in turning a much-needed spotlight on to the horrors of rampant sexual abuse by the Catholic clergy over the decades".

In fact, pedophilia among Catholic clergy was formally addressed in the mid-1990s with the establishment of the Melbourne Response and Towards Healing. The Royal Commission commenced its work around 15 years later. And it did not only put its "spotlight" on the Catholic Church, even though this turned out to be the prime focus of its inquiries. By the way, the *Boston Globe's* "Spotlight" team first published its revelations about clerical child abuse in the Catholic Archdiocese of Boston in January 2002 – almost six years after the creation of the Melbourne Response.

Indeed the Royal Commission looked at Knox Grammar School in Sydney, FitzSimons' alma mater – which, it was discovered, had a nest of pedophile teachers at the school until the 1990s. Knox Grammar is a Uniting Church institution. Five of its teachers were convicted of child sexual assault. Dr Ian Paterson, Knox headmaster at the time of the offending, gave evidence to the Royal Commission that he did not report instances of sexual assault to NSW Police, provided references for pedophiles, shifted staff offenders to different positions within the college and said he was unaware of the mandatory reporting laws for child sexual abuse that were introduced in NSW.

FitzSimons first wrote about Paterson in the *Sydney Morning Herald* on 25 April 2015. It was a remarkably soft account of his time at Knox Grammar when Paterson was head:

> And yet the Dr Paterson I knew, the principal for over three decades, was a very strong disciplinarian, a fine educator, and he ran a very tight ship. I simply cannot put that man together with the figure that has emerged from the Royal Commission – one who had allowed teachers who had groomed students to continue employment there, and even wrote a glowing reference for one he allegedly knew had had sexual relations with a student. *Dr Paterson*, do that? [sic]. I don't get it. If those specific allegations are true, I can't forgive it. No one could. But, if true, there is tragic irony in it.....

Note FitzSimons' use of the word "if" with reference to the grooming of boys at his old school. Moreover, he detected a "tragic irony" of a kind which he never acknowledged with respect to a Catholic school. On 4 April 2015, FitzSimons concluded a *Sydney Morning Herald* column with a mea culpa – of a minor kind:

> Last week I wrote that in my time at Knox, Dr Paterson ran a tight ship. He did, above decks. What was going on below decks was truly appalling and unforgivable. He told us, constantly, "As ye reap, so shall ye sow."

This time there was no reference to any "tragic irony". But the fact that FitzSimons referred to the ironic tragedies with respect to instances of historical child sexual assault at Knox Grammar in the mid-1970s suggests that he had one stance with respect to Uniting Church schools and another one with respect to Catholic schools.

• **Paul Kennedy** (ABC TV journalist, author)

Page 147 of *Hell on the way to Heaven*, states that from mid-1996 and "for the next decade and beyond, George Pell and the Catholic Church would be my [Foster's] opponents". Kennedy co-authored the book with Chrissie Foster. At the time of publication he appeared regularly on ABC programs. In December 2017, he presented the ABC TV documentary *Undeniable: Inside Australia's Biggest Cover-up* concerning child sexual abuse in religious and state institutions. Ben Knight was the executive producer.

Chrissie Foster appeared with Kennedy in *Undeniable*, including a scene at the end of the program when former prime minister Julia Gillard, who set up the Royal Commission, visits her home in Melbourne. Anthony Foster had died suddenly in late May 2017.

Undeniable essentially went over the ground covered by the Royal Commission and, to a lesser extent, the Victorian Parliamentary Inquiry. Certainly, it touched on some religious non-Catholic institutions and some non-governmental and government organisations. But the emphasis was on the Catholic Church – and the final scene depicted a Victorian Police escort for Anthony Foster's State funeral procession.

Paul Kennedy enthusiastically endorsed Peter Fox's *Walking Towards Thunder* – which had to be withdrawn from sale on account of various false allegations concerning a senior member of the NSW Police.

Like Louise Milligan and Sarah Ferguson, Paul Kennedy is very much an ABC journalist of the activist genre. On the morning of Wednesday 22 August 2019, Kennedy commented on ABC TV's *News Breakfast* about the previous day's decision by the Victorian Court of Appeal to uphold the jury's verdict in the re-trial of *The Queen v Pell*. He told viewers that the Melbourne Response was established "around the same time" as the date on which the second jury found that Pell had attacked A and B in St Patrick's Cathedral. Chrissie Foster had made a similar allegation earlier in the program.

The implication in Kennedy's comment was that Pell had established the Melbourne Response as some kind of cover for his criminal behaviour. Kennedy's statement was incorrect. The Melbourne Response was created, with the support of Victoria Police, in October 1996. The assaults for which Pell was convicted took place in December 1996 and February 1997.

I wrote to Kennedy about this on 29 August 2019 – concluding my email as follows:

> ...the Melbourne Response was created at least six weeks before – not around the same time as – the matters on which Pell was subsequently convicted. In other words, there was no causal connection between the two. Moreover, in October 1996, there were no allegations against Pell before secular or clerical authorities.
>
> In view of the fact that you have been one of the leading Pell critics in the media – and that you assisted Christine Foster with her book *Hell on the way to Heaven* – you have a responsibility to be precise when commenting on both *The Queen v George Pell* and *George Pell v The Queen*. The fact is that the Melbourne Response could not have been created to deal with any events in St Patrick's Cathedral in December 1996.

As is the wont of many an activist ABC journalist when criticised about errors, Kennedy did not respond to, or even acknowledge, my email.

- **Sarah Ferguson & Tony Jones** (ABC journalists)

On Tuesday 17 March 2020, ABC TV commenced its series *Revelation,* which it described as "a three-part documentary investigation into child sexual abuse within the Catholic Church. The ABC publicity stated that, in *Revelation*, Sarah Ferguson "comes face to face with two of Australia's most notorious serial pedophiles". They were former priest Vincent Ryan, who once worked in the Maitland-Newcastle Diocese and served over a decade in prison – and Bernard McGrath, a former St John of God brother who is serving up to four decades jail time for offences against children in Australia. The victims of both men were boys.

Revelation is very much a cult of personality journalism. Ferguson presented and directed all three episodes. She constantly appeared on camera and did all of the interviews. As TV critic Debi Enker wrote in Nine Newspapers on 15 March 2021, this is a form of television documentary in which a decision has been made "to make the reporter a prominent presence and also to employ evocative dramatic re-creations".

Revelation was an expensive taxpayer funded documentary with the team travelling to Rome and Dublin. But it revealed little that was new – except for the opportunity for viewers to get an insight into the minds of such criminals as Ryan and McGrath.

However, the benefit of this is far from clear. As Ferguson herself has acknowledged, some experts believe that pedophiles often display narcissistic traits. No surprise, then, that both men agreed to long-form interviews. It was the first – and probably the last – TV interview which either will give. A brush with "fame" – or, rather, infamy – despite the disgrace.

Reviewing the first episode in *The Age* "Green Guide", Barney Zwartz, a Pell critic, referred to the "portentous nature of the narration – in particular, Ferguson's opening sentence: "There are men living among us like Lucifer's fallen angels". This sounds clever – but what does it mean? Zwartz also referred to the portentousness of the "relentless music". And he queried whether viewers would learn anything from Ryan's self-serving account of his crimes – and doubted "the value of whole exercise".

The first episode in the series was titled "The Children have been used by the Devil" (it mainly focused on Ryan), the second "A Dangerous Place to be a Child" (it mainly focused on McGrath) and the third "Goliath" (which targeted Pell). Initially the ABC declined to say what "Goliath" was about – but it was hardly a surprise when it was announced that the person in question was Cardinal George Pell.

The second and third episodes were scheduled to be aired on Tuesday 24 March and Tuesday 31 March but one was delayed because of the showing of a special documentary on the 2019-20 bushfires in southeast Australia.

The next available Tuesday was 7 April – but this was the day set down for the High Court decision, early that morning, in *Pell v The Queen*. It seems that the ABC wanted "Goliath" to be shown before the High Court's decision was announced. In view of the Victorian DPP's poor performance before the High Court, there was an anticipation in some legal circles that the conviction would be quashed – which would have dented "Goliath"'s impact. For whatever reason, the ABC moved "Goliath" forward to Thursday 2 April.

"Goliath", which was written by ABC journalist Tony Jones, was yet another ABC contribution to the Pell pile-on. The program focused on a man whose first name is Bernie who appeared on the program. The ABC promoted "Goliath" with this claim about Bernie: "Pell accuser tells his story for the first time". False. Pell was interviewed by Victoria Police in Rome on 19 October 2016 about Bernie's story and not only emphatically denied the allegations but he also rigorously disputed the details of the case put by Victoria Police after it interviewed Bernie. The other man who accused Pell of historical sex crimes, PC, had also been interviewed by Victoria Police and had given evidence against Pell at the committal proceedings. Again, there was nothing "new" in his account.

When promoting "Goliath" on ABC Radio Sydney's *Drive with Richard Glover* on 31 March 2020, the following exchange took place:

> *Richard Glover:* Both these men [Bernie and PC] agreed to talk to you about what must have been a very difficult time in their lives.
>
> *Sarah Ferguson:* It was a long journey, Richard. And one of the lawyers involved in these stories described the survivors as lionhearted. And it's a phrase I really hold on to because it is lionhearted. But the key character in tonight's story, the one with the long story of interactions with George Pell, is both articulate and a man without bitterness. He has some anger, but no bitterness. And it makes him an extraordinarily compelling witness.

There are two problems here. First, Ferguson claimed that Bernie and PC were "survivors" of Pell's (alleged) crimes. Not so. They were complainants against Pell concerning matters which Pell had not been tried or convicted. Second, in describing Bernie as "an extraordinarily compelling witness", Ferguson followed Louise Milligan in maintaining that the credibility of a witness turns on their demeanour. This approach was criticised by all seven High Court judges less than a week later – as it had been by Justice Weinberg in the Victorian Court of Appeal. Justice Virginia Bell was particularly critical of regarding a witness as "compelling" during the two day hearing in *Pell v The Queen*. Similar criticisms of emphasising a complainant's demeanor had been made by the High Court in *M v The Queen* (1994) and in the 2003 civil case of *Fox v Percy* (where the majority comprised Chief Justice Murray Gleeson, Justice William Gummow and Justice Michael Kirby.)

In fact, there is nothing new in "Goliath". Victoria Police charged Pell relating to the allegations of Bernie and PC. A full day was booked to hear Bernie's testimony before Magistrate Wallington in *The Police v George Pell*. But the Victorian DPP dropped the case before the hearing. Magistrate Wallington committed Pell to go to trial with respect to PC's allegations that he was sexually assaulted by Pell in the YMCA Pool in Ballarat. But, in time, the Victorian DPP discontinued this charge – which also had been vigorously denied by Pell when interviewed by Victoria Police in Rome.

In "Goliath", Ferguson produced no forensic evidence or independent witness testimony against Pell concerning Bernie and PC. As pointed out above, these allegations were not regarded by the Victorian DPP (which was hardly friendly to Pell) as strong enough to go to trial. But they were good enough for Ferguson to blacken Pell's name on the eve of the High Court decision. For example, in "Goliath" Ferguson said that the boys in the YMCA Pool were "often supervised by Father Pell". There was no independent evidence to support this claim.

In the program, Ferguson interviewed Pell-antagonist David Marr – but not one of the commentators who doubted the majority decision of the Victorian Court of Appeal. It was yet another return-of-favours so beloved of the inner-city secularist left. After all, Marr had done an "in conversation" event with Ferguson at Sydney's left-wing bookshop Gleebooks on the occasion of the release of the 2019 edition of his book *The Prince*.

After the High Court decision in *Pell v The Queen*, the ABC withdrew "Goliath" for editing – before being put back on to the ABC Iview streaming service where it remains. In the re-cut, Ferguson again incorrectly referred to Bernie as a "new witness" and declared that "he is a compelling witness". Either she had not read the High Court judgment or chose to ignore its findings with respect to demeanour. Moreover, Ferguson claimed that Bernie was to have been a "key witness" to the *Swimming Pool Case* which was dropped by the Victorian DPP due to lack of evidence. This is simply not the case. The "tendency" evidence against Pell in this matter was not considered sufficient by Chief Judge Kidd to go before a jury. But Bernie was not one of the potential witnesses in this case.

In the original of "Goliath", no mention was made in the body of the program that Cardinal Pell had vehemently denied all the allegations of Bernie and PC that were put to him in Rome by Victoria Police – and the police did not have a comeback. Despite the additional time to put together the program for the Iview version, the second edition of "Goliath" also did not refer to the Rome interview in the body of the episode – and the same postscript was run at the end of a 90 minute re-cut program as had appeared when it first aired on 2 April 2020. This was unprofessional journalism.

For evidence that "Goliath" was a hatchet job on Pell, it is not necessary to look beyond what Jones wrote, and Ferguson said, about the re-trial of *The Queen v Pell* in the County Court of Victoria which had resulted in Pell's conviction:

> *Sarah Ferguson:* When Pell finally did have his day in court, his tightly woven defences publicly unravelled. On December 2018, Pell was convicted of sexually abusing two choirboys in Melbourne Cathedral in the 1990s.

This statement is false. During Pell's mistrial and re-trial, his defence did not unravel. That's why the likes of *The Age's* John Silvester, who was not a Pell supporter, expressed such surprise at the jury's verdict, after a lengthy duration, in the second trial. The truth is that it was the prosecution's case which unravelled – spectacularly so before the High Court. Ferguson made no mention of this in the re-cut of "Goliath".

Despite all the publicity hype, *Revelation* made little impact. Episodes one and two revealed nothing that had not been raked over concerning the Catholic Church in the Royal Commission and in the media (especially the ABC). And "Goliath" passed virtually without trace since it was overshadowed by the High Court's unanimous decision to quash Pell's conviction. "Goliath" merely made yet more implausible allegations against Pell, devoid of evidence.

Ferguson and Jones committed the same error as Milligan. In "Goliath" they regarded Bernie as compelling and believed what they wanted to believe. Just as in *Cardinal,* Milligan regarded A as compelling and believed what she wanted to believe. No member of this ABC trio could accept that some individuals have false memories while some others are delusional.

Cardinal Pell watched "Goliath", the final segment of the *Revelation* documentary, while in HM Prison Barwon. His immediate response can be found in one of the final entries of his *Prison Journal* on 2 April 2020:

> I am finishing today's journal after breaking to watch the *ABC TV* program *Revelation.* Two of the fellows who had accused me, and whose cases had been dropped, featured in a long program which covered much of my life, generally, but not always, presenting me in the most unflattering light. Bernie's accusations are so fantastic, ranging from accusations at St Joseph's Home, where I had no role, officially or informally, and only visited one or two times (possibly) in my twelve years in Ballarat, to accusations at St Patrick's Cathedral, Ballarat, where I never lived and had no role.
>
> The program could scarcely have been worse, although no new ground was broken, and the bizarre allegations against me in places

where I neither lived nor worked will help in the short and especially in the long run because they are so false and counter-productive. The *ABCs* exploitation of Bernie, that poor man, is disgraceful.

There seems to be no alternative to suing, although we have to receive a good verdict from the High Court to enable this. Some years of struggle lie ahead and financing the struggles might be beyond me, as there are limits to the burdens friends can be asked to bear.

And that's the problem. The ABC receives over $1 billion from the Commonwealth government each year. It has a large legal section for an organisation of its size and self-insures. That is, the ABC does not have defamation insurance and pays for any defamation settlements out of its budget. Moreover, on occasions the ABC pays for external legal advice which can be very expensive. It's extremely difficult for any taxpayer to sue the taxpayer funded public broadcaster. Consequently, the likes of Ferguson, Jones and Milligan are virtually untouchable since they are protected by employer liability and very few Australians have the money to sue the ABC.

• **Suzanne Smith** (author, former journalist)

Revelation was the ABC's last big media hit on George Pell. However, the pile-on continued for a while, even after the High Court decision. In August 2020, ABC Books published Suzanne Smith's *The Altar Boys*. Smith is a former ABC journalist who worked for many years on the ABC TV *Lateline* program.

The Altar Boys is a detailed account of the appalling number of Catholic clerical pedophiles who offended against children (mainly boys) in the Maitland-Newcastle diocese from around the mid-1960s to around the mid-1990s. They included Vincent Ryan and John Farrell. In her preface, Smith wrote: "During my time as a journalist I have reported on the epidemic of clerical abuse in the Anglican Diocese of Newcastle, and I'm not claiming that the abuse committed by Catholics in the region was worse than that committed by Anglicans." This statement is correct – Smith did report on Anglican, as well as Catholic, clerical child sexual abuse.

While *The Altar Boys* contains considerable new information, it lacked the big story capable of attracting media attention. Enter Cardinal Pell. Chapter 26 is titled "A Meeting with the Pope". It covered an alleged meeting between Pope Francis and Fr Glen Walsh (1961-2017) in Rome on 9 February 2016. Walsh had been called as a witness in the trial of Archbishop Philip Wilson who had been charged with covering up for a pedophile priest. Wilson was convicted but had the magistrate's decision overturned in the NSW District Court.

Walsh, apparently a victim of sexual assault when a young trainee brother, was a troubled and sick person when he visited Rome in early 2016. According to Smith, he told his closest friends and family that he had received a request from the Vatican to have a private interview with the Pope concerning the Wilson Case – and that a meeting took place on Tuesday 9 February 2016. Smith reported that Walsh had said that he had given Pope Francis only a brief summary of why he needed to testify against Wilson. He wanted to say more but didn't since he said that he was worried that the interpreter had links to the Maitland-Newcastle diocese.

As Smith reports in *The Altar Boys:*

> The Pope listened and asked him who had been supporting him on this journey. Glen replied again with the scantest of details.... Glen told several friends that when he'd left the meeting with the Pope, Cardinal Pell had been waiting outside. He had said to Glen, "Look what I have done for you," and lifted his hand towards Glen's face so the priest could kiss his ring, the ritual expected when one met a cardinal of the Catholic Church. But Glen said he had refused to kiss the ring and just walked out of the room, out of the Vatican offices, and into the daylight.

The Sydney Morning Herald and *The Age* were given early notice of Smith's work. On 19 August 2020, both Nine newspapers carried a Page One report by Harriet Alexander titled "What are you planning to say? Pope quizzed whistle-blower priest, book claims". In the third paragraph of her report, Alexander wrote that this was an "explosive claim". But the first two paragraphs indicated that there was some doubt at the *Sydney Morning Herald* and *The Age* about the story. Here they are:

> A low-ranking parish priest who agreed to give evidence against an archbishop accused of concealing child sexual abuse was mysteriously summoned to the Vatican before he was due to testify and **allegedly** quizzed by Pope Francis about what he was planning to say in court, a new book claims. [emphasis added]

> As Fr Glen Walsh emerged from the 2016 meeting, Cardinal George Pell was **allegedly** waiting outside. "Look what I have done for you," Cardinal Pell said, and lifted his hand for the priest to kiss his ring. [Emphasis added]

Harriet Alexander's page one story was illustrated by a photo of Walsh in Rome with St Peter's Basilica in the background. The caption read: "Father Glenn Walsh at St Peter's before the 2016 meeting." The intention of the image was to give verisimilitude to the story about the Sydney priest meeting the Pope. But it's the kind of photo which could have been taken of any tourist in Rome.

The Altar Boys repeats an error common to many contemporary journalists, including the ABC's Louise Milligan. Suzanne Smith put in direct quotation marks what Cardinal Pell allegedly said to Fr Walsh – as told by Walsh to several close friends sometime after the alleged event occurred. They later spoke or wrote to Smith. To repeat, the claim is that some of the late Fr Walsh's closest friends told Smith about what Walsh had said to them about what Pell had (allegedly) said to Walsh. This is hearsay upon hearsay. But Smith believes what Walsh told some close friends is true – despite a total lack of evidence.

In correspondence, Smith has told me that she did not attempt to contact Pell or the Pope's staff before breaking her explosive story in *The Altar Boys*. It's possible that Pell, who has a distrust for sections of the media which is entirely warranted, would not have responded to Smith. But at least the author could have tried to contact Pell and the Pope's staff. It's called professional journalism.

I have checked Smith's assertion with Pell. The facts are as follows.

The Vatican's official records show that the Pope celebrated Mass at the Altar of the Chair in St Peter's Basilica, with a group of Capuchin friars, on Tuesday 9 February 2016. During the morning he was with the Council of Cardinals (termed C9) in the Santa Martha Guest House. Cardinal Pell attended this meeting. The official records show that the Pope met with the Missionaries of Mercy in the Sala Regina Apostolic Palace at 5.30 pm that day. There is no record of any meeting with Fr Walsh or an interpreter. It is understood that Francis does not grant meetings with individuals on Tuesdays.

Smith refers to Walsh as having walked out of the Vatican offices after the meeting. The Pope does not meet people in his office. Official meetings take place in the library on the second floor of the Apostolic Palace – which is not open to visitors.

Pell has also advised me that he "did not organise any meeting for Fr Walsh with the Holy Father" – as the book *The Altar Boys* implies. Pell also told me that he did not meet with Walsh at any time in Rome. Pell attended the C9 meeting on the morning of Tuesday 9 February 2016, had two afternoon engagements and went to the Santa Cecilia concert hall in the evening. It was a very busy day. This information is taken from Pell's diary.

Pell concluded his email to me, dated 9 April 2021, as follows:

> It is not now the custom of cardinals to ask priests to kiss their ring, and I never had that practice; certainly not to a priest I knew and had befriended, such as Fr Walsh. Although he was not a priest of Sydney Archdiocese, I took him in and gave him a parish, which he left suddenly and without notice.
>
> To exit from the library where the Pope meets official guests, and the records show the Pope was in the Apostolic Palace on that afternoon of 9/2/'16, you have to pass through at least six large rooms where there are monsignors, gentlemen-in-waiting and Swiss Guards. You have to use the lift and it takes at least five minutes to emerge into "the daylight" still within the Vatican.
>
> Fr Glen was a good sad man, and his story is a complete fantasy. I

certainly was no part of it, although I never had a cross word with him during the many times we met.

Like many journalists who have written about Pell over the decades, Smith has believed what she wanted to believe. She wanted to believe that, somehow or other, Pell had acted improperly concerning the Archbishop Wilson case. She willingly embraced the story – based on multiple hearsay accounts of what a man in ill-health told his friends about an alleged meeting with the Pope concerning which there was not a skerrick of evidence. Clearly Glen Walsh had a clear "recollection" of an event that never took place. This was poor, unprofessional journalism on the part of Suzanne Smith.

Other media members of the Pell pile-on did not challenge Smith's account. On 1 September 2020, the University of Technology Sydney (UTS) put on a function titled "Recording: Truth-telling with Suzanne Smith and David Marr". Yes, another case of a Pell-antagonist interviewing a Pell-antagonist about Pell. There is no evidence that Marr used the occasion to query Smith's account of Walsh's alleged meeting with the Pope which had appeared on the front page of two of Australia's leading newspapers.

On 11 September 2020, Smith did a soft interview on *Mornings with Virginia Trioli* on ABC Radio Melbourne 774. Trioli did not challenge Smith when she said that Walsh "was given a direct message basically by the Vatican to become a hostile witness" in the Philip Wilson case – despite the fact that there was no evidence to support this assertion. The interview included this exchange:

> *Virginia Trioli:* Well it's – let's not immediately interpret it as a threatening gesture, although, you know, some listening this morning might. But it's a pretty big deal for, you know, a reasonably low level priest to be called to the Vatican and have a personal interview, all the way across the other side of the world, when you've actually decided to do something as extraordinary as go to the police.
>
> *Suzanne Smith:* Well, there's 400,000 priests in the world.
>
> *Virginia Trioli:* Why him?

> *Suzanne Smith:* I wonder, why him? That's right. Yeah, that was his interpretation.

Yes, it was. But this does not mean that Glen Walsh's recollection was accurate. Clearly Suzanne Smith believed what she wanted to believe – without even trying to do any fact-checking

Quelle Surprise! ABC Dismisses All Criticism Of Its Handling Of The Pell Case

• Craig McMurtrie's Rationalisation

At 6 am on Saturday 11 April 2020, Craig McMurtrie – in his capacity as the ABC's editorial director – wrote an article for *ABC News Online* titled "Why the ABC's reporting on the George Pell Case wasn't a witch-hunt". It was presented as a "reflection" on the Pell Case in the light of the High Court decision. But it was a defence of the ABC by the ABC's editorial director. I wrote to McMurtrie the following day with a critique of his self-serving article. He acknowledged my email but declined to comment on my email or answer any of my questions.

On Saturday 18 April the ABC put out another statement on the Pell Case titled "Response from the ABC spokesperson" – which was essentially a re-write of McMurtrie's 11 April article. There followed an identical, but differently headed, statement on Monday 20 April 2020 which was attributed to Craig McMurtrie, titled "The ABC's reporting on Cardinal George Pell". It commenced:

> The ABC has always acted in the public interest in reporting on the police investigation into Cardinal George Pell and in investigating other allegations made against him. The ABC firmly rejects claims that it pursued a "witch hunt" against Cardinal Pell, that it engaged in "vigilante" journalism or that it's coverage was one-sided or unfair. At every stage of this story the ABC has presented a wide range of opinions on the case.

McMurtrie's statement was an exercise in self-delusion. The taxpayer funded public broadcaster had waged a campaign against Pell over the years – and now McMurtrie was asserting that its coverage had been fair and balanced.

There was even an error – prejudicial to Pell – in the third paragraph of the ABC's 20 April 2020 statement, which read as follows:

> The first allegations [sic] against Cardinal Pell surfaced in 2002 and were considered serious enough for him to step aside while a Church-initiated investigation was conducted. That inquiry concluded that the complainant was honest but that there was insufficient evidence to corroborate the claim.

On 21 April 2020, I wrote to David Anderson, the ABC's managing director and editor-in-chief, pointing out the error in the ABC's statement which was written by McMurtrie:

> This statement is inaccurate and should be corrected. The inquiry into the allegation – not allegations – against George Pell, dating back to 1960, was conducted by retired Victorian Supreme Court judge Alec Southwell QC. Mr Southwell, not a Catholic, regarded his inquiry as similar to a royal commission or statutory board of inquiry.
>
> The statement by the ABC spokesperson, dated 18 April, is selective in its quotation from Mr Southwell's report and omitted this central finding by Alec Southwell QC: "I accept as correct the submission by Mr Tovey [the complainant's counsel] that the complainant, when giving evidence of molesting, gave the impression that he was speaking honestly from an actual recollection. However, the respondent [George Pell], also gave the impression that he was speaking the truth."
>
> Alec Southwell QC's finding that George Pell was honest in his recollection was not in the ABC's document dated 20 April 2020. Nor is there any reference to Mr Southwell's comment that "some valid criticism" had been made of "the complainant's credibility". The ABC's statement distorts Mr Southwell's finding and, as a con-

sequence, is prejudicial to Cardinal Pell. In fact, Alex Southwell QC held that he was "not satisfied that the complaint has been established".

Mr Anderson did not reply but the ABC statement was altered to include Mr Southwell's finding that George Pell had given the impression that he was speaking the truth. Also, the claim that there had been "allegations" – not an allegation – about Pell's alleged behaviour in 1960 was corrected in one instance but not in another. The current statement on the ABC website, dated 20 April 2020, records in an endnote that McMurtrie's document was changed on 22 April 2020. Now the final sentence of the paragraph read:

> That inquiry concluded that both the complainant and George Pell gave the impression of speaking honestly but that there was insufficient evidence to corroborate the claim.

However, no reference was made to Southwell QC's queries about the complainant's credibility – or to Southwell QC's specific finding that he was not satisfied that the complaint [against Pell] had been established. After the High Court decision, ABC management put out a statement which, even after a correction, was still misleading in a matter prejudicial to Pell in that it did not cite Southwell QC's specific finding. It was another instance of the taxpayer funded public broadcaster in denial.

The ABC's statement of 20 April 2020 also defended what it termed the ABC's "major investigations into Cardinal Pell". They were *7.30* on 27 July 2016 (reporter Louise Milligan), *Four Corners* "Guilty: The Conviction of Cardinal Pell" on 4 March 2019 (reporter Louise Milligan) and *Revelation's* "Goliath" episode on 2 April 2020 (reporter Sarah Ferguson, written by Tony Jones). The statement did not specifically name Milligan, Ferguson or Jones. No mention was made of the fact that not one of the allegations promulgated by Milligan or Ferguson/Jones in their ABC TV programs, concerning their "compelling" witnesses, succeeded at law.

The ABC statement sought to rationalise the ABC's coverage of the

Pell Case by claiming that "many of the Cardinal's most prominent supporters have regularly appeared on ABC programs". But it did not concede that many of Pell's strong supporters were simply not invited on to the ABC. And the statement did not produce a list of the relative number of appearances by Pell's opponents and supporters against which his claim the ABC's coverage was not unbalanced could be judged. McMurtrie's defence of his employer was long on fudge but short on detail.

At times in the statement it was evident that the ABC's editorial director Craig McMurtrie, who drafted the document, was not conversant with the facts. One example illustrates the point. McMurtrie wrote:

> Historical critics of the Cardinal also were interviewed but were balanced with other perspectives. For instance, journalist and author David Marr appeared on ABC Melbourne *Mornings* [with Jon Faine] along with Terry Laidler and Francis Sullivan on 26 February and Archbishop Comensoli did an extended interview on 27 February [2019]....

According to McMurtrie, this line-up represented "balance". But the Pell-antagonist Marr was "balanced" by Sullivan and Laidler – both of whom were Pell critics. There was not one Pell supporter on this panel of three. Also McMurtrie failed to point out that the *Mornings with Jon Faine* presenter mocked some of Archbishop Comensoli's comments during the on-air interview.

McMurtrie mentioned that Fr Frank Brennan had declined invitations to appear on some ABC programs to discuss the Pell case. But he chose not to reveal that Brennan was boycotting the ABC at the time due to his view that the public broadcaster's coverage of this case was so jaundiced in its campaign against Pell that Brennan would not have his name used in an attempt to restore "balance" – only after Pell's acquittal.

For example, after the High Court decision, Brennan chose to give his one and only interview to Kieran Gilbert on Sky News – having declined an offer by *7.30's* Leigh Sales. When the suppression orders were first lifted in February 2019, Brennan willingly gave interviews to Raf Epstein on the ABC Radio Melbourne's *Drive* program and to Leigh Sales on *7.30*. But by the time of the High Court decision in April 2020, Brennan decided that the ABC was simply involved in trying to restore an image of "balance" which had not occurred and declined invitations from the public broadcaster. McMurtrie's statement concluded:

> Other coverage included an interview on *The Religion and Ethics Report* with Dr Bernadette Tobin from the Plunkett Centre for Ethics, a close friend of Cardinal Pell, and an analysis piece by ABC religion expert Noel Debien.

It was a misleading statement. Dr Tobin appeared once on the low rating but influential ABC Radio National's *Religion and Ethics Report* – but only after Pell's conviction was quashed. Moreover, Noel Debien has said that he felt "a pariah" at the ABC for not having declared that "George was guilty as charged". It would seem that the ABC's editorial director was not aware of the prevailing staff driven culture at the ABC that had the effect of silencing Noel Debien.

The ABC's statement had to be revised on three occasions before the final version was settled. To some, this would suggest incompetence – especially since the public broadcaster had plenty of time to prepare a statement. But it served a purpose in providing material for the ABC's very own *Media Watch* program hosted by Paul Barry in his own qualified clearance of the ABC's coverage of the Pell Case.

It's worth noting that, in his capacity as the ABC's editorial director, Craig McMurtrie presided over a situation whereby the ABC failed to report its own pedophile scandals, including the 1975 comment by then ABC chair Professor Richard Downing that "in general, men will sleep with young boys". Or the 2017 conviction of former ABC children's program producer Jon Stephens who pleaded guilty to the sexual abuse of a 13 year old actor while on official ABC duties in 1981.[19]

• **Paul Barry's ABC *Media Watch* Cop-Out**

ABC TV's *Media Watch* program commenced in 1989. Since then, all its presenters have been left-of-centre journalists, including such Pell-antagonists as David Marr and Richard Ackland. Paul Barry has been in the presenter's chair since 2013, around the time when the Pell pile-on commenced. During this time, Barry never expressed a concern about the media's overwhelmingly hostile coverage of the Pell Case, including that of the ABC – and never wondered whether such reporting would make it impossible for the accused to receive a fair trial.

In view of the Easter break, Monday 20 April 2020 was the first *Media Watch* program after Pell's acquittal. It was titled "Pell – the final verdict; The ABC has been condemned for leading a witch-hunt against George Pell. So, how does its coverage stack up against that charge?" Barry's verdict was that the ABC was not involved in a witch-hunt. He essentially agreed with McMurtrie's self-serving analysis. Another case of an ABC employee defending the ABC against criticism.

Viewers got an idea of what was to come when Barry opened with the assertion that: "Tonight we look at the man who's divided the nation". It wasn't Pell who divided Australia – this was a consequence of the decision by Victoria Police to charge Pell with historical child sexual assault offences on the basis of the flimsiest of evidence.

Then Barry threw the switch to sectarianism by stating that "Pell's supporters…are often Catholics". Well, some were. But some of Pell's vocal supporters, with respect to his conviction, were not Catholics – Janet Albrechtsen, former Labor MP Peter Baldwin, Andrew Bolt, Rowan Dean, Jeff Kennett, Amanda Vanstone, and Keith Windschuttle. So, what's religion got to do with it? – except when anti-Catholic sectarianism is involved.

Barry relied heavily on Craig McMurtrie's apologia for the ABC and made only two specific criticisms of the public broadcaster. Barry criticised the fact that Louise Milligan's March 2019 program on

Four Corners "did not canvas any of Pell's defence from the trial" but "lined up witnesses condemning Pell". And Barry said that "having given so much time to Pell's accusers since 2016, *7.30* should surely have devoted more than six minutes to his final acquittal".

The same could have been said for many other ABC programs including *Insiders* (executive producer Samuel Clark) which did not cover Pell's acquittal in its first program after the High Court decision – despite having put Pell on the show's run-down on a number of occasions in previous years. Likewise ABC TV's *Q&A* ignored Pell's acquittal – after a number of programs over the years with unbalanced panels critical of Pell and audiences replete with Pell-antagonists.

All up, Barry's critique of the ABC's coverage was soft. Channeling McMurtrie, Barry implied that the likes of Francis Sullivan, Paul Collins and Terry Laidler were Pell supporters. Not so, in that none publicly declared a doubt about his guilt prior to the High Court decision. Barry even had a positive word to say about his ABC colleague, leading Pell-antagonist Louise Milligan:

> …let's not forget that Louise Milligan and her producer Andy Burns won the Melbourne Press Club's 2016 Golden Quill Award for that *7.30* special. While Milligan's book *Cardinal* was also highly acclaimed, winning the 2017 Walkley Book Award and the Law Reporting Award from Sydney's Sir Owen Dixon Chambers. So Milligan's reporting was praised by lawyers and journalists alike.

The Golden Quill Award and the Walkley Book Award are gongs given to journalists by other journalists. Let's not forget, to use a Paul Barry term, that the *New York Times* journalist Walter Duranty won the Pulitzer Prize in 1932 for a series of articles on the Soviet Union under the communist dictator Joe Stalin which were manifestly false.

Moreover, as documented in Chapter 7, Milligan would not answer straight-forward questions about *Cardinal* and never was interviewed by, or participated in a panel discussion with, a well-informed critic of her work. Sure *Cardinal* was "praised by lawyers" – but only some lawyers. Barry should have been aware that the legal profession was deeply divided over Pell's conviction and the upholding of the jury verdict by a majority decision of the Victorian Court of Appeal. To suggest otherwise was ignorant and, consequently, misleading.

Paul Barry could not name one ABC presenter, reporter or producer who publicly questioned the case against Pell and expressed the view that he was not guilty beyond reasonable doubt – and was, therefore, an innocent man. Not one.

From the time of the establishment of the Royal Commission in early 2013 until Pell's acquittal by the High Court in April 2020, viewers of Sky News would have heard from presenters and contributors who were supporters of George Pell in that they did not believe that he was a pedophile. This Sky News list includes Andrew Bolt, Peta Credlin, Rowan Dean, Miranda Devine and Chris Kenny. But Sky News viewers would also have heard from presenters and contributors who were Pell-antagonists. The list includes Derryn Hinch, Kristina Keneally, Dee Madigan, Paul Murray (up to when Pell was charged when he ceased to comment on the case), Graham Richardson and Peter van Onselen.

However, there was not one presenter on any ABC outlet – television, radio or online – who publicly expressed doubt about Pell's conviction, let alone stated their opinion that he was innocent. This is something about which the ABC's *Media Watch* program was in denial.

Following McMurtrie, Paul Barry did not even mention what presents as ABC Comedy. The recently appointed BBC director-general Tim Davie commented in March 2021 that BBC comedy shows provide a "metropolitan, London-centric and left-wing view of the world". It's much the same with the ABC, albeit in a Sydney and Melbourne metropolitan way. Over the years, Shaun Micallef (who was brought up a Catholic) targeted the likes of Cardinal Pell and his supporters in his *Shaun Micallef's Mad As Hell* program. Likewise Charlie Pickering in his *The Weekly with Charlie Pickering* and Tom Ballard in his *Tonightly*. No other view was heard on ABC Comedy – in that not one of its presenters ever sneered at or mocked Pell's critics or anti-Catholic sectarians. All the (feigned) humour was on Pell and his supporters.

The insouciance of *Media Watch* presenter Paul Barry and his executive producer Timothy Latham concerning the ABC's coverage of the Pell Case is evident in the attachment to the transcript of "Pell – The final verdict" – which is on the ABC website. It is the ABC statement of 18 April, titled "Response from an ABC spokesperson", which contained the claims prejudicial to Pell were corrected in the ABC's second statement of 20 April 2020. The original comment prejudicial to Pell remained on the *Media Watch* segment on the ABC website at the time this book went to print.

The ABC's *Media Watch* program did not even know what was the ABC's final version of the ABC's reporting on the Pell Case. I wrote to Timothy Latham (ABC TV's *Media Watch* executive producer) advising that *Media Watch's* website contained an error concerning the Pell Case. He did not respond.

A Note on the ABC's Evidential Standards

In 2021, the ABC settled a defamation claim made by Christian Porter (then a cabinet minister in the Liberal Party-Nationals Coalition government) against the ABC and Louise Milligan. The ABC paid Porter's mediation costs. Porter paid no money to the ABC.

As part of the settlement, on 30 May 2021 the ABC placed an editor's note at the end of the Milligan article which stated that its "serious accusations" could not be substantiated "to the applicable legal standard – criminal or civil". Conceding that the taxpayer funded public broadcaster is prepared to make allegations against individuals which did not meet the criminal (beyond reasonable doubt) or civil (on the balance of probabilities) evidentiary standard. This is the (low) standard which applies to the programs on Cardinal Pell by Louise Milligan, Sarah Ferguson and others.

* * * * *

The massive media pile-on against Cardinal Pell led to a situation where no jury could be expected to assess the evidence with an open-mind, no matter how much the jurors tried to do so. The answer to Professor Greg Craven's question in this specific case is that, at times, the justice system cannot be heard above the media mob.

* * * * *

Sky News' Andrew Bolt and Cardinal George Pell

News Corp columnist and Sky News presenter Andrew Bolt (an agnostic) was one of Cardinal Pell's most vocal supporters in the media – of which there were very few. This interview was shown on Sky News over two nights on 13/14 April 2020. It was conducted at the Seminary of the Good Shepherd in the Sydney suburb of Homebush shortly after the High Court decision.

Gail Furness in Sydney and George Pell in Rome

Gail Furness SC, Counsel Assisting the Royal Commission, interviewed Cardinal Pell (who was in Rome) over four days. Here Pell takes an oath on The Bible at the commencement of the hearing on Monday 29 February 2016. It was 8 am in Sydney and 10 pm (Sunday 28 February 2016) in Rome. This was the cardinal's third and final appearance before the Royal Commission – one in person and two by video link.

An official photo of the Royal Commission chair The Hon. Justice Peter McClellan AM. The Royal Commission's findings with respect to Cardinal Pell lacked evidence, were contradictory and, in one instance, amounted to a denail of due process. There is no right of reply against the findings of a Royal Commission.

9

ROYAL COMMISSION OR ROMAN CATHOLIC COMMISSION?

"...I don't think the [Royal] Commission was an unequivocal blessing....I still feel that the Commission focused unduly on Catholicism and that it can't be entirely absolved of unconscious elements of anti-Catholicism that has been the default position of Anglo-Australian culture since the 19th Century."
- Dr Paul Collins, "The Royal Commission – a mixed blessing", *Pearls and Irritations*, 12 December 2017.

The Royal Commission Established

Labor Party Prime Minister Julia Gillard announced the establishment of the Royal Commission into Institutional Responses to Child Sexual Abuse on 12 November 2012. Its creation was supported by the Liberal Party's Tony Abbott, the leader of the Opposition. The Royal Commission commenced operations in early 2013 and held its opening sitting in Melbourne on 3 April 2013. It provided its final report on 15 December 2017. Originally funded for three years, the Royal Commission successfully sought a two-year extension – this was granted by Malcolm Turnbull's (politically conservative) Coalition

An official photo of the Royal Commission Counsel Assisting Gail Furness SC

government. All up, it cost $342.3 million – out of a maximum budget allocation of $372.8 million.

The Hon. Justice Peter McClellan AM was appointed chair of the commission. In his address to the Royal Commission's final sitting, Justice McClellan made the following comment:

> The sexual abuse of children is not just a problem from the past. Child sexual abuse in institutions continues today. We were told of many cases of abuse that occurred in the last 10 to 15 years in a range of institutions, including schools, religious institutions, foster and kinship care, respite care, health and allied services, performing arts institutions, childcare centres and youth groups.... The Royal Commission has been concerned with the sexual abuse of children within institutions. It is important to remember that, notwithstanding the problems we have identified, the number of children who are sexually abused in familial or other circumstances far exceeds those who are abused in institutions.

The remit of the Royal Commission was limited to focusing on the sexual abuse of children within institutions – even though the number of abused children in familial or other circumstances far exceeds those who are or were abused in institutions.

In announcing the establishment of the Royal Commission, Prime Minister Julia Gillard initially said that it would inquire into institutional responses to instances and allegations of child abuse in Australia. Shortly, however, she referred to "revelations of child abusers being moved from place to place" – an implied reference to the Catholic Church. Moreover, as mentioned earlier, the prime minister told the media conference that she had contacted Cardinal Pell in advance of her announcement. No other religious or non-religious leader was referred to. No mention was made of the Royal Commission's limited remit with respect to all forms of child sexual abuse throughout Australia. In her book *My Story* (Knopf, 2014), Gillard wrote that she "did not want the royal commission to be seen to be a witch-hunt into one Church but rather to have the breadth it truly needed". But this was an unintended consequence of her decision.

The composition of the Royal Commission was announced on 11 January 2013. Namely, The Hon Justice Peter McClellan AM (chair) – a judge of appeal in the Supreme Court of New South Wales. Plus The Hon Justice Jennifer Coate (judge of the Family Court of Australia), Bob Atkinson AO (former Queensland Police Service Commissioner), Robert Fitzgerald AM (Productivity Commission), Helen Milroy (consultant child and adolescent psychiatrist) and Andrew Murray (former Democrats Senator for Western Australia). Ms Gail Furness SC was appointed Senior Counsel Assisting the Royal Commission.

In this group of seven, only Fitzgerald was brought up a Catholic. The choice of Atkinson was surprising since, as McClellan pointed out in his final address to the Royal Commission, the police "often refused...to investigate" the complaints of abuse made by children and that "many children who had attempted to escape abuse were returned to unsafe institutions by police". The appointment of a retired police commissioner to the Royal Commission would have been akin to an appointment of a retired Anglican or Catholic bishop or archbishop to the same body. The latter did not happen.

Writing in *Pearls and Irritations* on 12 December 2017, the historian and author Paul Collins – who depicts himself as a progressive, not a conservative, Catholic – commented:

> There was…a lack of well-informed Catholics on the [Royal Commission] staff to the extent that sometimes a kind of caricature Catholicism emerged. Besides Commissioner Robert Fitzgerald, former NSW president of the Saint Vincent de Paul Society, there were only about two well-informed Catholics on the staff …

Dr Collins had Robert Fitzgerald and Stephen Crittenden in mind. Crittenden (who is referred to in Chapter 6) is well-informed and was brought up a Catholic. On 18 November 2013, not long before taking up a senior position in the Royal Commission, Crittenden wrote in the left-wing *Crikey* newsletter: "The fact is that Catholic clerical culture is a machine that produces sick people". Enough said. The point is that Fitzgerald and Crittenden, to a greater or lesser extent, were highly critical of the "Old Church" which Cardinal Pell was deemed to represent.

George Pell had told a media conference on 13 November 2012 that he accepted the creation of a royal commission into institutional child sexual abuse – provided that the Catholic Church was not the only cab on the rank. This turned out to be the case, however, particularly in view of the media's reporting of the five year long inquiry. Certainly some non-Catholic religious institutions – along with some secular and government organisations – came in for criticism. But nothing like the Catholic Church. The Royal Commission had one essential target – Cardinal Pell.

As Professor Greg Craven wrote in *The Weekend Australian* on 19 August 2017, "a problem with what became the Royal Commission's focus on the Catholic Church was that it all but crowded out other institutions with predictable results". He continued: "The rule is that if an inquiry gives the impression it is about one subject the public will take it as the word". Greg Craven's warning came true shortly after. On 2 July 2017, prominent Fairfax Media journalist Peter Fitz-

Simons wrote in the *Sun-Herald* that the achievement of the Royal Commission was to turn "a much needed spotlight into the horrors of rampant sexual abuse by the Catholic clergy over the decades". The implication was that only Catholic clergy commit the crime of child sexual abuse.

CEO Philip Reed Interferes in Public Debate

Wednesday 17 February 2016 was one of a miniscule of occasions when I was invited on to ABC TV or ABC Radio to discuss the Pell Case – in spite of the fact that I had covered the matter in my newspaper column in *The Weekend Australian*, my blog and in my Sky News television interviews with Andrew Bolt on numerous occasions. The ABC is not inclined to hear the views of ABC critics – especially those who criticised its coverage of the Pell Case.

Leigh Sales introduced *7.30* on 17 February 2016 by referring to the release of Tim Minchin's *Come Home (Cardinal Pell)* song which she said had berated the Cardinal as a coward for not returning to Australia, due to his heart condition, and instead deciding to appear before the Royal Commission by video link from Rome. Sales said that Minchin's "lyrics have upset Pell supporters". Then it was over to *7.30* reporter Matthew Wordsworth who told viewers that supporters of Pell had said that Minchin's song was "verbal abuse set to music". The latter comment was made to Wordsworth by me in a pre-recorded interview, which was cut. Those interviewed were – in order of appearance – Gerard Henderson, Amanda Vanstone, comedian Meshel Laurie, David Ridsdale and Peter Fox. The last three were Pell-antagonists.

Two of my comments made it to air. The second one was as follows:

> *Gerard Henderson:* That will be three appearances [by Pell] at the Royal Commission and one before the Victorian Parliamentary Inquiry. No-one else has been asked to make those kinds of appearances – and in this whole, in this whole process, no-one has

produced any evidence that Cardinal Pell acted in any way that was unlawful or improper.

On the morning of Friday 19 February 2016, I received an email from Philip Reed, in his capacity as the Royal Commission's chief executive officer, which purported to claim that there was "an error" in my *7.30* interview. Reed's argument was as follows:

> In fact, Cardinal Pell is not the only witness to have given evidence on multiple occasions before the Royal Commission. The Most Rev. Dr Phillip Aspinall, Archbishop of the Anglican Diocese of Brisbane and former Primate of the Anglican Church of Australia, has given evidence to the Royal Commission four times. Other senior representatives of church and government bodies have given evidence across multiple public hearings, including Archbishop of the Anglican Diocese of Brisbane and former Governor-General Peter Hollingworth in two public hearings.

Reed's email was an improper intervention in the public debate by a public servant employed by the Royal Commission – especially since he sent a copy of his email to *7.30* executive producer Joanne Puccini along with Leigh Sales and Matthew Wordsworth, presumably to put pressure on them to correct the "error". If such a letter were to be sent, it should have been signed by the Royal Commission chair or one of his commissioners.

I replied immediately that what I had said on *7.30* was correct – and sent a copy of my email to Puccini, Sales and Wordsworth. The Royal Commission had access to evidence given at the Victorian Parliamentary Inquiry in Melbourne and Pell had already given evidence to the Royal Commission in Sydney and in Rome (via video link) with another Rome appearance to follow (also via video link). Pell's appearances in Melbourne, Sydney and Rome had already amounted to 17 hours in total with four days being set aside for his second video-link appearance from Rome.

Archbishop Aspinall gave evidence on four occasions to the Royal Commission but his appearances took up only a fraction of the time devoted to Pell up until 19 February 2016 when Reed's email was sent – with, as it eventuated, a further 19 hours to follow in Pell's second Rome appearance. Hollingworth appeared twice before the Royal Commission – again only a fraction of the time devoted to Pell. I concluded my letter to Reed as follows:

> In conclusion, I am genuinely surprised that the CEO of the Royal Commission should object to me making a statement of fact on the public record – especially when the criticism is so trivial. I would be interested in knowing if you have publicly rebuked any other commentator who has referred in any way to the Royal Commission.

Reed did not respond to my letter of 19 February or to two follow up emails. I wrote to McClellan about this on 29 September 2016 but he only acknowledged the email exchange on 17 October 2016 by saying that he "was aware" of my "correspondence with Mr Reed". No one at the Royal Commission ever answered the question as to whether the staff had sought to correct the (alleged) errors of journalists or commentators other than myself. The question only required a "yes" or "no" response. *7.30* did not take up the issue and the matter was dropped.

Commissioner Robert Fitzgerald Concedes that Emphasis on Catholic Offending Not Supported by Research

There was another problem – and, again, it involved Catholicism. In his final address, Justice McClellan made this point about what he termed "Roman Catholic institutions":

> Many institutions we examined did not have a culture where the best interests of children were the priority. Some leaders did not take responsibility for their institution's failure to protect children. Some leaders felt their primary responsibility was to protect the institution's reputation, and the accused person.... The greatest number of alleged perpetrators and abused children, in Church managed facilities that we are aware of, were in Roman Catholic institutions.

For the record, Catholics in Australia tend to call their church the "Catholic Church". Traditionally, some non-Catholics have preferred to use the term "Roman Catholic".

In its *Final Information Update*, the Royal Commission had this to say under the heading "Institutions administered by religious organisations":

> Of those who told us they were abused in a religious institution, the majority (61.4 per cent) said they experienced abuse in a Catholic Church institution, followed by an Anglican Church institution (14.8 per cent).

In the Royal Commission's *Final Report: Preface and Executive Summary*, it is pointed out that much of the abuse occurred some three decades ago. The report also states that "the largest proportion of survivors" who attended the Royal Commission's private sessions "was aged between 50 and 59 years". The reference to "survivors" rather than "complainants" indicates that the Royal Commission accepted the veracity of all complainants who told it their stories.

Putting the mid-point of the Royal Commission at 2015 and the mid-point of the largest proportion of complainants at age 55 and placing the average age of complainants at the time of the alleged offending at 13 – then it is evident that most alleged offences occurred five years either side of 1973. That is, some four decades before the mid-point of the Royal Commission. Yet much of the media coverage implied that what was being examined were contemporary crimes.

In his final address to the Royal Commission, Justice McClellan did mention that he and his fellow commissioners had spent five years investigating what were primarily crimes of an historical nature. But this was not obvious to those who followed much of the media's coverage of the Royal Commission – with its emphasis on Cardinal Pell.

In late February 2018, Robert Fitzgerald addressed the Catholic Social Services Australia national conference in Melbourne. On 11 March 2018, his speech was reported on Page One of *The Sunday Age* under the heading "Church 'fails to face' abuse tragedy". Fitzgerald was quoted as having referred to the disease of clericalism and having described the leadership of the Catholic Church as arrogant. He also said that he was a practising Catholic.

As reported by the *Sunday Age:*

> He [Fitzgerald] said the church was the only institution he'd ever known to have the answers to such major problems "but refuse in fact to look to those answers, look to those solutions". The scale of abuse recorded by the Royal Commission across all institutions, secular and religious, was immense, affecting countless, tens of thousands of abused children, most of whom were now adults. But such abuse was particularly prevalent in Catholic institutions. Nearly 62 per cent of all people who notified the royal commission of abuse in a religious setting were abused in a Catholic institution.

On Wednesday 14 March 2018, I emailed Fitzgerald querying the 62 per cent figure:

> As you are aware from the evidence you heard as a member of the Royal Commission into Institutional Responses to Child Sexual Abuse, most of the offences in Catholic institutions took place in the 1960s and 1970s and there have been very few such crimes committed over the past two decades. I am particularly interested in the statistic you quoted – namely that nearly 62 per cent of all the people who notified the Royal Commission of abuse in religious setting were abused in a Catholic institution.
>
> I assume that the Royal Commission, with its large staff component, drilled down into this statistic. As you know, after the Second World War Catholics were about 25 per cent of the Australian population. However, due to the systemic Catholic education system, which was not reflected in other faiths, Catholics must have accounted for around 80 per cent of children educated in a religious setting in Australia. Catholics also had a much higher percentage of orphanages and hospitals than like institutions which operated in a religious setting.
>
> In view of this, I wonder whether the Royal Commission developed any statistics for assessing the percentage of children who were sexually abused in Catholic institutions compared with the percent-

age of children who were abused in a religious setting which was not Catholic. I assume that such a statistic is available. Otherwise, the 62 per cent figure which you quoted in your address to the Catholic Social Service Conference is all but meaningless.

Fitzgerald replied the same day. He wrote that he did not regard any of the Royal Commission's figures as "meaningless"- since "too many lives have been damaged for such a view" – whatever that might mean – and added:

> Regrettably there are no historic prevalence studies in Australia but we recommended such be undertaken in the future. It would be very dangerous to underestimate contemporary risks to children. As noted in the Report this is still a contemporary issue.

My query was not about contemporary risks to children but, rather, the Royal Commission's figures for historical child sexual abuse. Fitzgerald's response indicated that – despite a budget of up to $372.8 million – the Royal Commission had undertaken "no historical prevalence studies". Fitzgerald and his fellow commissioners did not know whether there were more cases of historical child sexual abuses in Catholic religious institutions, on a percentage of the population basis, than in non-Catholic religious institutions. In his final address, Justice McClellan highlighted the raw figures without saying that no attempt had been made to ascertain whether offending in Catholic religious institutions was more prevalent than in non-Catholic religious institutions on a percentage basis – or, indeed, in secular or government institutions.

Nevertheless, the Royal Commission's *Final Information Update* and Commissioner Fitzgerald's statement prevailed and media reports focused on the raw figures and also frequently stated, incorrectly, that the 62 per cent figure for Catholics offending covered all institutions and not just religious institutions. Some examples illustrate the point.

On 30 May 2018, ABC Radio *AM* presenter Sabra Lane said that "more than 60 per cent of sex abuse survivors who gave evidence to the Royal Commission reported the abuse happened in Catholic run institutions". To repeat, this was wrong since the claim had been made with respect to religious, not all, institutions.

The following day, on the ABC Radio Hobart *Mornings* program, presenter Leon Compton – during an interview with the Catholic Archbishop of Hobart Julian Porteous – stated that the Royal Commission had found that the Catholic Church "was the majority perpetrator of child abuse nationally". Wrong. The Royal Commission looked at child sexual abuse – not child abuse generally. Compton also referred to the "60 per cent of cases" without mentioning that this finding related to religious institutions. Similar errors were made at this time on the ABC Radio National *Breakfast* (presenter Hamish Macdonald) and *Drive* (presenter Patricia Karvelas) programs.

After some complaints were lodged, the ABC acknowledged the errors (except the Sabra Lane howlers) in its "Corrections & Clarifications" segment on its website. As is the custom, no correction was made on the programs where the errors had been made and the names of the presenters were not given. And no ABC presenter or reporter ever raised the issue of the proportion of offending in religious institutions on a per capita basis.

The "Stars" of the Royal Commission – Peter McClellan & Gail Furness

The "stars" of the Royal Commission were its chair and Counsel Assisting. Both demonstrated a degree of antipathy towards Cardinal Pell.

• Justice Peter McClellan QC

Peter McClellan was educated at Normanhurst High School and the University of Sydney where he graduated in Arts and Law. He was admitted to the Bar in May 1975 and appointed a judge of the NSW Supreme Court in January 2001. During the period leading up to the Royal Commission, McClellan appears to have undergone a metamorphosis on some matters of law.

In August 1990, McClellan delivered a paper on the NSW Independent Commission Against Corruption (ICAC). It was published in *Current Issues in Criminal Justice* in 1991 in an article titled "ICAC: A Barrister's Perspective". This was a critique of the ICAC but extended to other royal commissions along with commissions of inquiry. He wrote:

> In recent years there has been an increasing trend in government to invoke royal commissions of inquiry to investigate particular problems. The frequency of such inquiries and the sensational reporting which they have attracted has tended to create a belief in some people that this is an appropriate method of handling any matter of public controversy. This is a view expressed by the press.

While recognising that "royal commissions may affect great community good", McClellan argued that they might "cause considerable harm to persons unfairly trapped by a blaze of sensationalist publicity which can be created". He concluded by maintaining that commissions of inquiry should accept "that persons should only be convicted after due process in the relevant court". McClellan's concern about the deleterious impact on individuals unfairly trapped in the blaze of sensationalist media publicity had dissipated by the time Cardinal Pell appeared before the Royal Commission some two decades later.

There was a not dissimilar U-turn on the issue of memory. In August 2006, McClellan addressed the annual conference of the Local Courts of New South Wales – his paper was published in 2016 in Volume 80 of the *Australian Law Journal* under the title "Who is telling the truth? Psychology, common sense and the law". In his talk, McClellan referred to "the fallibility of memory". He commented on the "debate…as to whether repressed memories are reliable, or whether they are falsely induced by therapists". And he concluded that "only rarely, if ever, will a person go to the grave with a clear and unaltered recollection of what happened yesterday, let alone what happened years before in their youth".

During his speech, Justice McClellan also: (i) said there is a difference between "real truth" and "perceived truth" and that in time "perceived truth becomes our reality", (ii) supported the view that most liars can fool most people most of the time and rejected the view that most people can detect falsehoods, (iii) argued that young children are significantly more likely to be overconfident about the accuracy of their positive identifications than older people, (iv) stated that there is evidence from psychologists that people are more likely to believe the testimony of an attractive or likeable witness than an unattractive or unsavoury witness, (v) commented that hesitation might not indicate a lie but it might indicate that a witness is not 100 per cent certain about the evidence they are giving – even if they honestly believe it is truthful, (vi) warned about the ability of a person to implant a false memory in the mind of another, (vii) mentioned that false memories of trauma are possible and persons affected could not tell the difference between their false recollections and their true memories, (viii) reflected that the reality is that our memories are unstable and malleable and that even without external influences memory will fade over time and (ix) acknowledged that memories may also be altered by post-event factors.

McClellan's attitude to memory had changed dramatically by the time he chaired the Royal Commission. As Virginia Miller points out in her book *Child Sexual Abuse Inquiries and the Catholic Church: Re-assessing the Evidence* (Firenze University Press, 2021), the (then) Attorney-General Mark Dreyfus amended the Royal Commission Act to free the Royal Commission "from the task of investigating claims of child sexual abuse or cross-examining people who made such claims". She added:

> It must be acknowledged that the Australian Inquiry decided to call claimants of unsubstantiated child sexual abuse "survivors" as a sign of respect for victims of child sexual abuse. Some of the victims had otherwise not had their claims believed, or had been punished for making such claims, or had been treated with derision when making such claims. The Australian Inquiry did not want to re-traumatise these people by doubting the veracity of their claims. However…the implication of this use of the term "survivor" is that all of the claims are true claims.

Also, the Royal Commission accepted the counselling guidelines promoted by Cathy Kezelman – president of the Blue Knot Foundation, which represents adult survivors of child sexual assault. In her book *Innocence Revisited: A Tale in Parts* (JoJo Publishing, 2010), Kezelman says that she was sexually assaulted by her father with the endorsement of her paternal grandmother. This claim has been emphatically denied by the author's brother (the medical doctor Claude Imhoff) and mother (Lusia Puterman). The latter wrote to *The Australian* on 4 October 2017 that two decades ago "Cathy suffered a breakdown and began recovering repressed memories of sexual assault by her father, grandfather and others".

McClellan, who is on record as describing Kezelman as an "old friend" of the Royal Commission, was to be introduced by her when he spoke at the Australian and New Zealand Association of Psychotherapy in Sydney on 30 September 2017. It so happened that on the same day *The Weekend Australian Magazine* published an article by Richard Guilliatt titled "Through the past darkly" which raised questions about Kezelman's allegations about her family. Kezelman was a late withdrawal from introducing McClellan at the Sydney conference – she did not attend the conference, reportedly, due to ill-health.

In his September 2017 address in Sydney, McClellan abandoned his 2006 warning about the fallibility of memory. He argued that, with respect to child sexual assault, "victims [note the use of the word "victim" not "complainant"] often find it difficult to provide adequate or accurate details in relation to the offending". However, he said that such circumstances are common and do not indicate memory impairment or dishonesty. McClellan raised no doubts about the recovered memory process with respect to complaints by adults about sexual assault in their childhood.

The contradictions did not end there. In an address to the University of NSW's Law faculty in December 2011, McClellan was reported to have said that some trials are too complex for juries and they make poor decisions. The message was that juries too often convict the innocent. While on the NSW Court of Appeal, he was involved in overturning some convictions in the criminal jurisdiction. Yet in a speech to the Modern Prosecutor Conference in Melbourne in April 2017, McClellan criticised the fact that while the number of complainants alleging child sexual abuse had increased, the conviction rates had fallen. The message was that juries too often acquit the guilty.[20]

An example of Justice McClellan's apparent antipathy towards Cardinal Pell can be found in his exchange with the convicted pedophile Gerald Ridsdale when he appeared before the Royal Commission (via video link from Ararat Prison) for two full days on 27 and 28 May 2015.

On the first day, Gail Furness SC commenced her examination of Ridsdale by taking him through his various convictions for child sexual abuse dating back to 1993. She then asked Ridsdale about his early years as a seminary student and then as a priest. Ridsdale acknowledged that, while at Corpus Christi College, he knew that he had an attraction to boys rather than to women. The examination had not proceeded far when Justice McClellan intervened and asked Ridsdale if he had a confessor at the seminary.

The exchange suggests that McClellan was expecting that Ridsdale would say that he regularly confessed the sin of pedophilia and received absolution. In the Sacrament of Confession, those who confess sin to a priest are forgiven provided they do a designated act of repentance and vow to sin no more.

Ridsdale (born May 1934) said that he went to confession around once or twice a month while at the seminary but ceased to confess his sins within three to five years of leaving Corpus Christi College in 1958. The following exchange took place:

> *Peter McClellan:* And were you honest in what you confessed to your confessor?
>
> *Gerald Ridsdale:* No.
>
> *Peter McClellan:* What did you not confess to your confessor which you should have?
>
> *Gerald Ridsdale:* I didn't confess the sexual offending against children.

Immediately after, Furness asked Ridsdale as to whether, when he was ordained by Bishop O'Collins in July 1961, he had told anyone about his past sexual offending. The answer was in the negative. Soon after, Ridsdale said that he "never talked to anyone, and certainly not in the confession either, about offending against children".

It would seem that neither McClellan nor Furness expected the answers they received from Ridsdale. In a perceptive article titled "Gerald Ridsdale, Pedophile Priest, In His Own Words" (*Journal of the Australian Catholic Historical Society,* Vol. 36, 2015), Professor James Franklin wrote that, watching the livestream of the examination, Ridsdale "gave the impression of being an honest and cooperative witness, although notably affectless". Franklin noted that, at age 81, Ridsdale's "memory was very patchy" but he provided "a unique opportunity to see into the mind of a pedophile priest". Franklin added that Ridsdale was willing to admit that his actions were wrong and criminal "without appearing notably remorseful".

The examination of Ridsdale dragged on into the second day, Thursday 28 May 2015. Midway through the morning, after an adjournment, Justice McClellan asked Ridsdale whether he was "familiar with the principle of mental reservation". He replied, "The principle of what, Your Honour?". Ridsdale added, in response to a question, that he thought that mental reservation "was something we used to talk about in priesthood" but added "I can't remember what it is now".

According to Catholic teaching, a mental reservation may be evoked when a person deliberately uses words which in a sense are true – but not in the manner which they will be understood by the person spoken to. For example, a person may falsely claim that he or she does not know where a person is – if a person is being sought unjustly by an authoritarian government. The reservation is that the location of the person is not known with respect to someone who is trying to do harm to the person. Such equivocation is only warranted if the cause is just.

In the past, some non-Catholics were wont to accuse Catholics of engaging in an act of mental reservation when told something by a Catholic which they did not believe. It seems that McClellan was of the view not only that Ridsdale was lying to him but also that he was rationalising his behaviour in line with Catholic teaching in what might be called a "Jesuitical" – or "casuistical" – manner. Yet, Ridsdale's demeanour in the witness box did not indicate at his (then) age of 81 years that he was interested in, or capable of, such intellectual sophistication.

Justice McClellan had taken the unusual step for a royal commissioner of speaking privately to Ridsdale in Ararat Prison on 17 March 2015 – shortly before Ridsdale was to give evidence. On Thursday 28 May 2015, he quizzed Ridsdale about the concept of mental reservation – implying that Ridsdale might have said something personal to McClellan which he was not prepared to say to the Royal Commission:

> *Peter McClellan:* Answer this for me: you spoke with me in a private hearing some weeks ago, didn't you?
>
> *Gerald Ridsdale:* Yes, in Ararat when we had the private closed hearing.
>
> *Peter McClellan:* Had you spoken to anyone about the evidence you might give in that hearing before you came to that private hearing?
>
> *Gerald Ridsdale:* No, I've spoken to no one about it. I was told not to.
>
> *Peter McClellan:* Since that private hearing, have you spoken to anyone about the evidence you might give in this public hearing?
>
> *Gerald Ridsdale:* No. Again, I was told not to say anything about it.
>
> *Peter McClellan:* Have you had any phone calls with anyone when you might have discussed the evidence?
>
> *Gerald Ridsdale:* No.
>
> *Peter McClellan:* Not at all?
>
> *Gerald Ridsdale:* No, I haven't.
>
> *Peter McClellan:* Do you have people who make phone calls to you in the gaol?
>
> *Gerald Ridsdale:* No, no one can make a phone call to me, I have to phone out.

It came as some surprise that a former Supreme Court judge assumed that all prisoners have a right to receive phone calls. After saying that his only out-calls were to his sister, a retired priest and his lawyer, Ridsdale was asked about jail visits:

> *Peter McClellan:* ...Have you had any visitors in the gaol since then [17 March 2015].
>
> *Gerald Ridsdale:* I think the only visitor I've had since then would be [a retired priest based in Horsham].
>
> *Peter McClellan:* Anyone else?
>
> *Gerald Ridsdale:* No.
>
> *Peter McClellan:* By the way, you'll appreciate there will be a record of the people who have been to see you in gaol, don't you?
>
> *Gerald Ridsdale:* Yes, and also the people that I've phoned.

Around this time, there were media reports that Cardinal Pell had visited Ballarat in March 2015 – dropping in at his old school St Patrick's College. It seems that McClellan became suspicious that Pell (or someone close to Pell) had been in contact with Ridsdale in Ararat Prison by phone or in person before the convicted pedophile gave his testimony to the Royal Commission. Ararat is some 90 kilometres from Ballarat.

As it turned out, in this instance, Ridsdale was telling the truth. His visitors were always his sister and a retired priest, and his phone calls were also to his sister and another retired priest. Moreover, the prison records would support this claim.

That Justice McClellan appears to have considered, even for a (heated) moment, that Pell may have sought to interfere with Ridsdale's forthcoming testimony says a lot about his attitude to the cardinal. Pell is no fool. He would have known that prisoners' phone calls are recorded and that any visit to a prison by a high-profile person would have led to substantial media coverage since, almost certainly, it would have been leaked by someone in or near the prison.

Over two days, the Royal Commission attempted to discover a link between Pell and Ridsdale. Early in the hearing, Gail Furness asked

Ridsdale whether Pell was "at any stage your confessor". The reply was in the negative. No surprise there, because Ridsdale had already told the Royal Commission that he had not been to confession since at least 1963 – and at a time when Pell was in Europe and had never worked as a priest in Ballarat hearing confessions, or anywhere else, since he was not ordained at the time.

Early in the examination, on 27 May, Justice McClellan put it to Ridsdale that he knew what Pell was going to say on his behalf at the Magistrates' Court when he was first convicted in May 1993. Ridsdale replied that he did not know. That's correct – since Pell only walked Ridsdale to the Magistrates' Court, he did not give character evidence. With the Royal Commission's large staff, this is a fact which it would be expected that Justice McClellan would have known before the hearing.

After two full days of hearings, neither Justice McClellan nor Counsel Assisting Gail Furness was able to establish any close relationship at any time between Cardinal Pell and the notorious pedophile Gerald Ridsdale. Their paths had crossed from time to time when Pell was based in Ballarat – including living in the same presbytery for about a year. But they had never worked together. The examination wound up shortly after the luncheon adjournment on the second day having failed to establish anything about Ridsdale beyond that was already known concerning a pedophile who pleaded guilty and had been in the Victorian prison system for around a quarter of a century.

The Fosters attended many of the Royal Commission's hearings in support of victims and complainants of child sexual abuse. When Anthony died suddenly in late May 2017, his family was offered a State Funeral by Daniel Andrews, the Labor premier of Victoria. Andrews addressed the memorial service on 7 June 2017. Soon after, ABC presenter, Jon Faine – who was MC – made the following comment:

> Now Ladies and Gentlemen – the Honourable Justice Peter McClellan, who is chair of the Royal Commission into Institutional Responses to Child Sexual Abuse, has asked if he can make a tribute. And it is today's final tribute. Peter.

This was an unusual act for a royal commissioner whose final report – which turned out to be highly critical of George Pell – was not concluded until December 2017. Writing in *The Australian Online* on 13 June 2017, journalist John Ferguson commented in his "Today in Victoria" column:

> "Today in Victoria" can understand why Mr McClellan would attend such an occasion, perhaps sitting semi-anonymously, deep in the congregation. But his decision to speak took it to a questionable level. The royal commissioner said he was invited to speak by the family and any issue about the Foster family had been dealt with by the royal commission. Sure, but given that Mr Foster was (understandably) such a strident critic of the church, it begs the question of whether Mr McClellan should even have attended the funeral.
>
> The commission is still considering church matters and, indeed, many (mistakenly) believe that the inquiry is all about the church. It is ostensibly up to Mr McClellan to protect his independence. He certainly doesn't seem to have enhanced it. The final reports into Ballarat and the Melbourne Archdiocese have yet to be published and Mr Foster was active in both jurisdictions as a relentless advocate for victims.

The unredacted version of the Royal Commission's Report was not released until May 2020 – shortly after the High Court had quashed Pell's conviction. It was highly critical of George Pell – even though none of its findings with respect to the cardinal were supported by witnesses or documentary evidence.

- **Gail Furness SC**

Gail Furness SC graduated in Arts from the University of Queensland and Law from the University of Melbourne. In October 2010, she was appointed a senior counsel in NSW. Furness has practised principally in public law and in special commissions of inquiry and royal commissions.

Furness cross-examined Cardinal Pell, at times, in quite a ferocious manner which was widely attested to by a mainly supportive media. Her attitude towards Pell was evident from the Royal Commission's hearings into the Ballarat diocese and the Melbourne archdiocese.

With Pell in Rome and Furness in Sydney, the cardinal was asked about the pedophile priest Monsignor John Day (born 1904) – whose crimes are documented in the book *Unholy Trinity: The hunt for the pedophile priest Monsignor John Day* (Allen & Unwin, 2013) by former Victoria Police officer Denis Ryan and journalist Peter Hoysted. The authors relate how Monsignor Day got away with child sexual abuse because of a cover-up by the Catholic bishops of Ballarat (initially James O'Collins and later Ronald Mulkearns) and the corruption at the time of Victoria Police – which led to Denis Ryan being forced out of his job in the early 1970s.

Yet Furness' line of questioning seemed to be an attempt to establish that George Pell (born 1941) and a junior priest in Swan Hill from 1971 to 1972 knew all about the older man's crimes. Her initial point was that the parishes of Mildura and Swan Hill "adjoin one another" and that, therefore, Pell would have been familiar with Day's activities. Pell doubted this – saying that he thought "there's at least Robinvale parish in between". In fact, Swan Hill was separated from Mildura by two parishes – Robinvale and Red Cliffs.

The Royal Commission had hundreds of staff and millions of dollars at its disposal to devote to research. Yet Furness put the above proposition to Pell without even checking past editions of *The Official Directory of the Catholic Church in Australia*. Also, Swan Hill is some 225 kilometres from Mildura and communications 50 years ago were not what they are today. Furness' line was that Pell should have known of Day's alleged offending and done something about it. Pell did have some knowledge of the allegations. After all, they were no secret in the Mildura area and the matter had been referred to, without mentioning Day specifically by name, in the *Melbourne Observer* Sunday newspaper on 13 August 1972. Pell has told me that he was assured by a female Mildura parishioner, whose judgment he valued, that the (then) rumours about Day were untrue.

Irrespective of any rumour which Pell may have heard, he had nothing to do with Day's offending or with the long-term cover up of his crimes by the Diocese of Ballarat and Victoria Police. Yet Furness wanted to pin some of the responsibility for Day on to Pell. It was part of the tactic to demonstrate that Pell was primarily responsible for covering-up child sexual abuse in the Catholic Church – in the Ballarat diocese and elsewhere.

An example of Furness' handling of Pell in her role as senior Counsel Assisting can be witnessed by the following exchange which occurred on 2 March 2016. First up, Furness asked Pell to assume that the hostile testimony of one of his accusers (Timothy Green) was accurate and truthful. Then she asked a long question which contained four negatives. Let's go to the transcript:

> *Gail Furness:* I want to ask you a few questions based on the obvious premise from my perspective that Mr Green's evidence is both accurate and truthful. For the purposes of answering my questions, can you act on that basis?
>
> *George Pell:* No, I can't because I don't accept it. But I'm certainly keen to try to answer any question you propose.
>
> *Gail Furness:* Okay. You told Counsel Assisting on Monday that a person who was ignorant of something, where that ignorance was not wilful ignorance and where that wilfulness was not the result of not doing a job within your authority, would have no moral or other responsibility for failing to act in relation to Ridsdale. Do you recall that? You were asked questions about the responsibility a consultor might have. I can take you to the transcript if you need it.
>
> *George Pell:* Yes, I'm not exactly sure what you're saying. But I'm happy to – I'm happy to accept it as a working hypothesis….

It was one thing to be asked to accept an accuser's accusations, unsupported by independent evidence, as both accurate and truthful. And something else to be asked to respond instantly to a question which contained four negatives.

At the end of his 19 hour interrogation in Rome, Pell had given evidence to the Royal Commission for around 36 hours – not counting his appearance before the Victorian Parliamentary Inquiry. Yet, in spite of leading and, at times, confused questions – Pell made no admissions which could lead to findings against him based on evidence rather than assumption. This in spite of Furness' considerable advocacy skills.

Gail Furness' cross-examination of George Pell was applauded by many Pell-antagonists who attended or watched the hearings in Melbourne, Sydney or Rome and by members of the media which reported on the events or watched them on the Royal Commission's livestream or, occasionally, on television.

On 3 March 2016, Jenny Noyes reported in the *Sydney Morning Herald* that Furness had become a "hero-woman who won't take evasion or shrugs for an answer" – and that her approach to grilling Pell had "earned her a lot of fans…made her a household name". The *Sydney Morning Herald* journalist Bevan Shields tweeted this on 1 March 2016:

> *Bevan Shields:* Wow. Gail Furness getting stuck in to George Pell now: Says it's "implausible" he was not told why Ridsdale was being moved #auspol
>
> Mar 1, 2016

The following day, ABC reporter Danny Tran tweeted:

> *Danny Tran:* Applause from Ballarat as Gail Furness says Cardinal Pell's evidence & reasons for being deceived are "completely implausible" @abcnewsMelb
>
> Mar 2, 2016

On 2 March 2016, ABC journalist Anne Barker reported that Furness "is likely to be best remembered for her relentless questioning of… Cardinal George Pell".

But not all commentators believed that senior counsel to royal commissions should be getting stuck into witnesses or be the recipient of applause from observers. On 5 March 2016, *The Australian* published this letter from Kenneth Wiltshire, Professor of Public Administration at the University of Queensland Business School:

> During the conduct of a royal commission it is the role of counsel assisting solely to help the commission identify the facts of the matters and obtain information that may assist members of the commission in reaching their conclusions. It is not the role of counsel assisting to form judgments, reach conclusions, express personal opinions, intimidate witnesses, or express belief or disbelief in their testimony. The counsel assisting is the servant of the royal commission.
>
> These standards and code of conduct have not been apparent during the Royal Commission into Institutionalised Responses to Child Sexual Abuse and particularly during the questioning of Cardinal George Pell by counsel assisting. A royal commission is the most powerful instrument of inquiry in our system of governance and so must behave impeccably and responsibly at all times. In this case, it is clear that victims involved have suffered considerable trauma and distress, and because of their suffering many have expressed a desire to see someone suffer in return as an attainment of justice. This is an understandable human reaction, but it is not a basis on which to conduct a royal commission.

Francis Sullivan & the Truth, Justice and Healing Council

In early 2013, the Australian Catholic Bishops Conference (responsible for Catholic priests who work in archdioceses and dioceses) and Catholic Religious Australia (responsible for the priests, brothers and sisters in religious orders) set up the Truth, Justice and Healing Council. The TJHC was chaired by the Hon. Neville Owen with Elizabeth Proust as vice-chair and consisted of 11 members in all. It was given the role of coordinating the Catholic Church's response to the Royal Commission "with a commitment to justice and compassion for survivors" and concluded its work on 30 April 2018. The layman Francis Sullivan (born 1956) was the TJHC's chief executive officer during its existence.

The TJHC could have adopted one or another course of action with respect to the Royal Commission. It could have acknowledged the dreadful crimes committed against children by some Catholic priests and brothers over the years but added that the Catholic Church was among the first institutions – religious, secular or otherwise – to address these crimes when it set up the Melbourne Response and Towards Healing in 1996 and 1997 respectively. It followed, then, that the Royal Commission was essentially dealing with historical crimes which the Catholic Church had attempted to address over the previous two decades. After all, Gail Furness SC said as much when she addressed the Royal Commission on 16 February 2017 in what was termed the "Catholic Wrap":

> Between January 1950 and February 2015, 4,445 people alleged incidents of child sexual abuse in 4,765 claims. The vast majority of claims alleged abuse that started in the period 1950 to 1989 inclusive. The largest proportion of first alleged incidents of child sexual abuse, 29 per cent, occurred in the 1970s.

However, this was not the tactic adopted by Francis Sullivan. Instead TJHC's legal representatives adopted an attitude of least resistance. They did not proclaim the Church's success, led by Archbishop George Pell in Melbourne and Bishop Geoffrey Robinson in Sydney – prior to the establishment of the Royal Commission – in all but eliminating clerical child sexual abuse and in setting up schemes of compensation and counselling for persons who were accepted as victims. Rather the TJHC gave the (false) impression that clerical child sexual abuse was a matter which the Church had only recently addressed.

Moreover, the TJHC's lawyers did not cross-examine witnesses – however hostile their testimony. This was consistent with its acceptance of the notion that all complainants were survivors (or victims) – as indicated in the TJHC's mission statement. The TJHC's decision not to cross-examine led to a situation where there was no restraint on allegations made. This was particularly damaging to Pell since he was the Catholic with the highest profile who appeared before the Royal Commission.

George Pell engaged his own legal team – headed by Allan Myers QC who ably was assisted by Sam Duggan – which was only involved when Pell himself was before the Royal Commission. Mr Duggan did cross examine some of those men who claimed that Pell was aware of the offending by such Catholic priests as Gerald Ridsdale and Peter Searson. However, the extraordinary time spent by Justice McClellan and Gail Furness cross-examining Pell drowned out Duggan's own advocacy.

The overall impression given by the Royal Commission during its five years of hearings was that clerical child sexual abuse remained a problem in the Catholic Church and that it had done virtually nothing over the years to address the problem. This view was not contested by Sullivan, who was a Catholic critic of Pell. A few examples illustrate the point.

On 10 June 2014, Sullivan was interviewed by Philip Clark on ABC Radio Canberra. Clark made a number of inaccurate and defamatory remarks about Pell. Sullivan did not contest the claims. Later he apologised – saying: "This was a mistake. I should have responded to these claims because there is no evidence the cardinal has covered up anything and he has certainly not defended pedophiles". Clark made an on-air apology on 18 June 2014 and the online ABC's Corrections & Clarifications segment briefly covered the apology on 25 June 2014.

On Monday 1 June 2015, Sullivan was the recipient of a very long interview by Virginia Trioli, a Pell-antagonist, on ABC TV *News Breakfast* program. It took place in the morning after the *60 Minutes* program where Peter Saunders had called on Pope Francis to move Pell from his Vatican position, describing the cardinal as "almost sociopathic". Saunders had never met Pell.

First up, Trioli asked Sullivan whether Pell had maintained Pope Francis' approval. Sullivan responded that the cardinal's position was "very tight". During the remainder of the interview, Sullivan used the words "very tight" twice more – along with "pretty tight" (also twice) and "tight". Sullivan did not say what he meant by this – but it was evident that he was not supporting Pell. So much so that Trioli put this question: "Francis Sullivan, you're not strongly defending Cardinal George Pell against these criticisms – why not?"

Sullivan went on to criticise Pell for not openly expressing his feelings and implied that Pell knew of Ridsdale's crimes when he was in Ballarat – in spite of the fact that, as at 1 June 2015, Pell had not appeared before the Royal Commission on this issue to state his own position. Most viewers of the interview would have come to the conclusion that the TJHC was distancing itself from Pell.

On 10 March 2017, Sullivan addressed a function at the Villa Maria parish in the Sydney suburb of Hunter's Hill concerning the Royal Commission's final hearings in its "Catholic Wrap". His speech was a withering criticism of the historical and contemporary Catholic Church. There were references to Catholicism's "scandalous history" and "spiritual bankruptcy". But Sullivan made no mention of the Melbourne Response or Towards Healing – nor did he quote the comments of Gail Furness, made just three weeks earlier, that the vast majority of alleged incidents of clerical child sexual abuse in the Catholic Church had occurred in the 1950s, 1960s, 1970s and 1980s.

That is, few complaints had been made in the previous quarter of a century when Pell was a significant figure in the Catholic Church. Sullivan's disinclination to mention the Melbourne Response and Towards Healing (which Pell inherited when he moved to Sydney in 2001) had the consequence of implying that the Cardinal had not acted on this "scandalous" matter when, in fact, he had. This further blackened Pell's name. The approach adopted by the TJHC was consistent with an attempt to discredit the "Old Church", as represented by Pell, and to proclaim the TJHC's role in the "Modern Church" for finally tackling clerical child sexual abuse.

The Royal Commission and Cardinal Pell

The Royal Commission brought down four reports of specific relevance to Cardinal George Pell. Namely, (i) *Case Study No 8: Mr John Ellis' Experience of the Towards Healing process and civil litigation*

(January 2015), (ii) *Case Study No 16: The Melbourne Response* (July 2015), (iii) *Case Study No 28: Catholic Church authorities in Ballarat* (November 2017, non-redacted version released in May 2020) and (iv) *Case Study No 35: Catholic Archdiocese of Melbourne* (November 2017, non-redacted version released in May 2020). *Case Study No 8* and *Case Study No 16* were presided over by Justice Peter McClelland, Professor Helen Milroy and Commissioner Andrew Murray. *Case Study No 28* and *Case Study No 35* were presided over by Justice Peter McClellan, Justice Jennifer Coate and Commissioner Andrew Murray.

The Royal Commission did not attempt an all-embracing view of child sexual abuse within institutions. Rather it elected to undertake a number of case studies in order to provide specific examples of a wider problem. In view of this, it is understandable why the Royal Commission focused on the notorious pedophile priest Ridsdale in *Case Study No 28*. However, it is not at all obvious why it showed such interest in Fr Peter Searson in *Case Study No 35* since some of his clerical colleagues in the Melbourne archdiocese were accused of far more serious criminality.

Writing in *Eureka Street* on 31 July 2016, Fr Frank Brennan commented:

> The Commission has been so focused on Pell that they decided to make the abuse of the late Fr Peter Searson their primary focus when investigating the abuse by Melbourne priests. This was not because Searson was the worst abuser, but because he worked in the region of the Archdiocese where Pell had supervision as auxiliary bishop.

Brennan wrote this before the Royal Commission released its findings on the Melbourne Archdiocese.

The Royal Commission is best known for its focus on Cardinal Pell – as well as Catholic institutions. Literally thousands of pages of submissions, transcripts and findings were devoted to Pell and the areas in which he worked. In spite of this, no evidentiary or documentary evidence was found to develop a case against the cardinal.

- **The John Ellis Case –** *Case Study No. 8*

According to *Case Study No 8,* as a teenager between 13 and 17 years of age, John Ellis was sexually assaulted by Fr Aidan Duggan who was a Catholic assistant priest at Bass Hill in Sydney. Duggan was between 54 and 59 years old at the time. The abuse continued into Mr Ellis' early adult years. Ellis approached the Sydney archdiocese in June 2002, not long after Pell became archbishop. By this time Duggan had dementia. Ellis' case was initially handled by John Davoren, the archdiocese's director of professional standards. The Royal Commission issued its findings on the Ellis case in January 2015.

In March 2014, on his last day as Archbishop of Sydney before moving to the Vatican, Pell forwarded a statement to the Royal Commission in response to, and in compliance with, its Notice to Produce in which he wrote:

> I acknowledge and apologise to Mr Ellis for the gross violation and abuse committed by Aidan Duggan, a now deceased priest of the Sydney Archdiocese. I deeply regret the pain, trauma and emotional damage that this abuse caused to Mr Ellis. I met with Mr Ellis and his wife in 2009. I acknowledged to him then, and I repeat now, that in responding to his Towards Healing complaint, mistakes were made by me and by others in the Church that resulted in driving Mr Ellis and the Archdiocese apart rather than bringing healing. I acknowledge and regret those mistakes, particularly the unacceptable delay from the date of his complaint to assessment. Also, certain steps were taken in the litigation that now cause me concern and that I would not repeat.

> Once the litigation was over, Msgr Usher, the Chancellor of the Archdiocese, with my full support, sought to assist Mr Ellis, by meeting counselling costs and, over time, making payments to Mr Ellis amounting so far to some $570,365. I am pleased that we have been able to provide this assistance to Mr Ellis, which in the case of the counselling costs is ongoing, and hope it has brought him some measure of comfort.

> Lessons have been learned. Following the conclusion of Mr Ellis'

court case, I commissioned a review of the Archdiocese's Towards Healing files to see whether processes had been followed appropriately. As a result of that review, I made a submission in 2009 to the review of Towards Healing and made another submission regarding Towards Healing in 2011, suggesting improvements I thought could be made to address issues such as delay, an improved pastoral response to victims of abuse and the quality of investigations. In addition, at my direction, the Archdiocese of Sydney has taken steps to improve its own response to victims of abuse. I am committed to continual review and improvement in the way we deal with these matters.

For all the Sydney archdiocese's poor handling of the Ellis case, including recourse to the judicial system, the matter was effectively resolved by 2009 – some years before the Royal Commission commenced operations. Yet the Royal Commission's report of January 2015 runs for some 125 pages and contains 34 findings. Finding 33 is as follows:

> We agree with Cardinal Pell's evidence that "we", which we take to be the Archdiocese, the Trustees and he as Archbishop, did not act fairly from a Christian point of view in the conduct of the litigation against Mr Ellis.

It is one thing if a Christian leader, like Pell, concedes that his Church did not act fairly from a Christian point of view in the conduct of litigation against Ellis – which was dropped after Pell said that he had not been advised of the extent of the claim (he had thought that Ellis' compensation claim was much higher than was the case). But it is not the role of a secular investigating body – like a royal commission – to come to a finding about what is Christian behaviour and what is not.

Not for the last time the Royal Commission, when given the choice whether to believe Pell or another witness, went for the second option. In the Ellis Case, Monsignor Brian Rayner (who had preceded Monsignor John Usher as vicar-general) gave evidence that he had advised Pell fully about the dealings between the Sydney archdiocese and Ellis. Pell, on the other hand, said that to the best of his recollection he was not consulted about the financial amount that should be considered by way of compensation.

The Royal Commission said that it "seems unlikely" that Pell would not have been provided with this advice. So it went with Rayner's account – despite the fact that there was no independent witness or documentary evidence.

• The Melbourne Response – *Case Study No 16*

The Melbourne Response was set up by George Pell in 1996 shortly after he was appointed Archbishop of Melbourne. In *Child Sexual Abuse Inquiries and the Catholic Church*, Virginia Miller lists a range of "child safety measures" implemented by the Catholic Church in Australia – commencing with a formal discussion at the 1988 Australian Catholic Bishops Conference up until 2020 when both the Australian Catholic Bishops Conference (ACBC) and Catholic Religious Australia (CRA) released their responses to the Royal Commission's recommendations. It was titled *The Light from the Southern Cross: Promoting Co-Responsible Governance in the Catholic Church in Australia.*

Miller's timeline includes reference to the role played by Sydney clerics – Fr Brian Lucas and Monsignor Usher – in the development of protocols to deal with the issue. She also refers to Lucas' study tour to North America in 1992 to discuss the matter with the leadership of some United States and Canadian archdioceses.

In private correspondence and discussions, Lucas – who is not close to Pell – has advised that, in November 1987, along with Usher and at the request of Cardinal Edward Clancy in Sydney, he gave a presentation on clerical pedophilia to all bishops, including Pell who was then an auxiliary bishop in Melbourne. Lucas advised that a committee was set up at that meeting which, from 1992, was chaired by Bishop Geoffrey Robinson. This work found its way into the document *Towards Healing,* which came into effect in March 1997.

There is no reason to doubt the important work Lucas and others did in the late 1980s and early 1990s in this area. The point is that, outside the leadership of the Catholic Church, few if any would have known about it. The Melbourne Response, on the other hand, made an immediate impact on account of Pell's charisma and the prominent Victorians who became involved in its creation, including the then leadership of Victoria Police.

Initially Pell had discussions with the Victorian premier Jeff Kennett and governor Sir Richard McGarvie. He also consulted such QC's as Sir James Gobbo, Charles Francis and Joseph Santamaria. The Melbourne Response was implemented with the support of Victoria Police and the Victorian Solicitor General (Douglas Graham QC). The chair of the panel overseeing the Melbourne Response was always a prominent lawyer – Alex Chernov QC, David Habersberger QC, Susan Crennan QC and David Curtain QC. Not all the above were brought up Catholic.

Generally, the Royal Commission's findings with respect to the Melbourne Response were not positive – the implication being that Cardinal Pell and his colleagues could have done better. It found that the total average expenditure for each claim of child sexual abuse, including the direct and indirect costs of providing counselling and medical support through Centrelink, was approximately $100,000. When the Melbourne Response was established, ex-gratia payments were set at a limit of $50,000 – in line with the then cap on payments made under the Victorian Victims of Crime Compensation scheme. It later increased to $75,000, in line with changes to the State scheme. The Foster family was given a compensation settlement of around $1 million.

Of particular note concerning *Case Study No 16* is that Justice McClellan and his two commissioners again chose not to believe Pell. Early on in its report, the Royal Commission considered the public meeting that took place in Melbourne on 19 October 1996 which was presided over by Archbishop Pell and a number of other Church leaders. Chrissie Foster told the Royal Commission that the Church leaders did not engage with the audience during the forum and that they did not appear to want to listen to the parents' descriptions of their experiences at the Sacred Heart Catholic Primary School at Oakleigh where Kevin O'Donnell had been parish priest. As pointed out previously, O'Donnell sexually assaulted Emma and Katie Foster. Mrs Foster said that she had written a letter to what was called the Melbourne Forum in Oakleigh which she had asked someone else to read out on her behalf. And that, while this was happening, Pell and other Church leaders walked off the stage and did not return. There is no contemporary media report of such an event occurring.

Pell said that he did not recall the meeting as being unpleasant and had no recollection of anyone walking out while someone was speaking. His evidence was in line with that of Archbishop Denis Hart (who attended the meeting in his capacity as vicar-general). And also that of Helen Last (not a supporter of Pell) who worked at the Pastoral Response Office and reported at the time that she had received positive feedback from the victims and others at the forum.

In spite of Pell's statement being supported by evidence, the Royal Commission decided to believe Mrs Foster, finding:

> Notwithstanding these differing accounts, we accept Mrs Foster's recollection of the events. Given the circumstances of the public meeting and her personal interest in the reading of the letter, she is less likely to recall the events incorrectly...

The Royal Commission applied the civil standard of proof laid down by the High Court in the 1938 case *Briginshaw v Briginshaw*. This was referred to as "comfortable satisfaction" by Justice George Rich and as "reasonable satisfaction" by Justice Owen Dixon. The court divided four to one with Chief Justice John Latham dissenting. In his judgment, Dixon wrote that "reasonable satisfaction should not be produced by inexact proofs and indefinite testimony, or indirect references".

Writing in the *University of Notre Dame Australia Law Review* in October 2012 about *Briginshaw v Briginshaw*, Dr Chris Davies commented:

> ...what became established from this case is what is known as the *Briginshaw* test, namely that the more serious the allegation and its consequences, the higher the level of proof required for a matter to be substantiated. The standard is not beyond reasonable doubt, but the more serious the allegation, the more persuasive the proof must be.

In this instance, the Royal Commission came to a "reasonable satisfaction" that Pell's account of the October 1996 meeting was not accurate. Yet Pell's evidence was supported by one witness and the contemporaneous note of a second person – whereas Chrissie Foster's allegation was not supported by independent evidence.

There was to be more of the same when the Royal Commission looked at the Ballarat diocese and the Melbourne archdiocese. However, a finding that Pell failed to disclose pedophilia to the relevant authorities was a serious allegation and, under the Briginshaw test, should have required a persuasive degree of proof.

- **The Ballarat Diocese –** *Case Study No 28*

Gerald Ridsdale was first charged with child sexual abuse in 1993 – he pleaded guilty and was sentenced to a maximum of 12 months – and a minimum of three months – jail. He was charged again with multiple offences in 1994, 2006, 2014, 2017 and 2020. On all occasions Ridsdale pleaded guilty and he has been in prison since 1994. That is, around two decades before the Royal Commission was established. The commissioners made Ridsdale the focus of their deliberations when *Case Study No 28* commenced hearings in Ballarat in May 2015.

The Ballarat hearings, which commenced on 21 May 2015, made it possible for a number of individuals to give evidence which discredited Pell – in his absence – virtually at will. In time, the Royal Commission dismissed some of these claims. But these submissions and findings received scant, if any, media coverage – unlike the initial claims.

Writing in *The Age* on 2 June 2015, in an article titled "Questions for George Pell when he fronts the Royal Commission", Jane Lee summarised the serious allegations made against the cardinal during the inaugural hearings on the Ballarat diocese. They were (i) that he had attempted to bribe David Ridsdale not to reveal the crimes of his uncle Gerald Ridsdale, (ii) that he had ignored Timothy Green's warning about the pedophile religious brother Edward Dowlan, (iii) that he was involved in moving Ridsdale from parish to parish, (iv) that he had a close relationship with Gerald Ridsdale and (v) that he was present when Ridsdale raped a child.

Lee wrote: "Church lawyers declined to cross-examine… survivors on their accounts; this means they will rely on Cardinal Pell's own response to defend himself against them." The problem was that Pell was not due to give evidence in these issues for many months. By the time he did, huge reputational damage had already been done.

As Pell put it in a statement which he released on 20 May 2015:

> Over the last 24 hours I have been accused of being complicit in the moving of a known pedophile, of ignoring a victim's complaint, and of bribery. These matters again require an immediate response and it is important to correct the record particularly given the false and misleading headlines.

Pell refuted all the claims and stated that many of these issues had already been addressed by him at the Victorian Parliamentary Inquiry in 2013. He added: "I also note that under the terms of reference the Royal Commission can access all material from previous inquiries…." But the Royal Commission elected to cover these matters again.

The Royal Commission's *Case Study 28* ran for 531 pages (including endnotes). It made findings concerning Pell's involvements with Monsignor John Day, Fr Gerald Ridsdale, Br Brendan Dowlan and Timothy Green.

- John Day

Despite Gail Furness' rigorous cross-examination of George Pell concerning his knowledge about Monsignor John Day, the Royal Commission did not find that Pell could or should have done anything about this matter.

- Gerald Ridsdale

George Pell was never in a position of authority over Ridsdale – moreover he was seven years younger. The Royal Commission's essential interest was in the relationship between the two men during the time that Fr Pell was a consultor to Bishop Mulkearns between 1977 and 1984. He was one of up to ten Ballarat clergy who held such a position at any one time.

The essential criticism about Pell, when a priest in the Ballarat diocese, is that he covered up Ridsdale's crimes – including being involved in decisions to move him from parish to parish. In its case against Pell, the Royal Commission focused on two occasions where it claimed that Pell, in his capacity as consultor during a meeting of the consultors, was told of Ridsdale's offending by Bishop Mulkearns.

Pell attended his first meeting of the consultors to Bishop Mulkearns on 19 July 1977 – he had just turned 36 years of age. At this meeting, Mulkearns proposed that Ridsdale (then acting as the administrator of the Edenhope parish) be appointed parish priest of Edenhope. This was not a proposal to move Ridsdale to another parish – but rather to upgrade his status from acting parish priest to a tenured parish priest position. Also present were Monsignor Leo Fiscalini and Fathers Kevin Arundell, F. J. McKenzie, James Madden and Daniel Torpy. Fr Adrian McInerney attended as secretary.

The Royal Commission found with respect to the 19 July 1977 consultors' meeting:

> Cardinal Pell provided a variety of possibilities of what he expected may have been said at this meeting. His evidence was more emphatic as to what was not said. He gave evidence that he would be

surprised if Bishop Mulkearns deceived him. We share that surprise. It does not logically follow that a bishop would deceive his appointed consultors, particularly given that it would be likely that they would find out elsewhere.

Furthermore, given that Cardinal Pell would have been surprised if Bishop Mulkearns had deceived him, it is likely that he knew of Ridsdale's sexual transgressions. We are satisfied that, by this time, the consultors who had attended previous meetings, including Father Madden and Father McInerney, had been told of Ridsdale's sexual transgressions. It is inconceivable that these consultors did not know by this time, given the usual practice and the general knowledge in the community.

This finding showed a lack of understanding of how the Catholic Church operated over four decades ago. The Catholic Church then – and, to some degree now – operated like an absolute hereditary monarchy – except that the Pope is elected by the cardinals. Mulkearns was not into volunteering information – and there is no evidence that he was "likely" to have done so concerning Ridsdale's crimes of pedophilia. And no evidence that it was "inconceivable" that he did not do so. Such word usage as "not likely", "seems unlikely" and "inconceivable" is often weaponised when there is no hard evidence to support a finding.

The above statement – namely that it was "inconceivable" that the likes of Fr Madden and Fr McInerney were not aware of Ridsdale's crimes as at 19 July 1977, when a consultors' meeting was held, appears at Page 267 of *Case Study No 28*. However, earlier at Page 74, the following statement appears concerning Mulkearns' decision in 1986 to appoint Ridsdale as assistant priest of Horsham, where Madden was parish priest:

Father Madden gave evidence that Bishop Mulkearns did not explain to him why the appointment of Ridsdale as his assistant priest was being made. Bishop Mulkearns did tell him Ridsdale had received counselling. Father Madden deduced there must have been some difficulties or problems. However, Father Madden told us he was "very clear" that he first came to know that Ridsdale had engaged in wrongful activity with boys in 1988, when he [Ridsdale] left Horsham. It is appalling that Bishop Mulkearns, knowing of Ridsdale's history of offending, did not report to the police or adequately inform Father Madden of the risks posed by Ridsdale....

So there you have it. At Page 267 the Royal Commission found that it was "inconceivable" that Fr Madden did not know of Ridsdale's offending in July 1977. But at Page 74 the Royal Commission reported that it had accepted evidence from the very same Fr Madden that he did not know about Ridsdale's offending until 1988. The Royal Commission accepted that Mulkearns did not inform Madden of Ridsdale's sexual offending until 1988 – but earlier it had accepted that Mulkearns would have informed all the consultors in July 1977 about Ridsdale, including Madden and Pell.

The other priest to give evidence, Fr Daniel Torpy, also said that he was not aware of Ridsdale's offending until years after the July 1977 meeting. Fr Kevin Arundell was not asked to give evidence and Monsignor Fiscalini and Fr McKenzie were deceased.

At Page 247 of *Case Study 28,* the Royal Commission had this to say concerning a meeting of the consultors which probably took place in early 1975 concerning Ridsdale's appointment as parish priest of Inglewood:

> He [Fr McInerney] was asked by counsel for the Church parties if he had any recollection of Bishop Mulkearns ever saying anything to the effect that Ridsdale had some issue with sexual behaviour or sexual abuse, and he said he did not recall him [Mulkearns] saying that. Father McInerney was asked if at any meeting while he was bishop's secretary he had "any recollection" of Bishop Mulkearns or anyone else saying something to the effect that Ridsdale had or might have sexually abused children, he said no. He said he was not aware of Ridsdale's offending before Ridsdale was charged in early 1993.

Another inconsistency. At Page 267, the Royal Commission said that it was "inconceivable" that Fr McInerney – along with Fr Madden and (then) Fr Pell – did not know of Ridsdale's offending in July 1977.

However, earlier at Page 247, the Royal Commission did not challenge Fr McInerney's statement that he did not find out about Ridsdale's offending until early 1993.

It was much the same with the second (and final) consultors meeting involving Ridsdale which Pell attended on 14 September 1982 – when Mulkearns announced that Ridsdale would be moved from his position as parish priest of Mortlake and that negotiations were underway for him to take up a role with the Catholic Enquiry Centre in Sydney.

Evidence was given by Fr Eric Bryant, who attended the meeting, that Mulkearns had said that "there was a problem with homosexuality in the diocese". Bryant had reason to remember – since it was his first consultors' meeting. In the Catholic Church in the early 1980s, evidence of a priest having an adult homosexual relationship would have been regarded as a potential scandal and would have been sufficient reason to relocate the priest. Dr Howard Brady, a former priest, has advised me that even a heterosexual relationship between a priest and a woman would have been sufficient reason to move a priest, possibly at his own request.

Four out of eight attendees at the 14 September 1982 meeting gave evidence to the Royal Commission – Fr Daniel Arundell, Fr Eric Bryant, Fr Brian Finnigan and Fr George Pell. All denied that Mulkearns told them in September 1982 that Ridsdale had been molesting children – and there is no reference in the minutes that Mulkearns had given any reasons for his decision to relocate Ridsdale. Nor was there any other documentary evidence to this effect.

At pages 310-312 of *Case Study No 28,* the Royal Commission had this to say:

> There is no reason not to accept the evidence of Father Bryant that Bishop Mulkearns said to the meeting that there was a problem with homosexuality in the Diocese and that this was the reason it had become necessary to move Ridsdale from Mortlake. Father Bryant's testimony on this point was clear and straightforward, and it is not contradicted by the other witnesses who were present at the meeting.... Cardinal Pell gave evidence that the bishop did not give

> the true reason for moving Ridsdale – namely, his sexual activity with children – and that the bishop lied in not giving the true reason to the consultors.
>
> We do not accept that Bishop Mulkearns lied to his consultors. Monsignor Fiscalini, Father Nolan and Father Finnigan all knew of allegations or complaints about Ridsdale's conduct with children before the meeting. They knew why it was necessary to move Ridsdale from Mortlake and take him out of the parish and Diocese to a position where access to children was restricted. It is inconceivable in these circumstances that Bishop Mulkearns deceived his consultors by not telling them the true reason. There would be little utility in doing so.
>
> The secret was out in at least two parishes by 1978....
>
> We are satisfied that Bishop Mulkearns told the consultors that it was necessary to move Ridsdale from the Diocese and from parish work because of complaints that he had sexually abused children. A contrary position is not tenable.

The Royal Commission found that it was "inconceivable" and "not tenable" to hold that Mulkearns had deceived his consultors about the real reason to move Ridsdale out of Mortlake to Sydney. This in spite of the fact that none of those present at the meeting on 14 September 1982 gave evidence at the Royal Commission to this effect. Mulkearns was not asked about this matter when he appeared before the Royal Commission (via video-link) in February 2016. He was scheduled to make a second appearance but, due to ill-health, did not do so. The other three priests present at the meeting – Monsignor Leo Fiscalini, Fr Henry Nolan and Fr John Martin were deceased. There was no evidence to support the Royal Commission's findings about what was "inconceivable" and "not tenable" – and the finding was made in spite of the specific evidence of Bryant to the contrary and Pell's testimony that he had no recollection of such a statement made by Mulkearns.

The Royal Commission did not accept that Mulkearns had deceived Pell and others. However, it found that Mulkearns had deceived Catholic Church Insurances, the *Warrnambool Standard* newspaper,

Cardinal Edward Clancy in Sydney and Fr Bryant (when he was parish priest of Portland) about Ridsdale's pedophilia. In spite of this, and without evidence, the Royal Commission found that Mulkearns had not deceived Pell and had informed him of Ridsdale's criminality in July 1977 and again in September 1982 – since it was "inconceivable" that Mulkearns would have deceived his consultors. So the Royal Commission accepted that Mulkearns lied to others – but not to Pell.

There is even more confusion about Ridsdale in *Case Study No 28* – which had the effect of downplaying the incompetence of Victoria Police. At Page 54, the Royal Commission found that "by at least December 1992, Victoria Police were investigating Ridsdale in relation to child sexual offences". However, at Pages 57 and 249, the Royal Commission accepted that Victoria Police's Bendigo Criminal Investigation Branch [CIB] had received a statement from a young boy as early as 1976 that Ridsdale had indecently assaulted him. Victoria Police knew about Ridsdale at least a year before Pell attended his first consultors' meeting – and around 15 years before it interviewed Ridsdale.

It would seem that there was a lack of fact-checking in *Case Study No 28*. At Page 238, the Royal Commission states that "when Ridsdale was convicted in 1993 he was not sentenced to imprisonment". Incorrect – as a simple Web search would have revealed. In May 1993, Ridsdale was sentenced to a maximum of 12 months imprisonment with a non-parole period of three months. He was released from jail in the second half of 1993 and jailed again the following August after pleading guilty to more child sexual abuse offences.

- Br Edward Dowlan

Br Edward Dowlan was a member of the Christian Brothers religious order at St Alipius Parish School in 1972 and shortly after at St Patrick's College Ballarat. He is a notorious pedophile who has served long jail terms on multiple offences. Pell told the Royal

Commission that, in 1973, he heard rumours of Dowlan's offending at St Patrick's College – with respect to implementation of harsh discipline on children and "possibly other infractions also" of a sexual nature. Pell added that he did not receive any specific allegation of sexual assault by Dowlan.

Pell, who was a young priest at the time (he turned 32 in 1973) passed on the information to Fr Davey, the chaplain of St Patrick's College. The school was under the control of the Christian Brothers. The following year Dowlan was moved from Ballarat to Warrnambool. At the Royal Commission, Pell expressed regret that he did not do more – but it would have been unusual at the time for a young diocesan priest to follow up such a matter with the Christian Brothers religious order – which was not under the control of the Ballarat Diocese.

The Royal Commission made the following finding with respect to Pell and Dowlan:

> Cardinal Pell told us that, with hindsight, he should have done more. In particular, he told us he should have consulted Brother Nangle [the principal of St Patrick's College] and ensured that the matter was properly treated. Cardinal Pell said he regretted not doing more at the time. We agree that he should have consulted Brother Nangle and ensured that the matter was properly treated.

This was a harsh judgment since Pell had no specific knowledge of any crime committed by Dowlan and he said that he had been assured by Fr Davey that the matter was being handled by the Christian Brothers.

- Timothy Green

The Royal Commission also made this finding with respect to Pell and Dowlan:

> We are satisfied that in late 1974, in the Eureka Swimming Pool changing room at Ballarat, Mr Green said to Father Pell, "We've got to do something about what's going on at St Pat's", and, when

Father Pell asked what he meant, Mr Green responded, "Brother Dowlan is touching little boys". Father Pell said words to the effect of "Don't be ridiculous" and walked away.

In November 2017, the Royal Commission cited a comment which Timothy Green (aged about 12 at the time) allegedly made to Pell in late 1974 – close to half a century earlier. Mr Green's evidence, given as an adult, was that he and two friends were sitting on a bench when Pell walked into the swimming pool change room. Green said that, while he had his "back to him", he told Pell that Dowlan was touching up little boys. Green also said that Pell had replied that "Don't be ridiculous". Green conceded he never saw Pell on this occasion – and did not notice when Pell exited the change room. Moreover, Green spoke to his front when Pell was behind him in the changing room of a public swimming pool.

There were two boys sitting next to Green at the time of the alleged exchange of words. One is deceased. The other said that he had no recollection of any such verbal exchange. Yet the Royal Commission found against Pell without even considering the possibility of mistaken identity – even though Green had said he did not see the person to whom he spoke.

• The Melbourne Archdiocese – *Case Study No 35*

The Royal Commission's *Case Study No 35* runs for 283 pages (including endnotes). It made the following findings with respect to Pell's involvements with Fr Peter Searson and Fr Wilfred Baker.

- Fr Peter Searson

In *Case Study No 35*, the Royal Commission focused on Fr Peter Searson (born 1923), the parish priest of Doveton in Melbourne's southeast. As pointed out earlier, this was unusual since Searson was by no means the worst clerical child sexual predator in the Melbourne archdiocese. Yet he comes first in the Royal Commission's case study for the Melbourne archdiocese – ahead of such notorious pedophiles as Desmond Gannon and Kevin O'Donnell. For example, the chapter on Searson totalled 49 pages compared with the six page chapter on Gannon. Gannon was first convicted of child sexual assault in 1995 – before Pell was appointed Archbishop of Melbourne – and did not reside in the area for which Pell was auxiliary bishop. Consequently, it would have been difficult for the Royal Commission to pin anything on Pell for the Church's handling of Gannon.

George Pell was appointed an auxiliary bishop of Melbourne in 1987 – he was one of four who held this position. He was based in the south-east suburb of Mentone and also became the parish priest of St Patrick's and the Holy Angels on Childers Street. In 1997 a woman approached Victoria Police and reported that she had been raped by Searson in 1974 when she was 18 years old. Victoria Police did not lay charges. According to the Royal Commission, the woman personally reported the matter to Archbishop Frank Little around 1974 but he did nothing. Yet there is clear evidence that allegations against Searson were known to Little in 1974 and Victoria Police in 1997.

In his capacity as auxiliary bishop, Pell had some limited authority with respect to the south-east suburbs of Melbourne. But Archbishop Little had unfettered control over the archdiocese. Moreover, the Catholic Education Office (CEO) – not the various auxiliary bishops – had responsibility for Catholic schools throughout the archdiocese.

The Royal Commission's case in this instance against Pell turned on one meeting. On 20 November 1989, a delegation from the Holy Family Parish School at Doveton met with Pell in his capacity as the local auxiliary bishop. The meeting, which was arranged by the staff union, focused on workplace relations. It was alleged that Searson had behaved unprofessionally towards the Holy Family School's staff and students alike. In the latter case, it was said that he had shown children a body in a coffin and shot a bird in a classroom – it is not clear whether the bird was alive or dead. Also he was accused of an unnecessary use of children's toilets. There was no allegation of sexual abuse. The evidence indicated that Searson was a bully who harassed teachers. The meeting wanted Searson counselled but not sacked. It is now clear that Searson had offended against children – but this matter was not raised at the November 1989 meeting.

The Royal Commission made this finding concerning Pell's involvement with Searson:

> We are satisfied that, on the basis of matters known to Bishop Pell on his own evidence (being the matters on the list of incidents and grievances and the "non-specific" allegation of sexual misconduct), he ought reasonably to have concluded that action needed to be taken in relation to Father Searson.

This finding overlooked the fact that Pell had no authority to take action against Searson – even if he had been asked to remove him as parish priest, which was not the case. During the hearings Pell conceded that he should have been "a bit more pushy" concerning Searson. The Royal Commission found that Pell "should have advised the Archbishop to remove Father Searson and he did not". This overlooks the fact that Little would not have acted on any such recommendation. The Catholic Education Office and Victoria Police knew more about Searson at the time than Pell did – but took no action.

In an apparent effort to obtain more evidence against Pell, the Royal Commission went to the trouble of reconvening its inquiry into Searson and called four witnesses from the Catholic Education Office. This came to naught – since during the hearing it became clear that the CEO did not tell Pell about Searson. The witnesses said that they had neither briefed nor met with Pell on this matter in his position as auxiliary bishop for the southern region of the Melbourne archdiocese.

Monsignor Thomas Doyle, the former CEO director who is not a Pell supporter, told the Royal Commission that he had tried to get Archbishop Little to remove Searson from the Holy Family parish for some ten years, but no action was taken. In view of this, Doyle did not see the point of attempting to get Pell to approach Little on the matter because he did not believe that this would achieve anything.

In October 1996, soon after Pell was appointed archbishop of Melbourne, a complaint was made that Searson had hit two boys on the head. Searson was immediately instructed by Denis Hart (the vicar-general) to stay away from altar boys. The matter was referred to the archdiocese's legal advisers who recommended that it be investigated by the Melbourne Response's independent commissioner, Peter O'Callaghan QC. On 13 March 1997, O'Callaghan wrote to Searson telling him that he had advised Pell to place him on administrative leave. Pell did so the next day and commenced a process that Searson be removed from the priesthood. Searson took his case to the Vatican and won. But Pell declined to enforce the Vatican's instructions and Searson did not return to the priesthood. He died in 2009.

The evidence indicates that when Pell had the chance to move against Searson he did so – unlike others in church and state before him. Yet the Royal Commission went out of its way to associate Pell with Searson's actions. In its findings on Pell's involvement with Searson, the Royal Commission used such words and terms as "should" and "ought" on several occasions concerning what it believed Pell should/ought to have been aware of circa 1989. But it produced no evidence that he was aware. And Pell's statement that he could have pushed harder against Searson was made in the light of what he knew in retrospect – a qualification which was ignored in the Royal Commission's findings.

- Fr William ("Bill") Baker

Fr Bill Baker (born 1936) was a parish priest in Melbourne from the mid-1970s until the late 1990s. Unlike Searson, Baker did not work in the south east area of the Archdiocese where Pell was based between early 1987 and mid-1996. Baker was charged with child sexual offences against boys in 1998 and sentenced to imprisonment in June 1999. He was committed subsequently to stand trial on other charges but died in 2013 while the matters were still pending.

The evidence suggests that Archbishop Little was advised as early as 1978 about Baker's offending but declined to take any action. Peter O'Callaghan QC came to the view, when he was in charge of the Melbourne Response procedures, that Baker's sexual assaults on boys commenced around 1963.

The Royal Commission made this finding concerning Pell's involvement with Baker:

> We are satisfied that the Curia knew in August 1996 that Father Baker would probably be charged in relation to an incident at Brighton in 1965. We are satisfied that Archbishop Pell, Bishop O'Connell, Monsignor Connors, Monsignor Deakin, Mr Exell and Father Waters were at the meeting where this was discussed. Archbishop Pell had the authority to remove Father Baker. Despite that knowledge, Archbishop Pell did not stand down Father Baker at that point in time. Father Baker remained in his position at North Richmond – a parish with a primary school attached to it – until May 1997.

On 21 May 1997, O'Callaghan QC, having investigated the case, wrote to Pell concerning many allegations against Baker going back decades and recommended that he be placed on administrative leave pending further investigation. Pell accepted the advice on 22 May 1997, removed Baker's priestly facilities and ordered him to leave the North Richmond parish immediately.

In spite of Pell's prompt and decisive action when formally advised of Baker's behaviour, after an investigation had been completed, the Royal Commission found that he should have acted earlier.

However, when Baker's case was raised with Pell at the Royal Commission on 2 March 2016, Counsel Assisting did not ask Pell any questions about what he knew about, and how he handled, Baker while he was Archbishop of Melbourne. Nor was Pell queried about any discussions concerning Baker which may have occurred at the Curia meeting held on 19 August 1996. Moreover, Pell was not advised of, and given opportunity to reply to, the essence of the Royal Commissions' adverse findings with respect to this matter.

This evident lack of basic procedural fairness speaks volumes about how Cardinal Pell was treated by the Royal Commission and its Counsel Assisting. Clearly the concept of "reasonable satisfaction" was a very low bar to jump when it came to Cardinal Pell.

Enter Paul Bongiorno

The best known Australians to be mentioned at the Royal Commission were probably Cardinal George Pell, former Network Ten journalist Paul Bongiorno, former governor-general and Anglican archbishop Peter Hollingworth and Anglican Archbishop Phillip Aspinall. All but Bongiorno gave verbal evidence to the Royal Commission.

As pointed out in Chapter 5, Bongiorno spoke well about Pell when interviewed by Tess Livingstone for her 2002 biography. But within a decade Bongiorno was an active participant in the Pell pile-on.

Pell was born in 1941, Bongiorno 1944. Both were chosen by Bishop James O'Collins to study at the Urban University in Rome. In 1971, as a junior priest, Bongiorno shared accommodation with Ridsdale in the Catholic presbytery in Warrnambool. In 1973, as a junior priest, Pell shared accommodation with Ridsdale in the Catholic presbytery in Ballarat East.

On 21 May 2015, the first day of the Royal Commission's hearings on the Ballarat diocese, Bongiorno appeared in his (then) regular Thursday commentary slot on ABC Radio National's *Breakfast* program. The presenter was Fran Kelly, a Pell critic who was brought up a Catholic. At the time, Bongiorno was a contributing editor to Network 10 and a writer for *The Saturday Paper*. Yet he went beyond the remit to discuss contemporary national politics – and turned his focus on historical clerical child abuse in the Ballarat diocese. In response to a question from Kelly, Bongiorno had this to say:

> …I know Gerald Ridsdale. I lived in a presbytery with him in Warrnambool. I've had the victims approach me to appear for them in court cases. Let me tell you this, Fran, I had no idea what he was up to. And when people look at me quizzically, I say: "Well look, let me tell you this; there are married men and women now who sleep with their husbands and wives who don't know that their husband or wife is having an affair." Let me tell

you that Ridsdale never came into the presbytery in Warrnambool and said: "Guess how many boys I've raped today?" They hide it. It was certainly hidden from me. And when it came out, after I'd left the priesthood, I was shocked and I was ashamed.

On 25 May 2016, I had the following email exchange with Bongiorno:

> GH to PB
>
> Paul
>
> Just a quick query. When you spoke to Fran Kelly in May 2015 about Ridsdale – did you know in advance that Fran was going to raise this matter on air or was it a surprise?
>
> Best wishes
>
> Gerard Henderson
>
> PB to GH
>
> It was the first day of hearings in Ballarat. Fran knew my background and asked me if I minded her raising the issue. I have assiduously avoided church issues, Pell and I grew up together, I have never criticised him publicly, but I wanted to identify with the many good and faithful priests still serving and in a real sense are victims of their "fallen comrades". Everyone in the church including me has been on a learning curve. I personally told Gillard her RC was needed.

That's clear, then. Bongiorno was the recipient of what, in another context, might be called a question-on-notice. He used the occasion to declare, no doubt truthfully, that when they shared accommodation he had no knowledge that Ridsdale was a pedophile. In time, Bongiorno was to have an involvement with the Royal Commission.

On 29 October 2015, a man identified as BPL made a sworn statement to the Royal Commission. BPL, who was born in December 1956, said that he was "sexually abused by Ridsdale on three or four occasions in 1970 and 1971 in and around Warrnambool". BPL and his younger brother were altar servers at St Joseph's Church – where Monsignor Leo Fiscalini was parish priest and where Ridsdale was, for a time, one of the assistant parish priests. In addition to his duties as assistant priest at St Joseph's Church, Bongiorno was also the chaplain to St Joseph's Christian Brothers College in Warrnambool (where BPL went to school) along with the Young Christian Students (YCS) organisation.

BPL told the Royal Commission that, while on a camp in the early 1970s at Crossley just outside of Warrnambool, he told Bongiorno that he had been abused by Ridsdale and he believed that this was also the case with his younger brother. He added that Bongiorno replied that this was a real problem and that he and his fellow priest, Fr Brophy, had talked to Fiscalini about the matter and that Fiscalini said that he was sorting it out with the bishop. BPL also said that Bongiorno told him to raise the matter with Fiscalini. BPL said that when he eventually did so, Fiscalini advised him that Bongiorno had mentioned his claims to him.

On 24 November 2015, Bongiorno filed a statement with the Royal Commission. He said that BPL's name was "vaguely familiar" to him and that people of that surname lived in Warrnambool but added: "I cannot put a face to that name". He wrote: "That conversation [with BPL] did not happen with me. I would remember it. I would be deeply shocked by the alleged substance of the conversation". Bongiorno also wrote that, while a priest, he never had any discussions with Fiscalini about Ridsdale. With respect to Monsignor John Day, Bongiorno wrote this:

> I knew of Monsignor John Day before I went to Mildura on a couple of occasions in my role as director of Catholic communications in Ballarat. I didn't hear of any allegations of child sexual abuse involving Monsignor Day until after I left the priesthood [in mid-1974] when it was reported in the media.

The Royal Commission did not call either BPL or Bongiorno to give evidence under oath. This was unfair to George Pell – since Bongiorno could have provided information in public as to what it was like being a young influential priest in the Ballarat diocese among such priests as Ridsdale and such bishops as Mulkearns. Bongiorno's position was similar to Pell's. Namely, that he lived for a year with

Ridsdale without knowing that he was a pedophile and no specific allegation about Ridsdale's child sexual abuse was raised with him.

In February 2018, a doctor, who had been a specialist physician at Warrnambool in the 1970s, wrote to me. He said that he was involved in Catholic Church activities in Warrnambool in the 1970s and regarded Bongiorno as a friend. He added: "I don't know why the allegation and refutation were not tested before the Commission which relied instead on correspondence from the parties involved in formulating its conclusion or lack thereof."

The doctor advised me that he had written to Bongiorno care of *The Saturday Paper* expressing the view that it was "anomalous" that Bongiorno should be appearing on such a program as ABC TV's *The Drum* as a commentator on clerical child abuse in the Catholic Church without mentioning that he had given written evidence to the Royal Commission. The doctor also "queried why the altar boy [BPL] should invent his story". Bongiorno had appeared as a panellist on *The Drum* on 14 December 2017 which discussed the Royal Commission. The guest interviewee was Bernard Barrett of the Broken Rites organisation, a vehement critic of Pell.

The doctor wrote that Bongiorno's assistant at *The Saturday Paper* acknowledged the correspondence and said Bongiorno would respond – but this did not occur. The letter concluded: "I believe he [Bongiorno] was given an easy ride by the Royal Commission compared with the way other ex-Ballarat near contemporaries have been treated."

Bongiorno's November 2015 statement to the Royal Commission attracted scant media attention apart from my coverage of the matter in my column in *The Weekend Australian* along with documentation in my *Media Watch Dog* blog (particularly the issue of 27 May 2016). Andrew Bolt covered this in his syndicated column and on his television program. Alan Jones (then at Radio 2GB) also referred briefly to the matter when he appeared on the ABC TV *Q&A* program on 7 March 2016.

I mentioned Bongiorno's time in Warrnambool in the final paragraph of a letter which I wrote to *The Saturday Paper* in November 2016 concerning comments by its columnist Richard Ackland about Pell. Erik Jensen, the paper's editor, published the correspondence but deleted the fourth and final paragraph about Bongiorno – advising me by email that it was "unseemly and dishonest" and not relevant.

The Royal Commission dealt with the BPL/Bongiorno matter at Pages 241-242 of *Case Study No 28*. This was its conclusion:

> Our experience during this inquiry confirms ordinary human experience that memory can be unreliable after the passage of time. However, on the material available to us, we are unable to resolve the differing accounts of BPL and Mr Bongiorno.

This finding speaks volumes about the Royal Commission's attitude to Pell. It was not able to resolve the differing accounts of BPL and Bongiorno, having not called either man to give verbal testimony. But the Royal Commission was able to resolve the differing accounts of Timothy Green and George Pell in Green's favour, even though Green conceded when he appeared before the Royal Commission that he had not been facing Pell when the alleged conversation took place.

Letting the Media & Government Schools Off-the-Hook

The Royal Commission's focus on the Catholic Church in general and Cardinal Pell in particular stands in contrast to its decision not to inquire into child sexual abuse in the media or government schools.

The Jimmy Savile case in Britain involving the BBC, the Jon Stephens case in Australia involving the ABC and the conviction of Channel 7 *Hey Dad!* star Robert Hughes in 2014 on historical child sexual abuse offences suggest that an investigation into the media might have produced some valuable information.

On 12 December 2016, I emailed Philip Reed, the Royal Commission's CEO, as follows:

> Dear Mr Reed

> I would be grateful if you could advise me whether, before it reports to the government, the Royal Commission intends to inquire into the institutional responses of the media – including the ABC – to child sexual abuse. As you may or may not be aware, in 1975 the ABC ran a program by a self-confessed pedophile [Richard Neville] which was soft on pederasts and did not adopt a duty of care to the victims of their crimes. I would be grateful if you, or your staff, could advise me, by the close of business on Wednesday, whether this matter is likely to be inquired into by the Royal Commission before it concludes it hearings.
>
> Yours sincerely
>
> Gerard Henderson

The following day I received this reply:

> Dear Mr Henderson
>
> It is unlikely that the media will form the subject of the Royal Commission's final public hearings.
>
> Regards
>
> Ingrid Van Steenwyk – Media & Communication

That was it – no reasons were given for the Royal Commission's decision not to undertake even one case study into the institutional responses by the media to child sexual abuse.

There was a similar omission concerning government schools. In his article in the *MercatorNet* website on 29 May 2021, the Sydney barrister Michael McAuley – in a piece titled "Was the Royal Commission hand in glove with the 'Get Pell' campaign?" – commented:

> The Royal Commission focused, as regards schools, on religious schools. Why this happened has never been satisfactorily explained – and there is ample evidence that children in state schools have also been victims of sexual abuse. By way of example, victims of paedophile teachers in state schools in Tasmania are currently seeking an investigation as to why alleged paedophiles were moved between state schools from the 1970s to the 1990s.
>
> This is a matter that might have been investigated, not only in Tas-

mania, but in all states. It has been suggested the Royal Commission unreasonably targeted religious schools, especially those of the Catholic Church. Its final report fails to set out clear and publicly verifiable criteria which justified this focus.

The Royal Commission conducted 57 case studies – including 16 relating specifically to the Catholic Church. There were a number of case studies into non-Catholic religious (mainly Anglican and Uniting Church) and independent schools. But there were no specific case studies into government schools.

Michael McAuley is correct. On examining the history of convicted pedophile Darrel George Harington on 4 March 2020, *The Mercury* documented how the Tasmanian Department of Education moved known pedophile teachers from school to school between the early 1970s to the 1990s. The Royal Commission conducted a case study on The Hutchins School in Hobart, Tasmania (which is an independent boys school with an Anglican background) – but showed no interest in the Tasmanian state government's institutional responses to child sexual abuse in its own schools.

Cardinal Pell's "It Wasn't of Much Interest" Moment

George Pell stumbled only once during his four days (it was late night and early morning in Rome) in the witness box on the occasion of his third – and final – appearance before the Royal Commission. Pell's comment that Ridsdale's offending "wasn't of much interest" has been used against him. However, reference to the transcript indicates that Pell's statement was not what his critics made it out to be.

Let's go to the transcript where Gail Furness is cross-examining Pell about Ridsdale's offending when parish priest at Inglewood in 1975 – and whether Pell was aware of this some two decades later. The exchange took place on 1 March 2016 – Pell's second day in the witness box:

> *Gail Furness:* Is it the case in 1993, or after that year, you under-

stood that he [Ridsdale] had been committing offences for which he was now convicted and sentenced – is that what you understood in 1993 or thereafter?

George Pell: I did.

Gail Furness: That's a different question from the one I asked you, Cardinal. It was whether you had knowledge that it was common knowledge at Inglewood at that time.

George Pell: I did not know that it was common knowledge at Inglewood at that time because, if I'd known that, I would have known that there were offences.

Gail Furness: Did you subsequently –

George Pell: Possible offences.

Gail Furness: Did you subsequently know not that he offended at Inglewood – leave that to one side – but that it was common knowledge of his interfering with children at Inglewood?

George Pell: I - I couldn't say that I ever knew that everyone knew. I knew a number of people did. I was – I didn't know whether it was common knowledge or whether it wasn't. It's a sad story and it wasn't of much interest to me.

Gail Furness: What wasn't of much interest to you, Cardinal?

George Pell: The suffering, of course, was real and I very much regret that, but I had no reason to turn my mind to the extent of the evils that Ridsdale had perpetrated....

Pell has told me that he had intended to say that the "prurient details" of Ridsdale's crimes was something he did not want to focus on. But he didn't say this – and the comment was misinterpreted. Moreover, Pell's critics in this instance overlooked the time frame involved.

As the transcript demonstrates, Furness asked Pell what he knew "in 1993 or thereafter" about Ridsdale's offending in 1975 in Inglewood. In 1975 Pell, as a relatively junior priest of the Ballarat diocese, had no authority over Ridsdale.

On this occasion, Pell's language was loose. What he intended to say was that, when an auxiliary bishop in Melbourne in 1993, he had no reason to focus on the details of the crimes of a Ballarat priest in Inglewood in 1975, over whom he was never in a position of authority.

On Thursday 3 March 2016, Pell's last day in the Royal Commission witness box, he was asked about his comment of two days earlier. The response was as follows:

> *Gail Furness:* You said on Tuesday…that Father Ridsdale interfering with children at Inglewood was "a sad story and it wasn't of much interest to me". Do you remember saying that?"
>
> *George Pell:* I remember messing up this sequence completely. I regret the choice of words. I was very confused, I responded poorly. Just previous to this exchange, we were talking about '93-'94. Then it swung over to the incidents in '74-'75. It was badly expressed. I – in '93 I was a Melbourne official considering something that happened in Inglewood. I have never enjoyed reading the accounts of these sufferings and I tried to do that only when it was professionally and absolutely appropriate, because the behaviour is abhorrent and painful to read about.

In its final report, the Royal Commission made no adverse findings with respect to Pell's comment cited above – but it has been used frequently by his critics, including Louise Milligan.

After the Royal Commission: The Media Pile-On Continues

As stated earlier, the unredacted version of the Royal Commission's findings into the Ballarat diocese and the Melbourne archdiocese were released by the Commonwealth Attorney-General (on behalf of the Commonwealth, State and Territory governments) on the morning of Thursday 7 May 2020. This meant that nothing in the Royal Commission's report would be used in any future criminal charges against Pell, lest they prejudice any further trial.

As might be expected, the leading members of the Pell pile-on immediately welcomed the release of the unredacted findings of *Case Study No 28* and *Case Study No 35* – before any of them would have had the time to both read and analyse the documents. Also, some journalists appeared not to understand the nature of royal commissions – in particular that they bring down findings to a level well below reasonable doubt concerning which there can be no appeal. For example, Fairfax Media journalist Peter FitzSimons, in a tweet on 8 May 2020, referred to the "scathing judgment by the Royal Commission of Pell" – ignorant of the fact that royal commissions do not deliver judgments.

At 10.19 am on 7 May 2020, Louise Milligan tweeted that she was "just going through the report tabled right now on Pell and the Royal Commission has comprehensively rejected his evidence". This was warmly welcomed by Paul Bongiorno who, sneeringly tweeted: "What they didn't believe him? Seems to be a regular feature." Yet at 10.19 am Milligan would not have had time to determine whether or not the Royal Commission's findings were comprehensive.

Milligan's tweet was misleading. The Royal Commission did not "comprehensively" reject Pell's evidence under oath. It cited no independent witness or documentary evidence to support its findings. Instead, the Royal Commission found that Pell's evidence was, variably "inconceivable", "implausible", "not tenable", "unlikely" and so on – and that he "should" or "could" have done something or other. These are opinions only – unsupported by evidence.

Milligan's tweet was but the first of a series put out early on Monday 7 May 2020 by journalists who would not have had the time to consider the two reports in any detail. Lucy Carter (ABC) described the findings about Pell as "truly explosive", to Lucie Morris-Marr they were "simply damning…forensic and blunt" while Melissa Davey focused the findings about Ridsdale without detecting the contradictions. Even the entertainers weighed in. Tim Minchin tweeted: "Oh geez, what a F_cking shock" and actor Rhys Muldoon tweeted "Pell aided and abetted pedophiles. This is beyond dispute".

On Friday 8 May 2020, Milligan wrote an article titled "History will not be kind to George Pell, as royal commission reveals its secret findings" which was posted on the ABC News website. Milligan did not query any of the Royal Commission's findings and she did not notice the major inconsistencies in its report about what – and when – the

Ballarat consultors (including Pell) knew about Ridsdale. It was poor scholarship – but it remained on the ABC website at the time this book went to print.

Milligan was not the only member of the Pell-pile on to miss the gross inconsistencies in the Royal Commission's findings. In the left-wing *The Saturday Paper* on 9 May 2020, Erik Jensen wrote that when Pell "walked into the Melbourne Magistrates' Court in 1993 beside Gerald Ridsdale…George Pell knew that the priest had been abusing children in the church". In fact, Pell did not enter the court on this occasion and he knew, by then, of Ridsdale's offending since the accused had already pleaded guilty. Jensen produced no evidence to support his claim that Pell had known about Ridsdale's offending "for more than a decade prior to" Ridsdale's conviction and merely accepted the Royal Commission's view that Pell did know.

Writing in *The Monthly* in June 2020, in an article termed "The last word on George Pell", journalist Anne Manne accepted without question all the Royal Commission's findings against Pell but failed to mention that none had been supported by evidence. Not surprisingly, Manne's account in the left-wing publication was not the "last word" on George Pell.

Cardinal Pell's Response to the Royal Commission

For his part, Cardinal Pell's office released a brief statement on 7 May 2020, shortly after the release of the unredacted parts of *Case Study No 28* and *Case Study No 35:*

> Cardinal Pell said he was surprised by some of the views of the Royal Commission about his actions. These views are not supported by evidence. He is especially surprised by the statements in the report about the earlier transfers of Gerald Ridsdale discussed by the Ballarat Diocesan Consultors in 1977 and 82. The Consultors who gave evidence on the meetings in 1977 and 1982 either said they did not learn of Ridsdale's offending against children until much later or they had no recollection of what was discussed. None said they were made aware of Ridsdale's offending at these meetings.

> The then Fr Pell left the Diocese of Ballarat and therefore his position as a consultor at the end of 1984. As an Auxiliary Bishop in Melbourne 1987-96, Bishop Pell met with a delegation from Doveton Parish in 1989 which did not mention sexual assaults and did not ask for Searson's removal. Appointed Archbishop of Melbourne on 16 August 1996, Archbishop Pell placed Fr Searson on administrative leave in March 1997 and removed him from the parish on 15 May 1997.

In a mere 180 words or so, Cardinal Pell pointed to the essential flaws of the Royal Commission's report with respect to his involvements with Ridsdale and Searson. Justice McClellan and his colleagues found that Fr Pell and Fr Madden were both told by Bishop Mulkearns in 1977 that Ridsdale was a pedophile. But earlier in the report, it was found that Madden did not learn about Ridsdale's criminality until 1988. Moreover, the Royal Commission found that Fr Pell and Fr McInerney were both told by Bishop Mulkearns in 1982 that Ridsdale was a pedophile. But earlier the Royal Commission found that McInerney did not learn about Ridsdale's offending until 1993.

The Royal Commission had been allocated expenditure up to $373 million along with hundreds of staff. But Justice McClellan and his staff failed to recognise the glaring contradictions in its findings concerning what Pell was told by Bishop Mulkearns about Ridsdale.

If such contradictory findings had been in a court decision, an appeal against the judgment would almost certainly have succeeded. If they had appeared in a first-year university law essay, the student would probably have been failed or certainly required to undertake a re-write.

The Critiques of Frank Brennan, J.G. Santamaria QC & T.K. Tobin QC

In his *Observations on the Pell Proceedings* (Connor Court Publishing, 2021), the Jesuit priest and lawyer Frank Brennan wrote that "the Royal Commission needed a big scalp, and Pell's was the one they wanted". He also referred to the Royal Commission's "shoddy work" and suggested that it exhibited "animus...towards Pell".

In mid-2020, three prominent lawyers wrote a response to the criticisms of Cardinal Pell by the Royal Commission. The authors were Hon. J. G. Santamaria QC (a former justice of the Victorian Court of Appeal), Professor Greg Craven and T.K. Tobin QC. With respect to *Case Study No 28*, the lawyers wrote:

> When he gave evidence to the inquiry, Dr Pell denied that he had known of the crimes that were being committed in Ballarat. So, the finding that he did know carried with it the implication that he had given false evidence.
>
> There was no direct evidence that Dr Pell knew of the crimes when they were being committed: no witness said that Dr Pell knew. Equally, there was no document placed in evidence that reflected that he knew of the crimes. Accordingly, the finding that he did know was based on a series of inferences. We have closely examined the evidence given at the [Royal Commission]. In our opinion, the conclusions drawn...were not open to it. Either the facts said to justify the inferences were not established or the inferences were logically fallacious.

The Santamaria/Craven/Tobin paper concluded that the Royal Commission's findings concerning Pell were "unfair and unreasonable". The authors also stated that the Royal Commission had failed to acknowledge that the steps taken by Cardinal Pell in 1996 in establishing the Melbourne Response "for the protection of children...were unprecedented" at the time.

In short, the Royal Commission's findings against Pell were contradictory and deeply flawed. Yet they were welcomed immediately by the likes of Milligan, Bongiorno, Morris-Marr, Davey and Minchin who were involved in the Pell pile-on – not one of whom noticed the contradictions in Justice McClellan's findings concerning Pell.

And so it came to pass that Justice Peter McClellan presided over a five year long royal commission which generated sensationalist publicity that unfairly caused significant harm to Cardinal George Pell.

This is precisely what McClellan had warned about in his 1990 paper concerning the excesses of royal commissions and commissions of inquiry.

At that time, McClellan had declared that persons should only be convicted after due process in the relevant court. However, the *Royal Commission into Institutional Responses to Child Sexual Abuse* effectively "convicted" Pell – at least in the eyes of large sections of the public – in the absence of evidence while, on occasions, denying him due process.

George Pell, St Patrick's College Ballarat and the Royal Commission

Soon after Cardinal Pell was convicted by the jury in a re-trial, his name was removed from the honour board at St Patrick's College, Ballarat which he attended between 1949 and 1959. George Pell is the school's best known alumnus. On 26 February 2019, Henrietta Cook reported in *The Age* St Patrick's (then) principal John Crowley as saying: "The jury's verdict demonstrates that Cardinal Pell's behaviours have not met the standards we expect of those we honour as role models for the young men we educate."

In this instance, Crowley seems to have regarded himself as a higher authority than Australia's superior courts. While acknowledging that Pell had a right to appeal, he was of the view that a one word jury verdict (i.e. "guilty") had more substance than any future judgment of a court of appeal. And so the campus building known as the Pell Wing became the Waterford Wing and Pell's name was removed from the honour board for ordained students – for starters.

St Patrick's College, formerly run by the Christian Brothers religious order, is now controlled by Edmund Rice Education Australia organisation. The college did not change its decision to wash its hands of Pell when the High Court of Australia quashed his conviction in a unanimous decision. Instead the college authorities appear to have awaited the publication of the unredacted reports of the Royal Commission which were due to be released within weeks of the High Court judgment. This occurred on the morning of 7 May 2020. Later that day, Pell-antagonist Louise Milligan put out this tweet:

> *Louise Milligan: St Patrick's College* Ballarat *stands* by its decision to revoke honours bestowed on alumnus, George #Pell following release of Royal Commission redactions about what he knew – some of it involving his old school.

Milligan attached to her tweet a statement by St Patrick's College on the Royal Commission's findings – which ran for a mere 175 words. The second last paragraph was as follows:

> In 2019, the College revoked honours which it had previously bestowed on Cardinal George Pell. This included renaming a building and removing his status as a Legend of the Old Collegians Association. St Patrick's College stands by these decisions.

There is no indication that the authors of the St Patrick's College statement – issued on the day the Royal Commission's reports into *Case Study No 28* and *Case Study No 35* were released – had studied or even read the documents. Nor was any mention made of Cardinal Pell's refutation of the Royal Commission's findings – which published immediately after they were released.

It turned out that George Pell's time at St Patrick's College Ballarat was to be extinguished on the school campus due to the contradictory and evidence-free findings of the kind of commissions that Peter McClellan had once warned could cause considerable harm to a person unfairly trapped in a blaze of sensationalist publicity.

The Australian Catholic University, on the other hand, did not de-platform George Pell's various portraits and plaques when he was convicted, and they remained in situ on the university's campuses at North Sydney and Ballarat at the time of the High Court's unanimous decision.

On the same day that St Patrick's College formally banished George Pell, the school's authorities announced that they were "excited to reveal" the name of "two new College Legends". One was Detective Sergeant Kevin Carson – who was the author of two Victoria Police reports which grossly overestimated the number of suicides in Victoria which could be linked primarily to child sexual abuse by priests and brothers. This is discussed in Chapter 10. Victoria Police privately acknowledge the error, but Carson's mistake was not revealed publicly until John Ferguson broke the story three years later in *The Australian*.

So it was out with Legend Pell – and in with Legend Carson. On 7 May 2020, St Patrick's College gave the reason why Detective Sergeant Carson had been made a Legend of the College. But no reasons were given for the decision to permanently strip Cardinal Pell of this award – beyond the brief reference to the unredacted findings of the Royal Commission, which the authors of the statement may or may not have read.

Photo of Altar Servers/choir outside St Patrick's Cathedral

On its front page on Good Friday, 1995 The Age depicted the procession into St Patrick's Cathedral on Palm Sunday (9 April 1995). Note the choristers are up the front immediately behind the cross bearer and two candle bearers. The choristers are followed by the other altar servers, priests, the archbishop and the archbishop's attendees. In April 1995, Frank Little was Archbishop of Melbourne. George Pell continued this Solemn Mass tradition, which goes back many decades, when he became Archbishop of Melbourne in June 1996. Victoria Police did not interview any of the altar servers who participated in Solemn Mass at St Patrick's Cathedral in December 1996 despite the fact that they were physically close to Archbishop Pell before, during and after the Solemn Mass, and despite the fact that they (unlike the choristers) would have been in the priests' sacristy soon after mass.

Graham Ashton held senior positions in Victoria Police before being appointed Chief Commissioner by the Andrews Labor government in July 2015. Ashton referred to Cardinal Pell's complainants as "victims" even before Pell was interviewed by police and later incorrectly claimed that Victoria Police commenced investigations into Pell only after a complaint was received.

Shane Patton was appointed Victoria Police Commissioner by the Andrews Labor government on 27 June 2020. He led the three person Victoria Police team which interviewed Pell in Rome but did not attend the interview. As deputy commissioner, Patton declared at a high-profile media conference that Cardinal Pell would be charged with numerous offences of historical child sexual abuse against numerous individuals. Since Patton took no questions, the announcement could have been made by means of a media statement.

10

VICTORIA POLICE'S OPERATION TETHERING – OR "GET PELL" – CAMPAIGN

> "All 'complainants' are not 'victims'. Some complaints are false and thus those 'complainants' are not 'victims'. Throughout the judicial process the word 'complainant' is deployed up to the moment of conviction whereafter a 'complainant' is properly referred to as a 'victim'. Since the entire judicial process, up to that point, is engaged in determining whether or not a 'complainant' is indeed a 'victim', such an approach cannot be questioned.... Since the investigative process is similarly engaged in ascertaining facts which will, if proven, establish guilt, the use of the word 'victim' at the commencement of an investigation is simply inaccurate and should cease."
>
> - Sir Richard Henriques, formerly a judge of Her Majesty's High Court of Justice in England, in his *An Independent Review of the Metropolitan Police Service's handling of non-recent sexual offence investigations alleged against persons of public prominence*, 31 October 2016.

Among the cases reviewed by Sir Richard Henriques in 2016 was that of "Nick" – subsequently named as Carl Beech – which was discussed in Chapter 1. He falsely alleged that, as a boy, he had been sexually abused by a number of high profile British individuals – including the late Sir Edward Heath, Lord Bramall, Lord Brittan and Harvey Proctor. Detective Superintendent Kenny McDonald, the senior Metropolitan Police Service officer who initially investigated Beech's claims – in Operation Midland – had declared that they were "credible and true". It turned out that the complainant was a fantasist and a liar. No charges were laid against the alleged offenders – but those against whom allegations were made, living and dead, suffered huge reputational damage. The case is well covered in the 2020 BBC Two documentary *The Unbelievable Story of Carl Beech* – which is directed by Vanessa Engle. The ABC chose not to run this film on either its main or second channels. On 16 November 2020, I wrote to ABC managing director and editor-in-chief David Anderson suggesting that the ABC show the documentary in view of its interest in historical child sexual abuse cases. He did not reply.

Commissioner Ashton's Incorrect Statements Concerning Cardinal Pell

ABC TV devoted its entire *7.30* program on 27 July 2016 to allegations of sexual offending by Cardinal Pell during the 1970s in Ballarat and the 1990s in Melbourne. Graham Ashton, the Chief Commissioner of Victoria Police, watched the program and made this statement when interviewed by Neil Mitchell on Melbourne Radio 3AW the following morning – initially denying that Victoria Police had leaked information to Louise Milligan for her *7.30* expose:

> We [Victoria Police] haven't provided the ABC with materials. Anyone who saw the show last night on the ABC, which I did look at, it's clear it's – the source of that information is from the victims. You could see the emotions in their voices and see it in them last night. They're highly traumatised from what they are saying has happened to them and they're talking to the media about that.

The *7.30* executive producer tasked Louise Milligan to cover the reaction to her own story. On 28 July 2016, she ran a clip from the 3AW interview of Ashton referring to the two men (L.M. and D.D.), who made allegations that Pell sexually abused them in the Eureka Swimming Pool in the 1970s, as Pell's "victims". This statement was seriously prejudicial to Pell – since it indicated that Victoria Police believed the allegations against him to be true, in spite of the fact that Pell had not even been interviewed on the matter at this stage. Such an approach to a police investigation was criticised by Sir Richard Henriques in his review, where he stated:

> The purpose of the interview is to permit a complainant to give as full and detailed an account as possible as part of an impartial fact finding exercise. At present the public are told: "If you make a complaint you will be believed." I consider that they should be told: "If you make a complaint we will treat it very seriously and investigate it thoroughly without fear or favour".... Any policy involving belief of one party necessarily involves disbelief of the other party. That cannot be a safe system.

George Pell was not treated fairly or professionally by Chief Commissioner Ashton and his colleagues. Nor did Ashton provide an accurate account on the manner in which Victoria Police investigated the Pell Case. Police commissioners are not expected to be media performers. However, Ashton chose to appear regularly on Melbourne Radio 3AW (where he spoke to Neil Mitchell) and ABC Melbourne Radio 774 (where he spoke to Jon Faine). His comments on 3AW and 774 were widely reported by other media outlets.

On 9 April 2020, a couple of days after the High Court had quashed Pell's conviction, the following exchange took place on 3AW:

> *Neil Mitchell:* Why did the investigation or intelligence probe begin on George Pell in the first place?
>
> *Graham Ashton:* Well we received a complaint from victims. That's what led to the assessment. [Note that, even after the High Court judgment, Ashton was still referred to Pell's "victims".]
>
> *Neil Mitchell:* So, it didn't begin until the complaint came in?
>
> *Graham Ashton:* No, we weren't sitting there thinking: "We don't

like George Pell, let's investigate George Pell".

Neil Mitchell: Well you have been accused – not you personally, well maybe you personally as well – the police are running a vendetta against George Pell.

Graham Ashton: What a joke. We don't run vendettas against people. That's not what we're about. That's not what we take an oath to do. We take an oath to serve the community and that means we do it without fear or favour. And that means if we get allegations, we investigate them and that doesn't matter who that is, and nor should it in this country.

Neil Mitchell: Do you feel any sympathy for George Pell?

Graham Ashton: It's not a matter in which I give any personal thought to.

Neil Mitchell: Fair enough….

Ashton's statement is simply not true. As pointed out in Chapter 1, Detective Superintendent Paul Sheridan gave evidence under oath to the Magistrates' Court on 28 March 2018 that Victoria Police set up Operation Tethering, aimed at investigating Pell, in March 2013. This was over a year before Victoria Police received its first complaint against Pell – and it came from a man who had been discharged from a psychiatric hospital the previous day. The only complaint, which led to Pell going to trial, was made to Victoria Police by A in June 2015 – over two years after Operation Tethering had been established.

On 6 June 2020, a few weeks before he stepped down as Victoria Police's chief commissioner, Ashton gave what was termed a "final interview" to the *Herald Sun's* Mark Butler. This is how Butler's report commenced:

> Mr Ashton labelled claims police put a target on Cardinal George Pell's back "complete rubbish": "When a police force receives allegations and those allegations are serious, we examine them. If we find there's sufficient information to warrant an investigation, then we do it. It doesn't matter who it relates to. And it shouldn't matter."

Ashton's final comment on the Pell Case was also incorrect. As both

Ashton and Butler should have known, Victoria Police set up its "Operation Tethering" investigation before it received any allegations – serious or otherwise – about Pell.

To summarise, Operation Tethering was a criminal investigation in search of a crime. It was established over a year before any complaint was made about Pell. After A made a complaint in June 2015, Victoria Police decided to advertise for any men who were choristers at St Patrick's Cathedral between 1996 and 2001 (i.e. Pell's time as Archbishop of Melbourne) to come forward. None did. In the event, Pell was put on trial in the absence of any independent witness and in the absence of any documentary evidence.

As documented in Chapter 2, Victoria Police laid 26 charges against Pell with respect to nine persons (one of whom was deceased). Only five charges made it to trial involving two persons (one of whom was deceased). They were thrown out by the High Court in a 7 to Nil judgment. Yet Ashton told Mitchell on 9 April 2020 that Victoria Police's "brief stood up well". That's called denial.

As pointed out in Chapter 2, Magistrate Belinda Wallington said that she would commit an accused for trial except when the "credibility" of a witness giving evidence against the accused had been "effectively eliminated". Magistrate Wallington found that the credibility of Witness S.G. had been effectively eliminated. S.G.'s allegations against Pell included rape in a cinema while a film was showing. Wallington made a similar finding with respect to M.B. whom, she found, had a cavalier attitude to giving evidence. So, the Melbourne Magistrates' Court held that the credibility of the two Victoria Police witnesses had been effectively eliminated. Yet Commissioner Ashton told an unquestioning Neil Mitchell that Victoria Police's brief against Pell "stood up well".

Victoria Police vs The Archdiocese of Melbourne

As the saying goes, "there's history there" between Victoria Police in general, and Graham Ashton in particular, and the Melbourne Archdiocese. On 30 October 1996, Victoria Police issued a media release titled "Police Support Catholic Church Initiatives To Combat Sexual Abuse". This was a reference to the Melbourne Response set up by (then) Archbishop Pell on that day. The statement included the following comment:

> Police have welcomed the appointment of Peter O'Callaghan QC to the position of Independent Commissioner. They say that they are pleased to see the appointment of the commissioner will not in any way conflict with police investigations or actions in respect to sexual abuse. Police are hopeful that the appointment of the commissioner will assist identify those engaging in sexual abuse and result in them being dealt with by the law.

The cooperation between the Catholic Archdiocese of Melbourne and Victoria Police concerning the Melbourne Response ran from late 1996 until late 2010 when Victoria Police decided it would no longer engage in agreements with non-government and non-law enforcement agencies. This was communicated to Archbishop Denis Hart (Pell's successor) by Victoria Police deputy commissioner Sir Ken Jones on 6 October 2010.

Graham Ashton joined Victoria Police (from the Australian Federal Police via the Victorian Office of Police Integrity) in December 2009. He worked initially in forensic services and then became director of the corporate strategy and governance department. In April 2011, Ashton commenced in the position of the assistant commissioner crime command and in February 2012 became the deputy commissioner of specialist operations. According to the Victoria Police website, "during this time Graham led a victim focused approach resulting in changes to the handling of child sexual abuse cases". Note the use of the word "victim", not "complainant". Ashton was appointed chief commissioner of Victoria Police by Daniel Andrews' Labor government on 1 July 2015.

In his letter to Archbishop Hart of 6 October 2010, Sir Ken Jones wrote that "having examined the Melbourne Response in detail" he was "very satisfied that victims who chose to use this process are dealt with properly". Sir Ken was effectively dismissed by Victoria Police in May 2011 after falling out with the then commissioner Simon Overland (who resigned in controversial circumstances the following month).

On 24 August 2011, Ashton wrote a blunt letter to Archbishop Hart formally demanding that the Archdiocese of Melbourne "remove any reference to agreement(s) made between Victoria Police and the Catholic Church from this website or any other public document portraying that an agreement had been met".

Sometime later, on 13 April 2012, Graham Ashton gave an interview to Radio 3AW's Neil Mitchell in which he criticised the Catholic Church and stated: "I can't think of a single referral we've had from the Catholic Church in the last couple of years I've been around." This statement was not correct – as Hart pointed out in a letter to then Chief Commissioner Ken Lay on 15 May 2012. In his response to Hart on 26 July 2012, Lay did not contest Hart's refutation of Ashton's claims. Lay stepped down, due to a family illness, in August 2014 and the position was not filled on a permanent basis until Ashton took over the role in July 2015.

On 19 October 2012, Ashton gave evidence to the Victorian Parliamentary Inquiry. This appearance was preceded by the lodgement of an unsigned 12-page submission by Victoria Police – to which was attached two appendices. The terms of reference of the inquiry required that it examine the handling of child abuse by religious and other non-governmental organisations. In the second paragraph of the submission, Victoria Police made it very clear that its focus was on the Catholic Church. The next paragraph stated that "in the last 15 years over thirty religious leaders have been convicted of child sexual offences within Victoria".

This statement was not correct. Certainly, some priests (including Gannon, Ridsdale and Baker) and some brothers had been convicted. But no archbishop, bishop, auxiliary bishop, monsignor or vicar-general had been charged, let alone convicted – nor had the leader of any religious order.

There were numerous other errors in the submission when Ashton appeared before the Victorian Parliamentary Inquiry. Early on, he said that most of his presentation would focus on the Catholic Church. Ashton told the Victorian parliamentarians "since 1996 the Catholic Church of Victoria has upheld approximately 620 cases of criminal child abuse, none of which they have reported to police". This statement, which repeated his comment to Mitchell six months earlier, was incorrect. Ashton also said that "there were 43 in number" of "suicides as a result of clergy abuse" in Victoria. This shocking figure – which played a part in the Commonwealth government's decision to establish a royal commission – turned out to be a massive overstatement. But it received extensive coverage in the Melbourne media, particularly in *The Age*. It is not clear where Ashton got the figure of "620 cases".

On 28 April 2013, Peter O'Callaghan published a detailed 61-page response to Victoria Police's submission to the Victorian Parliamentary Inquiry and also to Commissioner Ashton's verbal evidence. Attached to O'Callaghan's submission was a 108 page document containing correspondence, submissions and the like.

O'Callaghan QC's submission is a devastating rebuke of Ashton's claims. For example, O'Callaghan wrote that of the 304 relevant upheld complaints made to the Melbourne Response up to 30 June 2012, (i) 97 were reported to Victoria Police, (ii) 115 were made in response to deceased alleged offenders, (iii) nine were made with respect to alleged offenders living overseas and (iv) four were with respect to alleged complainants who could not be identified. Of the remaining 79 complainants, 76 complainants were encouraged by O'Callaghan to go to Victoria Police – while one was provided with advice about how a complaint could be made to police, another had the complaint accepted without the need for a hearing and another was said to have made a complaint that was unlikely to constitute criminal assault.

O'Callaghan made the point that the Melbourne Response did not purport to be a substitute for criminal justice but, rather, a process "which enables victims of sexual abuse to receive ex-gratia compensation and obtain free counselling and psychological support". He described the assertion that no complaints had been referred to Victoria Police by the Melbourne Response as "false and misleading". It was a very strong statement by a prominent Victorian barrister. Neither Ashton nor Victoria Police responded to O'Callaghan's submission.

The Victorian Parliamentary Inquiry was not uncritical of the Melbourne Response. However, it did not accept Commissioner Ashton's account of Victoria Police's relationship with the Catholic Church. At Page 25 of the Victorian Parliamentary Inquiry's final report, which is quite critical of the Catholic Church, the following comment is made:

> It is clear that Victoria Police paid inadequate attention to the fundamental problems of the Melbourne Response arrangements until relatively recently in April 2012 and that, when they did become the subject of public attention, Victoria Police representatives endeavoured quite unfairly to distance the organisation from them.

Graham Ashton's evidence to the Victorian Parliamentary Inquiry about suicide of child sexual assault victims/complainants was also misleading. In September 2011, Detective Sergeant Kevin Carson, an old boy of St Patrick's College Ballarat, completed the first of two reports concerning suicides in Victoria which could be linked to pedophile clergy. A second report followed in February 2012. All up, Carson found that no fewer than 43 suicides in Victoria could be linked primarily to clerical child sexual abuse.

Details of Carson's report found their way into *The Age* on 14 April 2012. Three days later, the Ted Baillieu-led (politically conservative) Coalition government announced the establishment of the Victorian Parliamentary Inquiry. Ashton subsequently told the Victorian Parliamentary Inquiry on 19 October 2012 that Victoria Police had now "concluded their research" into "suicides as a result of clergy abuse". Ashton said that he did not want to provide details in an open forum at this stage – and that he needed "to tread a little carefully on the suicide issue".

In *The Weekend Australian* on 25 July 2015, John Ferguson revealed that a Victoria Police investigation, titled Operation Plangere and headed by Leading Senior Constable Tania Siegemund, found that the 43 deaths claim could not be verified. Siegemund's report was dated 1 November 2012. As Ferguson commented: "Police now concede the real figure is one confirmed suicide with church-related sex abuse as a contributing factor and say that more than 40 per cent of victims on the suicide list could not be identified."

Leading Senior Constable Tania Siegemund made this finding about Detective Sergeant Carson's investigation:

> There are significant limitations to the data supplied by Detective Sergeant Carson, which have resulted in a significant number of the nominated premature deaths for review remaining unable to be verified, as the persons of interest are unidentifiable. These include the identifying particulars of individuals such as dates of birth, full names and addresses, details of alleged offences or offenders and years of alleged childhood sexual abuse. It was not possible to identify 18 of the 43 persons in the report, as per the data limitations and intelligence gaps discussed above.

Operation Plangere report was forwarded to the Royal Commission where it was later located and found its way to John Ferguson. Commissioner Ashton did not publicly correct his October 2012 statement about 43 suicides to the Victorian Parliamentary Inquiry. Ferguson quoted a spokesperson for Ashton as saying that the commissioner clarified his comments of 19 November 2012 in a secret hearing of the Victorian Parliamentary Inquiry. Victoria Police chose not to advise the public of this error – which was not revealed until Ferguson's story was published over three years after Carson's report had been leaked to *The Age*.

The Tethering Commences – Led by Commissioner Ashton

Operation Tethering commenced in March 2013 – just months after Graham Ashton's appearance before the Victorian Parliamentary Inquiry where he proclaimed that Victoria Police's focus, when it came to child abuse by religious and other non-government organisations, turned on the Catholic Church. It so happened that the most senior Australian Catholic was Pell, then the Cardinal Archbishop of Sydney.

When Graham Ashton appeared before the Victorian Parliamentary Inquiry in October 2012, he was Victoria Police's Deputy Commissioner – a position he held when Operation Tethering commenced in March 2013. When, on Christmas Eve 2015, Victoria Police advertised for witnesses of child sexual assault at St Patrick's Cathedral in the 1990s with respect to "male victims" aged 14 at the time, Ashton was Commissioner of Victoria Police. Note, again, Victoria Police used the term "male victims" instead of the appropriate term "male complainants".

It was Ashton who sent Deputy Commissioner Patton, along with Detective Superintendent Paul Sheridan and Detective Sergeant Christopher Reed, to interview Cardinal George Pell in Rome in October 2016. And Ashton was Victoria Police Commissioner when Pell was charged on 29 June 2017 – which was announced by Patton at a media conference. Since the Victoria Police Deputy Commissioner took no questions, this was a staged media event. The announcement could have been made by means of a brief media release. But this would not have been consistent with Victoria Police's "Get Pell" campaign – which involved campaigning against him in public by means of actively seeking complainants.

Cardinal Pell Dominates Rome Interview – But in Vain

Cardinal Pell volunteered to be interviewed by Victoria Police. He was under no legal obligation to do so. The interview at the Hilton Hotel, Fiumicino Airport in Rome ran for four and a half hours – including Pell's substantial introductory and concluding remarks but excluding breaks. Pell was questioned concerning eight individuals, one of whom (B) was deceased.

Patton was not present at the interview which was led by Detective Sergeant Reed with only occasional comments by Detective Superintendent Sheridan. Reed was the designated lead investigator, but Sheridan was the senior officer. It was soon evident that Reed had scant knowledge of the Catholic Church and its practices. Moreover, he was not on top of his brief. A few examples illustrate the point in the order in which they occurred during the interview – beyond the examples cited in Chapter 2.

When questioning Pell about the allegations made by S.G. – whose evidence Magistrate Wallington was to find lacked credibility – Reed referred to Warrenheip, a suburb close to Ballarat. In the official Victoria Police transcript of the interview, Warrenheip is referred to on several occasions as "Warren Heap". The transcript reads as follows:

> *Christopher Reed:* Was there a parish at Warren Heap [sic] or similar? A Church or anything?
>
> *George Pell:* No, no. There was a parish at Bungaree and there was a station Church in Dunnstown.
>
> *Christopher Reed:* Okay, is that in the vicinity, is it?
>
> *George Pell:* It is in the general area, it'd be some, I think it's some miles from Warren Heap [sic]. But, I mean, a map could easily ascertain that.
>
> *Christopher Reed:* Yes, very easily, that's correct. I was just asking for your recollection, that's all.
>
> *George Pell:* Yes, sure.

Yes, sure. Reed had no idea of the distance between Warrenheip and the small town of Dunnstown – it's about six kilometres, or close to four miles. There is no reason why Reed should have been interested in Pell's "recollection" of the distance between Warrenheip and Dunnstown since Victoria Police never suggested that Dunnstown had any relevance to allegations made by complainants against Pell. Clearly, Reed was floundering around due to this lack of knowledge of the Ballarat area and his failure to examine a map before the interview.

It was much the same concerning Reed's interest as to whether there was a parish at Warrenheip. One check of *The Official Directory of the Catholic Church in Australia,* before departing Melbourne for Rome, would have revealed that the answer was in the negative. Reed also asked Pell about the number of outdoor pools in Ballarat in the 1970s. It should not have been beyond the resources of Victoria Police to work this out itself. Reed could have checked with his colleagues at the Ballarat Police Station for starters – or made inquiries at the City of Ballarat Council.

Reed put it to Pell that Gerald Ridsdale had concelebrated Mass with him at St James Church in Sebastopol (a southern suburb of Ballarat). Pell replied that he had never concelebrated mass with Ridsdale anywhere – and that, during the time Reed was talking about (i.e. 1978 and 1979), Ridsdale was parish priest at Edenhope – about 300 kilometres away and close to the South Australian border. Again, this information about Ridsdale was in *The Official Directory of the Catholic Church in Australia,* if Reed had bothered to look.

Reed put it to Pell that he had said that he would like to take a boy named John "away on a Bible Study weekend". To which Pell replied: "Good heavens. I've never been at a Bible Study weekend in my life." Reed seemed unaware that the concept of Bible Study belonged to the Protestant, not Catholic, tradition.

Reed also assumed that a priest in Ballarat would regularly visit other priests in the Western District – he did not seem to realise that the Western District is a long way from Ballarat – again, a look at a road map would have demonstrated the point. Ballarat is in Victoria's Central Highlands. And then there was the fact that Reed had no understanding whatsoever of what happened at a Solemn High Mass in St Patrick's Cathedral on a Sunday.

Reading the official transcript of the Rome interview reveals that Reed threw numerous allegations, some of an extraordinarily debauched kind, at Pell which he readily batted away. Reed did not argue the point – since he had no evidence to support the case that he was putting to Pell beyond the statements of complainants. Moreover, Sheridan, the senior officer in the interview – said virtually nothing.

Cardinal Pell dominated the Rome interview. In the sense that he emphatically refuted all kinds of allegations of sexual assault in public places concerning which there was no evidence beyond the words of the complainants. But, in a sense, he need not have bothered – since it appears that the powers-that-be at Victoria Police had decided to charge Pell even before the interview team departed Melbourne Airport. This was evident when, after Pell had comprehensively refuted all of Reed's propositions without challenge, the following exchange took place:

> *Christopher Reed:* …Now there is some more formal things we have to do. Now Cardinal Pell, you may be charged with the offences that we've discussed here today. You do not have to do or say anything unless you wish to do so. But whatever you say or do may be recorded and given in evidence. Do you understand that?
>
> *George Pell:* Yes, I understand it, yes, about the evidence I've given.
>
> *Christopher Reed:* Yes. Thank you.
>
> *George Pell:* Yes, I do.
>
> *Christopher Reed:* Do you want to say anything in answer to any possible charge?
>
> *George Pell:* No, that I'm certainly not guilty. I believe on many, many details I've been able to prove that the charges are false, and I believe that with more work and information, we'll be able to give even further information to enhance the strength of those denials especially at St Joseph's Home and from the [St Patrick's] Cathedral if in fact we need anything more from the Cathedral.
>
> *Christopher Reed:* Do you wish to make a further statement in relation to the matter?
>
> *George Pell:* No except that I'm not guilty….

The interview wound up at 2.19 pm (Roman time) on Wednesday 19 October 2016. Victoria Police laid 26 charges against Pell on 29 June 2017 – eight months later. Despite the length of time to collect further evidence, Victoria Police stumbled at the committal proceedings in the Melbourne Magistrates' Court which commenced on 27 March 2018.

Victoria Police at the Pell Committal Proceedings

The proceedings at the Melbourne Magistrates' Court are covered in Chapter 2. But the sloppy Victoria Police investigation is best analysed with reference to the way Detective Superintendent Sheridan, Detective David Rae and Detective Sergeant Christopher Reed performed in response to cross examination – in the order in which they appeared. Reed and Rae were Operation Tethering's primary investigators. Sheridan was the senior officer in charge of the case and reported to Commissioner Ashton.

• Detective Superintendent Paul Sheridan

Sheridan gave evidence on Wednesday 28 March 2018. Early on, he conceded, during cross-examination by defence counsel Robert Richter QC, that Operation Tethering "could" be termed a "Get Pell" campaign but added that he would not do so. Sheridan also acknowledged that Victoria Police had not sought Pell's diaries to check on his whereabouts at the time of the alleged assaults. Nor had it sought to examine the official diary of St Patrick's Cathedral to determine what role Pell had at the site at certain times. Also, Sheridan said that Victoria Police had not examined copies of the Catholic paper *Kairos Catholic Journal* which reported on activities in the Archdiocese of Melbourne. This was basic police investigation work – but not when it came to Cardinal Pell.

All this led to a situation where Pell's defence, not Victoria Police and not the prosecution, identified the only possible dates on which the alleged attacks on A and B could possibly have taken place at St Patrick's Cathedral in 1996 or 1997. Sheridan provided no explanation for such unprofessional police work.

• Detective Senior Constable David Rae

Rae appeared before the Magistrates' Court – after Sheridan – on Wednesday 28 March 2018. He had interviewed A.S. on Wednesday

28 March 2014. A.S. was the first person to make a complaint about Pell. As mentioned earlier, A.S. had just been released from a psychiatric hospital. Under cross-examination, Rae acknowledged that he drafted A.S.'s statement along with the statement made by D.D. Rae did not take a record of his first discussion with D.D. The following exchange demonstrates the insouciance of Victoria Police.

> *Robert Richter:* What does your note say that [D.D.] said? What does your note say?
>
> *David Rae:* Nothing, no.
>
> *Robert Richter:* Why?
>
> *David Rae:* I'm not in the habit of doing it.
>
> *Robert Richter:* Well, police habits are taught, aren't they? So if you're going to speak to someone like a complainant, you're taught to make notes of what they say. Correct?
>
> *David Rae:* As a general rule, yes.
>
> *Robert Richter:* Well, you didn't make any notes?
>
> *David Rae:* No.
>
> *Robert Richter:* Why?
>
> *David Rae:* No reason. That's my, ah – that's my practice....

Richter went on to describe Rae's "practice" as "appalling". It turned out that Rae also had not taken notes of his first meeting with L.M. Rae also acknowledged, under cross examination, that he had never asked A.S., D.D., L.M. or S.G. for details of any psychiatric assessments made about them. He then conceded that he had not taken a note of his initial conversation with A concerning the alleged crimes at St Patrick's Cathedral. At the end of the cross-examination, Rae acknowledged that Victoria Police did not test the evidence before moving Operation Tethering from an investigation to an operational stage.

- **Detective Sergeant Christopher Reed**

Detective Sergeant Christopher Reed's performance when interviewing Cardinal Pell in Rome and when appearing in the Victorian County Court in *The Queen v Pell* has been discussed earlier. He performed no better during the committal proceedings in the Victorian Magistrates' Court which took place in between the Rome interview and the trial.

Earlier in his testimony, Reed confirmed that it was Victoria Police, not the Office of Public Prosecutions, which decided to charge Pell. Reed said that he was directed to lay the charges by his superior officers within Victoria Police. Early on, Reed acknowledged that – contrary to the advice of the DPP – Victoria Police did not check the signed statements of some nuns at the Nazareth Boys Home who had said that Pell had little, if any, relationship with the institution. Also, Reed admitted that he never sought to check the robes which Pell wore as Archbishop of Melbourne during a Solemn Mass in the years 1996 and 1997.

Reed said that Bernard Barrett, a vehement critic of Pell who headed the organisation Broken Rites, was a source of information for Victoria Police. He also said that Victoria Police did not ask complainants in sexual assault cases if they had experienced psychiatric problems in their life.

At the end of the cross examination, it was evident that Reed essentially believed what complainants told him and had done scant checking of their allegations.

Victoria Police's Modus Operandi

It would seem that the essential aim of Victoria Police's "Get Pell" campaign was to lay charges against him. When this was done, Pell's reputation and standing in the community would have been tarnished – whatever the outcome of any trials. Moreover, the more charges laid, the greater would be the reputational damage. When announcing Victoria Police's decision, Deputy Commissioner Shane Patton commented on several occasions that Pell had been charged with "multiple" offences with respect to "multiple" individuals.

At his media conference, Deputy Commissioner Patton said:

> During the course of the investigation in relation to Cardinal Pell, there has been a lot of reporting in the media and a lot of speculation about the process that has been involved in the investigation and also the charging. So for clarity, I want to be perfectly clear. The process and procedures that are being followed in the charging of Cardinal Pell have been the same that have been applied in a whole range of historical sex offences whenever we investigate them.

This comment was misleading. Operation Tethering was set up over a year before any complaint about Pell was made to Victoria Police. Manifestly this is not the same process and procedures that Victoria Police used with respect to a whole range of historical sex offences. Also, Patton omitted the word "alleged" when referring to the historical sex offences. More shoddy police work.

Patton's references to "multiple charges and multiple complainants" stands in stark contrast to the fact that the prosecution only managed to put five charges concerning two complainants (one of whom was deceased) to a jury. It was a confident presentation concerning what turned out to be a hopelessly weak case.

As Keith Windschuttle wrote in *The Persecution of George Pell* (Quadrant Books, 2020):

> ...Patton's announcement was a calculated exaggeration of the real prospects of the police case against Pell. It was a public relations exercise designed entirely to influence public opinion. It was patently designed to destroy the name and reputation of the accused, who police are normally required to treat as innocent until proven guilty. It was also a message with a long-term objective of impressing anyone who might be recruited for jury service at the trial. Despite his hypocritical comments about Pell deserving "due process" and "natural justice", Patton was accusing him of being no different to the most infamous to the clerical paedophiles jailed in the 1990s for serial offences that took place over decades.... In his statement to the press on 29 June 2017, Patton was surreptitiously announcing that Victoria Police had, in Pell, found another priest like Ridsdale.

• **Victoria Police & the Royal Commission**

The timeline suggests that Victoria Police was conscious of the Royal Commission's proceedings when pursuing Pell.

The Royal Commission's public hearing into the Catholic diocese of Ballarat and the Catholic archdiocese of Melbourne – in so far as they involved Cardinal Pell – took place in Ballarat (19-29 May 2015) and Melbourne (7-16 December 2015) with a third hearing scheduled in Ballarat commencing on 23 February 2016 which was to be attended by Pell. Pell received a medical exemption not to attend in person and – as discussed previously – appeared via video link from Rome from 29 February to 3 March 2016.

In September 2015, shortly before Pell's scheduled appearance before the Royal Commission to discuss the Catholic diocese of Ballarat and the Catholic archdiocese of Melbourne, Victoria Police increased the tempo of Operation Tethering.

Towards the end of his sworn evidence at the committal proceedings, Detective Sergeant David Rae said that, by early September 2015, Victoria Police had decided to run its case against Pell on three matters. First, the Phillip Island allegations of nearly half a century earlier. Second, the Eureka Pool allegations re the years 1977 and 1978 – i.e. the summer of 1977/78. Third, the St Patrick's Cathedral allegations of 1996-1997.

Following the allegations against Pell made at the Royal Commission's hearings in May 2015, a number of male complainants approached Victoria Police. In June 2015, A went to the police concerning the St Patrick's Cathedral allegations. The following month, D.D. went to the police concerning the Eureka Pool allegations – followed soon after by L.M.

Clearly Victoria Police believed that there would be more complainants. At the committal proceedings, Richter presented Rae with a Victoria Police document dated September 2015 which proposed that the media releases be put out "in an attempt to identify witnesses and complainants" concerning the Phillip Island, Eureka Swimming Pool and St Patrick's Cathedral matters.

A.S. refused to speak to Victoria Police about the Phillip Island alleged incident. That left the other two matters in abeyance. In the meantime, Victoria Police decided to arrest Pell when he arrived in Australia for the Royal Commission hearings in late 2015.

The arrest of Pell in Melbourne, following his appearance at the Royal Commission's public hearings which was to be held at a location inside the Melbourne Magistrates' Court, would have been huge international and national news. It would also have been highly prejudicial to Pell. Pell's decision not to return to Australia at the time meant that Victoria Police had to investigate the case at this time without the benefit of an arrest followed by questioning.

Rae told Richter that Victoria Police had a power to arrest Pell for questioning and take him into custody for this purpose. If Pell declined to answer questions, he was to be released and charged on summons. Rae conceded that, as of September 2015, Victoria Police had only a prima facie case against Pell. The exchange concluded:

> *Robert Richter:* Prima facie just means on the face of it?
>
> *David Rae:* Yes, on the face of it. Yes, that's my understanding.
>
> *Robert Richter:* Except that you do not charge just on a prima facie, do you?
>
> *David Rae:* No.
>
> *Robert Richter:* No. Because you've got to undertake the actual arduous task of testing the evidence? –
>
> *David Rae:* Well, that's right.
>
> *Robert Richter:* And that did not happen here, did it?
>
> *David Rae:* No.
>
> *Robert Richter:* I have no further questions.

Rae's testimony makes it clear that Victoria Police decided to charge Pell in late 2015 on the basis of untested prima facie evidence – immediately after he had given evidence at the Royal Commission and was likely to have been subjected to cross-examination by Justice Peter McClellan and Counsel Assisting Gail Furness SC.

- **Victoria Police's Intention to charge Pell leaked after Advertising for Complainants**

When Pell did not return to Australia as had been expected, Victoria Police went ahead with its plan to trawl for complainants and witnesses by means of media releases and, it would seem, media leaks either directly to journalists or via legal teams working for complainants.

On Wednesday 23 December 2015, Victoria Police issued a statement appealing for information in relation to "allegations of sexual assault" at St Patrick's Cathedral in Melbourne between 1996 and 2001 – the time when Pell was Archbishop of Melbourne. This received front-page coverage in the Melbourne newspapers *The Age* and the *Herald Sun* on Christmas Eve 2015.

Also on 23 December 2015, *The Age* carried an article by the plaintiff lawyer and Pell antagonist Judy Courtin headed "St Patrick's Cathedral investigated for child abuse". She commented that the dates between 1996 and 2001 were noteworthy since they coincided with Pell's period as archbishop of Melbourne. This clearly named Pell as the target of Victoria Police's investigation. Courtin also referred to the SANO taskforce's "raids on several properties in Melbourne, including East Melbourne, where the archdiocesan offices are situated" – information which clearly came, either directly or indirectly, from Victoria Police. Courtin, who exhibited a certain hostility to the Catholic Church, concluded her article as follows:

> ... it is significant that serious child sex crimes were allegedly committed in the very bosom, or sacred temple, of the archdiocese, St Patrick's Cathedral. Further, these alleged sex crimes are said to have occurred at a time when, the public has been assured, the church's act was being cleaned up. And this was all under the reign

of a man who then went on to become a cardinal and a key figure at the Vatican.

The implication here was that St Patrick's Cathedral should be viewed as a crime scene. Also, Courtin attempted to link the alleged serious child sex crimes between 1996 and 2001 with the establishment of the Melbourne Response in 1996.

On 16 January 2016, *The Courier* in Ballarat reported a Victoria Police statement appealing for information in relation to "any alleged sexual assaults committed at the Eureka Stockade Pool between 1977 and 1980" – when Pell was based in Ballarat.

Then on Saturday 20 February 2016, just over a week before Pell was to give evidence to the Royal Commission via video link from Rome, the entire front page of Australia's top selling newspaper, the Melbourne *Herald Sun*, was devoted to an "exclusive" by Pell antagonist Lucie Morris-Marr. Titled "Police Probe Pell: Top-Secret Investigation Into Sex Abuse Claims Against Cardinal", the story referred to alleged "multiple offences" against minors "both by grooming and opportunity". Clearly this leak came, either directly or indirectly, from Victoria Police.

Victoria Police never produced any evidence that Pell had ever engaged in grooming children. Its essential case against Pell alleged that he was an opportunistic offender who sexually abused boys whom he did not know in such public places as the crowded Eureka Swimming Pool during summer and St Patrick's Cathedral on a Sunday at the end of a Solemn Mass which was replete with priests, altar servers and choristers – along with the congregation and visitors.

Clearly the Victoria Police dossier that found its way to Morris-Marr was dishonest – and, as such, highly damaging to Pell. Even before Victoria Police's three man delegation travelled to Rome, it was evident that if Pell was charged, it would be impossible for him receive a fair trial in Melbourne due, in part, to Victoria Police's unprofessional and incompetent handling of such a high-profile case.

• **An Incompetent Investigation – Some Examples**

When Detective Superintendent Sheridan and Detective Sergeant Reed interviewed Cardinal Pell in Rome on the alleged St Patrick's Cathedral assaults, among other matters, it was evident that the case against Pell was weak. This led to the ironic situation whereby Pell offered to help Victoria Police with its investigation by suggesting witnesses whom they could contact. Victoria Police did not take up the offer. This led to a flawed investigation. A couple of examples illustrate the point.

▪ Before Pell was charged, Sergeant Reed did a video recorded walkthrough of St Patrick's Cathedral with the complainant A on 29 March 2016. It was reported by Sergeant Peter Redwood as follows:

> Video recorded walkthrough conducted by the informant with [A] at St Patrick's Cathedral on 29-Mar-2016. Depicts [A] indicating the locations of interest within the cathedral including the following:
>
> - choir area;
>
> - corridor and route taken from choir robe to the choir area;
>
> - room in which he and [B] located the wine and were sexually assaulted by Pell;
>
> - the corridor and location within which where Pell sexually assaulted [A].

Reed believed that, after Solemn Mass, the procession proceeded within – not outside – the Cathedral. That is, it was an internal procession. Reed conceded during the trial that it was Robert Richter QC – and not Victoria Police – who asked A for the first time (during the committal proceedings) how he had exited the Cathedral after the alleged attack in the priests sacristy. A basic question – which was never asked during Victoria Police's investigations.

▪ It was Detective Superintendent Sheridan who prepared Victoria Police's summary of allegations against Pell which was provided to Richter in Rome. Clearly Sheridan, the senior officer during the interview, incorrectly believed that there had only been an internal procession.

Pell told Victoria Police in Rome that a Solemn Mass at St Patrick's Cathedral involved not only choristers (like A and the late B) but also other priests (i.e. concelebrants), altar servers, money collectors and the like. In spite of this, Victoria Police did not interview any altar servers or money collectors. The Master of Ceremonies Charles Portelli and the sacristan Max Potter were interviewed after Pell's Rome interview – but neither gave evidence which supported the case against Pell.

It was left to Pell's defence to suggest former altar servers Jeffrey Connor and Daniel McGlone as witnesses. Their evidence was found convincing by Justice Weinberg in his Court of Appeal dissent and by all seven judges of the High Court.

The following exchange took place during *The Queen v Pell* in the County Court of Victoria on 29 November 2018:

> *Robert Richter:* ... You had not tracked down any altar servers at all?
>
> *Christopher Reed:* No, that's correct.
>
> *Robert Richter:* But the altar servers were a very, very important part of this investigation?
>
> *Christopher Reed:* Well, not during the investigative stage, no, we were concerned with the choir boys specifically, because the events that have been alleged occurred surrounding the choir boys, not the altar servers that were in a different location and had a different role.
>
> *Robert Richter:* But there weren't any choir boys present when this happened, alleged to have happened?
>
> *Christopher Reed:* – Well, there weren't any altar servers.
>
> *Robert Richter:* There weren't any of those present?
>
> *Christopher Reed:* There weren't any altar servers alleged to be present either.
>
> *Robert Richter:* Correct, but the altar servers took part in processions in the same way that the choirboys took part in the processions?
>
> *Christopher Reed:* – That's correct, yes.
>
> *Robert Richter:* And not just that the altar boys were more import-

ant because the altar boys were in a position to say what they did after mass in the priests sacristy?

Christopher Reed: – Evidence has been given to that effect, yes.

Robert Richter: Yes, and you accept that?

Christopher Reed: I accept that evidence that's given, yeah.

- The fifth charge against Pell was that he had groped A after Solemn Mass in St Patrick's Cathedral on Sunday 23 February 1997. Pell was presiding over – not saying – the Mass.

The Mass was celebrated by (then) Fr Brendan Egan. He subsequently left the priesthood but was employed in Melbourne at the time of the trial and readily contactable. Clearly Brendan Egan should have been interviewed by Victoria Police as a potential crucial witness – since he was very close to Pell during the 23 February 1997 procession in which Pell was alleged to have assaulted A. The following exchange took place in the County Court on 29 November 2018:

> *Robert Richter:* That Archbishop Pell is supposed to have pushed Mr J [i.e. A] into the wall and grabbed his private parts, and squeezed them hard, you'd want to speak to Father Brendan Egan, wouldn't you?
>
> *Christopher Reed:* Father Egan hasn't been spoken to.
>
> *Robert Richter:* Why?
>
> *Christopher Reed:* Ah, I don't have an answer for that. Because I haven't spoken to him.

Reed went on to concede that no one from Victoria Police investigated the allegation that Pell assaulted A in St Patrick's Cathedral on 23 February 1997:

> *Robert Richter:* ....Is there any record of anyone undertaking any investigation about J's [i.e. A's] allegations relating to February 1997?
>
> *Christopher Reed:* – Not that I'm – not that I can categorically recall now. No.

Robert Richter: Well, not that you recall at all?

Christopher Reed: Not that I can recall, no.

Robert Richter: Right. And if there had been, you'd have known about it?

Christopher Reed: Yes, you would.

Robert Richter: Yes. Thank you.

It says a lot about the Victorian legal system that Victoria Police charged Pell with a serious criminal offence (alleged to have occurred in February 1997) without investigating the case or interviewing any witnesses. And that Victoria Police's decision was not corrected by the Office of Public Prosecutions, the Director of Public Prosecutions, the Crown Solicitor, Magistrate Belinda Wallington along with Victoria's two most senior judges – Chief Justice Anne Ferguson and President of the Court of Appeal Chris Maxwell.

A Note on Victoria Police: The Catholic Church, Lawyer "X" and Operation Lorimer

Victoria Police was well aware of the crimes in the Ballarat diocese of the Catholic priests John Day and Gerald Ridsdale as from the early 1970s. However, some Catholics within the force conspired to thwart attempts by honest police – such as Denis Ryan (also a Catholic) – to lay charges lest this cause scandal to the church. This inaction was approved at the highest levels of Victoria Police for years at a time when many of its senior officers were not Catholics.[22]

It changed in the early 1990s when, following complaints to Victoria Police, Gerald Ridsdale and Desmond Gannon were charged and convicted (after pleading guilty) in 1993 and 1995 respectively. In 1996 Archbishop Pell set up the Melbourne Response in co-operation with Victoria Police. There has been virtually no clerical child sexual assault reported in the Melbourne archdiocese from the mid-1990s on.

Writing in his "Jack the Insider" column in *The Australian* on 9 April 2020, soon after Cardinal Pell's conviction was quashed, Peter Hoysted commented:

> When we move to the present and VicPol's Sano Task Force's pursuit of George Pell ending in ignominy, the question must be asked, did Victoria Police seek to erase its dismal history by the failed pursuit of one man, a prince of the Church?
>
> Consider an alternate reality where John Day had been charged and sentenced to a long term of imprisonment for his crimes against children in Mildura in 1972. Or if Ridsdale had been brought before the courts and prosecuted in Inglewood in 1975. Hundreds of victims would have been spared the trauma of abuse. There is no other way of looking at it.
>
> We understand the Catholic Church's failings, the miserable felonious business of covering up and moving clerical paedophiles onto other parishes and new groups of unsuspecting victims. What is barely known is the role of the police in facilitating those crimes. There's no shortage of guilt. More than enough to go around.

Earlier in his *Australian Online* column on 8 February 2017, Hoysted referred to what he described as the Royal Commission's stubborn unwillingness to investigate the link between clerical pedophilia and the police. Hoysted (who co-wrote *Unholy Trinity* with Denis Ryan) added:

> It [the Royal Commission] did examine the Day-Ryan scandal as part of their case study on the Ballarat Diocese. Denis Ryan read his statement into the record. He was not cross examined. His evidence was accepted. Forty years of pain, financial loss and emotional turmoil and it was all done and dusted in a Melbourne courtroom.

Unholy Trinity was published in 2013. Ryan eventually received an apology from Victoria Police in August 2016 – followed by a lump sum compensation payment by the Victorian Labor government in May 2018. Cardinal Pell has told me that, around the time of *Unholy Trinity's* release, Ryan wrote to him when he was Archbishop of Sydney. I understand that Pell replied expressing regret about Ryan's treatment by Victoria Police for trying to do his duty as a police officer.

Denis Ryan was examined at the Royal Commission by Counsel Assisting Angus Stewart SC – but not cross examined. During the examination, Stewart referred Ryan to a letter written in 2006 by (then) Victoria Police Chief Commissioner Christine Nixon to Russell Savage, a former police officer who was the Independent MP for Mildura in the Victorian Legislative Assembly between 1996 and 2006.

Commissioner Nixon advised Savage (a Ryan supporter) that she was "completely satisfied" that "Denis Ryan resigned from Victoria Police of his own accord" and had not been forced out because he wanted to take action against the pedophile Day. Ryan totally rejected Nixon's claim. His position was not challenged by Counsel Assisting.

As late as 2006 – Victoria Police would not accept that it had erred in failing to prosecute Monsignor Day in the early 1970s. Commissioner Nixon's letter to Savage was written a decade after Archbishop Pell had established the Melbourne Response. Clearly Victoria Police was in denial about the mishandling of clerical pedophilia for quite some time.

Operation Tethering was set up in March 2013 – a few years after Melbourne lawyer Nicola Gobbo – who was initially referred to as Lawyer X – had completed her third registration as police informer, this one covering the period between 2005 and 2010. This was during the time of what was termed the Gangland Wars in Melbourne – which took place between around 1999 and around 2010. Victoria Police engaged Nicola Gobbo as an informer despite the fact that, as a barrister, she represented some of the leading criminals involved in gangland murders, drug trafficking and the like.

It is grossly improper for a lawyer to inform on clients to police. This Gobbo knew – as did Victoria Police. During the time Gobbo was registered as an informer, some of her clients were convicted and sentenced to long terms of imprisonment. Over time, within and outside the criminal world, suspicion arose that Victoria Police had a special informer. The story was first revealed by Anthony Dowsley in the *Herald Sun* on 31 March 2014. But the name of the person was not revealed until later.[21]

For years, Victoria Police sought to keep the Lawyer X matter secret – taking some 28 actions against the *Herald Sun*. But eventually it failed in its legal attempts to do so at the Victorian Supreme Court and at the Victorian Court of Appeal. In time, the case ended up in the High Court of Australia – where, on 5 November 2018, all seven judges (Chief Justice Kiefel and Justices Bell, Gageler, Keane, Nettle, Gordon and Edelman – the same bench that sat in *Pell v The Queen*) denied Victoria Police special leave to appeal the decision of the Victorian Court of Appeal.

The issue involved was whether seven convicted criminals were entitled to know that their lawyer, Gobbo, was a police informer – in view of the fact that the use of Gobbo as an informer might have brought about a miscarriage of justice with respect to their convictions. The *Herald Sun* finally was able to report the full Lawyer X story (without mentioning the lawyer's name) on 4 December 2018. On 1 March 2019, after a five year legal battle with Victoria Police, the *Herald Sun* was able to reveal that Nicola Gobbo was Lawyer X.

Victoria Police's focus on Lawyer X occurred when Operation Tethering was underway. On 1 April 2014 at 1.29 pm, just hours after the *Herald Sun* broke the Lawyer X story, Charlie Morton (in his capacity as assistant director – Media & Corporate Communications Department, Victoria Police) sent this email to Commissioner Ashton advising that there should be no immediate response to the *Herald Sun* story:

> From: Morton, Charles
>
> Sent: Tuesday, 1 April 2014, 1.29 pm
>
> To: Ashton Graham, McRae Findlay, Fontana Stephen, Clegg Robert, Cartwright Tim, Lay Ken [Commissioner], Tabain Merita, Allen Catherine
>
> Hi Graham

> Happy to discuss, but on balance, I think for at least the next 24 hours we don't. First off, we're very limited in what we can say. Even our generalist answers provided to the Age yesterday have been skewed in today's paper to suggest we have confirmed the recruitment of witness x (see final para on p3). Dowsley has used all his best ammo already (I think). None of the other journos have got anything different or are prepared to use it.
>
> The Pell stuff is coming tomorrow and will knock this off the front page. Unless there are some serious appeals from convicted crims which might get up as a result of this, then I can't see this continuing with the same level of profile. There will be more, but I suspect we can weather it. I'd suggest we revisit it in 24 hours and see what it's looking like. Have discussed with Fin and he agrees. He's also looking at further injunction options.[22]
>
> Charlie

It is not known if Ashton replied to Morton's email. Moreover, no developments in the Pell Case took place on 2 April 2014. Nevertheless, Morton's note to Ashton indicates that senior figures in Victoria Police's media department were conscious of the fact that Cardinal Pell was, and would remain, a convenient distraction with respect to the organisation's attempt to cover-up the Lawyer X scandal.

At the time the High Court decision was brought down on 5 November 2018, Nicola Gobbo was referred to as "EF". The view of all seven of Australia's most senior judges amounted to a withering criticism of Victoria Police and its practices:

> ...EF's [Ms Gobbo's] actions in purporting to act as counsel for the Convicted Persons while covertly informing against them were fundamental and appalling breaches of EF's obligations as counsel to her clients and of EF's duties to the court. Likewise, Victoria Police were guilty of reprehensible conduct in knowingly encouraging EF to do as she did and were involved in sanctioning atrocious breaches of the sworn duty of every police officer to discharge all duties imposed on them faithfully and according to law without

favour or affection, malice or ill-will.

At the time, Graham Ashton was Police Commissioner. Some months after the High Court's unanimous judgment, as was his habit, Commissioner Ashton did a number of interviews on Radio 3AW (with Neil Mitchell) and ABC Radio 774 on the matter. In some interviews, Victoria's Police Commissioner entered into implied criticism of the High Court – most notably on 3AW on 28 March 2019:

> *Neil Mitchell* : She [Gobbo] went through 'til 2010 which was after the gangland wars.
>
> *Graham Ashton:* – there was significant underworld activity right through that period as well.
>
> *Neil Mitchell:* It's the old argument that the end justifies the means.
>
> *Graham Ashton:* The question is what was the means and what was wrong with the means.
>
> *Neil Mitchell:* The High Court had a view that it was atrocious behaviour by Vic Pol.
>
> *Graham Ashton:* And the courts have a view about this all the way through – it doesn't mean that we don't take a slightly different view of that.
>
> *Neil Mitchell:* You take a slightly different view to the High Court of Australia?
>
> *Graham Ashton:* Yeah.

Here Ashton was saying, as Victoria Police Commissioner, that he did not accept a unanimous decision of the High Court of Australia and that Victoria Police was entitled to reject a High Court decision by taking a "slightly different view". Ashton later said much the same following the High Court's unanimous decision in *Pell v The Queen* in April 2020.

Following the High Court's decision in the Lawyer X Case, in December 2018 the Andrews government set up the Royal Commission into the Management of Police Informants – headed by former Queensland Supreme Court judge, Honourable Margaret McMurdo.

Paragraph 4802 of her report, which was delivered on 30 November 2020, reads as follows:

> On the evidence, it is open to the [Royal] Commissioner to find that in his media interviews following the publication of the High Court's decision and during the conduct of the Commission, as Chief Commissioner of Police, Mr Ashton:
>
> 1. expressed the view that the "pub test" is a more acceptable standard of police conduct than what the rule of law requires
>
> 2. sought to justify potentially corrupt activity by Victoria Police on the basis that "the ends justify the means"
>
> 3. sought to avoid Victoria Police taking responsibility for the conduct of Victoria Police members which was correctly described by the High Court as atrocious and reprehensible
>
> 4. sent a message to Victoria Police members which might be understood by them to mean that they can safely ignore both the rule of law and the condemnation of the High Court and engage in "noble cause" corruption, and in so doing may be responsible for perpetuating a culture in Victoria Police in which "noble cause" corruption is acceptable
>
> 5. failed to discharge his responsibility to ensure that Victoria Police members act ethically and in scrupulous compliance with the law.

Currently there are over a thousand cases under investigation as to whether the person in question suffered a miscarriage of justice due to Victoria Police's registration of Gobbo as an informer. One of them was Jason Roberts, with whom Cardinal Pell interacted in Barwon Prison – see Chapter 1.

In July 2020, IBAC (the Victorian Independent Broad-based Anti-corruption Commission) presented a report by Commissioner Robert Redlich. Titled Operation Gloucester, the commission investigated improper evidentiary and disclosure practices in relation to the Victoria Police investigation of the murders of Sergeant Gary Silk and Senior Constable Rodney Miller. On 16 August 1998, these two Victoria Police officers were murdered while on active duty in the Melbourne suburb of Moorabbin. On 21 December 2002, Bandali Debs and Jason Roberts were convicted of the murders.

In 2015, IBAC commenced Operation Gloucester – an investigation into the allegations that some officers from the Lorimer Taskforce, engaged in preparing for the trials of Debs and Roberts, had been involved in misconduct by altering the content of witness statements and not disclosing this at the trial.

IBAC found that there were "serious failures by some officers of the Lorimer Taskforce to properly discharge their obligations when they failed to disclose all potentially relevant information to the prosecution, defence and the court in relation to the prosecutions of Mr Debs and Mr Roberts".

On 10 November 2020 the Victorian Court of Appeal (Justices T. Forrest, R. Osborn and A. Taylor) quashed Roberts' conviction and ordered a re-trial. In view of this, it is appropriate to await the outcome of the case before commenting on Operation Lorimer.[23]

Also of interest is that the members of Victoria Police involved in the Lawyer X matter petitioned the Royal Commission into the Management of Police Informants that they should not be named in its final report. The applicants argued about "the grave reputational risks and unfairness to them that will flow from the allegations being inevitably aired publicly by the media, when those allegations may not ultimately be accepted".

How interesting that members of Victoria Police are concerned about reputational damage resulting from allegations in the media about matters concerning which they might be cleared. But Victoria Police had no scruples in using the media to inflict grave reputational damage on Cardinal Pell. Even to the extent of Commissioner Ashton referring to Pell's "victims" before he was interviewed.[24]

Frank Brennan in Melbourne and Kieran Gilbert in Canberra

Frank Brennan S.J interviewed by Sky News' Kieran Gilbert from outside Newman College Melbourne on 8 April 2020 (the day after Cardinal Pell's acquittal). Fr. Brennan, the author of *Observations on the Pell Proceedings* (Connor Court, 2021), supported Cardinal Pell despite the fact that they disagree on some matters of theology.

Kerri Judd QC

Victorian Director of Public Prosecutions Kerri Judd QC. It was Ms Judd's decision to put the charges against Cardinal Pell to a re-trial in late 2018 which, in time, led to her poor performance leading the DPP's case before the High Court of Australia in March 2020. Melbourne Law School Professor Jeremy Gans has written that all seven High Court judges "were really on top of the factual details" of the case – "way more than Kerri Judd".

11

THE FALLIBILITY OF MEMORY AND COLLECTIVE GUILT

> The Roman Catholic Church has borne a heavy share of...retrospective opprobrium. For all sorts of reasons I dislike the Roman Catholic Church. But I dislike unfairness even more, and I can't help wondering whether this one institution has been unfairly demonized over the [child sexual abuse] issue, especially in Ireland and America... We should be aware of the remarkable power of the mind to concoct false memories, especially when abetted by unscrupulous therapists and mercenary lawyers. The psychologist Elizabeth Loftus has shown great courage, in the face of spiteful vested interests, in demonstrating how easy it is for people to concoct memories that are entirely false, but which seem, to the victim, every bit as real as true memories. This is so counter-intuitive that juries are easily swayed by sincere but false testimony from witnesses.
>
> - Richard Dawkins, *The God Delusion* (Bantam Press, 2006, Black Swan edition 2016, pp 355-336]

On 9 April 2012, the prominent atheist Richard Dawkins and one of the world's best known Catholics George Pell squared off on the ABC TV's *Q&A* program. Tony Jones, who later joined the Pell pile-on, was in the presenter's chair. The two men took questions from a live audience along with comments proffered by Jones.

At the start of the program, the presenter invited the audience to join the *Q&A* Vote Survey and answer the question as to whether religious belief makes the world a better place. At the end of *Q&A*, Jones announced that 76 per cent of viewers/listeners had responded in the negative. This was not surprising since the taxpayer funded public broadcaster attracts a significant secular, left-wing audience. Irrespective of the vote, it is fair to say that both men held their own in discussing the topic "Religion and Atheism" – as would be expected when intelligent and well-educated individuals take part in a debate.

The Phenomenon of "Remembering" Events that Never Happened

On *Q&A,* Richard Dawkins indicated that he was an equal-opportunity atheist. He was dismissive of all religions and his rejection of believers did not focus on conservative Catholics like Pell or even Christians in general. On *Q&A* Dawkins practised what he preached in *The God Delusion.* In the Pell Case, however, many of Pell's critics believed what they wanted to believe – in spite of the fact that the evidence against the cardinal was extremely weak and, at times, non-existent.

In the second paragraph of the High Court decision in *Pell v The Queen,* all seven judges wrote:

> A made his first complaint about the alleged assaults in June 2015. The prosecution case was wholly dependent upon acceptance of the truthfulness and the reliability of A's evidence. By the time A made his complaint, B had died in accidental circumstances. In 2001, B had been asked by his mother whether he had ever been "interfered with or touched up" while in the Cathedral choir. He said that he had not.

The prosecution case against Cardinal Pell turned completely on the accuracy of the truthfulness of A's memory. There was no other evidence against Pell – and a lot of evidence which suggests that he did not have the opportunity to commit crimes against A or the late B inside St Patrick's Cathedral after a Solemn Mass on Sunday.

At one stage in his legal career Justice Peter McClellan warned about the fallibility of memory. Yet he presided over the Royal Commission which did not query the claims of complainants who took their case to it – even though financial compensation was a real possibility for anyone who made a claim of sexual assault while in an institution. It is likely that nearly all the claims made to the Royal Commission were true. But it is also likely some of the claims were false for one reason or another.

The problem with accepting all memories as accurate has been analysed in numerous books and papers – including Daniel L. Schacter's *The Seven Sins of Memory* (Houghton Mifflin Harcourt, 2001) and Ros Burnett's edited collection *Wrongful Allegations of Sexual and Child Abuse* (OUP, 2016). In Australia, journalist Richard Guilliatt has done important empirical work in this area – including in his book *Talk of the Devil: Repressed Memory & the Ritual Abuse Witch-Hunt* (Text, 1996) and more recently articles in *The Weekend Australian Magazine* titled "The Unbelievers" (8 July 2017), "Through the past, Darkly" (30 September 2017) and "Tipped Scales"(18 July 2020).

The crucial arguments about memory can be found in the courts, since the consequences of legal cases are usually more important than the events of everyday life. However, a few Australian cases which did not end up in the legal system demonstrate how even highly intelligent and well educated individuals err when it comes to memory. A few examples illustrate the point.

Kevin Rudd became prime minister of Australia on 3 December 2007. As is the tradition, the prime minister was invited into the ABC Radio commentary box on one day during the Boxing Day Test cricket match at the Melbourne Cricket Ground later that month.

During a break in play on 27 December 2007, Rudd told ABC commentators Jim Maxwell and the late Peter Roebuck about how, as a 17 year old, he had travelled to the Brisbane Cricket Ground and watched 42 year old English batsman Colin Cowdrey face up to Australia's fast bowlers Dennis Lillee and Jeff Thomson during the First Test of the 1974-75 Ashes series, which ran from 29 November to 4 December 1974.

Here, Mr Rudd had a "clear recollection" of an event that never happened. Colin Cowdrey did not play in the First Test of the 1974-75 Ashes series in Brisbane. In fact, Cowdrey did not arrive in Australia, as a replacement batsman, until mid December 1974 when he played in the second Test in Perth.

Professor Robert Manne was voted on two occasions as Australia's leading public intellectual. In 2011, Manne claimed that I attempted to get him sacked as a columnist for *The Age*. He alleged, initially, that I had sent a dossier to *The Age's* opinion editor Paul Austin in 1993 making this demand. In fact, Austin did not hold this position at the time. Manne later claimed the document had been sent out in 1998. Manne also said that I sent a copy of the dossier to his friend Morag Fraser and that Austin had given a copy to him. So there were least three copies of the (alleged) dossier in existence – but Manne was not able to present one. Not surprising – since no such dossier ever existed and no such demand was ever made and he was not able to present any evidence to the contrary.

The writer Lily Brett (born 1946) and the psychologist Doris Brett (born 1951) are sisters who grew up in Melbourne. In their written work, Lily and Doris have quite inconsistent memories of their childhood and youth – particularly with respect to their mother. The Bretts have dramatically different recollections of the same events.

It should not be assumed that individuals who make false statements are conscious liars. Many people who make inaccurate allegations believe that they are telling the truth. It is their memories that are deficient – not their commitment to truthfulness, as they see it. And then there are those who have psychiatric problems or experience fantasies or whose memory has been adversely affected by alcoholism and/or drug addiction – and more besides. And then there are the wilful liars like "Nick"(Carl Beech).

"Guilt" by (Collective) Association

In Australia in the early 21st Century, there is a tendency to hold the Catholic Church primarily responsible for much of child sexual assault. Yet, as the Royal Commission itself conceded, most such crimes occur *in familia* situations.

Immediately after Cardinal Pell's conviction was made public, the ABC and *Sydney Morning Herald* journalist Richard Glover wrote an article on the case for *The Washington Post* (26 February 2019) – in the second paragraph of which he referred to Pell's dandruff. A few days later, Glover issued this tweet:

> *Richard Glover:* Those of us who were sexually abused when young have had a tough week. I'm quite angry with those who have made it worse, including one person I partly admired. Is it that hard to imagine how it feels?
>
> Mar 1, 2019

Now, Richard Glover is a clever, usually well balanced, man with a fine sense of humour. Yet the news that Pell had been found guilty in a re-trial of sexually assaulting two 13 year old boys in the mid-1990s led Glover to identify with those "who were sexually abused when young". It was as if the punishment of Pell somehow compensated for Glover's suffering many years previously.

The "one person" to whom Glover's anger was directed at seems to be me. Prior to Pell being charged, I used to appear occasionally on ABC Radio Sydney 702's *Drive with Richard Glover* program and – despite quite differing views – we got on okay. It seems that Glover took exception to comments about the Pell Case made in my *Media Watch Dog* blog on 1 March 2019 – which appeared early that evening in *The Australian Online*. One of my comments was that juries do not always make correct decisions – which is why a right of appeal exists.

Glover was blaming his knowledge of Pell's conviction, along with my comment that juries sometimes make errors, for increasing the pain he suffered when recalling the sexual abuse he endured when young.

Richard Glover told his story of life when young in his book *Flesh Wounds* (ABC Books, 2015, republished 2020). Glover, an only child, grew up in a dysfunctional, but relatively well-off, family. While at school in Canberra, he was propositioned by a couple of men – an unpleasant experience. After leaving school, he worked for a while in Queensland. Then he travelled to London, staying in accommodation arranged for him by his mother with an actor/director. The man made sexual advances on Glover who, at the time, had no other contacts in London. As Glover relates in *Flesh Wounds:*

> ...He was probably in his sixties, while I was nineteen. I can't call him a paedophile since I was old enough, at least under the law, to have made a run for it. I did learn later that exactly what happened to me had happened to a swag of young men, all from Australia. From the time he picked me up at the airport it took me five months to escape. Once he had you in the flat it was hard to break free. I still find it difficult to explain why....

It is appropriate to feel sorry for the predicament Glover faced when in London as a young man. But it is completely unreasonable for him to associate his past experiences with Pell's conviction. Unless Pell is to bear collective guilt for the sexual crimes and actions of others – both in Australia and overseas. Glover was not alone.

In *The Age* on 28 February 2019, journalist Bernadette Nunn wrote that "Pell's conviction is vindication for victims everywhere". On 2 March 2019, commenting in the Fairfax Media newspapers, Wendy Tuohy declared: "The 'village' it takes to raise a child may be more fragmented than it was in the past, but sex offences against children by people presented as moral authorities are still felt as an assault on all of us". Tuohy went on to make the false claim that Pell had given the court a reference for Ridsdale.

When Pell's appeal was dismissed by the Victorian Court of Appeal in a majority judgment on 21 August 2019, presenter Ellen Fanning introduced a segment on ABC TV's *The Drum* as follows:

> *Ellen Fanning:* We are joined by survivor of sexual abuse Brian.... Welcome back to the program, Brian. Brian, we saw joy and relief outside that courtroom from people who have been going along to

the Royal Commission, who have been supporting victims. What was your reaction to the Appeal Court's decision?

Brian was very pleased with the majority judgment of the Victorian Court of Appeal. But he was not a survivor from – or victim of – George Pell. Unless it is to be believed that Pell should carry responsibility for all victims and survivors.

Appearing on ABC TV *News Breakfast* on 18 September 2019, Melbourne University academic Gael Jennings discussed the news that George Pell had sought special leave to appeal his conviction to the High Court of Australia. She concluded her comments:

> *Gael Jennings:* …There's a very low rate at which they accept appeals because everyone appeals to the High Court. And that has to reach a whole set of criteria. And the talk among the legal community seems to be that it's going to be quite difficult to get this one up. But you know, I don't know, I'm not a lawyer. But, anyway, they're [Pell's legal team] doing what you'd expect them to do. But for the victims, you know, the victim support groups are saying this is disappointing.

Like Louise Milligan (see Chapter 7), Jennings got this wrong. On 13 November 2019 two High Court justices referred Pell's application for special leave to appeal to the Full Court for argument as on appeal. The important point is that when *Pell v The Queen* was considered by the High Court – what was at stake turned on whether Pell was guilty beyond reasonable doubt with respect to specific crimes. Yet Jennings focused on the view that, according to victims' support groups, Pell was somehow responsible for crimes – beyond the crimes he had been found guilty, by a jury, of having committed.

It was much the same when Cardinal Pell's conviction was quashed – *The Canberra Times* carried an article by Megan Neil on 8 April 2020 headed: "High Court's decision to release Pell 'devastates' survivors". The point here is that, according to the Australian judicial system, as of 7 April 2020, there are no "survivors" of sexual assault by Pell. Neil quoted Blue Knot Foundation president Cathy Kezelman as saying the High Court decision would be crushing for many survivors, given the immense courage it took to stand up to be heard. Kezelman added:

> Pell now has his freedom, but many abuse victims have never been free – trapped in the horror of the crimes which decimated their lives.

Clearly the president of the Blue Knot Foundation and adviser to the Royal Commission believed that Pell should not be free because the abuse victims of others were not free.

The High Court decision was discussed on *The Drum* on 7 April 2020. Ellen Fanning interviewed Chrissie Foster. As discussed earlier, two of Ms Foster's children were victims of sexual assault by the Catholic priest Kevin O'Donnell. She regarded the unanimous decision as an assault on all victims:

> *Chrissie Foster:* …I've had friends ring up in tears, crying. When you're involved, you take this all very personally because we've lived it, we've been there. We are there, it never goes away. For me, it's inside me with two of my children. And we just take this on board. It's a personal assault to us as well.
>
> *Ellen Fanning:* Do you think today's judgment of the High Court will have implications for future complainants?
>
> *Chrissie Foster:* I could see it putting people off. What is the point? It really feels like that. Why would you bother? Why would you put yourself through that?
>
> *Ellen Fanning:* You might not be happy with the outcome, but we have seen this go all the way to the High Court of Australia. Do you have faith in the legal system after today?
>
> *Chrissie Foster:* Well, I did have faith in the legal system because George Pell was convicted. And now, I don't know. What faith do you have? It was a guilty verdict. And then that was upheld in the appeals court here – and now it doesn't exist anymore. So what faith can you have in that? It's shifting sands. How can you stand on that? How can you rely on that?

Chrissie Foster was unchallenged by Ellen Fanning when she said that she had lost faith in the Australian legal system because the High Court of Australia quashed a guilty verdict of a jury. The fact is that appeal courts are part of the legal system – since it is recognised that, every now and then, judges, magistrates and juries make erroneous decisions.

Fanning then drew Foster's attention to Victorian Premier Daniel Andrews' statement of earlier that day that he believed all "victims". Foster responded:

> *Chrissie Foster:* Well, that brought tears to my eyes. And I think his message just speaks to us, of his understanding. But I just wanted to point out it was a beautiful message and I thank him for it and all he has done.

What the Victorian premier had done, in effect, was to dissent from a judgment of all seven judges of the High Court of Australia, two of whom (Justices Geoffrey Nettle and Michelle Gordon) were Victorians. Andrews would later appoint Nettle (after he retired from the High Court) to investigate whether any police or lawyers should be prosecuted in light of the findings of the Lawyer X Royal Commission.

Chrissie Foster and some of her supporters were shown on ABC TV *News Breakfast* on 29 January 2020 holding up a sign that read "Crime Scene". They had protested outside St Patrick's Cathedral the previous day against the Red Mass held in Melbourne at the beginning of the legal year. Presenter Lisa Millar agreed with the protestors that St Patrick's Cathedral was "the scene of the crime". So did her co-presenter Michael Rowland who referred to "these crimes" with reference to St Patrick's.

By 7 April 2020, it was evident that St Patrick's was not a crime scene and Pell was not a criminal. But neither Millar nor Rowland were inclined to wait for the High Court decision and neither ever corrected the comments they made. Nor has the program ever referred to the steps to Flinders Street Station as a crime scene – yet this was the place where a police officer was murdered in January 1974. ABC TV films outside the building without comment.

In his *Prison Journal* on Sunday 16 February 2020, Cardinal Pell observed:

> The chief justice of the Supreme Court of Victoria, one of the majority who refused my appeal, has been active in a different way, writing recently to her fellow judges urging them to consider their options carefully before attending the Catholic-sponsored Red Mass and suggesting that they not wear their gowns if they did attend. It is also a classic example of identity politics. The other religious ceremonies for the new law year commencement did not merit similar comment or concern.

It was not only complainants and victims – along with journalists – who ran the line that Cardinal Pell was somehow responsible for the crimes of others. In an article in *Women's Weekly* in May 2016, titled "Is George Pell an enemy of the church?", the writer Tom Keneally described his early life growing up Catholic in Australia and training to be a priest. He left the seminary before ordination. In time, Keneally became a member of the Pell pile-on.

In his preface to the updated 2019 edition of Louise Milligan's *Cardinal: The Rise and Fall of George Pell*, Keneally commented that, independent of the outcome of any appeal as to Pell's convictions for pedophilia, nothing will undo "the pain and damage the victims of Churchmen, those who sinned, those who covered up and massaged the sin, have created". Keneally did not provide any evidence to support his claim that Pell is somehow responsible for "the victims of Churchmen", none of whom were named.

Before Keneally got around to clerical child sexual abuse in the preface, he criticised Pell's position on climate change and his (alleged) attitude towards asylum seekers along with his role as "a notable neo-conservative, not just in ecclesiastical but in political matters as well". None of this had anything to do with Pell's conviction.

Keneally went on to criticise two former conservative Liberal Party prime ministers – John Howard and Tony Abbott – both of whom he said had sent "letters of support addressed to the court". John Howard did forward a character reference for Pell following his conviction. Abbott was not asked to forward any such reference – and did not do so. This error was not picked up by the (then) Melbourne University Press's managing director Louise Adler.

What is evident in Tom Keneally's comment is that he assessed Pell's conviction not so much with respect to clerical child sexual abuse but rather for its political impact, writing:

> Cardinal Pell is an inestimable loss…to the forces of the right, at a time they find themselves uniquely out of fashion with the Australian electorate.

Tom Keneally's preface was dated March 2019. On 18 May 2019, the conservative Liberal Party-Nationals Coalition government was returned to office with an increase in seats in the House of Representatives. What Keneally identified as the forces of the right in Australia clearly were not "uniquely" out of fashion with the electorate – and, if they had been, there was no connection to the Pell Case.

In his preface to *Cardinal*, Keneally declared that he stood with the publisher (Louise Adler) and the author (Louise Milligan) in part because they are "from the literary tribe" but also because their motives have been "poisoningly misinterpreted". He did not say how or by whom. It would seem that like Adler and Milligan (see Chapter 7), Keneally did not want to address any facts in the case inconsistent with Pell's guilt. Keneally is primarily a writer of fiction who showed little interest in assessing evidence. He channelled Milligan in believing complainant A – and in holding Pell responsible for the crimes of others.

On Saturday 1 March 2019, *The Weekend Australian* published my column titled "Pell's ordeal reinforces the case for judge-only trials" which, in part, criticised members of the pile-on. This met the following response on *Twitter* by former ABC and currently *The New Daily* journalist Quentin Dempster (which was endorsed by ABC identity

Russell Skelton):

> *Quentin Dempster:* Methinks Dr Gerard Henderson should register as an agent of influence for the state of The Holy See (Vatican) as now required by the Commonwealth of Australia for complete transparency.
>
> 2 March 2019, 5.51 pm.

This was another example of the low-grade anti-Catholic sectarianism which some Pell-antagonists, like Dempster, engaged in before and after the cardinal's conviction. Dempster did not contest the content of any of the views in my column.

Later that night, Milligan sent out a tweet citing Dempster's tweet. As is her practice, Milligan did not mention my name. But her message was clear – she described me as being on "the wrong side of history". Milligan seemed unaware that even the contemporary history of the Pell Case had yet to be resolved at the time.

On 6 March 2019, I emailed Milligan about her tweet – pointing out that it consisted "only of abuse" and adding that "no thoughtful journalist should believe that contemporary history is a closed entity". Milligan replied the same day – stating that this was "the first and last time" she would communicate with me and advising that she had asked *The Australian* to "instruct" me to stop "this unmitigated harassment".

Milligan's email referred to "those who have lost lives [and] who have suffered profound trauma in your culture war" and added: "I have just got off the phone from a grieving mother who is trying to make sense of this [i.e. Pell's conviction]."

I replied to Milligan the following day, making this point:

> I am not engaging in a culture war, and I have empathy for the victims of child sexual abuse. My only point is that defendants also have rights and that some people have false memories. Not every complainant is a victim – although the overwhelming majority are.

> If the grieving mother to whom you refer is the mother of one of the men concerning whom Pell was convicted – then I understand your point. But if she is not the mother of one of the two men Pell has been found guilty of assaulting – then there is no causal connection between her grief and Pell. Unless you hold the view that Pell is somehow responsible for the crimes of others.

Louise Milligan did not reply. Her position seems to be that it was okay for her to attack others but if she was criticised it was a case of harassment.

From Collective Guilt to the "Court of Public Opinion"

There is a connection between the concept of collective guilt and the notion that such an entity exists as a "court of public opinion". It's one thing when such a line is run by commentators in the public debate – and quite another when such ideas are raised by academics and lawyers who should know better.

Writing on the ABC *Religion & Ethics* website on 7 May 2021, the Melbourne-based Australian Catholic University academic Miles Pattenden reviewed the first volume of George Pell's *Prison Journal*. Early on, he had this to say:

> Here in Victoria, everyone seems to have made up their mind about George Pell. His hard-line moral and theological positions infuriate liberals inside and outside the Catholic Church, and hence his conviction on five counts of serious offences against children in 2019 presented a kind of wicked irony. But when, in 2020, the Australian High Court upheld Pell's appeal against his conviction with a 7-0 judgment, grave doubts were raised about the efficacy, competence, and impartiality of criminal justice in this state.
>
> Pell himself has returned to Rome but now seeks to maintain his place in the public eye through the publication of his prison journal. Nevertheless, many Australians — not least in Melbourne — remain as suspicious of him as ever. The court of public opinion

apparently cannot quite yet stomach the acquittal bestowed on him by the appellate judges.

There is no such entity as "the court of public opinion". What Pattenden's saying is that many Melburnians could not accept a High Court judgment that most of them would not have read. I wrote to Dr Pattenden on 11 May 2021 asking how he defined the court of public opinion. He did not respond.

Half way through his article, Pattenden made the following claim:

> The specific case against Pell always looked implausible, even to someone with limited knowledge of the mechanics of the Melbourne high mass or St. Patrick's Cathedral's topography. On the other hand, Catholic leadership in Australia — and worldwide — hardly seem to have faced a full reckoning for its collective complicity in turning a blind eye, or even covering-up, acts of frankly shocking depravity.
>
> Pell's acquittal on the narrow technical ground that he did not commit the crimes for which he was charged on the indictment was never going to provide closure or catharsis for the many Catholics and non-Catholics who sympathise with the scores of victims of other priests. For such persons, Pell's victory is, at best, a pyrrhic one. And how does his acquittal prevent crimes of the nature of the one of which he was accused from happening again?

This is an extraordinarily ignorant comment. Miles Pattenden conceded that the specific case against Pell "always looked implausible". Yet he went on to state that the Catholic leadership in Australia has not had to account for its handling of child sexual abuse. There is no causal connection between Pattenden's first and second points.

Also, Pell's maximum sentence to six years imprisonment was a precedent to clerics and non-clerics alike that serious jail time will follow serious child sexual assaults. When Pell was convicted in the re-trial, his legal team made it clear that it would not be appealing the severity of the sentence handed down by Chief Judge Kidd. The concern was with the verdict, not the sentence.

Moreover, it is meaningless for Pattenden to state that Pell was acquitted "on the narrow technical ground that he did not commit the crimes for which he was charged". That's not a technical ground for acquittal. That's the primary ground. Pattenden's reference to "the scores of victims of other priests" is a claim that Pell should be punished at law for the crimes of others. It was a view held by many of Pell's critics – but few were prepared to proclaim this position in public.

On 7 April 2020, the day of Pell's acquittal, an article appeared in *The Conversation* titled "How George Pell won in the High Court on a legal technicality". The authors were Ben Mathews (Professor, School of Law, Queensland University of Technology) and Mark Nicholas Bernard Thomas (Senior Lecturer, QUT). The article was published at 12.23 pm – just over two hours after the High Court had brought down its decision - it concluded as follows:

> Careful analysis of the full reasoning of the High Court is required to fully assess it. But for now, this extraordinary outcome is strange justice indeed. Pell has won today on a legal technicality….In contrast, the complainant has been believed by a jury, by a majority judgment, and by a substantial body of public opinion.

This is nonsense. Cardinal Pell's conviction was not quashed on a technicality. Rather, seven out of seven judges found that a jury, acting rationally, could not have been convinced beyond reasonable doubt that the crimes, claimed by the Victorian Director of Prosecutions, had been committed.

Moreover, if guilt or innocence is to be determined with reference to "a substantial body of public opinion" – then it would make sense to cease trials and determine guilt or innocence according to opinion polls. The reality of collective guilt suggests that, in any such situation, there would be many convictions for crimes committed by others than the accused.

Enter the Politicians

I cannot recall any person caught up in the Australian criminal law system who has faced such relentless hypercriticism for so long a period of time as Cardinal George Pell. This commenced before his trial and continued after his acquittal. It even took place during his re-trial.

The Pell Case was even the subject of political interference – some deliberate, some unintentional.

On Wednesday 8 February 2017, Senator Rachel Siewert, the Greens senator for Western Australia, moved this motion in the Senate:

> *Senator Siewert* (Western Australia – Australian Greens Whip): I move:
>
> That the Senate –
>
> (a) acknowledges that 4,444 people made allegations of child abuse by members of the Catholic Church, including the clergy, between January 1980 and February 2015;
>
> (b) notes that allegations of criminal misconduct against Cardinal George Pell have been forwarded to the Victorian Office of Public Prosecutions by the Victoria Police; and
>
> (c) calls on Cardinal George Pell to return to Australia to assist the Victorian Police and Office of Public Prosecutions with their investigations into these matters.

The motion was passed without dissent and without debate. At the time, the Liberal Party Senator Stephen Parry was president of the Senate and Malcolm Turnbull was prime minister of the Liberal Party-Nationals Coalition government which had a slim majority of seats in the House of Representatives.

It is assumed that neither the Coalition nor the opposition Labor Party saw any political benefit in opposing Greens Senator Siewert's motion. But it was an improper intervention by the legislature into the judicial realm.

At the time of Siewert's motion, Pell had appeared before the Royal Commission on three occasions in relation to its case studies and had given evidence to Victoria Police in Rome.

The cardinal was not legally bound to give evidence to the Royal Commission or to be interviewed by Victoria Police. What's more, Pell had no involvement of any kind in the overwhelming majority of the 4,444 cases referred to by Senator Siewert – some of which related to events before he was ordained a priest. Pell wrote to Senator Parry on 15 February 2017 refuting details in Siewert's motion. His letter was tabled in the Senate.

Very few of Australia's civil libertarians spoke up against the abuses of basic legal rights experienced by Pell. The Hobart-based barrister Greg Barns was one who did. The Brisbane-based Terry O'Gorman was another. Neither was a Pell supporter. On 9 February 2017, O'Gorman issued a media statement which included this comment:

> The wording of the Senate motion namely calling on Cardinal Pell to return to Australia to assist Victorian Police and the Office of Public Prosecutions was totally misguided and reflected the total lack of appreciation by those who voted for the Senate motion of the importance of observing the separation of powers doctrine which is fundamental to Australian democracy – but also indicates an appalling and, one suspects, a wilful ignorance of the processes of Police investigations and decisions to prosecute by the DPP.

O'Gorman's legal point was correct. The problem faced by the non-Greens senators was that, in February 2017, the media pile-on against Pell was at such a level that only the very brave – and probably politically foolish – politician would have opposed the Greens senator's motion.

The National Apology

Monday 22 October 2018 was set aside for the National Apology to Victims and Survivors of Institutional Child Sexual Abuse in Parliament House. Julia Gillard, who as prime minister had set up the Royal Commission, was the star of the occasion. Her role in establishing the Royal Commission was praised by Scott Morrison (who had become prime minister on 24 August 2018) and Opposition leader Bill Shorten at the event.

Writing in the *Sydney Morning Herald Online* on 22 October 2018, Jacqueline Maley described how the former prime minister received a standing ovation when she entered the Great Hall of Parliament where the function was held. Later Julia Gillard, according to Maley, was "mobbed". The event received widescale media coverage – including on the evening news bulletins.

The National Apology conducted on 22 October 2018 would have been planned by officials in the Department of Prime Minister and Cabinet many months in advance. But, per chance, it took place between the trial and re-trial of *DPP v George Pell*.

In his speech, the prime minister praised the Royal Commission and specifically referred to Chrissie Foster, without mentioning her name, as someone "whose two daughters were abused by a priest the family trusted". Mrs Foster was one of George Pell's prime antagonists. She attended both his trials. Scott Morrison concluded his speech at the National Apology function with these words: "I believe you. We believe you. Your country believes you."

Bill Shorten praised the Royal Commission – along with former prime ministers Kevin Rudd, Julia Gillard, Tony Abbott and Malcolm Turnbull. The Opposition leader told the assembled audience: "We are sorry for every time that you were not heard and not believed. We hear you now. We believe you. Australia believes you."

In view of the circumstances, it is not easy to imagine what Scott Morrison or Bill Shorten could have said about the accounts of those who were acknowledged to be "victims and survivors". Except to make no reference to belief, in view of the re-trial of *DPP v George Pell*. For the Prime Minister and Opposition leader to imply that all complainants are victims was capable of influencing the jurors for Pell's re-trial, who were sworn in at the County Court of Victoria on 8 November 2018.

As would be expected, Chief Judge Kidd instructed the impanelled jurors that they were to dismiss from their minds anything they might have heard about Cardinal Pell before his trial commenced. The problem here is that the concept of unconscious bias is now widely recognised with respect to matters of gender and racial discrimination – but not in the courts of law. Yet, like all of us, jurors can be influenced by unconscious bias – and the greater the direct and implied criticism of a public figure, the most likely this is to be the case.

Kerri Judd QC, Victoria's Director of Public Prosecutions, alone had the authority to drop the charges against Pell at the time – as she had been urged to do so after the first trial. Judd had decided that the case would go to a re-trial, and she did not change her position in spite of the additional problems posed to Pell receiving a fair trial due to the National Apology and its coverage by the media. In time, Judd may have come to regret her decision to insist on a re-trial – in view of her poor performance before the High Court arguing the prosecution's case.

Interviewed by Sky News' Kieran Gilbert on 8 April 2020, Frank Brennan said that "a big factor" in the jury reaching its guilty verdict was the fact that Pell did not give evidence at the trial – even though his Rome interview was shown in the court. As Brennan put it: "I suspect that some of the jurors thought: "We're sick of the Catholic Church having money to employ flash lawyers and they [Pell] then just sit there silent – and we are going to slot him." Brennan added that this was just speculation on his part.

In fact, no Catholic Church money was used to fund Pell's defence – but jurors would not have known this. Pell acted on legal advice – but Brennan's proposal to Pell that he go into the witness box had merit. Brennan was also of the view that the National Apology was on the minds of jurors during the days they were considering their verdict. As he told Kieran Gilbert:

> *Frank Brennan:* Now, what led the jury into such error in this particular case? We don't know. My own hunch and it's only a hunch – but I sat there during some of the first and second trials. My

hunch was, I think it was the second trial, was two weeks after Prime Minister Morrison had given his speech in the parliament, where he made the National Apology to those who were victims. And he said: "We believe you." So I think that was there in the mind of the jury: "Well, what does it mean to say, we believe you, other than to convict regardless of whatever conflicts there might be in evidence?"

This is an issue which Kerri Judd QC could have averted by discontinuing the trial. The Victorian DPP chose not to.

A Note on Victoria's Office of Public Prosecutions

On 28 November 2018, Chief Judge Peter Kidd expressed concern about the media release by Melbourne University Press concerning an award won by Louise Milligan for her book *Cardinal*. The Chief Judge also expressed his concern about tweets on the same subject which had been put out by Louise Milligan, Louise Adler and Peter FitzSimons – plus a retweet by Derryn Hinch. On 28 November 2018 – when the tweets were extant – the re-trial of *R v George Pell* was still under way. No action was taken by the DPP in this instance.

Soon after Pell's conviction was made public, the Victorian Director of Public Prosecution filed proceedings with the Supreme Court of Victoria with respect to 36 media respondents. The DPP sought a declaration that the media organisations breached a suppression order and that this had a tendency to prejudice or interfere with the administration of justice in the planned forthcoming prosecution of George Pell.

Following Pell's conviction on 13 December 2018, some news outlets gave extensive coverage to the fact that a prominent Australian had been convicted of a crime – but added that they were bound by a suppression order not to publish the name of the person concerned. The reason was that Pell was subjected to a second set of charges – and the announcement that he had been convicted on one set of charges could prevent a fair trial on a second set of charges.

This was well and good – but somewhat naïve. The Victorian legal system assumed that few if any Victorians knew of Pell's trial and subsequent conviction. In fact, there had been talk of the case on social media before and after – and even during – the trial.

As media commentator Stephen Brook wrote in *Crikey* on 6 May 2020:

> In the US, *The New York Times* and *The Daily Beast* reported the jury's guilty verdict but took extraordinary steps to prevent those stories from reaching Australia. *The Times* only published the story in print, and the paper stopped copies of the print edition from reaching Australia. *The Daily Beast* website geo-blocked the article from Australians. But in an era of online churnalism, it wasn't long before other sites copied the story and *Facebook* and *Twitter* were awash with news of Pell's conviction.

The Victorian DPP withdrew the charges against Pell in the Swimming Pool Case. But the DPP's action against the media outlets went ahead. In time, judgment was made against some media organisations and substantial fines imposed.

The Victorian Director of Public Prosecutions announced its decision to take action against certain media outlets on 26 March 2019. On 1 April 2019, I wrote to Anthony Loncaric (senior communications advisor, Office of Public Prosecutions Victoria) asking whether the Victorian DPP proposed to take steps with respect to what I termed "the apparent breach of the suppression order concerning George Pell that was drawn to the court's attention [by Pell's defence counsel] on 28 November 2018 which caused Chief Judge Kidd to express his 'real concern'". I pointed out that the jury was still impanelled on 28 November 2018 when the tweets went out and was yet to retire to consider its verdict. I acknowledged that the MUP release about *Cardinal* was taken down – but not before it has been on the Web for some time.

No response was received to my initial inquiry. So I emailed the Victorian DPP again on 4 April 2019. This is the full reply, sent the same day:

Hi Gerard

we don't wish to make a comment with respect to your query.

Regards

Anthony

So that was it. The DPP took action against certain media organisations for breaching a suppression order related to a trial which did not proceed. However, the DPP refused to comment about why no action was taken concerning comments made with respect to Cardinal Pell while his trial was still underway.

A Final Word

Writing in *Crikey* newsletter on 9 April 2020, in the aftermath of the High Court judgment, Sydney lawyer and Pell-antagonist Michael Bradley said that the decision was correct, but it demonstrated that the criminal law system was broken. He advocated that the Australian States and Territories adopt an inquisitorial system and junk the current adversarial one. Bradley wrote that, under the current legal process, an accused can be acquitted "without saying a word". He continued:

> Pell took that course, as was his right. He did not give evidence at his own trial; his version of events has never been revealed. All we know is what he said at a press conference, rather than under oath: that the crimes never happened.

This statement is wrong and misleading. Cardinal Pell voluntarily subjected himself to a detailed, prolonged record of interview with two Victoria Police officers interrogating him in Rome with respect to the alleged St Patrick's Cathedral offences on 19 October 2016. The cardinal answered in detail every question put to him; occasionally correcting errors made by Victoria Police. After Pell's conviction, Victoria Police placed a video of the interview that related to the St Patrick's Cathedral charges on its website. It seems that even an outspoken lawyer like Bradley was unaware of this. The interview can no longer be found on the Victoria Police website but can be located on *YouTube*.

From the time of Louise Milligan's *7.30* report on 26 October 2016 and the subsequent publication of her book *Cardinal*, accusations about Pell's (alleged) crimes at St Patrick's Cathedral were in the public domain. However, as Michael Bradley's article indicates, Pell's defence to the allegations had not been reported. If suppression orders had not been in existence, then Pell's forceful refutations of the charges as delivered to Victoria Police in Rome would have been in the public domain – since the video was played in the committal proceedings and the trials and, absent a suppression order, would have been reported.

Due to the suppression order, virtually no one was aware of the details of Pell's defence until after his defence was made public when Frank Brennan's article was published in *The Australian* on 27 February 2019 – followed by the analyses of the case by Andrew Bolt on Sky News' *The Bolt Report* and in his syndicated column in News Corp's newspapers.

Further details emerged in submissions to, and hearings of, the Victorian Court of Appeal and the High Court of Australia prior to Pell's acquittal. The most detailed critique of the prosecution's case can be found in Justice Mark Weinberg's minority judgment in the Victorian Court of Appeal – it was one of the most important dissents in the history of Australian criminal law.

It so happened that jurors at Pell's trials would probably have been aware of the aspects of the case against Pell – but almost certainly unaware of any aspects of his defence.

* * * * *

On 1 March 2019, shortly after a jury of twelve found Cardinal Pell guilty beyond reasonable doubt, *The Weekend Australian* published this letter by former Victorian Senior Crown Prosecutor Geoffrey Horgan QC:

> While not suggesting for a moment that the jury in the Pell Case was not satisfied of Pell's guilt beyond reasonable doubt, as a former crown prosecutor of major cases I find it difficult to understand how a jury could have reached that degree of satisfaction on the evidence of one complainant, without corroboration, and with internal inconsistencies and improbabilities in the allegations, that is, grievous sexual assaults in a public place.
>
> Was it because the vitriol directed at the cardinal over months and years made the verdict all but inevitable?
>
> Geoffrey Horgan QC, Melbourne

Gavin Silbert QC was a prosecutor for the Queen before returning to the Bar where he practised in criminal law doing both prosecution and defence work. He was appointed Victorian Chief Crown Prosecutor in 2008 and retired from this position in 2018. Since then he has practised law, concentrating on pro-bono briefs and matters of public interest.

On 23 February 2021, I wrote to Gavin Silbert concerning an article he had written for the Summer 2020/21 issue of *Victorian Bar News* titled "Pell v The Queen". The correspondence is published in full in Appendix 2. Gavin Silbert replied the same day – his email included this comment:

> …I have just finished reading *The Persecution of George Pell* by Keith Windschuttle which is as good an analysis as one could hope to find. We lawyers are used to defending clients and interpret their acquittals as a failure of the prosecution to prove guilt beyond reasonable doubt. I must say, that after reading this I was persuaded that not only was the standard of proof not met, but that Pell was an innocent man.

12

A DEATH IN ROME - A BURIAL IN SYDNEY AS THE PILE-ON CONTINUES AND CARDINAL PELL'S FINAL REFLECTION

Cardinal George Pell Describes Pedophilia as a Crime (February 2014)

"The crimes that were committed…by priests and others should never have occurred…It is a completely untenable failure whenever a child has been hurt by a sexual predator in the Church…I am serious about preventing these crimes."

- Cardinal George Pell's witness statement to the Royal Commission into Institutional Responses to Child Sexual Abuse, 14 February 2014.

* * * *

Royal Commission Chair Peter McClellan KC alleges that Cardinal Pell did not regard Pedophilia as a Crime (May 2023)

"Cardinal George Pell…gave evidence to the Royal Commission to the effect that the [Catholic] Church did not understand that the rape of a child was a crime, seeing it as a 'moral failing'."

- Peter McClellan KC, chair of the Royal Commission, in the Foreword to *Still Standing: A Mother's Fight to Bring the Catholic Church to Justice* by Chrissie Foster with Paul Kennedy (Viking, May 2023).

* * * *

Cardinal George Pell's Last Theological Battle Ends In Rome

Cardinal George Pell died in Rome's Salvator Mundi Hospital around 8.30 pm on Tuesday 10 January 2023 (Rome time), following a hip operation. The surgery was a success – after which he had lunch and did physio. Later Pell suffered a pulmonary embolism and died suddenly. The cardinal did not receive the Last Rites. He had been to see his confessor before the surgery. On the morning of the surgery, Pell celebrated Mass after which he remained for a long time in the chapel.

George Pell had experienced heart problems for many years and had a pacemaker installed in 2010. Initially he intended to have the surgery at St Vincent's Private Hospital in Sydney (where he had a dual knee replacement in late 2018, when on bail). However, Pell chose to have the procedure in Rome. At the time, there was speculation that Pope Francis might die in office – or retire due to failing health and mobility problems. Pell, having turned 80 years of age in July 2021, was no longer entitled to vote in the election for the papacy – such an entitlement applies only to cardinals under 80 years of age.

However, he would have been able to address the conclave of the Sacred College of Cardinals before it assembled in the Sistine Chapel to elect a new pope. There would also be meetings with the cardinals in Rome before the conclave commenced. It is understood Pell believed that Pope Francis had appointed a number of little known and inexperienced bishops to the cardinalate. Moreover, due to travel restrictions imposed by the COVID-19 pandemic, many had not been able to visit Rome or elsewhere outside their own countries. This would give so senior a figure as Pell – who was known to be close to the retired Pope Benedict XVI – an opportunity to influence the new cardinals as to whom they should support to succeed Francis.

But it was not to be. Pell's unexpected death followed shortly after the death on 30 December 2022 of Benedict XVI. It is believed that Pell – who had many contacts among the cardinals due to his important role in the Vatican stemming back for decades – had played a key role in Benedict XVI's election. Pope Benedict resigned on 28 February

2013 – being the first Vicar of Christ to do so since Pope Gregory XII in 1415. While being a strong supporter of Benedict XVI, Pell did not agree with the idea of popes resigning. Especially since Benedict continued to live in Vatican City not far away from Francis' residence and continued to dress in papal white. In Pell's view, Saint Peter should have one successor at any one time, not what appeared to be a couple of similarly dressed pontiffs – one active, the other retired.

After his acquittal by the High Court in early April 2020, Pell had taken up residence in the Sydney suburb of Homebush. He returned to Rome in October 2020 and based himself in his apartment there, which Pope Francis had insisted should remain untouched until the legal proceedings against the cardinal had concluded. Pell's idea was to spend half the year in Rome and the other half in Sydney. In the event, however, he spent more time in Rome – from where he made occasional visits to Europe and to the United States. Pell made a brief trip to Australia to take part in the requiem mass and Christian burial of his sister Margaret who died in the Victorian town of Bendigo on 18 December 2021. And then he went back to Rome – returning to Australia in early July 2022. He went back to Rome on 18 August 2022, some weeks earlier than what was initially planned.

Pell gave a couple of public speeches on what were to be his last appearances in Australia. On 6 August 2022, he addressed the Catholic Charity Aid to the Church in Need. Then on 17 August 2022 he gave the keynote address at the Capital Appeal Fundraiser of Campion College at the NSW Parliament House in Sydney. The Cardinal flew out of Sydney for Rome the next day – his remains returned five months later.

In his address to the Catholic charity, Pell acknowledged the importance of the Christian community. He declared "we are here to stay and to struggle, we are not going away" – and that the "gospel Protestants, the Evangelicals and the Orthodox Churches will be with us in these mighty battles". He added:

> I had long realised, as do nearly all the Protestants, that the issue is no longer between the English and the Irish in the Anglosphere, between the Proddies [Protestants] and the Micks [Catholics].

> Indeed, the gospel Protestants will be indispensable allies in the Christian survival and revival when it comes, as is the case in the pro-life battles in the United States. I have long described the confrontation as being between the Judeo-Christians and the anti-religious secularists.

I attended Pell's last hurrah in Australia at NSW Parliament House. The written speech was published in the March 2023 issue of *Quadrant* – but, on occasions, Pell broke from the text with a witty aside. The focus was on Australia in the 20th and early 21st centuries – but the speaker made it clear that his major concerns turned on "the Catholic church and the rise of a belligerent China".

Pell was critical of the contemporary Catholic Church currently headed by Archbishop Timothy Costelloe, the President of the Australian Catholic Bishops Conference – maintaining that it was "largely irrelevant to the preaching of the gospel". His particular focus was on the recent Plenary Council of Australia (involving both clergy and laity) which held its final meeting in Sydney the previous month.

Pell said that "Australia's finest theologian, a woman who happens to be orthodox (a position now regarded as conservative) was not invited to be a delegate". He added that "the nation's leading Catholic academic and an outstanding public intellectual (he was vice-chancellor at the Australian Catholic University) was barred from writing any council documents". No names were named. But references were to Professor Tracey Rowland at the University of Notre Dame (Australia) and Professor Greg Craven. Pell also regretted the absence of young priests at the plenary, whom he described as "one of the hopes of the future" along with "few Latin Church ethnic parishioners". He added with respect to the Plenary Council:

> Council members requested that the priesthood, family and education be discussed – to no avail – and naturally there wasn't a squeak on the approaching threats to religious freedoms in our schools, hospitals and retirement homes. A goodly percentage of the council's pacemakers (fixers?) [sic] were self-absorbed, not interested in missionary expansion, isolated from the real world, from the clash between good and evil, faith and darkness.
>
> One can see how the Church disintegrated in Belgium, Holland and

> Quebec. Jesus got a few mentions [at the Plenary Council], more than Jesus Christ, and faith was hardly mentioned at all, much less evangelisation or the unborn.

Nevertheless, the message was not overly pessimistic. Pell told his audience: "I do not believe that the battle is over, that the field has been lost". On his return to Rome, the following day, he would continue the battle.

Shortly before he died, Pell wrote an article for *The Spectator* magazine intending for it to be published in his name in the lead-up to the (then) forthcoming Synod on Synodality – to commence in Rome in late October 2023. The Synod was designed for Catholics to assess the position of the Catholic Church – from parishioners in the pews to bishops in their mitres – and was one of Francis' initiatives.

On the day after Pell's death, Pope Francis expressed his condolences in the telegram sent to Cardinal Battista, the Dean of the College of Cardinals – the traditional way for a pontiff to respond to the death of a cardinal. The Pope's message was written in Italian. *L'Osservatore Romano* published an English translation on 13 January. It read in part:

> I offer my sincere condolences, remembering with heartfelt gratitude his constant and committed witness, his dedication to the Gospel and to the Church, and especially his diligent collaboration with the Holy See in its recent economic reform, for which he had laid the foundations with determination and wisdom.

A requiem mass for Cardinal George Pell was held on Saturday 14 January at the Altar of the Chair at Saint Peter's Basilica. At the end of the mass, Pope Francis presided over the rites of what *L'Osservatore Romano* described as the *Ultima Commendatio* and *Valedicto*.

On 11 January 2023, *The Spectator* in London released the article which Pell had written for publication, under his own name. It was a critique of the 45-page document released by the Vatican in the lead-up to the Synod titled *Enlarge The Space Of Your Tent*. In his *Spectator* piece, Pell commented that the title had been produced with "no sense of irony". It commenced as follows:

> The Catholic Synod of Bishops is now busy constructing what they

think as "God's dream" of synodality. Unfortunately this divine dream has developed into a toxic nightmare despite the bishops' professed good intentions. They have produced a 45-page booklet which presents its account of the discussions of the first stage of "listening and discernment", held in many parts of the world, and it is one of the most incoherent documents ever sent out from Rome.

Pell was very critical of the document's relator (that is, chief writer and manager) Cardinal Jean-Claude Hollerich S.J. – whom, he wrote, had publicly rejected the basic teachings of the Church on sexuality. Pell commented that the document "was replete with neo-Marxist jargon" and displaced Christian notions of "forgiveness, sex, sacrifice, healing [and] redemption". In releasing the article, *The Spectator's* associate editor Damian Thompson wrote that Pell "was prepared to face the fury of Pope Francis and the organisers [of the Synod] when it was published".

There was more to come. Since the commencement of Lent in late February 2023, a document – written in the name of "Demos" – had been circulating in Vatican circles. It declared that the pontificate of Francis "is a disaster in many or most respects: a catastrophe".

Titled "The Vatican Today", the document consisted of 15 points. The writing style is different to Pell's – but reflects his known views. Cardinal Hollerich was described as "explicitly heretical" and regret was expressed that Francis had weakened the need for economic reform at the Vatican. "Demos" had this to say about Francis:

> The political influence of Pope Francis and the Vatican is negligible. Intellectually, Papal writings demonstrate a decline from the standard of St John Paul II and Pope Benedict. Decisions and policies are often "politically correct", but there have been grave failures to support human rights in Venezuela, Hong Kong, mainland China, and now in the Russian invasion [of Ukraine].

> There has been no public support for the loyal Catholics in China who have been intermittently persecuted for their loyalty to the Papacy for more than 70 years. No public Vatican support for the Catholic community in Ukraine, especially the Greek Catholics. These issues should be revisited by the next Pope. The Vatican's political prestige in now at a low ebb.

And there was some advice for the next pontiff:

> The Pope does not need to be the world's best evangelist, nor a political force. The successor of Peter, as head of the College of Bishops, also successors of the Apostles, has a foundational role for unity and doctrine. The new pope must understand that the secret of Christian and Catholic vitality comes from fidelity to the teachings of Christ and Catholic practices. It does not come from adapting to the world or from money.

Soon after Pell's death, the Italian journalist Sandro Magister declared on his *Settimo Cielo* blog that Pell was "Demos" – and that he had given permission to publish the document. This was contested by Pell's friend, the American Jesuit Fr Joseph Fessio S.J. He told the global Catholic news service EWTN, during an interview with Raymond Arroyo on 13 January 2023:

> I will take a sed contra [contrary view] on this. George Pell was a loyal son of the church. He would not publicly criticise the Holy Father and I doubt that he would put his signature to something, even anonymously, that would be public criticism.

A middle position was taken by George Weigel, another friend of Pell. Writing in *First Things* website on 16 January 2023 he commented:

> Judging from both the text and my conversations with the cardinal, it seems to me likely that the document was a result of conversations among more than a few members of the College of Cardinals. Certain formulations, however, are quite familiar to those who were in regular contact with Cardinal Pell and he seems to have been, on Magister's testimony, the final redactor of what came out of those conversations.

Cardinal Pell delivered his final homily on 7 January 2023 to the Magnificat Dominium Community in San Giovanni Rotondo, Italy. He praised popes John Paul II (Karol Jozef Wojtyla) and Benedict XVI (Josef Ratzinger). But did not mention Francis. He described "the heritage of Wojtyla and Ratzinger" as follows: (i) "they were Christians", (ii) "they were optimistic", (iii) "they understood the importance of the sacraments and, especially, of the Eucharist and (iv) "they understood the role of Peter's successor in the life of the Catholic Church".

In spite of this internal conflict within the Church over doctrine, Cardinal Pell received a great send-off. In Fr Robert A Sirico's edited collection *Pell: Contra Mundum* (Connor Court, 2023), the American author and commentator George Weigel wrote:

> Cardinal Pell's Requiem Mass was celebrated on 14 January 2023 in the apse of the Vatican Basilica, beneath Gianlorenzo Bernini's colossal bronze masterpiece, the *Altar of the Chair*. Non-papal liturgies, including cardinals' requiems, are always celebrated in that large space. But veterans of such events said that the congregation who assembled to bid farewell to George Pell, and to beg the Father of mercies to take his servant to the embrace of the Trinity, was the largest they had ever seen.
>
> Shortly before the Mass began, the *Sanpietrini*, the basilica workforce, were frantically setting up chairs behind the pews in the vast apse, the pews having long since overflowed. And thus the congregation filled the entire area between the *Altar of the Chair* and another Bernini triumph, the *baldacchino* over the papal high altar beneath the basilica's great dome. As one of the cardinal's longtime collaborators said, "When people fly in from all over the world on short notice, something is being said."

Shortly after Pell's funeral, Pope Francis gave an interview to Associated Press to mark the tenth anniversary of his election as pope. He acknowledged his theologically conservative critics within the church but said: "You prefer that they don't criticise for the sake of tranquility – but I prefer that they do it because that means there is freedom of speech". Asked about Pell, Francis acknowledged his criticisms but praised the recently departed as being his "right-hand man" in the cause of economic reform at the Vatican and added: "He was a great guy, great."

Follow the Vatican Money – To Where?

Nine months after Cardinal Pell's coffin departed Rome for Sydney, he remained news in Vatican City. On 22-23 October 2023, Paolo Totaro reported in the *Weekend Australian* that Pell's name was mentioned in a civil case in Vatican City. Former Vatican independent auditor-general Libero Milone had filed a legal action alleging unlawful dismissal. Milone had worked with Pell to investigate Vatican finances but had been dismissed.

Romano Vaccarella, a former Italian Constitutional Court judge, who appeared for Milone, said this:

> On the 19th of June in 2017 they do away with Milone; on the 29th of June they eliminate Cardinal Pell who is thrown into prison. All this within 10 days…what a coincidence.

The reference was to Victoria Police's decision to charge Pell with various counts of historical child sexual abuse – which led to him stepping down from his position of Prefect of the Secretariat for the Economy and returning to Australia to defend himself.

Libero Milone and his deputy Ferruccio Panico were arrested by Vatican guards and compelled to sign letters of resignation while in detention. The decision to dismiss the two was made by Cardinal Giovanni Angelo Becciu – an opponent of Cardinal Pell's attempts at economic reform at the Vatican.

As Dennis Shanahan reported in *The Australian* on 8 May 2022, Cardinal Pell raised concern that Becciu had transferred a sum of around $Aus 2.3 million from the Vatican to Australia between 2016 and 2017 – which, in Shanahan's words, "coincided with the investigation and trial of Cardinal Pell on sex abuse charges in Australia".

Pell was suspicious of why Becciu forwarded a substantial amount of money to Australia – but acknowledged that there was no proof about where it ended up. Tess Livingstone reported in *The Australian* on 26 December 2021 that Becciu wrote to Pell in December 2021 refusing to explain why he had authorised Vatican funds to be sent to Australia or where the money was sent. In the correspondence, Becciu wrote that he found Pell's "numerous interventions in many media…offensive to my personal dignity".

At the time this third edition of this book went to print, Cardinal Becciu was facing the personal indignity of being on trial at Vatican City for financial fraud and embezzlement.

News Of Cardinal Pell's Death Reaches Australia – And The Media Pile-On Is Born Again

I learnt that Cardinal Pell had died shortly after 9 am Australian Eastern Daylight Time via a text message from a Melbourne taxi driver who was a strong Pell supporter. He had been monitoring Melbourne Radio 3AW and *The Australian Online*. I had just come out of a meeting in North Sydney which was also attended by Anne Henderson. She suggested that there might have been post-operative complications, as was soon confirmed.

Within minutes, many of those who had been involved in the Pell media pile-on resumed their campaign.

At 9.36 am, shortly after Pell's death became news, Louise Milligan tweeted: "George Pell is dead. This will be a very triggering day for a lot of people. Thinking of them." Derryn Hinch immediately replied: "I wish he had lived for another 10 years of deserved public opprobrium." Lucie Morris-Marr concurred with Milligan – and used the occasion to publicise her 2009 book *Fallen,* which was published before Pell's acquittal by the High Court and not subsequently updated. Suzanne Smith, Magda Szubanski and Mike Carlton joined in the chorus.

The ABC's Paul Kennedy, a Pell-antagonist, was interviewed by Tony Jones (not the ABC presenter of the same name) on Nine's 3AW in Melbourne. Like the interviewee, the interviewer had taken part in the Pell pile-on. Kennedy is an activist journalist – but told Jones that he always tried to just point to the facts about Pell and remain unemotional about the issue. He didn't succeed, as the transcript indicates.

> *Tony Jones:* I can hear the emotion in your voice – is the overriding emotion, though, anger?
>
> *Paul Kennedy:* That's a difficult one…it's probably not for me to say.

Kennedy went on to comment: "I don't think it's anger." But added "I have to be emotional about it". No he shouldn't. A journalist is expected to act professionally – especially one employed by the taxpayer funded public broadcaster. In the interview, Kennedy described the Melbourne Response as "a disgraceful scheme". He claimed, without evidence, that Pell had been involved in "cover-ups" of child sexual abuse. He also implied that Pell was collectively responsible for the crimes of others. At the end of the interview, Kennedy thanked Jones for "always [having] been very good around this issue".

Tony Jones then interviewed Louise Milligan whom he described as "an author and investigative journalist who, in many ways, exposed much of the George Pell story via her book *Cardinal...* and also *Four Corners*". In fact, not one of Milligan's various allegations about Pell's alleged crimes made it through the Australian legal system – something that she has been unwilling to accept. In a soft interview, Milligan said that none of the Royal Commission's findings with respect to Pell "have been overturned". This demonstrated considerable ignorance of the Australian legal system. The Royal Commission was wound up in December 2017 – some time before the Commonwealth Government released its findings with respect to Pell shortly after his acquittal by the High Court. Pell had no right of appeal to the Royal Commission.

Milligan referred to the majority decision in the Victorian Court of Appeal to uphold the jury's verdict in the second trial – but ignored Justice Weinberg's devastating dissent. She did not mention the hung jury in the first trial or refer to the unanimous decision in the High Court in quashing Pell's convictions. Clearly Milligan, like many Pell-antagonists, does not accept the decision of Australia's highest court. Tony Jones gave Milligan every opportunity to fang Pell. No other view was heard.

On Nine's 2GB in Sydney, Ray Hadley continued his long-time campaign against Pell and censored any alternative view. Hadley interviewed Opposition Leader Peter Dutton on 2 February, the morning of the funeral. In response to a question, Dutton said he was attending the Requiem Mass due to Pell's contribution to Australian society, including education. Hadley commented that, if invited, he would not attend due to the Royal Commission's findings. A listener emailed the 2GB presenter saying that, for a different view, he might interview me. Hadley replied: "Mr Henderson's biased views are not welcome here". No other view was heard on *The Ray Hadley Morning Show.*

The ABC's *The World Today* interviewed historian (and former Catholic priest) Paul Collins along with academic Miles Pattenden, another Pell critic plus Paulina Guzik, a journalist with the United States Catholic magazine *Our Sunday Visitor.* Neither Collins nor Pattenden was a supporter of Pell – although neither Collins nor Pattenden ran a Milligan-style "Pell was guilty" line. Pattenden suddenly became an "expert" in the Pell Case – despite that he had only recently arrived in Australia from Britain – and criticised the Cardinal on issues not related to the St Patrick Cathedral charges.

For example, Pattenden maintained that Pell "was very heavily implicated in the sexual abuse of children in the Catholic Church as a bishop who perhaps didn't take the necessary actions against priests in his diocese". False. Pell first became bishop in charge of a diocese when appointed Archbishop of Melbourne in July 1996. He acted within three months against pedophile priests.

Collins got another run on ABC TV's *7.30* that evening when interviewed by David Speers – where he was professional enough to state that he and Pell had many disagreements. With respect to child sexual abuse, Collins supported the Royal Commission's findings against Pell without demonstrating that he had read the relevant material. No other view was heard.

In the introduction to the program, *7.30* showed grabs of Pell-antagonist David Marr and Pell supporter Greg Craven. Marr got three quarters of the available air time. Craven a quarter.

The following morning it was time for opinion pieces and obituaries. *The Age* and the *Sydney Morning Herald* commissioned Miles Pattenden to write an opinion piece. It was Pattenden who had made the extraordinary claim in April 2020 that Pell's convictions had been quashed by the High Court on "narrow technical grounds that he did not commit those crimes". See Chapter 11. Clearly such manifest ignorance did not stop the editors of Nine's newspapers giving him another go.

This time Pattenden wrote that Pell became a "heavyweight boxing champion" at school. Absolute tosh. Pattenden confused George Pell the priest with his father George Arthur Pell who became a professional boxer for a while – presumably due to misreading a *Wikipedia* entry. Pattenden also claimed that Pell was a "fan of the monarchy". In fact, he was a high profile republican during the 1999 referendum on whether Australia should become a republic with an Australian head of state. Pell had in fact moved the successful motion at the 1998 Constitutional Convention: "That this Convention supports the adoption of a republican system of government on the bipartisan appointment model in preference to there being no change to the Constitution." In time, Pattenden's howlers were removed from Nine's online edition.

It so happened that Pattenden also contributed an article on 12 January 2023 in the *Crikey* newsletter. While critical of Pell, Pattenden referred to his conviction as "a cruel and brutal miscarriage of justice…which raised grave doubts about the efficacy, competence and impartiality of our criminal justice system". This view about Pell's innocence did not make it into Pattenden's article in *The Age* or *Sydney Morning Herald*.

Turn to the obituary page of *The Age* and the *Sydney Morning Herald*. The writer was Barney Zwartz – a member of the Pell media pile-on who had falsely predicted that Pell's guilty verdict would not be overturned on appeal and opined that he had "reached the nadir of human disgrace". See Chapters 4 and 6. Nevertheless, in an opinion piece accompanying the obituary, Zwartz wrote that he was "sad" to learn of Pell's death. In the obituary he had this to say:

> Regarded by friends and colleagues as a convivial companion with a sophisticated palate for wine, Pell's public persona tended to be abrasive, his tone didactic. Many women, in particular, found him a bully. Watching Pell give evidence in 2016 to the royal commission, I wondered in *The Age* whether he was "handicapped by his unfortunate demeanour: his slow, heavy delivery – deliberate, even ponderous – and unemotional expression can seem pompous, overbearing and unfeeling".

So there you have it. Zwartz apparently regarded it as his melancholy duty to tell readers of Nine's obituary pages that Pell had a sophisticated palate for wine – but was an unsophisticated abrasive bully.

A different opinion was expressed later by Sister Patty Fawkner, the congregational leader of the Good Samaritan religious order. Writing on the *Goodsam's* website on 9 February 2023, she recalled that when appointed principal of a school in the Ballarat diocese in the early 1980s she had been given the impression that Pell was "a tough, hard-nosed, combative towering figure who was going places and not to be trifled with". But added:

> My impression of "George the ogre" was challenged later when I worked in a Ballarat diocesan office where his name was often mentioned. A young administrative assistant would not have a word said against Father Pell because of his generous and discreet kindness to her family when they fell on hard times. I heard many such stories over the decades.

Sister Fawkner wrote that "given the circumstances and logistics surrounding the abuse [she] thought the charges untenable" and added:

> I was also disturbed by what I perceived to be the bias and vendetta-like mentality of the Victoria Police and Victorian judicial system, and sections of the media. Some ABC journalists seemed to set themselves up as Pell's judge, jury and hangman. One of the Sisters in my Congregation who works in prison ministry visited Pell every week for the 57 weeks of his incarceration. Did she think him guilty or innocent? I don't know. She said that she appreciated his endurance in extremely difficult and isolating conditions, their times of shared prayer, and his graciousness towards her. "He had an inner peace," she said. "He was true to himself and consistent that he hadn't offended."

Sister Fawkner concluded her reflection as follows: "George Pell was neither evil incarnate, nor sinless and blameless. He was truly gifted and terribly flawed, like the rest of us." No such considered and balanced evaluation could be found in the news outlets that led to the media pile-on against the living Pell and which continued after his death – such as Nine newspapers (*The Age* and *Sydney Morning Herald*), the ABC, *The Saturday Paper*, *The Guardian Australia*, *The New Daily* and the like.

On 14 January 2023, the whole of *The Saturday Paper*'s front page and all of Page 4 was devoted to an article by Louise Milligan titled "The child abuse cases for which George Pell was never tried". It was yet another rant against Pell by Milligan.

She described the Royal Commission findings against Pell as "a masterclass in restraint" – mentioning that the commissioners had found it "inconceivable" that Pell did not know about some pedophile clerics and that his behaviour had been "unacceptable". Clearly, Milligan did not understand that the Royal Commission used such allegedly restrained words because there was no evidence to support its findings.

Milligan went on to refer to some allegations against Pell by men that had allegedly been abused by him when boys but "never got to trial". These matters turned on the claim that Pell had offended against boys in swimming pools in the Ballarat region in the 1970s. All of these allegations emerged after Pell's high-profile appearance for the first time at the Royal Commission. Milligan specifically referred to the case of "Bernie" – which formed part of Sarah Ferguson's case against Pell in her ABC TV documentary *Revelation*. See Chapter 8.

Milligan overlooked the fact that the swimming pool charges were dropped by Victoria Police or the Victorian Office of Public Prosecutions or the courts due to a lack of evidence to put cases to trial – despite the fact that Victoria Police was hostile to Pell and the Office of Public Prosecutions was willing to charge Pell over the St Patrick's Case in the face of a lack of evidence.

Milligan's *Saturday Paper* article was subjected to a withering critique by Melbourne Law School's Professor Jeremy Gans in a Twitter (now X) thread on 14 January. He focused on the ABC journalist's analysis of Chief Judge Peter Kidd's judgment in *DPP v Pell (Evidential Ruling No 1)* which led to the swimming pool charges being withdrawn by the Office of Public Prosecutions. Gans pointed out that Milligan had left out "the key bit of Kidd's reason". He added:

> ...It's a recurrent problem with Milligan's journalism. If there are facts that don't help her argument, she doesn't tell her readers She just leaves them out.

Professor Gans also criticised Milligan's analysis of the County Court trials along with the Victoria Court of Appeal and the High Court of Australia decisions. An assessment of Gans' coverage of the Pell Case demonstrates that he was objective – not taking sides for or against the cardinal. His criticism of Louise Milligan was this: "Milligan is a gifted writer. But I don't think she's a good court reporter."

Yet the ABC chose Milligan as its go-to journalist for covering the Pell Case. As is her wont, Milligan did not defend her work and simply ignored Jeremy Gans' critique of her legal reporting. According to Gans, Milligan blocked him on Twitter (now X).

It was not long before David Marr re-joined the pile on. On 16 January, he told Jane Lee for *The Guardian's* "Full Story" podcast:

> *David Marr:* He [Pell] was a danger to children. He was a danger to children. Not only himself but in his role as a priest, an auxiliary bishop and an archbishop, he was a danger to children. He did not protect them. He put them in danger. He left them in danger. His career is an iconic career of a very high-ranking prelate in the Catholic Church who did not protect children. Now, he had old fashioned theological views...

Marr provided no evidence to support his assertion that Pell "himself" was a danger to children. This claim was contrary to the High Court's unanimous decision and also overlooked the fact that there was no evidence submitted to the Royal Commission which could support such a claim. It would seem that, after Pell's death, Marr joined the likes of Milligan, Morris-Marr and Davey who had refrained from accepting the informed decision of Australia's seven most senior judges at the time.

George Pell's Last Journey – Into The Crypt Of St Mary's Cathedral

On Friday 20 January 2023, I received an email from The Most Reverend Anthony Fisher OP, the Catholic Archbishop of Sydney, inviting me and Anne Henderson to attend the Pontifical Funeral Mass for His Eminence Cardinal George Pell AC. Archbishop Fisher's OP acknowledged that he was a priest of the Dominican Order (i.e. the Order of Preachers). Cardinal Pell's AC was the Companion in the Order of Australia – Australia's highest civilian award. The Funeral Mass was scheduled for Thursday 2 February 2023 at St Mary's Cathedral commencing at 11 am.

As it turned out, even the cardinal's funeral and burial became a matter of controversy. Soon after news of Pell's death reached Australia, the Victorian Labor premier Daniel Andrews was asked at a media conference whether he had received a request that Pell be given a State funeral. The premier replied:

> No. And there won't be a state memorial service. I couldn't think of anything that would be more distressing for victim survivors than that. There's been no requests made, and these things are normally offered rather than asked for, and there will be no offer made.

So there you have it. No one asked the Victorian premier to provide a State funeral for Pell – who was to be buried in NSW, not Victoria where he had not lived for some two decades. But Andrews felt the need to volunteer that he would not provide one – adding that if invited he would not attend such an event. This led to an immediate response from Professor Greg Craven:

> I think Daniel Andrews is an insult in search of a target. So far as I know, no one wanted a state funeral, no one asked for a state funeral, and I for one would hope that he [Andrews] wouldn't have been invited to a state funeral.

On 12 January, Andrews said this with respect to complainants of child sexual abuse:

> We see you, we believe you, we support you and you're at the centre of not only our thoughts, not only our words, but our actions. We should never ever forget that predator brothers and priests were systematically moved around knowingly. It was part of a strategy from one working-class parish to the next. We should never ever forget that, and we will never ever forget Victims survivors of institutional child sexual abuse at the hands of the Catholic church.

It so happened that before the end of the year, evidence emerged of widescale child sexual abuse in Victorian state government schools – and that pedophile male teachers were moved by the Victorian Education Department from school to school. Andrews promised to issue a formal apology to the victims of abuse at Beaumaris Primary School but resigned from politics on 27 September 2023 without having issued the promised apology.

The Coalition government in NSW was not asked – and did not offer – a state funeral or a memorial service.

The Funeral Mass on 2 February was televised live by Sky News and live-streamed.

The previous day had seen the "Rite of Reception" of the body and the commencement of Lying in State at 9.30 am at St Mary's – followed by two masses for the dead (at 1.10 pm and 8 pm) along with an Evening Prayer and Vigil – otherwise called the Vespers (at 5.30 pm).

Fr Joseph Hamilton, priest-secretary to the late cardinal, delivered the Homily. Early on he had this to say:

> ... the office of Vespers today is a little different than usual. For 22 days now we have been inundated by plaudits, protests, and pundits surrounding the passing of our cardinal. Though locally this may seem like a tsunami of hatred, it fades to less than a ripple when viewed from the perspective of the global Church. For the vast majority of the worldwide Catholic family, Cardinal George Pell was another Clemens August Graf Von Galen, a lion of the Church, a magnet for vocations, a confessor bishop, a true cardinal priest.

Towards the end of the homily, Fr Hamilton recalled George Pell's return to Rome, some six months after his acquittal by the High Court's unanimous decision:

> Shortly after our cardinal's return to the Vatican, on October 12, 2020, Pope Francis called us to a private audience. As we made our way through the salons of the Apostolic Palace all the way to the antechamber of the papal study, the greeting "*ben tornato Eminenza*" could be heard over and over again: "Welcome back, Eminence." Our cardinal was held in enormous esteem and affection by the Pontifical Swiss Guard, who saw in him a reflection of their own oath to serve and protect—several guards told me so, including those on guard the morning of his Requiem Mass in St. Peter's Basilica.
>
> Before entering the papal study to meet Pope Francis, in a scene that will remain with me to the end of my days, Msgr. Leonardo Sapienza, regent of the papal household, stepped out to greet us and to lead us in. Suddenly, however, he paused, dropped to both knees in front of the cardinal, took his hand, kissed it, and said, "Welcome, welcome confessor of our Church."

Thursday 2 February 2023 was a very hot day in Sydney. Those with invitations were required to be at the cathedral's western door by 10.40 am – and were seated in pews up the front. St Mary's capacity is some 1,400 attendees in the pews. The general public attained access through the main door and occupied about two-thirds of the floor. A large crowd – estimated at around 6,000 – who could not get access to the Cathedral – stood, sat or knelt outside. The Sydney Archdiocese authorities provided bottled water to the congregation inside and outside the cathedral.

And then there were the demonstrators, some of whom were involved in clashes with the faithful outside the church. The protest was organised by the Community Action for Rainbow Rights (CARR). CARR was given ready access to the media. For example, Kim Stern – a CARR organiser – was interviewed on ABC TV *News Breakfast* the morning of the funeral.

It was a soft interview. Presenter Michael Rowland described Pell as "the head of the Catholic Church here in Australia" – an incorrect statement. And Rowland said nothing when Stern declared: "People hate the guy – so if you're interested in showing your opposition, you should definitely come out to the protest at 10.30 today." Not many did. Rowland and Stern gave the impression that Cardinal Pell was collectively responsible for the crimes of Australian Catholic clergy.

Following the threat of legal action by CARR which led to a compromise and an agreement with NSW Police, the demonstrators were given space on the Hyde Park side of College Street – close enough to be heard faintly within the Cathedral but separated from St Mary's by Pell's supporters – who included Maronite Lebanese, Croatian, Vietnamese and Filipino Australians.

Writing in the *Sydney Morning Herald* on 2 February, the leftist activist and one-time academic Simon Hunt (aka Pauline Pantsdown) justified the demonstration by references to Pell's "decades-long enabling of pedophile priests through a career-long inaction, as documented in the final royal commission report". If Hunt had read the Royal Commission's findings on Pell, he would have known that they were not supported by any witness or documentary evidence and contained serious inconsistencies. See Chapter 9.

The ceremony commenced with an entry procession of hundreds of priests dressed in white robes. Archbishop Fisher was the principal celebrant of the Solemn Pontifical Mass of Christian Burial. The official booklet contained statements by Pope Francis and Archbishop Fisher. The music before mass consisted of work by Felix Mendelssohn, Johann Sebastian Bach, Frank Bridge, Tim Attride and Edward Elgar. Dr Lisa Buxton, the executive officer of the Aboriginal Catholic Ministry Sydney, gave the Acknowledgement of Country.

Then Mass commenced. There were readings by Georgina Pell (the cardinal's niece) and Dr Michael Casey (a former private secretary to Pell) – and intercessions were invoked by Sarah Pell (Pell's niece), Danny Casey (who worked with Pell at the Vatican), Katrina Lee (formerly a media adviser to the archdiocese and friend of Pell), Dr Bernadette Tobin (an academic and friend) and Chris Meney (the chancellor to the Sydney archdiocese, who is Pell's second cousin).

Archbishop Fisher delivered the homily. He indicated that he would follow the wishes of the recently departed that "funeral homilies should focus on the Scriptures and the Catholic faith, especially regarding the Resurrection and God's mercy and not be a eulogy or canonisation ceremony for the deceased.". Fisher said: "So, this one last time, Your Eminence, I will try to do as I am told". And he did. Concentrating on Pell's initiatives – which he summarised – commencing with the establishment of Domus Australia in Rome:

> It took more than a bit of Christian shamelessness for the son of a Ballarat publican to take a Roman monastery with church, renovate it to Australian comfort standards, radically redecorate it, and so establish an Aussie watering hole—er, pilgrim house—in the heart of the Eternal City. It took boldness to get the bishops of Australia and St Mary's Cathedral Choir there for the opening. And it took sheer importunity to bang on the door of the Pope [Benedict XVI], asking him to bless and open the place—perhaps the only hotel ever opened by a pope!
>
> Yet ἀναίδεια [a Greek word meaning persistence] was on-brand for Pell, and it enabled him to bring us not only Domus Australia but three good seminaries, four new Catholic tertiary institutions, the Benedict XVI Retreat Centre, the John Paul Centre at Sydney Uni, several new institutes of consecrated women, a vastly expanded tertiary and youth apostolate and World Youth Day—like the Domus opening, stuffed full of pope, bishops and musicians, but with half a million idealistic young adults to boot!

The archbishop pointed out that while Domus Australia is a high-standard hospitality centre for Australian pilgrims in Rome – to tour its chapel and public spaces is also to revisit the history and faith of the Church in Australia. He added: "All around Domus we see representations of St Mary MacKillop and Australia's first bishops, priests, nuns and laity, of First Australians, convicts and migrants, and what they built."

The walls of the Domus Australia Chapel contain images of Pius V, John Joseph Therry, Bede Polding, Daniel Mannix, John Paul II, St Francis Xavier, St Patrick, St Dominic, St Brigid, St Therese of Lisieux, Mother Teresa, Mary Ward, John Henry Newman and Cardinal Xavier

Nguyen Van Thuan plus the martyrs – John Fisher, Thomas More and Edmund Campion. As the archbishop put it, "each painted hero in Domus Australia gives us a peek into what drove George Pell the man and priest: his passion for evangelisation, education, welfare, worship and witness".

Towards the end of Anthony Fisher's homily, there was this:

> Pope Francis recently called George "a great guy" to whom "we owe so much". Not everyone agrees. But if some experienced him as demanding, pugilistic or polarising, and others as faithful, hospitable and witty, it's now the turn of the saints to endure his teasing, lecturing or commands.

The solemn Pontifical Mass continued up to the Communion Antiphon at which the congregation sang a Pell favourite set to music by Edward Elgar – with words from the English convert John Henry Newman's 1865 poem *The Dream of Gerontius*. It commences:

> Firmly I believe and truly
> God is three, and God is One;
> And I next acknowledge duly
> Manhood taken by the Son.
> And I trust and hope most fully
> In that Manhood crucified;
> And each thought and deed unruly
> Do to death, as He has died.

After Communion, Words of Remembrance were delivered by Mr David Pell (Pell's brother) and The Hon. Tony Abbott AC.

Towards the end of his eulogy, David Pell said this about clerical pedophilia in the Catholic Church:

> We sympathise with the legitimate victims and are in complete abhorrence of the criminals. Our own family has not been immune to this evil. As a Catholic family brought up in Ballarat, we along with many other Catholic families had no idea of the evil curse that was perpetrated upon the innocent children of unaware parents, by secretive, deviant and manipulative criminals. We as a society will continue to spend the rest of our days healing people….

> I need to remind you that all ordained priests take a vow of obedience to their bishop. That is what George was doing when he accompanied that perpetrator [Gerald Ridsdale] to court. He was not his friend. He was appalled at what he heard in court... George did not know, as a junior consultor, of the perpetrator's crimes and the reason why he was being moved across parishes. .... I also need to remind you that the Catholic Church 40 to 50 years ago was completely different to today's Church, and that each bishop was in complete control of their own diocese – and were autocrats.

Then it was Tony Abbott's turn, Australia's 28th prime minister. The Catholic layman summed up his friend's achievements with reference to Australia and the Holy See:

> Here in Australia, he was the first archbishop to sack misbehaving clergy, and report them to the police, rather than hide them in another parish. In Rome, he tried to ensure that the collections from the faithful were used for the glory of God rather than the indulgence of the higher clergy. Most recently, he called a draft Vatican document further eroding the apostolic tradition a "toxic nightmare". He was never one to mince his words....
>
> He was made a scapegoat for the Church itself. He should never have been investigated in the absence of a complaint. He should never have been charged in the absence of corroborating evidence. And he should never have been convicted in the absence of a plausible case – as the High Court so resoundingly made plain.

At this moment, the congregation engaged in loud and long spontaneous applause – driven not so much by the invited guests but from the rank-and-file in the pews and outside. Many were Catholics, some were not. All felt a sense of injustice about what the usually mild and considered Fr Frank Brennan S.J. was to call in his article in the July-August 2023 edition *Quadrant* (titled "Cardinal Pell at the Hands of the Victorian Justice System") as "nothing more than an appalling police sting operation protracted by grossly erroneous judicial reasoning by Victoria's two most senior judges".

Then, towards the end of his speech, Abbott brought spontaneous laughter from the congregation when he said:

> ...the presence of so many here, from all walks and stations of

> life; many, not Catholic; some, not Christian; a few, without any religious faith at all, is an overdue tribute; and perhaps an admission that we should strive to do right in death, to those who've been wronged in life.
>
> His greatest triumph, in fact, was not to have held the highest ecclesiastical offices of any Australian; but to have kept his faith, in circumstances which must have screamed: "My God, my God, why hast thou forsaken me". Not to succumb to anger, self-pity or despair – when almost any other human would – and instead to have accepted this modern day crucifixion, walking humbly in the footsteps of Our Lord; that's the heroic virtue that makes him, to my mind, a saint for our times. And as I heard the chant [of the demonstrators] "Cardinal Pell should go to Hell", I thought: "Ah ha!, at least they now believe in the afterlife!" Perhaps this is St George Pell's first miracle.

A good joke, to be sure. But one that Archbishop Fisher felt the need to qualify – who told the congregation that he could hear the cardinal's message coming through his coffin – and it said: "No canonisations."

After Archbishop Fisher delivered The Prayer of Commendation, the coffin and procession left the Cathedral for The Rite of Committal which took place in St Mary's crypt. As Cardinal Pell's mortal remains were carried down the main aisle – once again, there was spontaneous applause which continued outside the Cathedral.

Due to limited space, Cardinal Pell's burial in the crypt under St Mary's Cathedral was a small affair for his family, close friends and clergy. *The Catholic Weekly* columnist Monica Doumit was there and she wrote about the occasion on 12 February 2023:

> There was the procession of the casket down to the crypt for final burial, with the jeers of a small crowd of protestors desirous to hound him literally to the grave overwhelmed by the sound of *Ave Maria* being sung by those in the forecourt. While one, faithful priest was lowered into the ground, 300 more belted the *Salve Regina* at the top of their lungs....

Earlier, Doumit commented on the occasion:

> Let's start with the planned protest organised by Community Action for Rainbow Rights. For all the publicity given by the media, it

attracted maybe 200 or 300 people. There were definitely fewer of them than the 375 bishops, priests and seminarians in attendance, whose procession into St Mary's Cathedral alone took much longer than the protest march through Hyde Park.

Then there were the thousands who showed up (official estimates put the crowd at 6,000 people). This was the biggest Mass Australia has seen since World Youth Day 2008, and it was held mid-morning on a work and school day. They came to the Cathedral and stayed, despite knowing that they would have to stand outside in scorching temperatures and could much more easily watched the whole thing from home....

Two former prime ministers attended Pell's funeral – John Howard and Tony Abbott. Of contemporary political leaders there was but one – Peter Dutton, the leader of the Liberal Party in opposition at the federal level. Prime Minister Anthony Albanese, who was brought up a Catholic and attended St Mary's Cathedral School, was represented by Senator Don Farrell, the deputy leader of the Albanese government in the Senate. The NSW State election was scheduled for Saturday 25 March 2023. The (then) Catholic premier Dominic Perrottet and (then) Labor opposition leader Chris Minns – both practising Catholics – did not attend and were represented by others. Writing in *The Australian* on 8 February 2023, Paul Kelly – one of Australia's most experienced journalists – reflected:

> The Pontifical Mass for Cardinal George Pell – a religious event and a public event – was a funeral ritual, a celebration of Catholic resilience but testimony to the now deeply fractured relations between secular power and the Catholic Church. The church's celebration of Pell's life was a magnificent event yet evidence of a diminished nation, its culture fragmented and its current secular leaders hiding in fear, unable to pay respects to the life of George Pell, who attained the most senior position in the Catholic hierarchy of any Australian.

Kelly went on to write that the secular reaction to Pell's death was driven by "politicians terrified of offering respect despite Pell being the target of the greatest miscarriage of justice in Australia since World War II and adverse findings by a royal commission that he knew of sexual abuse crimes, the finding relying on inference not evidence (there was none)".

For his part, Greg Craven looked at Pell's influence on the Catholic Church in an article in *The Australian* on 17 January 2023:

> One of the most interesting things about the death of the cardinal was the identity of those interviewed in the media. Of course, the ABC went to reliable purveyors of doom such as cemented critic of Catholics, David Marr, or the sad, scarpered ex-priest Paul Collins. But two things were noticeable when the "ordinary" laity were interviewed. First, they were overwhelmingly Pell-positive. Second, they did not have Irish names like Collins or Craven. The immediate origins of these on-the-ground Catholics were The Philippines, Vietnam, Latin America, the Middle East… They were determined and articulate. Most of all, they were young, hopeful and, in Catholic terms, orthodox.

When Pell first became a bishop, the Catholic Church in Australia was primarily Anglo-Celtic with an Italian/Polish influence. By the time he died, it was very much a multicultural church with respect to practising Catholics – as was evident in the attendance at the Pontifical Mass of Christian Burial on 2 February.

Peter McClellan and Michael Rowland Verbal a Dead Man

The unanimous decision of the High Court to quash Cardinal Pell's convictions for historical child sexual abuse had the effect of blunting the allegations by Pell-antagonists that he was a pedophile. Such claims did not disappear – but they were muted.

This remained the case after Pell's death. Most participants in the continuing Pell pile-on focused instead on the findings of the Royal Commission to attack the deceased cardinal. None conceded that the Royal Commission produced no evidence to support its findings or conceded that Peter McClellan KC produced a report which was seriously flawed with respect to Pell.

McClellan's ongoing antagonism towards Pell was evident when he wrote the foreword to the book written by Chrissie Foster – with the ABC's Paul Kennedy – titled *Still Standing: A Mother's Fight* to *Bring the Catholic Church to Justice* (Viking), 2023. This book came out on 2 May 2023 – close to four months after Pell's death. In his foreword, McClellan wrote:

> The history of the sexual abuse of children within the Catholic institutions is one of devastating criminal offending by individuals and catastrophic mismanagement by Church leadership. Cardinal George Pell, the most senior Australian Catholic of his generation and for some years the Director of the Aquinas Campus of the Institute of Catholic Education, and other senior clerics gave evidence to the Royal Commission to the effect that the Church did not understand that the rape of a child was a crime, seeing it as a "moral failing". I remain unable to comprehend how any person, much less one with qualifications in theology, could consider the rape of a child to be a mere moral failure and not a crime.

This damaging statement with respect to Pell is not true – as McClellan would have known if he had checked the documents of the royal commission which he headed.

On 24 February 2014, Pell filed a 28-page long witness statement with the Royal Commission consisting of 173 paragraphs. Paragraphs 13 and 14 contained the following comments:

> I have apologised a number of times for these terrible crimes and I apologise to the victims again with all my heart....The crimes that were committed....by priests and others in the community should never have occurred. The Catholic community should be one of the safest places for children and young people and it is a completely unacceptable failure whenever a child has been hurt by a sexual predator in the church. There is always more to be done and better ways of doing things. I am serious about preventing crimes and our efforts have already had a good measure of success.

On 24 March 2014, Pell gave evidence to the Royal Commission where the following exchange took place:

> *Gail Furness SC:* At paragraph 16 of your statement, you refer to having been regularly involved as the bishops of Australia worked to deal with "this scandal, these crimes". Do you see that in paragraph 16?
>
> *George Pell:* Yes.

> *Gail Furness SC:* By "this scandal, these crimes", are you referring to sexual abuse of children by clergy?
>
> *George Pell:* Clergy and teachers and Catholic personnel.

There are some other exchanges between Furness and Pell of a similar kind.

Chrissie Foster appeared on the TV *News Breakfast* program on 4 May 2023 to promote her book. She was interviewed by Pell-antagonist Michael Rowland. Let's go to the transcript:

> *Michael Rowland:* Peter McClellan, who of course chaired the Royal Commission [into Institutional Responses to Child Sexual Abuse], has written a lovely foreword to the book. And he says, he writes in particular about George Pell – and other senior Catholics – giving evidence to the fact that they saw the rape of a child as a moral failing, not a crime. And Peter McClellan writes how he still can't get his head around that – and lots of people still can't, right?
>
> *Chrissie Foster:* And I can't either....

Rowland, like many journalists in the Pell pile-on, simply believed what McClellan wrote – without fact-checking. But the error was McClellan's. He seriously damaged the reputation of a man who was dead and, obviously, could not defend himself by seeking a correction or initiating legal proceedings.

The Royal Commission's Failure to Inquire into Government Schools leads to new Inquiries in Tasmania, Victoria and NSW

In Chapter 9, reference is made to the fact that the Royal Commission did not inquire into the institutional responses concerning child sexual abuse in government schools – sometimes referred to as state schools. Attention was drawn to the fact that the Tasmanian Department of Education had moved known pedophile teachers from school to school from the early 1950s until the 1990s.

On 26 September 2023, the Tasmanian government released the report of the Commission of Inquiry into the Tasmanian Government's

Responses to Child Sexual Abuse in Institutional Settings which was established in March 2021 and headed by a former senior judge, The Hon. Marcia Neave. This focused on historical child sexual abuse in such government institutions as the Launceston General Hospital and Ashley Youth Detention Centre – but included some state schools. In June 2021, before Neave's report, there was the Independent Inquiry into the Tasmanian Department of Education's Responses into Child Sexual Abuse – it was headed by Professor Stephen Smallbone and Professor Tim McCormack. The Smallbone/McCormack report, released on 7 June 2021, was highly critical of the Tasmanian Department of Education.

Both reports, inter alia, covered the case of government school teacher Darrel George Harington who was moved from school to school by the Tasmanian Department of Education for many years. In 2015, Harington pleaded guilty to multiple charges of historical child sexual abuse with respect to several victims. The McClellan Royal Commission commenced operations in early 2014. One of Harington's victims informed the Neave inquiry that he had told his story to the Royal Commission. Nothing happened.

McClellan's Royal Commission did two Case Studies covering Tasmania – one on The Hutchins School (which has connections with the Anglican Church) and the other on the Church of England's Boys' Society. The McClellan Royal Commission did not do a case study into any government institution in Tasmania. It was much the same in Victoria and NSW.

On 21 September 2022, Stuart Grimley, then a Derryn Hinch's Justice Party member of the Victorian Legislative Council, moved a motion calling on the Andrews government to investigate child sexual abuse in Victorian state schools. In his speech, Grimley said that the Royal Commission headed by McClellan "did not properly investigate abuse in government institutions".

On 4 February 2023, Daniel Andrews said that he would formally apologise on behalf of the Victorian Government to all survivors of institutional sexual abuse – including those in government schools.

But he resigned as premier and as a politician on 27 September 2023, before doing so.

On 28 June 2023, the Andrews government announced the establishment of a Board of inquiry into Historical Child Sexual Abuse at Beaumaris Primary School (in Melbourne) to be headed by Kathleen Foley SC. The inquiry was specifically charged with investigating the Victorian Department of Education during the 1960s and 1970s in relation to historical child sexual abuse at Beaumaris Primary School at the time. The inquiry was announced after a two year campaign by complainants with respect to four male teachers at the school. It was initially extended to cover a further 18 schools and then to an additional six schools where the teachers were employed. Even so, the terms of reference remain very narrow.

On 2 August 2023 the *Herald Sun* in Melbourne reported that former students of some 70 state schools are pursuing historical child sexual abuse claims against the Victorian Government.

On 9 September 2023, *The Weekend Australian* published an article by McClellan titled "Commission did investigate abuse in state schools". It was a response to my *Weekend Australian* columns of 29 July and 2 September 2023 which were critical of the Royal Commission for ignoring government schools. He had this to say:

> Henderson writes of the Royal Commission did not hold one "case study" into a government school, which he described as a "grievous error of omission". He is not correct. The royal commission was aware of the potential for criticism if it did not hold a case study into any state school but it did not receive allegations that would have justified the cost of a public hearing into a state school. However, as the final report records, the royal commission did examine three NSW public schools in a case study.

In Case Study 45, the Royal Commission referred to private hearings into three NSW government schools. However, in all three instances the Royal Commission's focus was on sexual behaviour between children and other children – and how this was handled by the NSW Department of Education. There was no investigation into reported acts of pedophilia by principals and/or teachers in NSW.

In any event, this investigation took up just six pages of Case Study 45's 100 pages – the rest was devoted to three Christian Schools. I emailed (as well as posted) a letter to Mr McClellan on 13 September concerning his article. There was no response.[25]

On 13 September 2023, I received an email from a retired senior schoolteacher in regional Victoria who gave me a name and phone contact. Let's call him XY. XY contested McClellan's claim in *The Weekend Australian* that the Royal Commission "did not receive allegations that would have justified the cost of a public hearing into a state school".

XY advised the Royal Commission of child sexual abuse that had occurred when he was a senior teacher in a Victorian regional government primary school. The abuse was covered up and the offender was moved to a school in Melbourne. There the abuse continued. Eventually the teacher was convicted. The case was reported on page one of the *Herald Sun* in Melbourne on 31 March 1997 – that is more than a decade before the Royal Commission commenced operations.

It turned out that XY was invited by the Royal Commission to attend a hearing in Melbourne. It paid travel costs and one night's accommodation – and he met at least one of the commissioners, whom he named. In time, XY received a pro-forma thank you signed by McClellan, which I have seen. But nothing happened. As with Tasmania, no case studies were done into the institutional responses by the Victorian Education Department with respect to the schools where the convicted pedophile had taught.[26]

The same is true of NSW. In July 2018, NSW Police established Strike Force Southwood to identify and investigate allegations of sexual assaults and student/teacher relationships at government schools on Sydney's Northern Beaches in the 1970s and 1980s. The inquiry includes Cromer High School, where Chris Dawson once taught. In 2023, Dawson was convicted of murdering his wife and, later, of unlawful sexual activity with a female student. It is understood that Strike Force Southwood is currently investigating some 20 former teachers at three government secondary schools in this small area of NSW.

It appears that the Royal Commission did not inquire with any State or Territory education department as to whether they had any files on principals/teachers who may have sexually abused students.

Clearly, when it came to investigating institutional responses into child sexual abuse in government schools – the Royal Commission, headed by Peter McClellan KC, was not fit for purpose.[27]

How Pell-Antagonists Refused to Report or Review Books which Discredited the Media Pile-On.

The publication of this book was greeted with derision by some – even before it was published or read. In a post on 25 November 2021, Lucie Morris-Marr declared: "Apparently Gerard Henderson is releasing a book about the media 'pile-on' and will go to town about myself and others…Bring it on."

The following day, Amanda Meade – *The Guardian Australia's* media editor – sneered about the forthcoming publication and its publisher. Her comments included: "No, it's not on his favourite topic the ABC, but it is all about how the ABC covered his friend Cardinal George Pell. Henderson has been a fierce critic of ABC journalist, Louise Milligan, whose book *Cardinal* won the Walkley book award."

Chapter 6 of this book (which was published in December 2021) contains the list of some 120 journalists and commentators who took part in the Pell pile-on. The list includes *The New Daily's* Lucie Morris-Marr and *The Guardian Australia's* Melissa Davey and David Marr. Not one of this trio provided any criticism of the book when published – not even Morris-Marr whose "bring it on" challenge faded to naught – and both *The New Daily* and *The Guardian Australia* ignored the book.

Indeed, the leading institutions in the Pell pile-on effectively "cancelled" the work. It was not even mentioned – let alone reviewed – on the ABC or in *The Age, Sydney Morning Herald,*

Guardian Australia, The Saturday Paper, The New Daily and more besides.

A similar fate befell Fr Frank Brennan's *Observations on the Pell Proceedings* (Connor Court, 2021) and Keith Windschuttle's *The Persecution of George Pell* (Quadrant Books, 2020). Brennan is a well-regarded author and commentator. Windschuttle's work was highly praised by Gavin Silbert KC – in spite of the fact that Silbert was critical of some material on the case published in *Quadrant* which is edited by Windschuttle. See Appendix 2.

The Persecution of George Pell was the first of three books on the Pell Case published after the High Court decision. Windschuttle received one ABC interview – by Andrew West on Radio National's *The Religion and Ethics Report* on 17 February 2021 - following which there were many complaints from middle level ABC management, ABC journalists and listeners along with the baying anti-Pell mob on social media. After that, all discussion on the Pell Case on the taxpayer funded public broadcaster stopped. Windschuttle did not receive any more interviews – and Frank Brennan and myself scored ducks (in cricket terminology).

At the time, I took up the matter with David Anderson, the ABC's managing director and editor-in-chief. He did not respond. I spoke to three ABC contacts about the matter in mid-2023 – over a year after my book was published. These were the responses:

• One senior ABC journalist said to me that the book was great but added that it was not possible to interview me about it due to what would be strong opposition from ABC staff and ABC management along with ABC listeners and viewers.

• Another high-profile ABC journalist texted me that the unwillingness of the ABC to discuss books on the Pell Case by Frank Brennan and myself was of concern – but added the situation was "tricky". It was not clear why a discussion on considered and documented books on the Pell Case after the High Court's unanimous decision should be "tricky". I was told that the issue was being worked-on. But nothing happened.

- And a third well-known ABC presenter said that it was not clear how a discussion on my book could be fitted into his radio program. When I asked the presenter whether this also applied to the two ABC television channels, as well as some 60 ABC radio stations, there was no reply.

Over the years, Frank Brennan has appeared regularly on the taxpayer funded public broadcaster – with special interest in his views on Indigenous issues. But even he could not score an ABC interview on his *Observations on the Pell Proceedings* which has run to two editions.

Among the 120 people named by me as part of the Pell media pile-on, some 40 were ABC journalists – led by Louise Milligan and Sarah Ferguson. But not one of the "ABC 40" told me that anything in the book was factually incorrect or even exaggerated.

This avoidance of public debate and discussion about one of the most important criminal law cases in Australian history – especially on the ABC and in Nine newspapers and *The Guardian Australia* – was mere intellectual cowardice.

A Note on the Victorian Legal System

As documented in Chapter 10, at one time in 2014 Victoria Police hoped that the allegations against Cardinal Pell would help to divert attention – for a while at least – from its Lawyer X scandal.

The engagement of defence lawyer Nicola Gobbo to inform on some of her criminal clients to Victoria Police ran counter to the legal principle that everyone is entitled to a fair trial in which it is up to the prosecution to establish its case in the criminal jurisdiction beyond reasonable doubt. The actions of Victoria Police in this instance were effectively condemned by the High Court in a unanimous judgment on 5 November 2018. See Chapter 10.

Writing in *The Australian* on 22 June 2023, Damon Johnston reported how Victoria Police spent millions of dollars of taxpayers' money to prevent Victorians from finding out about the Lawyer X scandal until the High Court's decision to end the media embargo. Johnston was editor of the *Herald Sun* newspaper at the time.

Eventually, the Andrews Labor government set up a royal commission headed by former Queensland judge Margaret McMurdo to look into the matter. It recommended the establishment of an Office of the Special Investigator (OSI) to examine whether there was sufficient evidence to prove that offences had been committed by Gobbo and/or by current or former police.

Geoffrey Nettle KC, a former High Court justice who reached compulsory retirement age in November 2020, was appointed to this position. Under the legislation covering the OSI, Nettle was prevented from filing a charge concerning alleged offences – unless this was agreed by the Victorian Director of Public Prosecutions, Kerri Judd KC.

On 20 June 2023, Nettle wrote to the clerks of the Victorian Legislative Council and Legislative Assembly advising that he considered it "pointless" for the OSI to continue and that it should be wound up. He said there was sufficient evidence to lay charges against several individuals. However, Nettle's recommendations had been overruled by Kerri Judd KC, the Victorian DPP. Shortly after, the OSI was closed.

And so it came to pass that one of the greatest scandals in Australian criminal law has come to naught. As Johnston wrote, "it's difficult not to conclude that the cover-up [by Victoria Police] has worked for police".

Nettle is widely regarded as one of the finest legal minds in Australia. Yet his view on the need to lay charges was finally dismissed in condescending correspondence by Judd dated 26 May, 2023. In this letter, Judd went to the extent of suggesting that Nettle might have been proposing what amounted to "an abuse of process" in this instance. This led to an emphatic repudiation by Nettle in correspondence dated 29 May 2023. He told Judd that the strength of her arguments "do not improve with repetition".

In a letter to Nettle dated 16 March 2023, Judd had written that there was no reasonable prospect of conviction due to the shortage of evidence. This despite the fact the OSI submission ran for some 5,000 pages.

Writing to Nettle on 26 March 2023, Judd claimed the "passage of time … would have to be taken into account in determining whether it is in the public interest to proceed with a prosecution". In fact, the passage of time was longer in the Pell case than with respect to the Lawyer X matter. As pointed out earlier, Judd declined to take into account the passage of time between alleged crimes and trial dates when continuing the prosecution against Pell in 2018 for crimes allegedly committed in 1996/97.

In an article in the *Herald-Sun* on 26 June 2023, the Victorian State political editor Shannon Deery quoted someone whom he described as a seasoned Melbourne legal expert as saying: "The complete lack of judgment and objectivity down at the OPP gets plainer each week."

For his part, the then premier Daniel Andrews publicly sided with Kerri Judd. This stands in contrast with Andrews' decision to effectively criticise the High Court's unanimous judgment in *George Pell v The Queen*. Both were instances of an improper intervention by a political leader in a legal matter.

In the state of Victoria, there appears to be one law for Victoria Police and another for the late Cardinal George Pell and some others.

The Last Word

My last personal discussion with George Pell took place in north west Sydney on 19 June 2022 at a small conference of Catholic priests. He gave the first talk and I delivered the second. After the lunch, Monica Doumit spoke.

Pell's address was on the state of contemporary Catholicism in Australia and elsewhere – it was similar to his last address in Australia at the NSW Parliament House. Except that he spoke without reference to politics and without humour. Following the talk, there was a question/discussion period during which the cardinal treated his priestly audience as equals.

I was to follow-up with a talk called "The Media and the Pell Case". Over coffee, following his talk, Pell said to me that he might not attend my address – but did not give a reason. I responded that it did not matter to me whether he was there or not. In the event, he sat towards the back of the room.

In the discussion period, I was asked a direct question – and gave a direct answer. One of the priests wanted to know what I thought about the Cardinal's 405 day incarceration for crimes which he did not commit. My reply was along the lines: "Well, I wouldn't want to serve 405 days in effective solitary confinement when I knew I was innocent. Prison is harsh enough for the guilty, let alone the innocent. However, I believe it was for the best that he suffered in this way. For, without an emphatic quashing of the convictions by all seven High Court judges in a single judgment, he [Cardinal Pell] would never have been able to claim full vindication."

The point here is that, as Justice Mark Weinberg said in his Victorian Court of Appeal dissent, juries do not have to give reasons for decisions – judges do. It was only when the case against Pell by Victoria Police and the Victorian Director of Public Prosecutions was fully revealed that it became evident that George Pell had been wrongly convicted and that he should never have been charged, so weak was the evidence.

Pell's innocence is evident in the detailed reasons provided by Justice Weinberg and all seven judges of the High Court of Australia. Put simply, Pell could not have been at the scene of the crimes – and nor could have his alleged victims.

After the morning session, I was allocated a seat at the luncheon table next to Pell. We were joined by a couple of young priests. Early on, there was a conversation – which went something like this:

Gerard Henderson: George, I hope you didn't mind what I said at the talk about the "upside" of you serving over a year in prison. But I was asked a question – and I gave my honest opinion.

George Pell: No, Gerard. It didn't bother me at all. Indeed, I have been thinking much the same recently. What's more, if I had never served time, I would not have written my *Prison Journal* – and I'm very glad I did that.[28]

* * * *

Pope Francis prays at Cardinal Pell's coffin – St Peter's Basilica, Rome, 14 January 2023. Despite their theological differences, Francis described George Pell as "a great guy, great". Vincenzo Pinto via Getty Images.

Pope Francis blesses Cardinal Pell's coffin with holy water at the end of his Requiem Mass at St Peter's Basilica, Rome – 14 January 2023. Vatican Media.

The procession enters the Solemn Pontifical Mass of Christian Burial, St Mary's Cathedral Sydney, 2 February 2023. The principal celebrant was the Most Reverend Anthony Fisher OP, Archbishop of Sydney. Image by Giovanni Portelli

Part of the large crowd following Cardinal Pell's Requiem Mass outside St Mary's Cathedral in the hot Sydney sun – 2 February 2023. Image by Giovanni Portelli.

Cardinal Pell's coffin is lowered into the crypt in the presence of family members (from left) Julie Pell, Nicholas Pell, Sarah Pell, Judy Pell and David Pell. Georgina Pell is not in the photo. Image by Giovanni Portelli.

Charles Firth and Lachlan Hodson, who in Barry Humphries' phrase identify as comedians, undertake a little noticed stunt as part of The Chaser team on the eve of Cardinal Pell's funeral. The joke was that they were burying the evidence against Pell found by the McClellan Royal Commission. In fact, the Royal Commission produced no forensic, documentary or witness evidence to support its hostile findings with respect to Cardinal Pell.
See Chapter 9.

Young and not-so-young comedians at the book launch: Paige Hally and the late Barry Humphries.

Margaret Cunneen SC launched *Cardinal Pell, The Media Pile-On & Collective Guilty* with some encouragement from Barry Humphries at Australian Catholic University North Sydney – 7 December 2021.

APPENDIX 1

THE QUESTIONS ABOUT *CARDINAL: THE RISE AND FALL OF GEORGE PELL* WHICH LOUISE MILLIGAN DECLINED TO ANSWER

Writing in *The Australian* on 16 April 2020, columnist Greg Sheridan made the following comment:

> Louise Milligan, an ABC journalist, wrote a book damning Pell. It...was based in part on allegations now dismissed in court. Yet she was used on the ABC as though she were an impartial reporter. Even worse, because she was an ABC employee, the ABC itself never hosted a serious critical evaluation of the book.
>
> Gerard Henderson wrote powerful critiques of Milligan's book, saying there were factual errors and asking her how much investigation she did before accepting allegations as fact, and how she could reconstruct, verbatim, decades-old conversations from one-sided sources.
>
> If the ABC was behaving professionally, it would have invited Henderson on to make his critique there. But the ABC is a herd of independent minds. They never seriously disagree and never criticise each other by name, though they criticise everyone else by name. Milligan's book was never searchingly critiqued on the ABC. Given the massive power of the ABC, this is an abuse of power.

Set out below is the email Gerard Henderson sent to Louise Milligan on 30 May 2017. As discussed in Chapter 7, the author declined to answer the letter but handed it on to her publisher Louise Adler at Melbourne University Press – who also declined to address any of the questions asked of her best-selling author. Note that *Cardinal* won numerous media awards including the Walkley Book Award and the Gold Quill for 2017 and was admired by such leading journalists as Annabel Crabb, David Marr, Peter FitzSimons, Kate McClymont and Quentin Dempster. The only changes to the letter are corrections to the numbering of the questions.

Gerard Henderson to Louise Milligan – 30 May 2017

Louise

I have recently completed reading your *Cardinal: The Rise and Fall of George Pell* (Melbourne University Press, 2017).

By the way, there are several references in your book to the (then) Bishop Pell walking Gerald Ridsdale to court at Warrnambool in 1993. As a simple *Google* test will reveal, this Ridsdale case was heard at the Melbourne Magistrates' Court in 1993.

* * * * *

I note that it has always been journalistic practice to send "a list of questions" to people on whom you intend to write about.

I intend to write about *Cardinal* in my *Media Watch Dog* blog shortly. Consequently, I have set out below a list of questions concerning your book. They are as follows:

1. At Page 4, you refer to the allegations concerning (then) Archbishop Pell's alleged sexual assault of a choir boy at St Patrick's Cathedral sometime between 1996 and 2001 as "George Pell's ugly secret". How is this statement consistent with your comments, following the publication of your book, that Cardinal Pell is entitled to the presumption of innocence? Also what is the justification for writing at Page 227 that some of Pell's accusers "will" be cross-examined by the Cardinal's Queen's Counsel? – since he has not been charged.

2. In view of the serious allegations in *Cardinal* – and to the fact that you acknowledged on the ABC TV *News Breakfast* program on 17 May 2017 that your book is written "from of the complainants' point of view"– what is your policy about anonymous sources?

For example, *Cardinal* contains references to "one senior member of a religious order" (Pg. 20), "another Royal Commission source" (Pg. 41), "one of the most senior priests on the Curia of the Melbourne

Archdiocese at the time" (Pg. 51), "one Church official" (Pg. 88), "officials in the church" (Pg. 281), "a friend...who is a mother in the neighbourhood" (Pg. 290), "someone who works around the Royal Commission" (Pg. 297), "the father-in-law of an ABC journalist (Pg. 313), "people who knew [George Pell] in his Ballarat days" (Pg. 329) – and more besides – plus the occasional "many". The allegations at Pages 88 and 281 – which go to George Pell's character – are most damaging. But they are unsourced.

In view of the serious allegations in your book, do you believe that it is professional to allow anonymous individuals – none of whom claim to be victims – a chance to condemn George Pell in such a way that a reader has no chance of judging their credibility or motives?

3. What is your position on memory? At Page 101 – when rationalising an inaccurate description of George Pell by one of his accusers – you write: "Memory does strange things when it comes to visual descriptions of people". Yet, elsewhere in *Cardinal*, you accept as accurate the recollections of individuals who have seen George Pell on television in recent times and claim that this is the person they came across 30 to 40 years previously.

4. What is your position on the use of direct quotation marks? At Page 47, you place in direct quotes the recollection of a critic of Cardinal Pell who relates – word for word – a conversation which Pell had with her cousin. This despite the fact that (i) the alleged conversation took place over two decades ago, (ii) the woman concedes to being in the room next door to where the conversation took place and (iii) Pell was (allegedly) determined that the person could not hear what he said to her cousin. This would be uncharacteristic behaviour – in view of the fact that you maintain Pell has a "steel-trap mind" and would be unlikely to speak so loudly that he could be heard between rooms while (allegedly) attempting to have a secret conversation.

Likewise in Chapter 6 – on the basis of hearsay upon hearsay – how do you construct the precise words that (then) Fr Pell used some three decades ago? Is this professional journalism?

5. What is your attitude to time? At Pages 129-130 you write that Cardinal Pell was fit enough to turn up at an event in Ballarat "just before he gave video link evidence" from Rome to the Royal Commission on account of not being medically fit to travel to Australia. Cardinal Pell was in Ballarat in March 2015 and he was due to give evidence to the Royal Commission in December 2015 – nine months later.

This is an important point – since you imply that George Pell suddenly developed a heart condition which prevented him from flying from Rome to Australia for hearings of the Royal Commission. So, do you believe it accurate to state that March 2015 is "just before" December 2015 – and insufficient time for a 73 year old man, who already had experienced two heart attacks, to suffer a further deterioration in health?

6. What is your evidence that the Catholic Church could afford to splash around $20,000 a day on Allan Myers QC as legal counsel before the Royal Commission for Cardinal Pell? (Pg. 131). Were you told this by the Catholic Church and/or Mr Myers? Or did you just make this up?

7. In view of your sustained criticism of the (then) Bishop Pell's handling of Fr Peter Searson in Melbourne when he (Pell) was an auxiliary bishop – why did you fail to mention that, when he became Archbishop of Melbourne, George Pell sacked Searson and refused to abide by a Vatican decision that he be re-instated? (Pg. 260). Was this a deliberate omission or did you forget this fact – which was not challenged before the Royal Commission?

8. In dealing with the decision of former Judge Alan Southwell QC's finding that Phillip Scott's complaint – with respect to an alleged assault in 1961 – against (then) Archbishop Pell was not upheld, you write:

> So in the end, the character assassination of Scott was successful – it achieved its aim – to keep Pell as Archbishop of Sydney. (Page 103)

The clear imputation is that Judge Southwell's decision was affected by the (alleged) character assassination of Mr Scott which occurred outside the hearing. What evidence do you have that there was any causal relationship between the alleged character assassination of Mr Scott in the media – and Judge Southwell's decision? Do you believe that Judge Southwell would have been so unprofessional to allow media reports to influence his finding? If so, what is your evidence for this assertion?

9. On Page 19 you write that George Pell "infamously shared the [Ballarat East] presbytery with [Gerald] Ridsdale for a year." At Page 142 you (incorrectly) state that Gerald Ridsdale shared a presbytery for a year with Paul Bongiorno in Ballarat East. It was, in fact, Warrnambool where Ridsdale and Bongiorno shared accommodation – as the evidence before the Royal Commission makes clear. Why is (then) Fr Pell's accommodation with Ridsdale "infamous" – but not (then) Fr. Bongiorno's accommodation with Ridsdale?

10. On Page 15 you write that "one seminarian in Pell's year **seems to remember** Pell and [Anthony Salvatore] Bongiorno going on holiday together one summer". **(Emphasis added).** Do you maintain that what an anonymous source "seems to remember" warrants quoting in what is presented as a serious book of contemporary history?

11. Do you believe that such words as "if" and "perhaps" are warranted in what is presented as a professional work by one of the ABC's leading investigative reporters?

* * * * *

It would be appreciated if you could reply to the above questions before the close of business on Thursday 1 June 2017.

Gerard Henderson

APPENDIX 2

GAVIN SILBERT Q.C. ON CARDINAL PELL AS "AN INNOCENT MAN"

As discussed in Chapter 11, Gerard Henderson wrote to former Victorian Chief Crown Prosecutor Gavin Silbert Q.C. concerning an article he had written about the Pell Case in the *Victorian Bar News*. The full correspondence is published below:

Gerard Henderson to Gavin Silbert QC – 23 February 2021

Dear Mr Silbert

I read with interest your article "Pell v The Queen" in the *Victorian Bar News* Issue 168.

I assume that someone has drawn your attention to the typo in the second paragraph. It states that "A had not made his first complaint [against Cardinal George Pell] until 2005…". This should read 2015.

On another matter. I was surprised by your claim that the media coverage of the Pell Case was "entirely uninformed". This comment apparently relates only to those journalists who believed that Pell should not have been convicted. And not to those who, like Louise Milligan, believed that he was guilty as charged. Moreover, you make no reference to whether the substantial hostility to Pell in the media brought about a situation where he could not receive a fair trial.

Two of the main critics of the Cardinal George Pell's prosecution from the beginning to end were Fr Frank Brennan SJ and Professor Greg Craven. Their arguments were consistent with the subsequent dissent of Justice Mark Weinberg in the Victorian Court of Appeal and with all seven judges in the High Court of Australia.

Fr Brennan and Professor Craven have legal qualifications and neither has referred to "A"(or "J" as he was referred to in the County Court) as "a liar". Consequently they cannot be said to have engaged in the "gutter journalism" to which you refer in your article – without naming names.

I was also interested in this comment in that part of your article where you defend the actions of Victoria Police and the Victorian Director of Public Prosecutions in the charging and prosecution of Pell:

> An examination of the critiques serves little purpose at this time.... The Director of Public Prosecutions was accused of failing to exercise proper prosecutorial discretion prior to indicting; the verdicts confirm that the reasonable prospects of conviction test was satisfied.

As you will be aware, Cardinal Pell was originally charged with 26 offences with respect to nine complainants. All were withdrawn before the Magistrates' Court, or struck out by the Magistrate, or effectively ruled out by the County Court (when it disallowed the tendency evidence) before being dropped by the DPP or quashed by the High Court.

This would suggest that the Victorian DPP's case against Pell warrants some form of critique since few prosecutions have such a failure rate – but you seem to hold a different view.

I assume that you are the same Gavin Silbert QC who was interviewed by Louise Milligan for her book *Witness* (Hachette Australia, 2020) where the following comment appears:

> Gavin Silbert SC, then [i.e. in 2017] the Senior Crown Prosecutor, sent the Pell brief back to the police, to tell them they could charge if they wished.
>
> "The allegations of the complainant, if accepted by a jury, were sufficient," Silbert much later told me in an interview for this book. "I didn't have to form a judgement on whether it would be accepted by a jury – just, taking it at its highest, and assuming they were accepted, they were sufficient."
>
> Silbert also believes that "Witness, J", the choirboy complainant against Pell, was a very compelling witness. "I thought so," he said, "I mean, the jury accepted him at the end of the day."

I note here that in explaining the decision to advise Victoria Police that they could charge Cardinal Pell if it wished – reference is made only to the five charges concerning the complainant "J" which include four charges concerning the deceased "R".

They amounted to 5 out of 26 charges laid by Victoria Police. Do you still hold the view that, the Senior Crown Prosecutor acted correctly in advising Victoria Police that it could lay charges with respect to all 26 charges? Or just the five that made it to the mistrial and the trial?

For example, as you will be aware, Magistrate Belinda Wallington ruled out Charges 7 to 14 as "not of sufficient weight for a jury to convict". The same was the case with Charge 15. Magistrate Wallington set a high bar indeed for not putting charges to a jury – namely that "the credibility of a witness is effectively destroyed". Clearly the Magistrate was not impressed by the evidence of the complaints with respect to these charges. This matter is not referred to in the *Victorian Bar News* article.

On another matter, Ms Milligan reports Gavin Silbert as believing "that 'Witness J', the choirboy complainant against Pell, was a very compelling witness". Somewhere between two and ten jurors in the first trial did not hold this view. Likewise Justice Weinberg in the Victoria Court of Appeal – who, like the jurors in both trials, saw J's evidence via video link. Likewise all seven judges of the High Court of Australia. [Author's note: This final sentence is incorrect – the High Court did not view the video.]

As you will be aware, in *Pell v The Queen* the High Court warned against putting weight on the demeanour of a witness – as had the High Court in the civil case of *Fox v Percy* in 1983 – the majority comprised Gleeson C.J, Kirby J. and Gummow J.

I am planning to write about the Pell Case in the future. The purpose of this note is to offer you the opportunity to respond to my comments if you so wish.

Yours sincerely

PS: I have a humble LL.B and I have never described J as a "liar". I believe that some individuals have clear "recollections" of events that never happened, and I am well aware of the fallibility of memory. You don't have to regard a complainant as a conscious liar to cast doubt on his or her recollections of events. No doubt, you are aware of this. My view on demeanour is consistent with the view of the High Court of Australia.

Gavin Silbert QC to Gerard Henderson – 23 February 2021

Dear Mr Henderson,

Thank you for your email and I am more than happy to speak with you; regrettably I am rather pressed for time at the moment so am not able to give you more than a very brief response.

First, I am aware of the typo in the first paragraph; A's complaint was first made in 2015, an error that was drawn to my attention by Mark Weinberg.

Much of the media coverage was uninformed and I do not restrict that comment to those who believe he should have been convicted. Both Father Brennan and Greg Craven wrote informed pieces but some of the other commentary was lacking in intellectual rigour on " both sides". I thought there was some appalling commentary in *Quadrant*. That said, I have just finished reading *The Persecution of George Pell* by Keith Windschuttle which is as good an analysis as one could hope to find.

We lawyers are used to defending clients and interpret their acquittals as a failure of the prosecution to prove guilt beyond reasonable doubt. I must say, that after reading this I was persuaded that not only was the standard of proof not met, but that Pell was an innocent man.

My comment on the committal was premised on the fact that the first jury convicted and that the matter was not taken away from either jury by the judge; that suggests that the legal test was satisfied.

I am certain that I am the same person interviewed by Louis Milligan for her book *Witness* but I have not read the book and am reluctant to comment. All I would say is that Victoria Police have the sole function of charging in Victoria and their recent practice of attempting to obtain the imprimatur of the DPP and/or Crown Prosecutors is without any legal justification; they have sought to do this of late to protect themselves from criticism particularly in matters of political sensitivity or high public interest. My invariable practice was to tell Victoria Police that it was a matter for them and to refuse to offer any advice.

The fundamental premise of an unsafe and unsatisfactory appeal is that the appeal court should proceed on the basis that if a jury has accepted a witness' evidence, then it should not arrogate to itself the right to disbelieve that evidence but should weigh the totality of evidence to ascertain whether the jury, accepting the complainant's evidence as credible and reliable, should nonetheless have had a reasonable doubt. The High Court proceeded on this entirely conventional basis.

I am very happy to speak with you and regret that I could not give you a more detailed response.

With best wishes,

Gavin Silbert QC

Gerard Henderson to Gavin Silbert QC – 23 February 2021

Dear Mr Silbert

Thanks for your prompt reply to my email of earlier today.

I understand how busy you are and I do not propose to engage you further on this issue. You have covered the matters which I raised – and I am very grateful for this.

Best wishes

Gerard Henderson

* * * * * * *

NOTES

1. In 2012 the Victorian government, led by the Liberal Party premier Ted Baillieu, set up the Inquiry into the *Handling of Child Abuse by Religious and Other Non-Government Organisations* – to be conducted by the Family and Community Development Committee of the Victorian Parliament. Its membership comprised Liberal Party MP Georgie Crozier (chair), Labor Party MP Frank McGuire (deputy chair), Liberal Party MP Andrea Coote, Labor Party MP Bronwyn Halfpenny, National Party MP David O'Brien and Liberal Party MP Nick Wakeling. McGuire, Halfpenny and Wakeling were members of the Legislative Assembly. Crozier, Coote and O'Brien were members of the Legislative Council. The report of the committee, released in November 2013, was titled *Betrayal of Trust*. In this book the entity has been described as the Victorian Parliamentary Inquiry.

2. In early 2002 (over five years after Archbishop Pell had established the Melbourne Response to deal with complaints about Catholic priests, religious and lay workers in the Archdiocese of Melbourne), the *Boston Globe* commenced a series of articles on child sexual abuse in the Catholic Archdiocese of Boston. They were written by the newspaper's Spotlight Team. This work inspired the 2015 film *Spotlight*. Subsequently the *Boston Globe's* investigative staff wrote the book *Betrayal: The Crisis in the Catholic Church – The Findings of the Investigation that Inspired the motion picture Spotlight* (Black Bay Books, 2015).

3. The first complaint against George Pell was made in 2002 by a man who alleged that he had been groped by Pell in 1961 or 1962 on a church camp at Phillip Island when he was 11 or 12 years of age. The complainant was made after a hostile report about the (then) Archbishop of Sydney on the Channel 9 *60 Minutes* program. The allegations about Phillip Island with respect to George Pell are discussed in Chapter 6.

4. In the Victorian jurisdiction (unlike other Australian states) a distinction is made between the Director of Public Prosecutions (a person) and the Office of Public Prosecutions (an organisation). The function of the OPP is essentially to assist in the work of, and carry out work on behalf of, the DPP. In view of this, the term Director of Public Prosecutions or DPP in this book covers the operations of the DPP and OPP – unless indicated otherwise.

5. Fr Frank Brennan S.J. AO, a Jesuit priest and lawyer, is currently rector of Newman College, a residential college at the University of Melbourne. When it was announced that a suppression order had been placed on the reporting of *The Queen v Pell* and that the trial could

not be reported, Brennan met with Pell and suggested that he ask a retired County Court judge to monitor the proceedings. The idea was to bring about a situation where it would be possible to provide accurate information about the case once the proceedings had ended and the suppression order lifted.

Cardinal Pell got back to Fr Brennan and said that his advisers had told him that Brennan was best placed to undertake this task. As Pell put it, Brennan "would go over better with the literati and glitterati". This was a reference to the fact that Brennan is a human rights lawyer. Moreover, he is a theological liberal – not a theological conservative (like Pell).

As Brennan wrote in his *Observations On The Pell Proceedings* (Connor Court, 2021): "By exchange of letters amongst the President and Vice President of the Australian Catholic Bishops Conference and my Jesuit provincial, I was asked 'to offer commentary on the conduct of the (Pell court) proceedings once the suppression orders have been lifted', noting that 'Any commentary needs to be seen, as much as is possible, to be clear, objective and impartial'." Frank Brennan's position with respect to Pell entailed that he had immediate access to the transcripts of evidence given at the trial – except for the testimony of the complainant A (who was referred to as J in the appeal courts).

6   Vivian Waller is a solicitor and principal of Waller Legal. She was formerly an associate with Maurice Blackburn and completed her articles at Slater & Gordon. As Keith Windschuttle documents in *The Prosecution of George Pell*, in 2012 Waller put a submission to the Victorian Parliamentary Inquiry in which she accused Pell of having been present in 1969 when a boy was raped by the notorious pedophile Brother Robert Best at St Alipius Primary School in Ballarat East. Pell was not in Australia in 1969 – he was studying at Oxford University. When the error was pointed out to the Victorian Parliamentary Inquiry by Katrina Lee (then the media director for the Catholic Archdiocese of Sydney) Vivian Waller did not apologise for her error or even admit that she got it wrong. Cardinal Pell provided the *Herald-Sun* with his passport to prove that he was not in Australia during the late 1960s and early 1970s. See *SBS News Online* "Pell pulls out passport to disprove claims", 27 June 2015.

7   Annexure A of the Victorian Court of Appeal's judgment in *George Pell v The Queen* sets out in alphabetical order the witnesses referred to in the court's judgment. The list excludes the complainant (A) along with other witnesses who gave evidence at trial but who were not specifically referred to in the Court of Appeal's reasons. All the witnesses who are referred to in this book are listed below (apart from the complainant A and the deceased B).

	Surname	Given names	Role and age in 1996
1	Bonomy	Robert Anthony	Chorister 1990–1998, 15 years old in December 1996
2	Connor	Jeffrey Ian	Altar server 1994–November 1997, 40 years old in December 1996
3	Cox	Geoffrey Arnold	Assistant organist and choirmaster 1995–1999, director of music 1999–2014
4	Dearing	David Michael	Chorister between 1993–2000, 14 years old in December 1996
5	Dearing	Rodney David	Chorister June 1993–2002 and father of David Dearing, 44 years old in December 1996
6	Derrij	Farris	Chorister from 1994 (grade 5) until the end of year 12, 12 years old in 1996
7	Doyle	Christopher Leigh	Chorister 1994–1999, 14 years old in December 1996
8	Finnigan	Peter Michael	Choir member from 1990 – 1996, Choir Marshal from 1993/1994 – 1996
9	Ford	Stuart Michael	Chorister 1994 – 2000, turned 14 years old in December 1996
10	La Greca	Andrew Chorister	1993–2000, 13 years old in December 1996
11	Mallinson	John Whalley	Organist 1976–1999, choirmaster 1987 – 1999, 62 years old in December 1996
12	May	John Lawrence	Sacramental wine maker
13	Mayes	David Nicholas Andrew	Chorister 1994–2000, 13 years old in December 1996
14	McGlone	Daniel Newman	Altar server from 1987 until 1997, 27 years old in December 1996
15	Nathan	Anthony Lord	Chorister 1993–2000, 13 years old in December 1996
16	Parissi	Luciano	Chorister 1991–2001, 16 years old in December 1996
17	Portelli	Charles	Assistant priest January 1993–June 1996, Master of Ceremonies to Archbishop Pell September 1996–2000
18	Potter	Maxwell Francis	Sacristan 1963–2001, 62 years old in December 1996
19	Reed	Christopher Ashley	Informant
20	Thomas	Aaron Roger	Chorister 1993-2001, 13 years old in December 1996

8   However, when sentencing Pell on 13 March 2019, Chief Judge Kidd made a serious error – which is documented in Keith Windschuttle's *The Persecution of George Pell*. The trial judge was essentially putting the case of the complainant and the prosecution which led to Pell's conviction when he said:

> You then committed further indecent acts with J[i.e. A]. You told J to take off his pants and you started touching his genitalia **with your hands**. This is charge 3 on the Indictment. **While this was occurring,** you began touching your own genital area **with your other hand**. These acts occurred over a minute or two. This is charge 4 on the Indictment. Both charges 3 and 4 are Indecent Act charges. (Emphases added).

As Keith Windschuttle commented in *The Persecution of George Pell*:

> Now, George Pell is a man with only two hands. If he started touching the boy with his "hands", then "while this was occurring" he would not have been able to touch his own genitals with his "other hand". He would need three hands to do what the judge claimed. This was not an error in the transcript. Anyone who replays the video of Kidd's remarks will find it clear that he said Pell was touching the boy's genitals with his hands, plural, while his "other hand" was on his own penis. This was no slip of the tongue that doesn't matter....Kidd was sentencing a man to prison for an offence, which in the judge's own words, was physically impossible for him to have committed.

Chief Judge Kidd's error was unrelated to Pell's conviction. But it demonstrates the trouble which the complainant and the prosecution had in explaining how the assaults happened – which led to the sentencing judge's confusion in his sentencing remarks in explaining what the complainant and the prosecution were alleging – and what the jury found.

9   See Gerard Henderson's *Santamaria: A Most Unusual Man* (Melbourne University Press, 2015, p. 14).

10 Mick McGuane (born 1967) was an Australian Football League star who played 152 games for Collingwood, including in the 1990 premiership team. Matt Rosa (born 1986) played a total of 207 AFL games for the West Coast Eagles and the Gold Coast Suns.

11 This is a reference to the Council of Trent, which ran from 1545 to 1563 – it formalised the Catholic Church's response to the Reformation and is said to have been the high watermark of the Counter Reformation. The Tridentine Creed, which summarised the work of the Council of Trent, was published in 1564. The Council of Trent, among other things, determined the format of clerical seminaries that remained in operation until the Second Vatican Council in the 1960s.

12 The story of the Catholic Social Studies Movement (The Movement)

and the National Civic Council is told in Gerard Henderson's *Santamaria: A Most Unusual Man*. The CSSM was formed in the early 1940s and became the NCC in 1957.

13 Quoted in William J. McCarthy *James Patrick O'Collins: A Bishop's Story* (Spectrum Publications, 1996) which contains a foreword by Bishop Ronald Mulkearns.

14 The Curia of an archdiocese comprises the archbishop, assistant bishops, vicar-general and the archbishop's secretary. In the first edition of *Cardinal*, Louise Milligan wrote that Pell accompanied Ridsdale to the Warrnambool Magistrates' Court (in the Diocese of Ballarat). It was the Melbourne Magistrates' Court on William Street in the Central Business District (in the Archdiocese of Melbourne).

15 This matter is discussed – and the relating correspondence published, in the author's *Media Watch Dog* blog of 17 August 2021. It can be found on The Sydney Institute's website.

16 Bernard Barrett (born 1934) is a retired academic. He is a voluntary researcher for Broken Rites, a not-for-profit organisation which supports complainants of child sexual abuse. Bernard Barrett was involved with C who made allegations about George Pell at Phillip Island in 1961 or 1962 – and with A (i.e. J) who made allegations about George Pell at St Patrick's Cathedral in 1996 and 1997.

In an ABC Radio interview with John Cleary on 3 February 2013, Barrett said that Broken Rites claimed credit for contributing to the establishment of the Victorian Parliamentary Inquiry and the Royal Commission. During The *Police v Pell* in the Melbourne Magistrates' Court, Barrett provided no audible response to Robert Richter QC's question: "You do have a passion about the Catholic Church, don't you?" At one stage during the hearings, Richter said to Barrett "You're a disgrace" – complaining that Barrett was "not answering any questions".

17 In his appearance on *7.30,* David Marr was asked by Leigh Sales "whether one could get one's penis out" of the robes that Pell wore at the Solemn Mass. Marr replied that "it was authoritatively stated by the three judges on the bench that you can actually have a piss while wearing this gear – and that being possible then, without other kinds of details, other things are possible as well". The Victorian Court of Appeal made no such finding. I pointed this out by email to *7.30* executive producer Justin Stevens – but Marr's error was not corrected.

18 This transcript has been put together from *YouTube* footage. The interview was pre-recorded and cut before it went to air. It demonstrates an incident in the Pell pile-on in which the interviewee was given only a fraction of the time taken by *The Project's* panelists, all of whom

agreed with each other about Pell's guilt and none of whom anticipated that Pell could wage a successful appeal.

19   I discussed the ABC's failure to cover its own historical and current cases of child sexual abuse in my paper titled "The Media and Religion in Australia" which is published in *Upholding the Australian Constitution: Proceedings of the Thirtieth Conference of The Samuel Griffith Society* – August 2018, Volume 30 (The Samuel Griffith Society, 2019).

20   Justice McClellan's address to the University of New South Wales Law Faculty was reported by Adam Harvey on the ABC website on 14 December 2011 titled "Judge wants to cut juries from complex trials".

21   For the most comprehensive coverage in book form see Anthony Dowsley and Patrick Carylon *Lawyer X* (HarperCollins, 2020).

22   This April 2014 Victorian Police email among other documents, was revealed at the Royal Commission into the Lawyer X case. In his *Quadrant Online* piece, Douglas Drummond expressed the view that Graham Ashton accepted Charlie Morton's advice about weaponising the Pell case to "deflect public scrutiny onto the [Catholic] Church and away from Victoria Police's own wrongdoing" with respect to Lawyer X. He referred specifically to the ABC News report of 12 December 2019 titled "Emails reveal how Victoria Police tried to keep revelations about Lawyer X off the front page".

23   In July 2022, Roberts was acquitted of the murder of Silk and Milner following a re-trial in which the defence counsel argued that "the stench of police misconduct" made the evidence of the police witnesses unreliable.

24   On 28 August 2020, *Quadrant Online* published an article by Douglas Drummond titled "The Egregious Failures of Victoria Police". From 1981 to 1992, Drummond was Queensland's Special Prosecutor following the Commission of Inquiry into Possible Illegal Activities and Associated Police Misconduct (the Fitzgerald Inquiry) which was presided over by Tony Fitzgerald QC. Subsequently, Drummond was a judge of the Federal Court of Australia between December 1991 and April 2003.

In his article, Douglas Drummond is highly critical of the handling by Victoria Police of allegations of child sexual assault up until at least 2002. And he points out that both the Royal Commission into Institutional Responses to Child Sexual Abuse and the Victorian Independent Broad-based Anti-corruption Commission (IBAC) showed scant interest in investigating Victoria Police's responses to historical child sexual abuse.

NOTES 475

25   Gerard Henderson's letter to Peter McClellan, dated 13 September 2023, can be accessed via The Sydney Institute's website in the Correspondence section of *Media Watch Dog,* 15 September 2023.

26   Russell Jackson, of ABC Investigations, wrote three substantial reports on the Victorian Education Department on 27 August 2023, 11 September 2023 and 4 October 2023 – pointing to its failure to deal with pedophile teachers. They were published on the ABC News website – but not covered on the main ABC TV or radio outlets.

27   The McClellan Royal Commission was not restricted by its terms of reference from investigating government schools – unlike the inquiry conducted by the Victorian Legislative Council's Family and Community Development Committee. It was known as the *Betrayal of Trust* report. But its full title was *Inquiry Into the Handling of Child Abuse by Religious and Other Non-Government Organisations* and reported in November 2013. This inquiry was established by the Victorian Coalition Government during the premiership of Ted Baillieu.

28   George Cardinal Pell's Prison Journal was published by Ignatius Press in three volumes. Volume 1 titled " The Cardinal Makes His Appeal" covers the period 27 February to 13 July 2019; Volume 2 "The State Court Rejects the Appeal" – 14 July 2019 to 30 November 2019 and Volume 3 "The High Court Frees an Innocent Man" – 1 December 2019 to 8 April 2020. Volume 1 was published in 2020, the remaining volumes in the following year. It contains an introduction by George Weigel who contributed an afterword in Volume 3.

Cardinal Pell told the author that he very much liked Anne Henderson's review of his Prison Journal Volume 1 in the March 2020 issue of Quadrant. Her final paragraph was as follows:

> Cardinal George Pell's Prison Journal is a remarkable read. While written in such a deprived and austere setting—both physically and emotionally—the text is full of uplift and insights into the human condition. In a Western world of material and instant gratification, it reminds us how much the strength of human existence—morally and physically—relies (and has always relied) on an ability to handle and grow from suffering.

ACKNOWLEDGEMENTS

I decided to write this book on 13 November 2019 when two High Court justices referred George Pell's application for special leave to appeal his conviction (in the County Court of Victoria for historical child sexual abuse) to the Full Court of the High Court for argument as an appeal. As one who has spent almost half my life living in Melbourne, I was of the view that, once the case got out of the jurisdiction of Victoria, Cardinal Pell had a very good chance of having his conviction quashed. Provided the High Court took on the case. However, I only commenced writing on 7 April 2020 – when, in a unanimous judgment, the High Court of Australia overturned both the jury's finding in Pell's re-trial and the majority judgment of the Victorian Court of Appeal.

I had commenced writing about the media pile-on against George Pell in my newspaper column from around the time he took up the position of Catholic Archbishop of Sydney in March 2001. There followed the establishment of the Royal Commission into Institutional Responses to Child Sexual Abuse, the decision of Victoria Police to charge Cardinal Pell and the subsequent court cases.

During this time, a number of people provided me with information concerning the Royal Commission and the trials. Initially, I was helped by Katrina Lee, the one-time leading Sydney-based journalist who became communications and media adviser to the Archdiocese of Sydney and personal adviser to Cardinal George Pell. Katrina Lee is the kind of adviser that everyone needs – in that she is prepared to give an informed opinion without worrying about how it will be received.

Fr Frank Brennan S.J. also provided me with much material about the Royal Commission and the trials. I made use of his collection of articles/speeches in his book *Observations on the Pell Proceedings* (Connor Court, April 2021) including his map of St Patrick's Cathedral which appears at the front of the book. Frank Brennan, who does not agree with Cardinal Pell on some theological matters, showed considerable intellectual courage in supporting the Cardinal concerning the allegations against him. Frank also read the manuscript, offered advice and corrected some errors.

Without the support of Katrina Lee and Frank Brennan it would not have been possible to publish this book at this time – less than two years after the High Court decision and the release of the un-redacted sections of the Royal Commission's final report pertaining to Pell.

I was also assisted by the coverage of Monica Doumit in *The Catholic Weekly* – she is a fine, hard-working journalist who writes very well. Keith Windschuttle's *The Persecution of George Pell* (Quadrant Books, 2020) is an important book based on thorough research which I found most valuable. In his capacity as editor of *Quadrant* magazine, Keith Windschuttle published a number of important articles on the Pell Case. I relied on Tess Livingstone's 2002 biography on George Pell for some of the material in Chapter 5.

I am very grateful to T.K. Tobin QC who read the manuscript and found some errors while providing most helpful advice. The same is true of Dr James Franklin, who is editor of the important *Journal of the Australian Catholic Historical Society*. Also, thanks to Sister Mary of Christ at the Carmelite Monastery in the Melbourne suburb of Kew who provided details of Cardinal Pell's first day after his release from prison.

A number of individuals provided information over the years – not all of whom wanted to be mentioned here. Special thanks to Adrian Barrett, Sam Duggan, Rosemary Eliott, James Franklin, Malcolm Kerr, John Previte, Glenn Mathias, Chris Meney, Monsignor Charles Portelli and Paul Santamaria QC.

Lalita Mathias, my excellent executive assistant for over three decades, typed the manuscript and advised on the text. She also did much valuable research with respect to the various legal cases. The very talented Paige Hally designed the cover, and both read and advised on the manuscript. Naomi Killin went through 20 years of my files to locate newspaper clippings, journal articles and transcripts pertaining to George Pell and proof-read the manuscript.

Anne Henderson (nee Keppel) has been heavily involved in all my written output since we first met while undertaking casual employment at the Campion Press Bookshop in Melbourne in December 1965. Anne – who has published important studies on, among others, Robert Menzies, Enid Lyons and Joseph Lyons – made many valuable suggestions on the book and checked the manuscript.

It was great to work with Anthony Cappello and his team at Connor Court. Connor Court is a brave and influential publisher which fulfills an important role in the public debate. Thanks also to Garry Cousins (of Garry Cousins Indexing) who prepared a comprehensive index against a tight deadline.

I am also grateful to George Pell who checked Chapter 5. I was aware of the Cardinal's career in Sydney – but needed to have the material in Chapter 5 concerning his time in Ballarat, Rome, Oxford and Melbourne checked.

Finally, a special thanks to John Howard OM AC – Prime Minister of Australia between March 1996 and December 2007 – for his Foreword. I worked for John Howard between 1984 and 1986 and have always admired his political skills, intelligence, sense of history and professionalism.

All Souls' Day, 2 November 2021

A NOTE ON THE NEW EDITION

I decided to add a chapter to this book on learning of Cardinal Pell's death in January 2023. The original 11 chapters remain as they were when *Cardinal Pell, The Media Pile-On & Collective Guilt* was published in November 2021. Except for the correction of some misspellings and a few minor changes. No one has advised me of any significant errors of fact or sought any changes to the text.

All Saints' Day, 1 November 2023

INDEX

A (complainant – originally referred to as J)
  as a compelling witness 30, 69, 106, 120, 241–2, 280
  claims assault happened in sacristy 230
  credibility of 82–4, 96–7, 103, 105–8, 120
  doubts date of alleged offence 226
  evidence of in County Court 65–7
  High Court on the evidence of 23, 396
  makes complaint against Pell 8
  Milligan on 70, 228–9, 280
  Pell holds no ill-will towards 35
  prosecution accepts claims of 59
  Rae fails to record conversation with 376
  responds to Pell's acquittal 35
  returns to St Patrick's with detective 383
  Soutphommasane on 256
  transcripts of evidence not released 64
  video testimony of 68, 74–7
  Wallington on the evidence of 57–8
  Weinberg on the evidence of 23
Abbott, Tony 37, 192, 246, *246*, 251–4, 269, 297, 405, 412
ABC
  anti-Pell activist journalists 132, 165–7
  as a conservative-free zone 197
  as a taxpayer-funded broadcaster 281
  at Pell media conference 190
  Clark apologises for remarks about Pell 322
  comedy programs 293
  Corrections & Clarifications segment 307, 322
  Craven criticises reporting of 25, 33–4, 97
  dismisses criticism of its reporting 286–94
  evidential standards of 294

  gives little coverage to Pell supporters 32, 289–90, 293
  meagre coverage of Pell's acquittal 292
  misreports Royal Commission findings 306–7
  on Pell's appeal to the High Court 116–17
  settles defamation claim against Milligan 294
  sympathetic coverage of *Cardinal* 165–6
  Whitlam takes out writ against 183
  withdraws *Goliath* for editing 279
  see also specific journalists; specific programs, e.g. AM, Four Corners
ABC News Online 286
academics 407–9
Ackland, Richard 166, 291
Adams Phillip 166
Adler, Louise 166, 187, *194*, 216, 230, 405, 414, 419
Agagianian, Cardinal Gregorio Pietro 151
The Age 29, 94–5, 132, 168, 177–8, 213, 254, 276, 280, 282, 331, 357, 368, 370, 381, 398, 400
agnosticism 154–5
Akerman, Piers 269
Alberici, Emma 166, 185, 190
Albrechtsen, Janet 31, 195, 269, 291
Alcorn, Gay 220–2
Alexander, Harriet 282–3
Allison, Lyn 40, *40*
The Altar Boys (Smith) 281–4
altar servers 80, 98–100, 119, 125–6, 360, *360,* 384–5
Aly, Waleed 15, 62, 166
AM (radio program) 167, 186, 306
Anderson, David 220, 287, 362
Andrews, Daniel 36–8, 42, 54, 212, 315,

391, 403
Anglican Diocese of Newcastle 281
Ansell, Benjamin 113
anti-Semitism 148
applications for discontinuance 59–61, 70–4
Aquinas College 157–8
Ararat Prison 206, 311, 313
Armidale diocese 181–3
Arundell, Father Kevin 332, 334–5
A.S. (complainant) 375–6, 380
Ashton, Graham 97, 271, 360, *360,* 362–71, 375, 389–92
Aspinall, Archbishop Phillip 302, 344
Assumption of the Blessed Virgin Mary 147
Atkinson, Bob 299
Austin, Paul 398
Australia Human Rights Commission 257
The Australian 88, 96, 115, 191, 204, 235, 239, 247, 310, 319–20, 359, 386–7, 406, 417, 419
Australian and New Zealand Association of Psychotherapy 310
Australian Book Review 214
Australian Catholic Bishops' Conference 179–80, 320, 327
Australian Catholic University 158, 247–8, 358
Australian Dictionary of Biography 7
Australian Financial Review 81, 90, 230
Australian Labor Party 138
Australian Law Journal 308
Australian Lawyers Alliance 190
The Australian Online 181, 316, 387, 399
Australian Rules Football 139–40, 177
Australian Wine Cafe 7

B (deceased former chorister – originally referred to as R) 9, 57, 65–7, 90, 228–9
B.A. (complainant) 50
Bacon, Wendy 166
Baird, Julia 44
Baker, Su 230
Baker, Father William ('Bill') 342–3
Baldwin, Peter 31, 291
Ballarat 13, 31, 50–1, 136, 157, 168, 373
Ballarat diocese 330–9, 352, 379, 386

Ballard, Tom 166, 293
Barker, Anne 319
Barns, Greg 34, 220–2, 263, 411
Barrett, Bernard 183, 222, 347, 377
Barron, John 166
Barry, Paul 224, 290–4
Barwon Prison 2–3, 26, 193, 280
BBC 293, 348, 362
Be Not Afraid (Pell) 138, 143
Beazley, Kim 135
Beech, Carl 38, 111, 361–2, 398
Beech, Eric 188
Belgium 156
Bell, George 93
Bell, Justice Virginia 1, 5, *25,* 119–20, 123–4, 126, 278, 389
Benedict XVI, Pope 133, 157
Beran, Cardinal Josef 150
Bernie (complainant) 246, 277–81
Betrayal of Trust inquiry 184
Bickmore, Carrie 166
Biddulph, Steve 166, 254–5
Big Ideas (radio program) 186
Black Inc. 206
Blue Knot Foundation 310
Boas, Gideon 242
Bolt, Andrew 3–4, 31, 94, 134–5, 195, 204, 234–5, 238, 269, 291, 293, 295, *295,* 301, 347, 417
The Bolt Report (television program) 181, 238, 417
Bolton, Robert 230
Bongiorno, Paul 145–6, 166, 201–2, 210, 224, 344–8, 353
Boonen, Ben 132
Boston 272
Boston Globe 272
Boyce, Christopher 101–4, 115, 122
BPL (complainant) 345–7
Bradley, Michael 166, 416–17
Brady, Howard 335
Brady, Veronica 144
Bramall, Lord 38, 111, 362
Breakfast (radio program) 28–9, 167, 201, 218, 268, 307, 344
Brennan, Father Frank 31–3, 44–5, 96–8, 195, 204, 237, 241–2, 269, 289–90, 324, 355–6, 394, *394,*

413–14, 417
Brennan, Sir Gerard 32
Brett, Doris 398
Brett, Lily 398
Briant, Alexander 152
Briginshaw v Briginshaw 329–30
Brittan, Lord 362
Broken Rites 176, 183, 222, 347, 377
Broken Rites Newsletter 177
Brook, Stephen 415
Brown, Tara 166, 266–7
Bryant, Father Eric 335, 337
Buck, Robbie 218
Buckingham, Sue 254
Bungaree 159
Burchill, Scott 166
Burke, Kelly 166
Burke, Molly 137
Burnett, Ros 397
Burns, Andy 209
Burnside, Julian 166, 258–9
bushfires 277
Butler, Mark 364
By Wendouree, Memories 1951–1963 (Molony) 143
Byron Bay Literary Festival 231

C (complainant) 176–7
Cameron, Julie 59
Campion, Edmund 152–4
The Canberra Times 168, 257–8, 401
Cardinal (Milligan) 40, 58, 88, 144, 165, 187, 194, 209–17, 223–4, 227–30, 280, 292, 404–5, 414–15, 417, 419
Carleton, Richard 167, 172–3
Carlton, Mike 167
Carmelite Monastery, Kew 26–8
Caro, Jane 167
Carr, Archbishop Thomas 26
Carrick, John 158
Carroll, Archbishop Francis 179
Carson, Kevin 359, 369–70
Carter, Lucy 353
Carvalho, Karina 25, 33
The Case of George Pell (Davey) 63, 68–9, 230, 240–5
Case Study No. 8 323–7

Case Study No. 16 324, 327–30
Case Study No. 28 324, 330–9, 348, 352, 354, 356, 358
Case Study No. 35 324, 339–43, 352, 354, 358
Cassidy, Barrie 28, 31, 167, 192, 250–2
Castel Gandolfo 149
Cathedral Trial 8, 14–18, 60, 64–74, 88
Catherine of Siena, Saint 170
Catholic Church
 addresses clerical child sexual abuse 272, 321, 386
 anti-Catholic feeling 207, 406
 compensates Foster family 173, 328
 Ellis gives warning about collective guilt 47
 Holy Communion 135–6
 implements child safety measures 327
 in England 152
 Kidd warns jury about collective guilt 42–3, 98, 117
 mental reservations 312–13
 organisational structure 142, 161, 179–80, 182, 333
 Peter Fox's allegations regarding 186
 Pope issues *Nostra Aetate* declaration 148
 relationship with Victoria Police 365–70
 responses to clerical child sexual abuse 272
 Solemn Mass viii, 16–20, 67, 70–3, 79–80, 82, 89–90, 383–4
 teachings of 26, 130, 134–6, 143, 147
 Tony Windsor on 186
 Truth, Justice and Healing Council 320–1, 323
 undue focus of Royal Commission on 297, 299–301, 303–7, 348–50
 see also Melbourne Response; Towards Healing; Vatican I; Vatican II
Catholic Church Insurance 336
Catholic Education Office 340–1
Catholic priests 140–1, 146–7, 153–4, 264–6, 268–9
Catholic Religious Australia 320, 327

Catholic Social Services Australia 304
Catholic Social Studies Movement 138, 150
Catholic Theological College, Clayton 159
celibacy 144, 198–9
Centenary Mass 131
Chamberlain, Lindy 5–6, 8
Chamberlain v The Queen 6, 109
Champion, John 42, 48
Chandler, Andrew 93
Channel 9 News 232
Chernov, Alex 328
child sexual abuse *see* clerical child sexual abuse
Child Sexual Abuse Inquiries and the Catholic Church (Miller) 309, 327
Christchurch terrorist attack 243
Christian Brothers 132, 158, 180, 337–8, 346, 357
Church of England 93, 154
Clancy, Cardinal Edward 136, 171, 179, 327, 337
Clark, Philip 167, 322
Clark, Samuel 292
clerical child sexual abuse
    by male Catholic clergy 168–9
    Catholic Church addresses 272, 321, 386
    in Armidale diocese 181–3
    in Ballarat diocese 330–9
    in Maitland-Newcastle diocese 181, 185, 187, 189, 281
    in Melbourne archdiocese 339–43, 352, 365–70, 379
    in Parramatta diocese 182–3
    influence of media on trials 46–7
    Kidd's warning about collective guilt for 42–3
    Pell addresses 321
    Victorian Parliamentary Inquiry into 184, 260, 274, 302, 331, 367–71
    see also Melbourne Response; Towards Healing; *specific offenders*
CNN 233
Coate, Justice Jennifer 299, 324
Coghlan, Gorgi 167, 249–50
coincidence evidence 85–7
collective guilt 43, 47–8, 65, 98, 117, 178, 219, 398–407, 409
Collins, Matt 29, 90
Collins, Paul 292, 297, 300
Come Home (Cardinal Pell) (song) 162, 164–5, 249, 269–70
Comensoli, Archbishop Peter 289
communism 150
complainants 163, 188, 214, 241, 277–8, 304, 309–10, 361
    see also names of specific complainants; witnesses
Compton, Leon 307
Connor, Jeffrey 258, 384
The Conversation 409
The Conversation Hour (radio program) 40
Cook, Henrietta 357
Cooke, Richard 167
Cor Ad Cor Loquitur 149
Corbett, Rachel 167, 249–50
Cornish, Jean 88–9
Corpus Christi College 140–6, 159–61, 311
Costello, Peter 135
Costigan, Frank 214
counselling 169
Country Party 138
County Court of Victoria 9, 14, 39, *40*, 41, 63–70, 113, 244, 279
The Courier 382
Court of Appeal of the Supreme Court of Victoria 3–4, 6–9, 16, 24, 29–30, 39, 59–60, 75, 81, *92*, 100–14, 122–3, 205, 225, 240, 254, 389
'court of public opinion' 407–9
Courtin, Judy 167, 381–2
COVID-19 pandemic 1, 28, 119
Cowdrey, Colin 397–8
Cowen, Sir Zelman 135
Cox, Geoffrey 57
Crabb, Annabel 167, 419
Cranmer, Bishop Thomas 152
Craven, Greg *25*, 31, 33–4, 96–8, 195, 204, 247–8, 254, 295, 300, 356
Craven, Peter 213–14
Credlin, Peta 31, 293
Crennan, Susan 328
cricket 397–8
Crikey 300, 416
Criminal Procedure Act 2009 100

Crittenden, Stephen 167, 177–8, 199, 300
Crowley, John 357
Cudmore, Monsignor Gerald 168–70
culture wars 5
Cunneen, Margaret 185–7
Curnow, Sarah 222
Current Issues in Criminal Justice 308
Curtain, David 328
Czechoslovakia 150

D (complainant) 226
The Daily Beast 415
Daily Mail 237
Dalai Lama 144
Daly, Bishop Noel 159
Daniel, F. 86
D'Arcy, Bishop Eric 159
Davey, Father Brendan 338
Davey, Melissa 63, 68–9, 102, 167, 207–8, 230, 233, 239–45, *245,* 353
Davie, Tim 293
Davoren, John 325
Dawkins, Richard 395–6
Day, Monsignor John 316–17, 331–2, 346, 386–8
D.D. (complainant) 53–5, 209–11, 362, 376, 379
de Chardin, Pierre Teilhard 151
Dean. Rowan 31, 291, 293
Deane, Justice William 6, 109–10
Debien, Noel 195–6, 245, 290
Debs, Bandali 393
Dei Filius 147
delays, in making allegations 66–7, 83, 114
demeanour, of witnesses 110–13, 241–2, 278–9, 313
Democratic Labor Party 138, 150
Dempster, Quentin 167, 217, 219, 405–6, 419
Devine, Miranda 31, 195, 269, 293
Di Natale, Richard 253
Director of Public Prosecutions (NSW) 46
Director of Public Prosecutions v George Pell 39, 46, 64–70, 74–89, 414
Director of Public Prosecutions (Victoria) 13, 48, 61, 94, 98, 386, 413–16
Dixon, Father Martin 145
Dixon, Justice Owen 329
do Rozario, Michael 11

Dodd, Andrew 186
Domus Australia, Rome 156–7
Donohoe, Brendan 37
Doogue, Geraldine 199–200
Doubt: A Parable (Shanley) 112–13
Doumit, Monica 31
Dowlan, Brother Edward 331, 337–8
Downing, Richard 290
Dowsley, Anthony 389
Doyle, Monsignor Thomas 341
DPP v Pell (Evidential Ruling No. 1) (County Court) 16, 39, 59, 85, 88
DPP v Pell (Sentence) 15, 42
DPP v Tyrrell 114
Dreyfus, Mark 254, 309
Drive (radio program) 70, 260, 277, 290, 307
Drive with Richard Glover (radio program) 399
The Drum (television program) 44–5, 162, 165, 204, 219, 347, 400–3
Duggan, Aidan 325
Duggan, Sam 322
Duranty, Walter 292
Durkin, Patrick 81

East Germany 150
Easter (2020) 26
Edelman, Justice James 1, 5, *25,* 117, 389
Edmund Campion (Kilroy) 152
Edmund Rice Education Australia 357
Edwards, Astrid 232
Egan, Brendan 17, 61, 385
Elizabeth I, Queen 152–3
Ellis, Angela 48, 74, 86, 101
Ellis, John 323, 325–7
Ellis, Judge Roy 44–7, 74
England, Catholicism in 151–4
Engle, Vanessa 362
Enker, Debi 276
Epstein, Rafael 167, 290
Eros Foundation 176
Eton College 152–3
Eureka Pool 55, 58, 209–10, 338–9, 363, 379–80, 382
Eureka Street 324
ex-cathedra pronouncements 147
executions 7–8

Fahey, John 98, 248
Faine, Jon 29, 31, 40, 167, 289, 315, 363
Fairfax Media 97, 198, 400
faith 143, 154
The Fall and Rise of Derryn Hinch (Hinch) 264
Fallen (Morris-Marr) 10, 14, 59, 63, 83–4, 194, 234–9
Fanning, Ellen 167, 219, 400–3
Farrell, John Joseph 181–3, 190, 281
Farrelly, Elizabeth 167
Feast of Corpus Christi 130
Feik, Chris 199
Fennell, Steven 255
Fennell v The Queen 29
Ferguson, Chief Justice Anne 6, 18–19, 75, 92, 101, 103–4, 106–11, 125, 167, 220, 386
Ferguson, John 316, 370
Ferguson, Sarah 156, 167, 207, 209, 246, *246,* 275–81, 288, 294
Final Information Update 304, 306
Final Report (Royal Commission) 304
Finnigan, Father Brian 335–6
Finnigan, Peter 57
Finnis, John 31
First Things 115
First Vatican Council *see* Vatican I
Fiscalini, Leo 332, 334, 336, 344, 346
Fischer, Tim 135, 237
Fisher, Archbishop Anthony 141, 182
Fisher, John 154
Fitzgerald, Robert 299–300, 303–6
Fitzgerald, Ross 139
FitzSimons, Peter 10, 167, 271–3, 300–1, 353, 414, 419
Flesh Wounds (Glover) 399–400
Fletcher, James 48
Flint, David 31
Foley, Martin *194,* 211–12
football 139–40, 177
Forbes, Clara 158
Fordham, Ben 252
forensic disadvantage 66–7, 83
Forrest, Justice T. 4, 393
Foster, Anthony 173–4, 267, 274, 315, 328
Foster, Chrissie 173–4, 187, 253, 260, 274–5, 315, 328, 328–30, 402–3, 412
Foster, Emma 329
Foster, Katie 329
Four Corners (television program) 167–70, 180–3, 222, 224, 288, 291–2
Fox, Julian 182
Fox, Peter 167, 185–7, 189, 198, 253, 274, 301
Fox v Percy 278
Francis, Charles 328
Francis, Pope 10, 36, 133–4, 141, 266–7, 282–3, 322
Frangopoulos, Angelos 261
Franklin, James 31, 312
Fraser government 158
Fraser, Malcolm 135–6
Fraser, Morag 398
Friel, Chris S. 31
Furness, Gail 296, *296, 298,* 299, 311–12, 314–23, 332, 350–2

Gageler, Justice Stephen 1, 5, *25,* 389
Galbally, Paul 26, 62, *62,* 100
Gannon, Desmond 340, 386
Gans, Jeremy 5, 36–7, 50, 63, 81, 112, 394, *394*
Gare, Shelley 31
The Garrett (podcast) 232
gay activists 129–32
Gay with God (Punch) 144–5
George Bell, Bishop of Chichester (Chandler) 93
George Pell (Livingstone) 131, 145, 168–9
George Pell v The Queen (Court of Appeal) 1, 5, 39, *92,* 100–13, 115, 117, 269
Geraghty, Chris 167, 264–6
'Get Pell' campaign 9–10, 14, 70, 178, 361–93
Gibson, Mark 48, 64, 74–9, 81, 99–101, 122, 125–6, 227, 244
Gilbert, Kieran 32, 289, *394,* 413
Gillard, Julia 188–9, 192, 198, 274, 297, 299, 411–12
Gleebooks 279
Gleeson, Chief Justice Murray 278
Glen Waverley seminary 141
Glennon, Michael 169–70
Glover, Richard 167, 259–61, 277, 399–400

Gobbo, Sir James 328
Gobbo, Nicola (Lawyer X) 388–91
The God Delusion (Dawkins) 395–6
Golden Quill Award 292, 419
Goliath (documentary) 167, 246, 276–80, 288
Good Shepherd Seminary, Homebush 27–8
Gordon, Justice Michelle 1, 5, *25,* 117, 124, 389, 403
government schools 349–50
Gracer, Kartya 26, *62*
Graham, Douglas 328
Grant, Troy 185
Green, Jonathan 167
Green, Timothy 318, 331, 338–9, 348
Greenslade, Stanley Lawrence 151
Greiner, Kathryn 31
The Guardian Australia 46, 102, 168, 192, 196, 198, 204–8, 222, 233, 239, 245, 270
Guilliatt, Richard 310, 397
guilt, collective *see* collective guilt
Gummow, Justice William 278
Gun Alley (Morgan) 7

Habersberger, David 328
Hachette Australia 187, 230
Hadley, Ray 167, 224, 250–2
Harington, Darrel George 350
Harmer, Wendy 167, 218, 261, 268
Hart, Archbishop Denis 142, 156, 179, 184, 329, 342, 366–7
hearsay evidence 215–16, 228, 283
Heartfelt Moments in Australian Rules Football (Fitzgerald) 139, 141
Heath, Ted 38, 111, 362
Heenan, Cardinal Archbishop John 152
Heiss, Elsie 254
Hell on the Way to Heaven (Kennedy and Foster) 187, 274–5
Helliar, Peter 167, 249–50
Henderson, Anne 31
Henderson, Gerard 31, 192, 200, 203, 217, 234, 238, 269–70, 405–7, 419, 424, 428
Hennessey, Jill 42, 212
Henriques, Sir Richard 361, 363
Henry VIII, King 154
Henson, Bill 208

The Henson Case (Marr) 208
The Herald 8
Herald Sun 9, 209, 234–5, 364, 381–2, 389
Hey Dad! (television program) 348
Hickey, Archbishop Barry 156
High Court of Australia
  accepts Weinberg's reasoning 115
  acquits Pell 1, 3–6, 22–4, 26, 60–1, 127, 242–3, 357, 409
  appeals to generally 241
  considers decision of Court of Appeal 122–3
  denies Victoria Police leave to appeal 389–91
  hears *George Pell v The Queen* 39, 115–27
  judges on the Court *25*
  Marr responds to verdict of 206, 243
  on demeanour of witnesses 278
  on the evidence of A 23, 396
  Pell antagonists unable to accept verdict of 222, 225, 232–3, 242–3, 256–7, 263–4, 401–2, 407–9
  Pell applies for leave to appeal to 16, 401
  Pell's hearing before 41
  response to judgement of 28–38, 258
  Ross appeals to 7
  Walker and Shann apply for leave to appeal to 116–19
Hilton Hotel, Fiumicino Airport 11, 371
Hinch, Derryn 167, 261–4, 269, 293, 414
Hinch Live (television program) 261–3
Hochhuth, Rolf 149
Holdenson, Paul 101
Hollingworth, Peter 302–3, 344
Holloway, Nicholas 130
Holy Communion 135
Holy Family Parish School, Doveton 341
Homebush seminary 232
homosexuality 335
Honi Soit 162
Horgan, Geoffrey 417–18
Howard government 133, 192
Howard, John 135, 250–3, 269, 271, 405
Hoysted, Peter 31, 316, 386–7
Hughes, Robert 348
Hume, Cardinal Archbishop Basil 130, 132

Hungary 150
Hunter Valley 185, 189
Hutcheon, Jane 145
The Hutchins School, Hobart 350
IBAC 392–3
ICAC 308
Imhoff, Claude 310
Independent Broad-Based Anti-Corruption Commission (IBAC) 392–3
Independent Inquiry Into Childhood Sexual Abuse (UK) 267
Indigenous Australians 192
Industry Super Holdings 233
Innocence Revisited (Kezelman) 310
Inquiry into the Handling of Child Abuse by Religious and Other Organisations 184, 260, 274, 302, 331, 367–71
Inside Story 81, 112
Insiders (television program) 181, 192–3, 196, 201–3, 250–1, 292
Institute of Catholic Education 157–8
institutional abuse 42–3
Isaacs, Justice Isaac 7

J (complainant – see A) 8
Jarrett, Bishop Geoffrey 156
Jennings, Gael 167, 401
Jensen, Erik 30–1, 167, 354
Jesuits 180
Jews 148–9
John XXIII, Pope 147
John Francis Tyrrell v The Queen 29, 113–15
John Paul II, Pope 89, 129, 133, 160, 168, 171, 178
Jolley, Mary Ann 167, 180, 182
Jones, Alan 347
Jones, Barry 135–6
Jones, Chris 167
Jones, Sir Ken 366–7
Jones, Tony 167, 246, 252–4, 277, 279–81, 288, 395–6
Jones, Tony (3AW) 167, 428-9
Josephites 180
Journal of the Australian Catholic Society 312
journalists *see* media
A Journey from the Pulpit to the Bench

(Geraghty) 265
Judd, Kerri 5, 32, 42, 48, 50, 74, 101, 104, 119–26, 394, *394,* 413–14
judicial independence 46–7
juries
 Barns on 34
 first Pell trial 14, 65–6, 68–70
 Kidd on 15–16, 257, 262, 272
 McClellan on 310–11
 second Pell trial 14, 16–18, 74–5, 81–3
 unconscious bias 413

Kairos Catholic Journal 375
Karvelas, Patricia 307
Kaufmann, Leah 98, 247–8
Kaye, Stephen 113–14
Keane, Justice Patrick 1, 5, *25,* 120–1, 124, 389
Keck, James 113
Kelly, Craig 248–50
Kelly, Fran 28–9, 167, 201, 251, 344
Kelly, John A. 159
Kelly, Michael B. 131
Kelly, Michael H. 167, 268–9
Kelly, Ned 5, 8
Kelly, Paul 31, 191
Kemp, Richard 45
Keneally, Kristina 167, 253–4, 270, 293
Keneally, Tom 404–5
Kennedy, Bishop Henry 182
Kennedy, Bishop Michael 182
Kennedy, Paul 167, 187, 250–1, 274–5
Kennett, Jeff 31, 135, 291, 328
Kenny, Chris 293
Kezelman, Cathy 310, 401–2
Kidd, Chief Judge Peter
 condemns mob mentality 39–40, 59
 considers tendency evidence 279
 delivers charge to the jury 81–3
 dismisses prosecution's case 86–8
 expresses concern over media release 414
 forbids showing of Powerpoint presentation 79–81, 100
 hears *DPP v George Pell* 65–70
 hears Pell's re-trial 74, 78–9, 84, 223–4, 261
 Howard provides reference to 250
 instructs jury against bias 413

interviewed on *The Project* 15–16, 62
makes remarks on closed court 64
on the role of the jury 15–16, 257, 262, 272
portrait of *62*
sentences Pell 90
warns against collective guilt 42–3, 98, 117, 219
Kiefel, Chief Justice Susan 1, 3, 5, *25,* 122, 125, 127, 389
Kilroy, Gerard 152
Kirby, Justice Michael 278
Kiss, Vince 265–6
Knight, Ben 274
Knight, Dom 167
Knox Centre 17
Knox Grammar School 272–3
Knox, Malcolm 30–1, 34
Kohlberg, Lawrence 158
Kolbe, Maximilian 154
Kurti, Peter 31
Kurtz, Howard 163

La Croix International 268–9
Laidler, Terry 289, 292
Lane, Sabra 209, 306–7
Last, Helen 190, 329
Lateline (television program) 167, 185, 190
Latham, Timothy 294
Latimer, Bishop Hugh 152
Laurie, Meshel 167, 301
Lawyer X 388–91, 403
Lay, Ken 367
Lee, Jane 331
Lee, Katrina 41, 237
Leo XIII, Pope 133
Lexis Nexis Butterworths Concise Australian Legal Dictionary 31, 85
Liberal Party 138, 405
Liberty Victoria 259
Light 158
The Light from the Southern Cross 327
Lillee, Dennis 397
Little, Archbishop Frank 136, 159–61, 168–70, 174, 184, 340, 342, 360
Little, Detective Sergeant Inspector Jeff 187
Livingstone, Tess 31, 88, 131, 140, 145, 148–52, 155, 168–9, 198, 344

L.M. (complainant) 53–6, 209–11, 362, 376, 379
lockdowns 119
Loncaric, Anthony 415–16
Loreto Convent, Ballarat 139
Lorimer Taskforce 393
L.T. (complainant) 54
Lucas, Father Brian 327–8
lynch mob mentality 39–43, 48, 59, 91, 247
Lyons, John 167, 171–2

M (complainant) 226
M v The Queen 218, 241, 278
Macdonald, Hamish 167, 249–50, 307
MacKillop, Mary 156, 207
Madden, Father James 332–4, 355
Madigan, Dee 44, 167, 269–70, 293
Magistrates Court of Victoria 8–10, 39, 41, 48, 58–9, 63–4, 225, 230, 374–5, 377
Maitland-Newcastle diocese 181, 185, 187, 189, 281
Maley, Jacqueline 412
Mallinson, John 57
Manne, Anne 167, 354
Manne, Robert 398
Manning, Cardinal Henry 147
Mannix, Archbishop Daniel 26, *128,* 134, 138, 141, 146, 148, 150, 170
Marks, Russell 167
Marr, David 63–5, 102, 113, 156, 167, 192–4, *194,* 196–209, 213, 218–19, 242–3, 245, *245,* 278–9, 285, 291, 419
Marshall, Leslie 163
Martignoni, Miles 245, *245*
Martin, Father John 336
Martin, Louis 27
Martin, Zelie 27
Martin, Ray 167, 220
martyrs 152–4
Mary I, Queen 152
Mary, Saint 156
Mathews, Ben 409
Maxwell, Justice Chris 6, 11, 18–19, 75, *92,* 101, 103–4, 106–10, 125, 220, 259, 386
Maxwell, Jim 397
Mayne, Stephen 167

M.B. (complainant) 53–4, 365
McAuley, James 170
McAuley, Michael 349–50
McCallum, Mungo 165, 167
McCarthy, Joanne 167, 181, 186–7, 204–5
McCarthy, William 66
McClellan, Justice Peter 296, 298–9, 303–4, 306–16, 322, 328, 355–8, 396
McClymont, Kate 167, 419
McCusker, Malcolm 31
McDonald, Kenny 362
McGarvie, Sir Richard 328
McGlone, Daniel 115, 258, 384
McGrath, Bernard 275–6
McGregor, Jeanavive 222
McGuinness, Phillipa 167, 179–80
McInerney, Father Adrian 332–5, 355
McInerney, Father Jim 142
McKenzie, Father F.J. 332, 334
McKenzie-Murray, Martin 167
McKinnon, Alex 167
McMurdo, Margaret 391–2
McMurtrie, Craig 286–92
Meagher, Father Danny 28
media
    adverse publicity of Chamberlain case 8
    adverse publicity of Ross case 8
    antagonists deny presumption of innocence 28–31, 271
    anti-Pell publicity 162, *162,* 246, *246*
    child sexual abuse in 348–9
    Craven expresses concern over 97
    DPP takes action against media outlets 415–16
    Ellis on media influence 46–8
    follow Pell after release from prison 26–8
    influence on judicial independence 46–7
    journalists antagonistic towards Pell 163–8, 195–246, 248–94
    journalists as activists 164, 166, 190, 217–18, 221, 234, 237, 242, 274
    journalists supportive of Pell 293, 295
    Kidd interviewed on *The Project* 15–16, 62
    Pell investigation leaked to 234–5, 382
    respond to Pell's acquittal 28–31, 401–3
    respond to Royal Commission's findings 352–4
    see also ABC; *specific journalists; specific newspapers; specific radio and television programs*
Media and Entertainment and Arts Alliance 238
Media Watch (television program) 198, 224, 290–4
Media Watch Dog (blog) 181, 215, 347, 399
Melbourne 168
Melbourne archdiocese 339–43, 352, 365–70, 379
Melbourne Assessment Prison 2, 37, 117, 206
Melbourne Observer 317
Melbourne Response 11, 43, 170, 174, 180, 190, 260, 267, 272, 274–5, 321, 323, 327–30, 342, 356, 366, 368–9, 386
Melbourne University Press 187, 194, 211, 216–17, 230, 414, 419
Meldrum, Molly 264
memory 45, 82–3, 111–12, 215, 308–10, 395–8
Menadue, John 264
Meney, Chris 27
mental reservations 312–13
Mentone 161, 340
Menzies, Sir Robert 138
Mercator Net (website) 349
The Mercury 350
Metropolitan Police (UK) 38
Micallef, Shaun 167, 293
Middleton, Karen 44, 167, 251–2
Mildura 317
Millar, Lisa 167, 187, 250–1, 403
Miller, Rodney 393
Miller, Virginia 309, 327
Milligan, Louise
    ABC defends investigations of 288
    ABC settles defamation claim against 294
    as a Pell antagonist 165–7, 207–33, 245, 358, 406–7
    as an activist journalist 165–6
    as author of *Cardinal* 40, 165–6, 187,

194, 414, 419
Barry on 291–2
correspondence with Henderson 406–7, 419
evidential standards of 294
interviews complainants on *7.30* 54–6, 417
interviews Pell's classmates 144
on revoking of honours by St Patrick's College 358
on the evidence of A 70, 228–9, 278, 280
portrait of *40*
position supported by Keneally 405
posts tweets before Pell's re-trial 414
previews High Court case 116–17
raises swimming pool allegations 58, 87–8
responds to findings of royal commission 353–4
Milroy, Helen 299, 324
Minchin, Tim 162, *162,* 164–5, 167, 249, 269–70, 301, 353
Mindszenty, Cardinal Jozsef 150
Mitchell, Chris 239
Mitchell, Neil 362–4, 367, 391
Molan, Jim 225, 252
Molony, John 143
Monash University 158
The Monthly 165, 168, 354
Moore, Charles 93
More, Thomas 154
Morgan, Kevin 7
Mornings with Jon Faine (radio program) 289, 363
Mornings with Leon Compton (radio program) 307
Mornings with Virginia Trioli (radio program) 218, 285–6
Morris, Linda 265
Morris-Marr, Lucie 7, 10, 14, 41, 59, 63–4, 68, 83–4, 167, 194, *194,* 207, 209, 233–9, 353, 382
Morrison, Andrew 190
Morrison, Scott 119, 411–12
Morrow, Julian 167
Morton, Charlie 389–90
Motto, Megan 44
Mottram, Linda 167
The Movement 138, 150

M.R. (complainant) 57
Mrs B (mother of deceased former chorister – originally referred to as R) 228–30
Muldoon, Rhys 353
Mulkearns, Bishop Ronald 156–9, 168–9, 184, 317, 332–7, 355
Mundine, Warren 31
Munificentissimus Deus 147
Murdoch, Rupert 234–5
Murphy, Chris 167
Murphy, Justice Lionel 6
Murray, Andrew 299, 324
Murray, Paul 167, 269–70, 293
My Country (Marr) 207–8
My Story (Gillard) 299
"My Time in Prison" (Pell) 115
Myers, Allan 321–2

National Apology to Victims and Survivors of Institutional Child Sexual Abuse 411–14
National Association for People Abused in Childhood 266
National Civic Council 150
National Committee for Professional Standards 175–6
National Party 405
national public register, of sex offenders 262
National Tertiary Education Union 247
Nazareth Boys' Home, Ballarat 50–2, 58, 377
Neighbour, Sally 168–70, 222
Neil, Megan 401
Netherlands, Catholicism in 151, 156
Nettle, Justice Geoffrey 1, 5, *25,* 121–2, 124, 389, 403
Network 10 162, 164, 168, 249, 344
Neville, Richard 349
The New Daily 41, 68, 168, 194, 217, 233, 237, 405
New South Wales Independent Commission Against Corruption 308
New York Times 292, 415
Newcastle diocese *see* Maitland-Newcastle diocese
Newcastle Herald 181, 187, 204
Newman, Cardinal John Henry 134, 147,

151
News Breakfast (television program) 166–7, 187, 250, 274, 322–3, 401, 403
News Corp 94, 235
newspapers 168
Niall, Richard 113–14
Nicholas, Mark 409
Nine Network 168, 171–2
Nine Newspapers 29–30, 168, 198, 254–5, 276
Nixon, Christine 388
Nolan, Father Henry 336
Northern Territory Emergency Response (2007) 192
Nostra Aetate 148
Noyes, Jenny 319
NSW Court of Appeal 310
NSW Crimes Act 44
NSW Director of Public Prosecutions v Wilson 44
NSW District Court 282
NSW Police 185–7, 232
Nunn, Bernadette 400

O'Brien, Peter 241
Observations on the Pell Proceedings (Brennan) 355–6
O'Callaghan, Peter 342–3, 368–9
O'Collins, Bishop James 138, 146, 150, 157–9, 312, 317, 344
O'Connor, Cardinal Archbishop John 131
O'Doherty, Stephen 44
O'Donnell, Father John Kevin 173–4, 329, 340, 402
O'Farrell, Barry 185
O'Gorman, Terry 411
Old Melbourne Gaol 7–8
One Plus One (television program) 145
onus of proof 118, 122–3, 206
Operation Gloucester 392–3
Operation Midland 362
Operation Plangere 370
Operation Tethering 9, 178, 361–5, 370–86, 388
opportunity witnesses 66–7, 104
Osborn, Justice R. 4
Overland, Simon 367
Owen, Neville 320

The Oxford Companion to the High Court 6
Oxford University 151–3

Palmer, Tim 167
papal infallibility 147
Parramatta diocese 182–3
Parry, Stephen 410–11
Paterson, Ian 273
Pattenden, Miles 407–8
Patton, Shane 10–11, 13, 360, *360, 371,* 377–8
Paul Murray Live (television program) 261, 269–70
Paul VI, Pope 148–9, 152, 154
P.C. (complainant) 54, 277–8
Pearls and Irritations (blog) 264, 300
pedophilia *see* clerical child sexual abuse
Pell, David John (George Pell's brother) 138–9
Pell, Cardinal George
  accompanies Ridsdale to court 173–4, 190, 315, 354
  accused of covering up Ridsdale's crimes 172–3, 332–7
  acquitted by High Court 1, 3–6, 22–4, 26, 60–1, 127, 357, 409
  addresses clerical child sexual abuse 321
  allegations against 13, 16–19, 50–8, 89–90, 108, 164, 172, 175–8, 185, 191, 209–10, 215, 223, 226, 238, 274, 277, 331
  alleged meeting with Walsh 282–5
  anti-communism of 150
  anti-Pell publicity 162, *162,* 246, *246*
  appeals to the High Court 115–27, 401
  appeals to the Victorian Court of Appeal 100–12, 222, 400
  appointed Prefect of the Secretariat for the Economy 10, 133–4
  as an assistant priest 156–7
  as Archbishop of Melbourne 18–19, 129, 134–5, 168–71, 327
  as Archbishop of Sydney 171, 179–80
  as principal of Institute of Catholic Education 157
  as rector of Corpus Christi College 159–61

as the subject of *Goliath* documentary 276–7
at Corpus Christi College 140–6
at Good Shepherd Seminary 27–8
at school 139–40
attends Pontifical Urban University 146, 148–51
becomes a cardinal 178–9
blamed for events in Armidale and Parramatta 180–3
bullying of defenders of 195
calls media conference 175–6
cares for O'Collins in Bishop's House 158–9
charged by Victoria Police 13–14, 193, 202, 211, 213, 257, 278, 365, 374, 377–8
childhood 138–9
commentators question appeal by 255–7, 262, 269
commitment to social justice 133–4
committal hearing 41, 50–1, 57–9, 374–7
completes doctorate at Oxford 151–3
completes masters at Monash 158
concerns over fairness of trial 247–8, 412–15
conducts mass at St Patrick's 16, 18–19, 21–2
consecrated a bishop 160–1, 340
considers not appealing to High Court 115
convicted of child sexual abuse 3, 204, 237, 247–8, 251, 408
delivers panegyric at Santamaria's funeral 135, 155
demeanour of 112–13
denies communion to non-Catholics 136
denies communion to Rainbow Sash wearers 131
doubts about conviction of 94–8, 249, 417–18
endures mobs outside court 41
engages own legal team 321–2
establishes Domus Australia in Rome 156–7
gives evidence to Royal Commission 165, 296, *296,* 301–3, 316–20, 335, 350–2, 356, 379
gives evidence to Victorian inquiry 184
granted bail for medical reasons 84
hears decision of High Court 3–4
held responsible for crimes of others 398–407, 409–11
hounded by media crews 26–8
in prison 2–4, 14, 28, 205–6, 243, 280
informed of royal commission by Gillard 189
interviewed by Bolt 295, *295*
interviewed by *Four Corners* 181
interviewed by police in Rome 10–13, 21–2, 71–2, 229, 246, 279, 371–4, 383, 416–17
interviewed on *Sunday* 171–2
journalists antagonistic towards 163–8, 195–246, 248–94
journalists supportive of 293, 295
leaves Barwon Prison 26
lobbies for asylum seekers 133
McClellan's antipathy towards 311–15
media response to acquittal of 28–31
meets Foster family 173
meets Paul VI 149
name removed from honour board 357–8
notoriety of trial 5
objects to leak by Victoria Police 234
on agnosticism 154–5
on English Catholics 152–3
on football 139–40
on Pope Francis 134
on public perception 129
on *Q&A* 395–6
on the John Ellis case 325–6
ordained a priest 151
oversees creation of statues 170
parents of 136–8
prosecuted by Victoria Police 48–59
refutes claims made by royal commission 331
responds to establishment of royal commission 189–91, 300
responds to findings of the royal commission 354–5
responds to *Goliath* documentary 280–1
responds to his acquittal 35
responds to Marr's essay 199

rests at Carmelite Monastery 26–7
retrial of 74–89, 412
returns to Ballarat from Oxford 155
Royal Commission focuses on 323–43
'secret trial' of 63–5
Senate motion calls for return of 410–11
sentenced to imprisonment 89–91
sets up Melbourne Response 11, 43, 171, 174, 327–8, 386
studies French in Paris 148
supporters of speak out 31–4
theological conservatism of 66, 84, 132, 134, 151, 154–5, 159–60, 170
timing of alleged assaults 19–21, 71–3, 123–5, 244
trains to become a priest 140–6
tried in the County Court (Cathedral Trial) 14–18, 64–74
vestments of viii, 96–7, 377
visited by Abbott in prison 37
visits residents in HIV-AIDS refuge 132
with Bob Santamaria 128
Witness A lodges complaint about 8
writes booklet on the Josephites 156
writes for college journal 149
writes tracts on Catholic education 158
Pell, George Arthur (George Pell's father) 136–8
Pell, Margaret (George Pell's sister) 138–9, 150
Pell, Margaret Lillian (née Burke) (George Pell's mother) 136–8
Pell v The Queen 5, 22–4, *25,* 26, 29, 34, 36, 39, 116–17, 193, 208, 232–3, 239, 246, 277–9, 389, 391, 396, 401
Pelly, Michael 81
The People v George Pell (song) 165
Percy, Tom 31
Perrett, Janine 167
The Persecution of George Pell (Windschuttle) 378, 418
Phelps, Kerryn 167
Phillip Island allegations 13, 175–8, 198, 215, 379–80
Pickering, Charlie 167, 293
Pius IX, Pope 147, 151
Pius XI, Pope 133
Pius XII, Pope 147, 149

PM (radio program) 167
police *see* Victoria Police
The Police v George Pell 39–40, 48–59, 246, 278
politicians 410–12
Pontifical Commission for the Protection of Minors 266
Pontifical Urban University, Rome 146, 148–51
Portelli, Charles 18, 22, 57, 78–9, 89, 108, 115, 120–1, 258, 384
Porteous, Archbishop Julian 307
Porter, Christian 294
Potter, Maxwell 18, 20, 22, 57, 66, 79, 90, 107, 115, 258, 384
Powerpoint presentation 79–81
practice, as evidence 120–1
presumption of innocence 28–31, 38, 118, 177, 243, 271
The Prince (Marr) 198–202, 206, 279
Principe, Remy 139
Prison Journal (Pell) 2, 4, 8, 27–8, 128, *128,* 142, 154, 156, 160, 170, 280–1, 404, 407
probative value, of evidence 86
Proctor, Harvey 362
The Project (television program) 15–16, 162, 164–5, 168, 248–50, 271–2
Propaganda College 146, 148–51
Protestants 137, 152
protests *40,* 46
Proust, Elizabeth 320
public opinion *see* 'court of public opinion'
Puccini, Jo 209, 302
Pugh, Clifton 128
Punch, Julian 144–5, 167
Puterman, Lusia 310

Q&A (television program) 252–3, 292, 347, 395–6
Quadrant 94, 170
Quarterly Essay 199
Quebec 156
The Queen v Pell 244, 249, 279, 384–5

Radio 2GB 224, 252, 347
Radio 3AW 28, 362–4, 367, 391
Radio 774 40, 218, 285, 363, 391
Rae, David 375–6, 379–80

Raheen (house) 146
Rainbow Sash Movement 129–32, 134, 176
Rayner, Monsignor Brian 326–7
The Reckoning (podcast) 245
Red Mass 403–4
Redlich Robert 392
Redwood, Peter 383
Reed, Christopher 10–12, 71–3, 371–7, 383–6
Reformation 152
Reid, Philip 302-3. 349
The Religion and Ethics Report (radio program) 290
Religion & Ethics (website) 407–8
The Religion Report (radio program) 177
The Representative (Hochhuth) 149
Reucassel, Craig 167, 204
Revelation (television program) 156, 167, 239, 246, 275–6, 280–1, 288
Rice-Davies, Mandy 34
Rich, Justice George 329, 384–5
Richardson, Graham 167, 293
Richter, Robert 10–11, 48–9, 59–61, *62*, 70, 74, 77–8, 82, 86, 92, 225–8, 375–6, 380, 383
Ridley, Bishop Nicholas 152
Ridsdale, David 172–3, 301, 331
Ridsdale, Father Gerald
  accompanied to court by Pell 173–4, 190, 315, 354
  as a parish priest 157, 373
  awareness of crimes of 169, 201–2, 355, 386
  Bongiorno on 344–7
  flaws in royal commission findings regarding 355
  gives evidence to royal commission 311–15
  in Ararat Prison 206
  Marr continues to link Pell with 205
  Marr refers to in *The Prince* 198
  Mulkearns on 169
  Pell accused of covering up crimes of 172–3, 236, 323, 332–7, 354
  Pell responds to royal commission findings regarding 354
  Pell's response to offending of 350–1

Reed questions Pell about 373
  royal commission focuses on 324, 330–1
  shares accommodation with Pell and Bongiorno 157, 201, 210, 224, 344
  Victorian Parliamentary Inquiry findings on 184
Riley, Mark 251–2
Roberts, Jason 4, 392–3
Robinson, Bishop Geoffrey 43, 171, 176, 321, 327
Roebuck, Peter 397
Rome 10–13, 21–2, 71, 146–7, 150, 156–7, 165, 229, 279, 296, 319, 371
Rosenbloom, Henry 244
Roskam, John 31
Ross, Colin Campbell 5–8
Rowland, Michael 167, 187, 403
Rowles, Jason 54
Royal Commission into Institutional Responses to Child Sexual Abuse 297–359
  allegations made against Pell at 164, 195, 331, 355
  Bongiorno gives evidence to 344–8
  Brennan on 355–6
  calls claimants survivors 309
  case study approach 324
  Case Study No. 8 324–7
  Case Study No. 16 324, 327–30
  Case Study No. 28 324, 330–9, 348, 352, 354, 356, 358
  Case Study No. 35 324, 339–43, 352, 354, 358
  composition of 299
  cost of 298
  counselling guidelines 310
  Crittenden works for 178, 300
  emphasis on historical crimes 304–6, 321, 323
  extended by two years 297
  final report 304, 316
  findings of 352–4, 356
  FitzSimons misunderstands remit of 272
  focus on Pell 323–43, 355–7
  Furness as senior Counsel Assisting 296, *296, 298*, 299, 311–12, 314–23, 332, 350–2

Gillard establishes 188, 297
Henderson on 187, 192, 301–2
Hoysted on 387
investigates Ballarat diocese 330–9, 352, 379
investigates Melbourne archdiocese 339–43, 352, 365–70, 379
lack of Catholics on staff 300
McClellan as chair of 307–16, 322, 329, 355–8, 396
media response to 188–9
omits inquiries into media and government schools 348–50
Paterson gives evidence to 273
Pell gives evidence to 11, 165, 296, *296,* 301–3, 350–2, 356, 379, 410–11
Pell responds to establishment of 189–91, 300
Pell responds to findings of 354–5
releases findings regarding Pell 31, 172
remit of 298–9
Ridsdale gives evidence to 311–15
Ryan gives evidence to 388
Truth, Justice and Healing Council's response to 320–1, 323
undue focus on Catholicism 297, 299–301, 303–7, 348–50
Royal Commission into the Management of Police Informants 391–3, 403
Royal Exhibition Building, Melbourne 129
Royal Oak Hotel, Ballarat 137–8
Rudd, Kevin 397–8, 412
Rugg, Eliza 113, 232
Ryan, Sister Angela 176
Ryan, Denis 316, 386–8
Ryan, Vincent 275–6, 281

Sacred College of Cardinals 178
Sacred Heart Catholic Primary School, Oakleigh 329
Sacred Heart Teachers College, Ballarat 157
Sales, Leigh 167, 190, 204–5, 267, 289–90, 301–2
SANO *see* Sexual Abuse Non-Government Organisations Task Force
Santamaria: A Most Unusual Man (Henderson) 216
Santamaria, B.A. ('Bob') *128,* 135, 138, 150, 155
Santamaria, Joseph Gerard 328, 356
Sarre, Rick 29
The Saturday Paper 30, 44, 168, 344, 347–8, 354
Saunders, Peter 266–7
Savage, Russell 388
Savile, Jimmy 348
Saville, Margot 167
Schacter, Daniel L. 397
Schillebeeckx, Father Edward 155
Schwartz Media 168, 197
Schwartz, Morry 165
Scott, Mark 181
Scribe 244
Searson, Father Peter 322, 324, 339–42, 355
Second Vatican Council *see* Vatican II
sectarianism 66, 137, 164, 207, 291, 406
secularism 164
'Sergeant Schultz defence' 202
The Seven Sins of Memory (Schacter) 397
7.30 (television program) 53–6, 58, 87, 165, 167, 183, 190, 204–6, 209–11, 213, 223, 267, 288, 290, 292, 301–3, 362–3
sex, in Catholic teachings 130, 335
Sexual Abuse Non-Government Organisations Task Force 9, 222, 381
sexual revolution 148–9
S.G. (complainant) 50–3, 365, 372
Shanahan, Angela 31
Shanley, John Patrick 112
Shann, Ruth 16, 48, 60–1, *62,* 70, 74, 79–81, 86, 92, *92,* 99, 101, 116, 118, 126, 225
Shaun Micallef's Mad As Hell (television program) 293
Shelton, Lyle 31
Sheridan, Greg 204, 419
Sheridan, Paul 9–11, 21, 364, 371–3, 375, 383
Sherwin, Ralph 152
Shields, Bevan 319
Shorten, Bill 253, 412
Siegemund, Tania 370
Siewert, Rachel 410–11
Silbert, Gavin 418, 427–8

Silk, Gary 393
Silvester, John 94–5, 280
Sinozic, Lil 88–9
The Sisters of St Joseph in Swan Hill (Pell) 156
60 Minutes (television program) 168, 172–6, 266–7
Skelton, Russel 167, 406
Sky News 3–4, 32, 94, 181, 238, 261, 269, 289, 293, 301, 413, 417
Smith, Chris 167
Smith, Doug 222–4
Smith, Justin 28, 31, 167
Smith, Suzanne 281–6
Southwell, Alec James 176–8, 199, 287–8
Soutphommasane, Tim 167, 255–7
Sowersby, Tony 246
Speakman, Mark 46
Special Commission of Inquiry into matters relating to the police investigation of certain child sexual abuse allegations in the Catholic Diocese of Maitland-Newcastle 185–6, 189
Spencer, Pauline 40, *40*
Spencer, Sue 181
Squires, Wendy 167
S.S. Strathden (ship) 146
St Alipius Church, Ballarat East 157, 210, 224
St Alipius Primary School, Ballarat 158, 337
St Columba's Seminary, Springwood 265–6
St James Church, Sebastapol 373
St Joseph's Church, Warrnambool 344
St Joseph's College, Geelong 113
St Joseph's College, Warrnambool 346
St Kevin's College, Melbourne 8
St Martin's in the Pines, Ballarat 157
St Patrick's and the Holy Angels Church, Mentone 161, 340
St Patrick's Cathedral, Ballarat 280
St Patrick's Cathedral, Melbourne
    alleged sexual assaults in 3, 8–9, 14, 16–18, 56, 58–9, 61, 78, 82, 89–90, 108, 210–11, 226, 229–30, 244, 379–81, 417
    doors vandalised 28

official reopening 131
Pell conducts mass at 16, 18–19, 131
Pell consecrated a bishop at 161
plan of vi
Powerpoint presentation of 79–81
procession of altar servers 360, *360*
protest held at 403
Reed does walk-through with A in 383
timing of alleged assault vi, 20
St Patrick's College, Ballarat 139, 143, 337–8, 357–9
St Patrick's Seminary, Manly 160
standard of proof 118, 177, 329 30, 418
State College of Victoria 158
Stefanato, Angelo 139
Stenhouse, Father Paul 31
Stephens, Jon 290, 348
Stepinac, Cardinal Aloysius 170
Stewart, Angus 388
Stone, Robert 43–4
Stonyhurst College 152
Strike Force Lantle 187
suicides 368–70
Sullivan, Francis 252–4, 289, 292, 320–3
Sun-Herald 271, 301
Sunday (television program) 171
The Sunday Age 304–5
Sunday Telegraph 189
suppression orders 41, 64, 85, 88–9, 93, 247, 289, 414–17
Supreme Court of Victoria 389
    see also Court of Appeal of the Supreme Court of Victoria
Swan Hill 156, 317
Swimming Pool Case 55, 58–60, 64, 74, 85–8, 279, 415
Sydney Gay and Lesbian Mardi Gras 133
The Sydney Institute 181
The Sydney Morning Herald 10, 29, 34, 132, 168, 177, 181, 198, 200, 213, 254, 265, 271, 273, 282–3, 319, 412
Szego, Julie 167
Szeps, Josh 167
Szubanski, Magda 167

Talk of the Devil (Guilliatt) 397
Tandberg, Ron 167
Tasmanian Department of Education 350

Tate, Michael 155
Taylor, Justice A. 4, 393
Taylor, Chris 167
Taylor, Lenore 192, 239
tendency evidence 55, 85–7, 279
Tennison Woods House 98
Thakur, Ramesh 31
Therese, Saint 27
Thompson, Geoff 167, 180–2
Thomson, Jeff 397
Throsby, Margaret 231
The Times 415
Tirtschke, Alma 7
Tobin, Bernadette 290
Tobin, T.K. 356
Tonightly (television program) 293
Torpy, Father Daniel 332, 334
Torquay Surf Club 223
Towards Healing (document) 327
Towards Healing (program) 171, 182–3, 272, 321, 323, 325–6
Tran, Danny 319
The Trial of George Pell (Davey) 207
Trioli, Virginia 166–7, 218, 222, 228, 285–6, 322–3
Truth, Justice and Healing Council 320–1, 323
truth, real and perceived 308–9
Tuohy, Wendy 167, 400
Turnbull government 297
Turnbull, Malcolm 410, 412
Twitter 5, 117, 220–2, 405–6, 415
Tyack, Les 222–3
Tyrrell, John Francis 38, 113–15, 255
Tyrrell v The Queen see *John Francis Tyrrell v The Queen*

The Unbelievable Story of Carl Beech (documentary) 362
unconscious bias 65–6, 413
Undeniable: Inside Australia's Biggest Cover-up (documentary) 274
Unholy Trinity (Ryan) 316, 387
Uniting Church 272–3
University of Technology Sydney 285
Urban VIII, Pope 146
Usher, Monsignor John 325, 327

van Onselen, Peter 293

Van Steenwyk, Ingrid 349
Van Thuan, Francis Xavier Nguyen 154
Vanstone, Amanda 31, 291, 301
Vatican I 147, 151
Vatican II 131, 141, 147–8, 151–2, 154, 158, 160, 268–9
Victoria Police 361–93
  acknowledge Carson's error 359
  advertise for witnesses of child sexual assault 365, 371, 381
  alleged fabrication of evidence by 7
  apologise to Ryan 387
  at Pell's committal proceedings 375–7
  B's testimony to 67
  charge Pell 13–14, 193, 202, 211, 213, 257, 278, 365, 374, 377–8
  Craven expresses concern over 97
  early inaction of 386–8
  engage Lawyer X as an informant 388–91, 393, 403
  fail to interview witnesses 88–9
  fail to investigate before laying charges 61, 375, 377, 380
  fail to lay charges against Searson 340–1
  flaws in investigations of 383–6
  'Get Pell' campaign 9–10, 14, 70, 178, 361–93
  IBAC's Operation Gloucester 392–3
  in *DPP v Pell* 78
  interview Pell in Rome 10–13, 21–2, 71–2, 229, 246, 279, 371–4, 383, 416–17
  investigate complaint by Witness A 8–9
  investigate Ridsdale 337
  involvement in Melbourne Response 260, 275, 328, 366–7, 386
  leak investigation to media 234–5, 382
  modus operandi of 377–8
  Operation Tethering 9, 178, 361–5, 370–86, 388
  prosecute Pell 48–59, 122
  provide escort for Anthony Foster's funeral 274
  refer to complainants as victims 362–3, 371
  respond to Melbourne Response 366
  Sexual Abuse Non-Government Organisations Task Force

9, 222, 381
submission to Victorian Parliamentary Inquiry 367–9
support counselling for Ridsdale 169
Victorian Bar News 418
Victorian Parliamentary Inquiry into child abuse 184, 260, 274, 302, 331, 367–71
Victorian Victims of Crime Compensation scheme 328
Vietnam 154

Walker, Bret 16, 92, *92,* 101–2, 116, 118–19, 126–7
Walking Towards Thunder (Fox) 187, 274
Walkley Book Award 238–9, 292, 419
Waller, Vivian 35, 167, 222, 252
Wallington, Belinda 19, 40, *40,* 42, 48–9, 53–9, 65, 85, 115, 226–7, 278, 365, 372, 386
Walsh, Father Glen 282–6
Ward, Roz 167
Warden, Ian 167
Warrenheip 372
Warrnambool Standard 336
The Washington Post 259–60, 399
Waterford, Jack 167, 257–8
The Weekend Australian 201, 207, 214, 217, 219, 235, 237, 244, 301, 347, 370, 397, 405, 417–18
The Weekend Australian Magazine 310
The Weekly with Charlie Pickering (television program) 293
Weigel, George 32
Weinberg, Justice Mark 6, 18, 23, 30, 58–60, 81, *92,* 93, 100–1, 103, 105, 108–16, 218–22, 240–1, 256, 258, 278, 384, 417
Werribee Park 141
Westacott, John 167
Westminster Cathedral 130
Westmore, Peter 32
Whelan, Judith 167
White Australia Policy 149–50
Whitlam, Antony 182–3
Whitlam Labor government 158
Whitlam Report 182–3
Wilcox, Cathy 167
Wilde, Oscar 48

www.ingramcontent.com/pod-product-compliance
Ingram Content Group UK Ltd.
Pitfield, Milton Keynes, MK11 3LW, UK
UKHW021315180426
11947UKWH00015B/1242